Mathematics for A and AS level

Statistics

The School Mathematics Project

PUBLISHED BY THE PRESS SYNDICATE OF THE UNIVERSITY OF CAMBRIDGE
The Pitt Building, Trumpington Street, Cambridge CB2 1RP, United Kingdom

CAMBRIDGE UNIVERSITY PRESS
The Edinburgh Building, Cambridge CB2 2RU, United Kingdom
40 West 20th Street, New York, NY 10011-4211, USA
10 Stamford Road, Oakleigh, Melbourne 3166, Australia

First published 1997

Printed in the United Kingdom at the University Press, Cambridge

Typeset in Sabon 10/12$\frac{1}{2}$ pt

A catalogue record for this book is available from the British Library

Adapted from the original 16–19 Mathematics material by Chris Belsom

Main authors   Chris Belsom   Fiona McGill
                        Robert Black   Paul Roder
                        David Cundy   Mary Rouncefield
                        Stan Dolan   Jane Southern
                        Ron Haydock   Nigel Walkey
                        Chris Little

Team leader   Chris Belsom

Project director   Stan Dolan

ISBN 0 521 56616 9

Acknowledgements
The publishers would like to thank the following for permission to use copyright material:

text on page 1   from *Revised English Bible*, Oxford University Press
                      and Cambridge University Press, 1989;

photographs on page 41 (l)   AIP Meggers Gallery of Nobel Laureates;
                      (r)   Ann Ronan/Image Select;
photograph on page 42   Dr Seth Shostak/Science Photo Library

Contents

Introduction for the student

The material in this book provides a suitable preparation for the statistics content of most A level and AS level courses in mathematics; it is based on four units from the SMP *16–19 Mathematics* course – *Living with uncertainty*, *The Normal distribution*, *Probability models for data* and *Statistics in action*.

The book is a self-contained resource, consisting of explanatory text and exercises. All exercises are provided with solutions at the end of the book. The textual material is written in such a way that you yourself become involved in the development of the ideas; *it is a text to be worked through, rather than read passively*. You learn mathematics by actually *doing* it, and this is constantly encouraged through the text.

Throughout the body of the text, as material is being developed, you will meet blocks of questions indicated as follows:

 .4A

The probability distributions for two packs of cards are shown below. *Y* is the score on a card from the yellow pack.

. . .

The questions in these **development sections** are designed in such a way that ideas are opened up, explored and developed before results or observations are formalised. They are a crucial part of the learning process, making you more familiar with the ideas that you will eventually apply in more straightforward and conventional exercises. Answers, or more detailed solutions, are provided at the back of the book both for these sections and for the exercises. You should check your work as you go along, correcting as necessary. Do not resort to looking at the solutions too readily when you encounter a problem – wrestling with a difficulty is a better way of resolving it than giving up too early.

At various points in the text you will also be directed towards a number of **tasksheets**. These contain support or enrichment material.

We hope that you will find the material in this book (and the approach adopted) a challenging, enjoyable and rewarding introduction to the study of statistics.

1 Living with uncertainty

.1 Statistics and data analysis

1.1.1 Introduction

If the study of statistics is no more than the collection of data, then it can be considered to have had a long history. The Domesday Book of William the Conqueror is an early example of a good attempt to collect information about a population. The Bible provides evidence of even earlier examples, like the following from the New Testament:

> *In those days a decree was issued by the emperor Augustus for a census to be taken throughout the Roman world.*
>
> Luke 2:1

or this extract from the Old Testament:

> *... as the Lord had commanded Moses. He drew up the lists ... in the wilderness of Sinai. The total number of Israelites aged 20 years and upwards fit for service, recorded in the lists of fathers' families, was 603 550.*
>
> Numbers 1:19, 45–46

Such enumerations are still practised today and a national census of the population is conducted in the United Kingdom every ten years. The ready availability of statistics of this kind helps to keep us informed of trends and changes in society which might influence our thinking and behaviour. It is important to be able to 'read' statistical information, for example about the dangers of smoking or about the association of heart disease with certain life styles, and to make informed judgements upon it. Your study of statistics should help you to do this.

One of the early statisticians, better known for her other activities and achievements, was Florence Nightingale (1820–1910). As part of her efforts to improve the conditions for patients, she collected data in various hospitals on the causes of death and illness. She realised that it was always necessary to *use* and *interpret* information after it had been collected.

> *The War Office has some of the finest statistics in the world. What comes of them? Little or nothing. Why? Because the Heads do not know how to make anything of them ... What we want is not so*

much an accumulation of facts, as to teach the men who are to govern the country the use of statistical facts.

Florence Nightingale

It is, of course, the **interpretation** of statistics that is at the heart of much controversy. Everyone knows the harsh reference to statistics made by Disraeli:

There are lies, damned lies and statistics.

Daily newspapers are a regular source of statistical information. Data are collected, published and commented upon in connection with just about everything imaginable. People's eating habits, road accidents, crime and cricket all come in for statistical analysis by the press.

Statistics is not the aimless collection of data for its own sake, or simply for general interest. The collection of data is normally made in response to a problem that needs to be investigated or to a hypothesis that is to be tested. It is the **collection** and **analysis** of data, followed by the making of **judgements**, **decisions** or **inferences**, which form the subject-matter of statistics. This can be summarised in the following way:

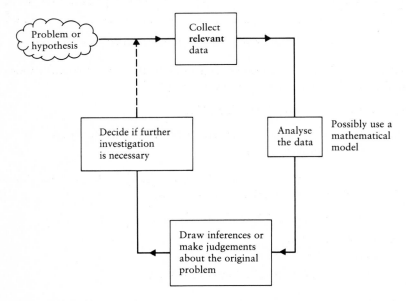

The study of statistics will involve you in a consideration of each of the areas mentioned in the diagram. Projects and your own statistical investigations will give you the opportunity to engage in the full cycle of a statistical enquiry.

1.1 Exercise 1

The following diagrams are based on statistics from the government publication *Regional Trends* (1996).

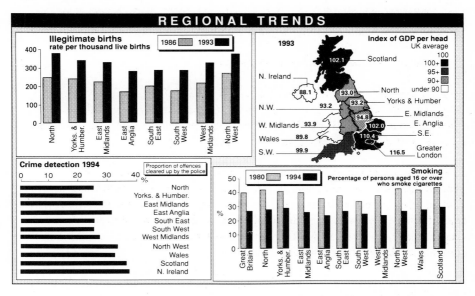

Study the diagrams and then answer the questions based on this material.

1 In 1986, approximately what percentage of all births in the East Midlands were described (in the diagram) as illegitimate?

What is the corresponding figure for 1993?

In 1993, which English region registered the greatest and which the least percentage of illegitimate births?

2 The average gross domestic product (GDP) for the UK is fixed at 100. Figures for the regions are given in relation to this figure.

(a) What is the average GDP for those living in:

(i) Greater London,
(ii) Northern Ireland?

(b) Comment on any regional differences in GDP.

3 In 1994, Yorkshire and Humberside had the worst 'clearance' rate for criminal offences.

(a) What percentage of crimes was cleared up by the police in:

(i) the South East,
(ii) Scotland,
(iii) the North?

(b) Does the table give you any information about the numbers of crimes committed in these regions?

(c) How do you think data could be collected on:

   (i) the clear up rate,

 (ii) the number of crimes?

Do you see any problems?

4 The government decides to launch a new anti-smoking campaign.

(a) Is there any evidence in the table for directing the advertising to particular regions?

(b) What other information on smoking habits might be useful in advising the government on how to conduct its campaign?

1.1.2 Exploratory data analysis

Many statistical studies are prompted by debatable issues. Is there a connection between lung cancer and smoking? Are men worse drivers than women? Does lead in petrol affect the mental development of children?

In order to answer questions of this kind you need to collect data, analyse it and then draw conclusions.

In most cases it is useful to have methods available for exploring the data and looking for possible patterns and trends before any detailed statistical analysis begins. Pictorial representations of data are often used to convey important features of the information rapidly.

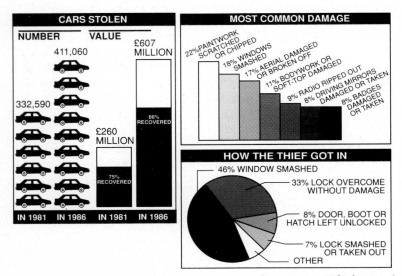

Car security, *Which?* March 1988

Techniques known as **Exploratory Data Analysis** (EDA) have been developed which make it possible to organise sets of data rapidly so that patterns can be spotted easily. The techniques of EDA are covered in this section prior to a study of more detailed methods of statistical analysis.

For example, the data in the table provide information about the weather in two seaside resorts.

July		Bournemouth				Torquay			
		Sun (h)	Max. °C	°F		Sun (h)	Max. °C	°F	
Wed	1	10.1	23	73	sunny	10.0	22	72	sunny
Thurs	2	10.6	20	70	sunny	7.8	19	66	sunny
Fri	3	13.3	22	72	sunny	13.7	19	66	sunny
Sat	4	14.1	21	70	sunny	14.5	20	68	sunny
Mon	6	15.4	27	81	sunny	15.1	24	75	sunny
Tues	7	11.8	25	77	sunny	12.3	26	79	sunny
Wed	8	11.0	26	79	sunny	11.5	25	77	sunny
Thurs	9	13.6	26	79	sunny	11.5	22	72	sunny
Fri	10	13.1	22	72	sunny	8.8	19	66	sunny
Sat	11	6.9	22	72	sunny	–	–	–	–
Mon	13	8.7	23	73	bright	6.9	22	72	bright
Tues	14	14.0	23	73	sunny	13.5	22	72	sunny
Wed	15	1.6	20	68	showers	0.7	19	66	rain
Fri	17	8.0	20	68	sunny	7.8	20	68	showers
Sat	18	2.6	18	64	showers	2.3	12	63	showers
Mon	20	0.6	17	63	rain	1.6	20	68	bright
Tues	21	2.7	19	66	bright	3.8	20	68	bright
Wed	22	–	16	61	showers	2.2	20	68	cloudy
Thurs	23	0.2	18	64	drizzle	0.5	19	66	cloudy
Fri	24	0.2	18	64	cloudy	2.0	19	66	bright
Sat	25	–	20	68	dull	3.0	22	72	cloudy
Mon	27	8.7	21	70	sunny	5.5	19	66	bright
Tues	28	2.8	21	70	bright	4.6	22	72	bright
Wed	29	3.2	22	72	cloudy	5.1	23	73	sunny
Thurs	30	3.9	22	72	showers	5.1	21	70	bright
Fri	31	4.4	21	70	bright	7.6	19	66	bright

A simple pictorial representation of the temperatures (°C) for Bournemouth might be a bar chart.

25 – 29 ☐☐☐☐

20 – 24 ☐☐☐☐☐☐☐☐☐☐☐☐☐☐☐☐☐

15 – 19 ☐☐☐☐☐☐

A **stem and leaf diagram** (or **stem plot**) is similar to this but has the advantage of retaining all the detail of the original data.

Stem (tens)	Leaf (units)
2	5 6 6 7
2	0 0 0 0 1 1 1 1 2 2 2 2 2 3 3 3
1	6 7 8 8 8 9

Key: 1 | 6 means 16 °C

Stem and leaf diagrams always use equal class intervals.

The previous example used class intervals of 5 °C and the leaves were arranged in numerical order.

 .1A

Draw a stem and leaf diagram for the data for Bournemouth using intervals of 10 °C, i.e. 10–19, 20–29.

Also draw diagrams using intervals of 1 °C and of 2 °C.

Which diagram do you think gives the best pictorial representation of the data?

Stem and leaf diagrams can be used to compare two samples by showing the results together on a 'back-to-back' stem plot. In the following example, the twenty-six temperatures for Bournemouth are compared with the twenty-five temperatures for Torquay.

Daily maximum temperatures for July

Bournemouth   Torquay

```
              7  6  6 | 2 | 6
                    5 | 2 | 4  5
3  3  3  2  2  2  2  2 | 2 | 2  2  2  2  2  2  3
1  1  1  1  0  0  0  0 | 2 | 0  0  0  0  0  1
              9  8  8  8 | 1 | 9  9  9  9  9  9  9  9  9
                 7  6 | 1 |
                      | 1 |
                      | 1 | 2
```

5 | 2 means 25 °C   1 | 9 means 19 °C

In this month the temperatures in Bournemouth were a little higher than in Torquay.

The stem plot gives an impression of:

- the average of the data;
- the variability of the data;
- whether or not the data are symmetric.

1.1 Exercise 2

1 The table gives the heights (in centimetres) of twenty married couples.

(a) By considering the data in the table, say which of the two sets of heights is more variable.

(b) (i) Draw stem and leaf plots for the heights of the husbands and wives separately.
   (ii) Which set of heights is more variable?
   (iii) Which has the higher middle value?
   (iv) Find the median in each case.

(c) Consider the data as a set of the heights of 40 adults and draw a 'combined' stem and leaf plot. Comment on its shape.

Wife	Husband
159	180
162	165
142	161
159	173
158	174
139	173
170	173
155	179
156	184
154	177
159	178
163	175
158	168
161	171
152	171
171	175
143	173
158	182
164	164
156	174

(d) If the group of adults is representative of the population, which of the distributions below is likely to represent that of adults' height? Explain your choice.

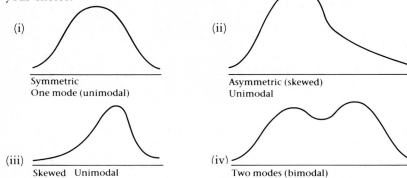

(i)

Symmetric
One mode (unimodal)

(ii)

Asymmetric (skewed)
Unimodal

(iii)

Skewed   Unimodal

(iv)

Two modes (bimodal)

A unimodal distribution which is not symmetric is said to be **skewed**.

2 Use a stem plot to compare the examination marks of two classes.

Class 1   80 62 53 76 76 31 59 78 84
             66 71 50 79 69 87 64 56 65
             58 78 75 60 51

Class 2   71 68 56 79 73 51 48 83 64
             58 75 45 91 80 59 34 55 73
             81 62 64 69

(a) Which class has performed better in the examination?

(b) Which class appears to be less variable in terms of pupil attainment?

3 The following (in thousands of pounds) are starting salaries for graduates in 'sales' and 'technical' jobs.

15, 11, 9, 12, 7.5, 8, 10, 16, 11, 12, 10, 9, 10, 14, 9.5, 13, 8.5, 8, 8.5, 12, 11, 9, 11, 7, 10, 13.

Draw a stem plot for the data. Comment on its shape. Is it what you would have expected?

1.1.3 Numerical representation of data

Sometimes it is important to condense a large data set into a few numbers which give an impression of the original set. It is useful to have a single number which can represent the *average* of the data, and you already know three possible such numbers – the **mean**, the **median** and the **mode**.

For example, in a group of five families, the number of people in each family is 2, 5, 6, 5 and 4. For this data set,

the mean family size is $\frac{1}{5}(2 + 5 + 6 + 5 + 4) = \frac{22}{5} = 4.4$,

the median family size is 5,

the modal family size is also 5.

 .1B

There are two interesting ways of obtaining 'averages' by minimising certain functions. These involve the idea of **absolute value**, which you may have met as the function ABS when using a calculator or computer. An alternative name for the function is the **modulus**.

The modulus of any real number a, written $|a|$, is defined as follows.

$$|a| = \begin{cases} a \text{ if } a \geq 0 \\ -a \text{ if } a < 0 \end{cases}$$

For example,

$$|2.5| = 2.5, \qquad |-3| = 3$$

You will see that the expression $|a - b|$ represents the (unsigned) *distance between a and b* on the number line. For example, consider this table of values for $|x - 4|$:

x	...	−1	0	1	2	3	4	5	...
$|x - 4|$	...	5	4	3	2	1	0	1	...

The size of each of the families in the example above can be represented on the number line as shown below.

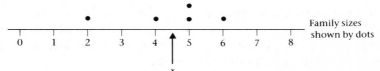

You wish to find a number x somewhere on the line as a representative number for family size. The question to consider is where to place x. To make the marked points cluster around x as closely as possible, you might try minimising the sum of all the distances of the points from x.

1 Using a graphic calculator or computer, plot the graph of
$$y = |x - 2| + |x - 4| + |x - 5| + |x - 5| + |x - 6|$$
for values of x from 0 to 8.

For what value of x is y a minimum?

What is the median value for the data set 2, 4, 5, 5, 6?

2 (a) Consider the data set 1, 3, 6.

   (i) What is the median value?
   (ii) Plot the graph of $y = |x - 1| + |x - 3| + |x - 6|$. What value of x makes y a minimum?

   (b) Investigate other small data sets and make notes on your findings.

Instead of minimising a sum of distances you might try minimising a sum of **squares of distances**.

3 (a) Consider the data set 1, 2, 5.

   (i) Plot the graph of
   $$y = (x - 1)^2 + (x - 2)^2 + (x - 5)^2$$
   What is the value of x at the minimum point?
   (ii) What statistical measure of the data set have you obtained?

   (b) Investigate other small data sets and make a note of your observations.

The three commonly used 'averages' are each appropriate in different circumstances and for different purposes.

Some desirable properties of a number which is used as a 'representative' number for data are:

• it should use all the data values;
• it should not be too influenced by 'wayward' values;
• it should be easy to calculate.

The **mode** is often used in situations where there are no numerical values; for example, the most common eye colour in a class or the university subject which attracts most students.

With examination scores, for example, you are concerned with *total* score and so need a high **mean** mark. The mean is most frequently used in statistical work.

The **median** is usually very easy to calculate and is used for EDA work. It has the advantage that it tends to be little affected by a few abnormal items of data – it is more robust than the mean. In finding the median you *have* to use ranked data, that is data which are placed in order (for example, the finishing position of a runner in her last 10 races).

1.1 Exercise 3

1 Fifty people who entered a raffle were asked afterwards how many winning tickets they had bought. Forty-one had none, six had one and three had two.

Calculate the mean, median and mode of the number of winning tickets per person.

Which is the most suitable measure of the average in this case?

2 In an aptitude test, twenty people were asked to do a jigsaw puzzle and the time taken by each was recorded, with the following results:

Time (seconds)	13	34	40	43	45	46	48	49	51	52
	52	53	58	63	72	75	76	78	104	

As can be seen, only nineteen people completed the jigsaw.

(a) Calculate the mean and median of these data and decide which you think is the most appropriate measure of average, giving your reasons.

(b) The twentieth person gave up after 148 seconds. Should this information have been included in your calculations? Give reasons for your answer, stating how the observation would affect the mean and the median.

3 The distribution of the ages of the inhabitants of a south coast seaside town has the following shape:

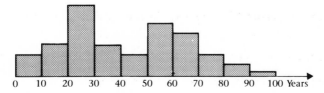

Comment on the shape of the distribution and how you might measure the average age for the inhabitants of this town.

1.1.4 Box and whisker diagrams

A **box plot** or **box and whisker diagram** is a pictorial representation of data based upon five numbers: top of range, upper quartile, median, lower quartile and bottom of range. These are illustrated in the box plot of times for reaction to a stimulus (in hundredths of a second) shown below.

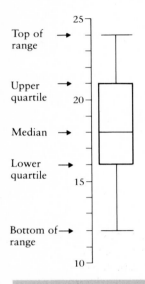

A quarter of the values lie between 12 and 16, a quarter between 16 and 18, a quarter between 18 and 21 and a quarter between 21 and 24 (hundredths of a second).

> The middle 50% of the data lies within the box. The length of the box (the **interquartile range**) is a measure of the variability or spread of the data.

The box plot for a perfectly symmetric distribution would look something like the one drawn below.

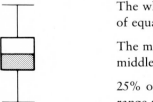

The whiskers are of equal length.

The median is in the middle of the box.

25% of observations are in the range represented by the shaded box.

If the distribution had most of its values at the lower end of the range the box plot might be as shown in the second diagram. Again, 25% of the values are in the range of the shaded box.

To obtain the 'representative' numbers which are used on the box and whisker diagram you often have to work from large collections of data.

The following analysis illustrates the procedure.

Medical statistics are used for purposes as varied as deciding between alternative treatments, determining appropriate premiums for medical insurance schemes and estimating future medical provision.

Length of stay (days)	No. of males	No. of females
0	6	4
1	15	2
2	4	3
3	2	4
4	5	2
5	8	1
6	16	4
7	12	2
8	9	5
9	11	5
10	10	0
11	18	0
12	7	2
13	2	3
14	5	2
15	7	0
16	1	2
17	3	0
18	1	1
19	1	0
21	1	0
22	2	1
23	0	1
24	1	1
26	1	0
28	1	1
29	0	2
37	2	0
41	1	0
45	0	1
72	0	1
Totals	152	50

This table, which shows the lengths of stay in hospital following a myocardial infarction (heart attack), was provided by St Thomas' Hospital, London, from their Hospital Activity Analysis database.

A **cumulative frequency diagram** can be used to represent such data pictorially. If you need practice in drawing and using cumulative frequency diagrams, it is provided on tasksheet S1.

▶ 1.1 Tasksheet S1 – Cumulative frequency diagrams (page 299)

The number of male patients staying *up to* a certain number of days in hospital is plotted against the length of stay in days.

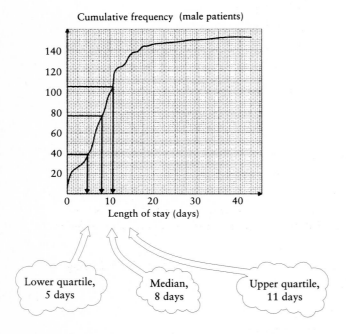

The box plot for length of stay for males is:

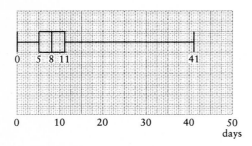

From a stem and leaf plot with the results already written in numerical order it is easy to extract the values of the median and quartiles, although it is important to note carefully the *direction* in which the numbers follow on. It may help to imagine the data written out on a line.

Consider the following back-to-back stem plot for data obtained during an experiment on reaction times.

Adult reaction times

Females (*n* = 19)   Males (*n* = 20)

```
              4   4 │ 2 │
  3  3  3  3  2   2 │ 2 │ 2  2  2  2  2  3
           1  1   0 │ 2 │ 0  1
                  8 │ 1 │ 8  8  8  9  9
        7  7  7   7 │ 1 │ 6  7  7
              4   4 │ 1 │ 4  4  5
                    │ 1 │
                    │ 1 │
                    │ 0 │ 8
```

1 | 4 means 14 hundredths of a second

Median   There are 20 reaction times for males. The two middle values are the 10th and 11th (18 and 19 hundredths of a second) and so the median is 0.185 second.

Lower quartile   There are 10 values below the median. The middle values are the 5th and 6th (16 and 17 hundredths of a second) and so the lower quartile is 0.165 second.

You should obtain the **upper quartile** from the data and confirm the following values for the data.

Reaction times in seconds

	Males	Females
Upper quartile	0.220	0.230
Median	0.185	0.210
Lower quartile	0.165	0.170

1.1 Exercise 4

1 Box plots for the experimental data on the speeds of two types of bullet are as shown.

What can be deduced from the box plots alone?

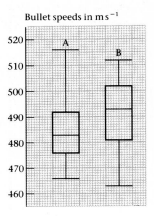

Bullet speeds in m s^{-1}

2 Box plots for the maximum daily temperatures during one month, for London and Copenhagen, are as shown.

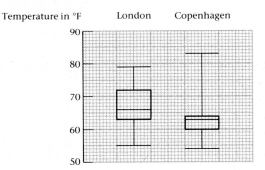

(a) Which city had the highest recorded temperature? Which city was generally hotter? Carefully justify your answer.

(b) Which city had the greater range of temperature? Which city would you consider to have had the more variable temperature? Carefully justify your answer.

3 The back-to-back stem plot drawn below gives the daily hours of sunshine measured at the Weston Park Meteorological Station in Sheffield.

<u>January</u>   <u>July</u>

```
                                    13 │ 6
                                    12 │ 0
                                    11 │ 1 5
                                    10 │ 1
                                     9 │ 7
                                     8 │
                                     7 │ 0 3 6 7 9
                              2      6 │ 2 6
                            8 7      5 │ 5 6 7 8 8
                                     4 │ 3 8 8
                            3 0      3 │ 1 3
                          4 3 1      2 │ 5 6
                          9 7 5      1 │ 6
8 7 5 5 4 3 1 0 0 0 0 0 0 0 0 0 0 0  0 │ 0 0 1 6 8
```

6│2 means 6.2 hours

(a) What conclusions can you draw directly from the stem plot?

(b) For each month, find:
   (i) the median,
   (ii) the lower quartile,
   (iii) the upper quartile.

(c) Using a common scale, draw box plots for the daily hours of sunshine for January and July.

(d) What are your conclusions from the box plots?

4 The table below provides information about alcohol consumption in a number of countries in 1978 and 1985.

Use box plots for 1978 and 1985 to draw some conclusions about any changes in total alcohol consumption.

	Alcohol consumption Litres per head of 100% alcohol		
	1978	1985	% change
France	16.3	13.9	−15
East Germany	11.5	13.4	+17
Portugal	9.9	13.1	+32
Hungary	12.2	12.3	+0.8
Spain	14.3	11.8	−17.5
West Germany	12.9	11.3	−12.5
Austria	10.4	11.1	+6.7
Belgium	10.2	10.8	+5.8
Switzerland	10.4	10.8	+3.8
Czechoslavakia	11.6	9.9	−14.7
Denmark	8.9	9.8	+10.0
Italy	12.0	9.4	−21.7
Australia	9.8	9.2	−6.2
Argentina	11.2	8.7	−22.4
Bulgaria	9.2	8.7	−5.7
Netherlands	8.9	8.4	−5.9
New Zealand	8.5	8.1	−4.8
Canada	8.4	7.8	−7.7
USA	8.2	7.7	−6.1
UK	7.2	7.1	−1.4
Eire	7.7	6.9	−10.4
Greece	6.1	6.8	+11.4
Poland	8.3	6.7	−23.8
Finland	6.3	5.9	−6.4
USSR	6.2	5.7	−8.1
Yugoslavia	7.8	5.3	−32.1
Sweden	5.9	4.8	−18.7
Japan	5.6	4.4	−21.5
Norway	4.0	4.1	+2.5

Brewers' Society Statistical Handbook 1986
The Sunday Times: 26 June 1988

After working through section 1.1 you should:

1 be aware of the importance of statistical information, its impact and influence on the planning and organisation of our lives and the insights it gives into the way we live;

2 appreciate that statistics involves the four stages of:

- collecting relevant data,
- analysing the data,
- making inferences,
- deciding if a further investigation is necessary;

3 be able to construct stem and leaf plots from data and use these plots to indicate average tendency, variability and symmetry of the data;

4 be able to construct and interpret box and whisker diagrams from raw data, cumulative frequency diagrams and stem and leaf plots;

5 be able to choose an appropriate average, mode, mean or median, for a given data set;

6 understand the terms symmetric, skewed, unimodal and bimodal as applied to distributions.

1 Living with uncertainty

.2 Data analysis revisited

1.2.1 Grouping data

A census of the United Kingdom population is taken every 10 years. The collection and analysis of census data is undertaken by a special government department – The Office for National Statistics. The questions asked on the census form are sometimes the cause of considerable national debate; for example, whether or not to include questions on the ethnic background of householders.

The census is wide-ranging and covers many aspects of our lives such as population patterns, mortality rates, number of home-owners, salary levels, and unemployment statistics. Information is normally presented on a regional and national basis.

The data can be used in various ways. Examples might be planning for demographic changes, or deciding on transport development for a particular region. The data can also be used to examine national or local trends and to answer questions such as, 'How many mothers work outside the home?' 'Are people getting married later in life?' and so on. Some of the questions on the census form are designed to obtain information about living conditions in people's houses; for example, whether or not the house has a bathroom or toilet. Housing is classified as 'substandard' if it lacks at least one of the basic amenities (for example, hot water, inside toilet, kitchen, etc.).

The following figures, classified by region, give the number of substandard households (per 1000 households) in 1991.

Non-metropolitan counties (39)		Metropolitan districts (36)	
Avon	138	Bolton	247
Bedfordshire	134	Bury	154
Berkshire	113	Manchester	289
Buckinghamshire	87	Oldham	248
Cambridgeshire	162	Rochdale	201
Cheshire	145	Salford	270
Cleveland	192	Stockport	118
Cornwall	179	Tameside	210
Cumbria	165	Trafford	113
Devon	147	Wigan	200
Derbyshire	204	Knowsley	44
Dorset	116	Liverpool	293
Durham	225	St Helens	223
East Sussex	153	Sefton	158
Essex	106	Wirral	138
Gloucestershire	134	Bradford	175
Hampshire	122	Calderdale	195
Hereford and Worcester	147	Kirklees	183
Hertfordshire	73	Leeds	123
Humberside	198	Wakefield	134
Isle of Wight	158	Barnsley	200
Kent	147	Doncaster	164
Lancashire	199	Rotherham	182
Leicestershire	220	Sheffield	238
Lincolnshire	167	Birmingham	206
Norfolk	178	Coventry	156
Northamptonshire	144	Dudley	116
Northumberland	150	Sandwell	191
Yorkshire	125	Solihull	25
Nottinghamshire	191	Walsall	146
Oxfordshire	107	Wolverhampton	188
Somerset	125	Gateshead	186
Staffordshire	176	Newcastle upon Tyne	201
Shropshire	145	North Tyneside	158
Suffolk	176	South Tyneside	206
Surrey	84	Sunderland	183
Warwickshire	121		
West Sussex	72		
Wiltshire	104		

1 .2A

Draw a stem and leaf diagram for the data about the metropolitan districts. Comment on the suitability of a stem and leaf diagram for these data.

When dealing with large amounts of data, it is often much more convenient and sensible to collect the data values in groups. A possible grouping for the census data from the non-metropolitan counties is given below.

Number of substandard households (per 1000) in the non-metropolitan counties

Number of households (per 1000)	Frequency
60–79	2
80–99	2
100–119	5
120–139	7
140–159	9
160–179	7
180–199	4
200–219	1
220–239	2

Notice that here the groups are of equal width (60–79, 80–99 and so on) but often this is not the case. If there are few values in a group then several groups can be combined. For example, the data on substandard households could be re-grouped as follows:

No. of households (per 1000)	Frequency		No. of households (per 1000)	Frequency
60–99	4	*or*	60–139	16
100–119	5		140–179	16
120–139	7		180–239	7
140–159	9			
160–179	7			
180–239	7			

.2B

1 What should you consider when deciding what group widths to use?

2 Group the data on the metropolitan districts into a suitable grouping of your choice.

1.2.2 Representing grouped data – histograms

The lengths of 20 screws were measured. The results are shown below in a frequency table, together with a diagram to illustrate the data.

Length (mm)	Frequency
0–20	5
20–25	5
25–30	8
30–35	2

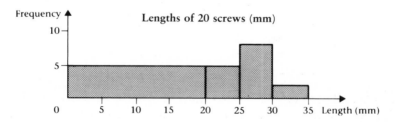

Lengths of 20 screws (mm)

This simple frequency diagram gives a distorted picture of the data. It gives the impression of a large number of screws in the 0–20 mm range. Worse, it suggests that there are 5 screws of length 0–5 mm, another 5 of length 5–10 mm and so on. In fact there are only 5 in the whole 0–20 mm range!

Representing the frequency by the height of the block causes problems when the data are grouped into *unequal* group intervals. It is the actual size or *area* of the block which is needed to represent the frequency.

$$\text{Frequency} = \text{area of block} = \text{width of interval} \times \text{height of block}$$

$$\text{Height of block} = \frac{\text{frequency}}{\text{width of interval}} = \text{frequency density}$$

Applying this idea to the distribution of screw lengths, the following frequency densities are obtained.

Length (mm)	Interval width	Frequency	Frequency density
0–20	20	5	$\frac{5}{20} = 0.25$
20–25	5	5	$\frac{5}{5} = 1.00$
25–30	5	8	$\frac{8}{5} = 1.60$
30–35	5	2	$\frac{2}{5} = 0.40$

The diagram is as follows:

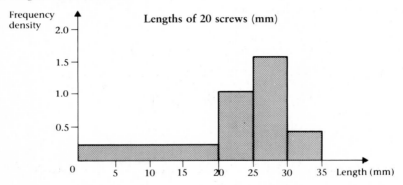

With the frequency density diagram above, there is no distortion as there was in the earlier diagram. This sort of diagram *should* be used when data are grouped into unequal **class intervals**.

A diagram where the frequency is represented by area is called a **histogram**. Note that there are *no gaps* between the groups and the vertical axis represents frequency density, *not* frequency.

When handling quantitative data you need to be aware of the existence of two distinct types of data – **continuous** and **discrete**.

Continuous data can, theoretically, be *any* values within a continuous range. Discrete data can only take *certain* values within a range. Examples of measurements which would produce continuous data are height, weight, and time. Examples of discrete measurements are marks on a test $(0, 1, 2, \ldots)$ or numbers in a family $(1, 2, 3, \ldots)$.

It is *always* important to consider the nature of the data, especially when drawing histograms. In the last section you saw how to draw a histogram for continuous measurements. The next example shows how to handle discrete data and also illustrates how to deal with the common problem of a group for which the interval is not fully defined.

Example 1

In a traffic survey, the number of cars passing a point in a one-minute interval was recorded over 120 successive intervals. The results were as follows:

Number of cars (N)	0–9	10–14	15–19	20–29	30+
Frequency (f)	18	46	35	13	12

Draw a histogram for these data.

Solution

To avoid gaps in the histogram the intervals are re-defined in a convenient way. This is illustrated in the sketch below for the 10–14 range (possible values 10, 11, 12, 13 and 14 only).

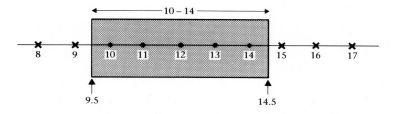

The first interval would therefore be re-defined as −0.5–9.5 to include all ten discrete data values from 0 to 9.

The frequency table becomes:

Class interval	−0.5–9.5	9.5–14.5	14.5–19.5	19.5–29.5	29.5–49.5
Frequency	18	46	35	13	12
Frequency density	$\frac{18}{10} = 1.80$	$\frac{46}{5} = 9.20$	$\frac{35}{5} = 7.00$	$\frac{13}{10} = 1.30$	$\frac{12}{20} = 0.60$

Notice that the last group (30+) has been defined to be of width 20, twice the width of the 20–29 group. This seems reasonable as it is likely that some of the eight values in this group are greater than 39; otherwise the data would all fall in the interval 30–39 and this would have been given as the group description.

Number of cars passing in a one-minute interval

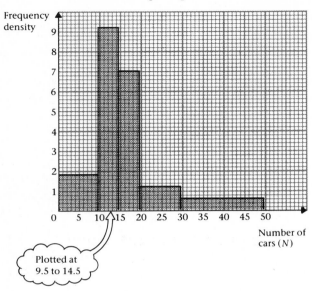

1.2 Exercise 1

1

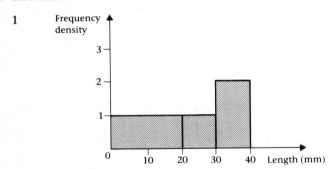

For the histogram shown:

(a) how many of the lengths are in the intervals

    (i) 20–30 mm   (ii) 30–40 mm   (iii) 0–20 mm

(b) what is the total frequency?

2 For the histogram shown, find the total frequency.

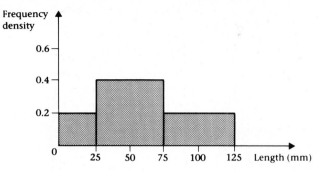

3 Construct histograms for the following data sets.

(a)

Volume (cm^3)	f
0–5	5
5–10	5
10–20	10
20–30	20
30–40	10
40–60	5

(b)

Number of cars per hour	f
50–59	10
60–79	30
80–99	20
100–139	10

4 Rainfall data are provided below for 50 weather stations in the north of England and 50 in the south. Each figure represents total rainfall (in mm) for June.

(a) Decide on a sensible grouping, which should be the same for the north and south. (Consider using unequal widths if this is sensible.)

(b) Construct frequency tables based on your choice of group size.

(c) Draw histograms for both data sets separately.

(d) Comment briefly on the two distributions.

Northern weather stations (mm of rain)

59	106	109	74	104	115	94	225	140	217
146	149	140	121	132	78	114	86	87	126
120	101	125	108	105	112	97	83	77	88
106	123	95	113	105	144	117	107	174	176
108	87	110	95	78	103	87	83	87	80

Southern weather stations (mm of rain)

89	89	111	93	73	121	103	80	108	88
75	79	103	107	70	82	97	59	90	53
67	46	43	65	112	115	99	217	83	61
98	90	95	87	86	77	96	70	111	74
81	70	72	87	68	85	100	67	54	109

5 Draw histograms to represent the data on substandard housing in the non-metropolitan counties and metropolitan districts provided on page 21. Use the same grouping for both histograms. Comment briefly on the two distributions.

1.2.3 Averages and spread

You have seen that the mean, median and mode are all measures of the 'average' value of a set of data. The mean is particularly important in statistical work and a special symbol is introduced for it.

Suppose the observed values are $x_1, x_2, x_3, \ldots, x_r, \ldots, x_n$.

$$\text{Mean} = \frac{\text{Sum of observed values}}{\text{Number of observations}}$$

'x bar' – for the mean of the values

$$\bar{x} = \frac{\text{Sum}(x_1, x_2, \ldots, x_n)}{n}$$

$$\bar{x} = \frac{1}{n} \sum x$$

Sigma x – for the sum of the observations

Keys for $\boxed{\bar{x}}$ and $\boxed{\sum x}$ are on your calculator.

Check that you can use *your* calculator to obtain $\sum x$ and $\bar{x}$ for a set of values.

The following are the scores awarded to two gymnasts in a competition.

First gymnast	9.7	9.5	9.7	9.8	9.9	9.6
Second gymnast	8.8	9.2	8.8	9.8	9.4	9.8

The scores can be shown along a number line as follows.

First gymnast

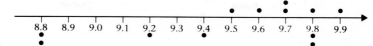

Second gymnast

The scores of the second gymnast are much more spread out. It is useful to have a *number* to represent **spread**: for this you need to define a reference point and consider how spread out the observations are about the reference point.

The obvious points about which to measure spread would seem to be the median and the mean, as they represent 'average' values for the data.

You have already met one measure of spread which is measured about the median – the interquartile range. It has the disadvantage of being insensitive to changes in the 'outer' 50% of the data. A possible measure of spread around the mean is

the sum of the differences from the mean, i.e. $\sum (x - \bar{x})$

With this, however, positive and negative differences cancel each other out and the result is *always* zero. This problem with negative differences can be solved in two ways, by considering either

the sum of the squares of the differences $\qquad \sum (x - \bar{x})^2$

or the sum of the absolute value of the differences $\quad \sum |x - \bar{x}|$

Also, a measure of spread should not be dependent on the number of values in the sample, so an 'average' needs to be taken.

It is conventional to take the mean as the reference point. One measure of spread considers the mean of the deviations from the mean. This is the mean absolute deviation. A second and more important measure takes the *mean of the squared distances from the mean*. This is the **variance**.

Example 2

Calculate the mean and variance of the ages of seven children at a holiday playgroup. These ages are 1, 2, 2, 3, 5, 6 and 9 years.

Solution

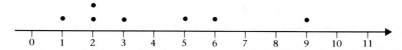

For these data,

$$\bar{x} = \tfrac{1}{7}(1 + 2 + 2 + 3 + 5 + 6 + 9) = 4$$

The sum of the squared distance of each point from the mean is

$$(1 - 4)^2 + (2 - 4)^2 + (2 - 4)^2 + (3 - 4)^2 + (5 - 4)^2 + (6 - 4)^2$$
$$+ (9 - 4)^2 = 48$$

The mean squared deviation from the mean is $\frac{48}{7} = 6.86$.

So, for the data given, the mean age is 4 years and the variance is 6.86 years^2.

Statisticians use the variance *and* the *square root of the variance*, called the **standard deviation**, to measure spread. Both are important measures and are in common use.

> The mean of the sum of the squared distances from the mean is called the variance. It is conventional to use the square root of the variance as a measure of spread around the mean. This is called the standard deviation.
>
> Standard deviation = $\sqrt{\text{variance}}$

 .2c

1 Find the mean and standard deviation of the scores for each gymnast given on page 28.

2 Obtain by direct calculation the standard deviation for each data set below and comment on how well the standard deviation seems to measure spread.

(a) 5, 5, 5, 5, 5, 5, 5   (b) 1, 2, 3, 4, 5

(c) 1, 2, 3, 4, 5, 6   (d) 2, 4, 6, 8, 10

3 Investigate, by considering a number of data sets, what happens to the mean and the standard deviation when:

(a) all the values in the data set are increased by the same value, for example 2, 5, 7 becomes 12, 15, 17;

(b) all the values are multiplied by the same number, for example 2, 5, 7 becomes 6, 15, 21.

Write down your conclusions.

You should have observed the following results for the mean and standard deviation.

When all data values are multiplied by a constant a, then the new mean and the new standard deviation are a times the original mean and standard deviation.

When a constant value, b, is added to all data values, then the mean is also increased by b. However, the standard deviation does not change.

Intuition tells you that these results are obvious, although they will be proved later when we have an algebraic formula for the variance and standard deviation. If you think about data points on the number line, it should be clear that adding a constant to each simply moves each point along the line; the points do not become more spread out. So the mean increases by the constant while the standard deviation does not change.

When you multiply by a constant (for example, a), then the distance between each point increases by a factor of a; the points are more spread out and the spread is a times as great. The mean and standard deviation increase by a factor of a.

The phrase 'standard deviation' is often abbreviated to s.d. and the symbol used to denote standard deviation is, by convention, the letter s. The result above can then be expressed as

Original data values	$x_1, x_2, \ldots, x_n$	mean $= \bar{x}$	s.d. $= s$
Data values if multiplied by a	$ax_1, ax_2, \ldots, ax_n$	mean $= a\bar{x}$	s.d. $= as$
Data values if b is added	$x_1 + b, x_2 + b, \ldots, x_n + b$	mean $= \bar{x} + b$	s.d. $= s$

1.2 Exercise 2

1 A student measures the resistance of a piece of wire, repeating the experiment six times to check her results. Her results are:

Resistance (ohms)   54.2   53.7   55.0   53.7   54.0   54.6

(a) Find the mean and standard deviation of the readings.

(b) She discovers that each reading in the table is 10% too high, because of faulty equipment. Write down the new mean and standard deviation.

2 A teacher's class has 32 pupils, having a mean age of 14.0 years and a standard deviation of 0.25 years. Write down the standard deviation of the ages of the same 32 pupils two years later.

3 The temperature is recorded at 12 weather stations in and around London on a given day. The mean recorded temperature is 12 °C, with a standard deviation of 0.5 °C. Write down the mean temperature and the standard deviation in degrees Fahrenheit.

1.2.4 Formulas for variance and standard deviation

Sometimes it is necessary to have a formula for the variance. This is important not simply in *calculating* a variance; it can also be useful in general mathematical work, for example to see how the variance relates to other measures. You can obtain a formula as follows.

Suppose a set of data values is $x_1, x_2, x_3, \ldots, x_n$, having a mean value of $\bar{x}$.

The squared differences from the mean are:

$$(x_1 - \bar{x})^2, (x_2 - \bar{x})^2, \ldots, (x_n - \bar{x})^2$$

The total of these squared differences is $\sum (x - \bar{x})^2$.

> This means add up all the squared differences $(x - \bar{x})^2$

So the mean of the squared differences is $\dfrac{\sum (x - \bar{x})^2}{n}$.

$$\text{Variance} = \frac{\sum (x - \bar{x})^2}{n}$$

$$\text{Standard deviation} = \sqrt{\left(\frac{\sum (x - \bar{x})^2}{n} \right)}$$

An algorithm for direct calculation of the variance using this result is illustrated.

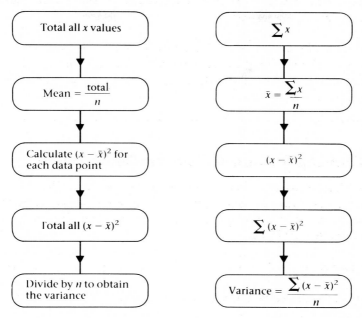

.2D

1 Use this algorithm to calculate the variance of the following values.

(a) 2.1,   3.8,   3.9,   6.2

(b) 30,   29,   47

2 Comment on any difficulties in obtaining the variance using this algorithm.

The algorithm provided is not efficient and you might look for an alternative expression.

Having an algebraic form for the variance means that you can, by some manipulation, consider other ways of expressing the result, and this is illustrated below.

$$\text{Variance} = \frac{\sum (x - \bar{x})^2}{n} = \frac{1}{n} \sum (x - \bar{x})(x - \bar{x})$$

$$= \frac{1}{n} \sum (x^2 - 2x\bar{x} + (\bar{x})^2)$$

$$= \frac{\sum x^2}{n} - \frac{\sum 2x\bar{x}}{n} + \frac{\sum (\bar{x})^2}{n} \qquad ①$$

Since $\bar{x}$ is a constant, it may be taken out of the sum in the second term as a factor.

$$\frac{\sum 2x\bar{x}}{n} = 2\bar{x}\frac{\sum x}{n} = 2\bar{x}\bar{x} = 2(\bar{x})^2$$

Consider the term $\dfrac{\sum (\bar{x})^2}{n}$. This is simply $(\bar{x})^2$, a constant, added to itself n times and the result divided by n, so

$$\frac{\sum (\bar{x})^2}{n} = \frac{n(\bar{x})^2}{n} = (\bar{x})^2$$

With these simplifications, expression ① for the variance becomes

$$\text{Variance} = \frac{\sum x^2}{n} - 2(\bar{x})^2 + (\bar{x})^2$$

$$= \frac{\sum x^2}{n} - (\bar{x})^2$$

This is a very useful form and saves a great deal of work when evaluating the variance by direct calculation.

$$\text{Variance} = \frac{\sum(x-\bar{x})^2}{n} = \frac{\sum x^2}{n} - \bar{x}^2$$

Example 3

The weights (in kilograms) of the eight forwards in a school rugby team are 65, 60, 70, 58, 61, 52, 72 and 70.

Calculate the mean weight and the standard deviation of the weights.

Solution

$$\text{Mean} = \tfrac{1}{8}(65 + 60 + \ldots + 70) = \tfrac{508}{8} = 63.5 \, \text{kg}$$

$$\text{Variance} = \tfrac{1}{8}(65^2 + 60^2 + 70^2 + 58^2 + 61^2 + 52^2 + 72^2 + 70^2) - 63.5^2$$

$$= \tfrac{32\,598}{8} - (63.5)^2$$

$$= 42.5$$

$$\text{Standard deviation} = \sqrt{42.5} = 6.52 \, \text{kg}$$

1.2 Exercise 3

1 The ages of the children at a party were 2, 3, 3, 4, 5, 5, 5, 6, 7, 8, 8, 9, 9 and 10 years. Find the mean and standard deviation.

2 15 sacks of potatoes were taken from a lorry and weighed. The masses were 49, 52, 47, 53, 55, 48, 50, 50, 54, 52, 51, 52, 49, 50 and 53 kg, to the nearest kilogram.

   (a) Calculate the mean and standard deviation of these masses.

   (b) If the lorry could take a maximum load of 5 tonnes, how many sacks would you recommend loading on it?

3 Five people in a lift have a mean weight $\bar{w} = 70$ kg. The standard deviation of their weights is 10 kg.

   (a) Find their total weight, $\sum w$, and $\sum w^2$.

   (b) A man weighing 80 kg leaves the lift. Calculate the mean and standard deviation of the weight of those remaining.

4 30 pears in a tray have a mean mass of 105 g and a standard deviation of 6.1 g. Calculate the total of the squared deviations from the mean of their masses.

   If another tray contains 20 pears with mean mass 105 g and standard deviation 8.4 g, find the total of the squared deviations from the mean for all 50 pears in the two trays, and deduce their standard deviation.

5E From the formulas for mean and standard deviation, prove that

   (a) if $y = x + k$, then $\bar{y} = \bar{x} + k$ and the standard deviations of x and y are equal;

   (b) if $z = kx$, then $\bar{z} = k\bar{x}$ and the standard deviation of z is k times the standard deviation of x.

1.2.5 The mean and variance for grouped data

The table shows the number of shots played in each of fifty rallies between two tennis players before and after a coaching session. Only the grouped data for the length of each of the fifty rallies are recorded, not the original results.

Number of shots in rally	Number of rallies	
	Before coaching	After coaching
1–10	32	5
11–20	12	20
21–30	3	15
31–40	2	3
41–50	1	5
51–60	–	2
Total	50	50

Use the **mid-interval value** as representative of the length of rally in the group. The 'before coaching' table becomes

Before coaching

Group	Midpoint	Frequency
1–10	5.5	32
11–20	15.5	12
21–30	25.5	3
31–40	35.5	2
41–50	$\frac{41+50}{2}=45.5 \Rightarrow$ 45.5	1

Take each of the rallies in the 1–10 group as having 5.5 shots. Then the total number of shots played for these 32 rallies is *estimated* to be $32 \times 5.5 = 176$.

The data can now be entered into your calculator as

> 32 rallies of 5.5,
> 12 rallies of 15.5, and so on

 .2E

Find out how to use your calculator to obtain means, variances and standard deviations for grouped data.

Enter the data in your calculator and confirm that the values of the mean rally length and the standard deviation are 11.1 and 9.2 respectively.

For direct calculations, the formula for the variance for grouped frequency distributions would be obtained as follows.

Let the group mid-value be x. Let the number of data values be f.

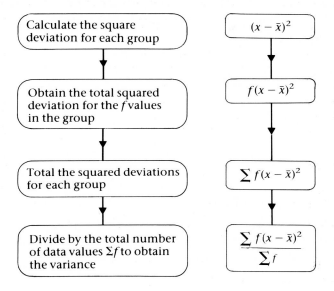

$$\text{Variance} = \frac{\sum f(x - \bar{x})^2}{\sum f}$$

An alternative form (equivalent to that obtained on page 34), which is more useful in calculations and often more accurate, is

$$\text{Variance} = \frac{\sum fx^2}{\sum f} - \bar{x}^2$$

1.2 Exercise 4

You should use the statistical functions on your calculator for this exercise.

1 (a) For the tennis data on page 36, calculate the mean and standard deviation of the length of rallies after coaching.

   (b) Has the coaching made a difference in this case? Justify your answer.

2 The projected population distribution of England and Wales for the year 2025 is given below. Calculate:

(a) the total population,

(b) the mean and standard deviation of the age of the population.

Age group (years)	Frequency (thousands)
0–14	9 928
15–29	9 953
30–44	10 075
45–59	9 808
60–74	8 989
75–89	4 289
90–99	469

Be careful with age calculations!

This group has people from 15 to *just* below 30.

The midpoint will be

$\frac{15+30}{2} = 22.5$ yrs

3 The age distribution of the population of England and Wales in 1986 is given below.

Age group (years)	Mid-value x (years)	Frequency (thousands)
0–14	7.5	9 410
15–29	22.5	11 835
30–44	37.5	10 202
45–59	52.5	8 147
60–74	67.5	7 171
75–89	82.5	3 114
90 +	95	184

Take the group for 90+ to be 90–99 years old

(a) Why is it reasonable to take the last group to be 90–99 years?

(b) Calculate the mean and standard deviation of the population in 1986.

(c) Using your answers to questions 2 and 3(b), comment on what is expected to happen to the age distribution in England and Wales as the years pass.

4 In a statistical investigation of the works of Charles Dickens, a student records the lengths of a number of randomly chosen sentences taken from one of his novels. The results are indicated below.

Sentence length (number of words)	Frequency
1–5	2
6–10	7
11–20	46
21–30	27
31–40	19
41–50	7
50+	2
Total	110

Choose a suitable upper value for the last group and calculate estimates for the mean and standard deviation of the number of words per sentence of this work.

Give two reasons why the estimates might be inaccurate.

After working through section 1.2 you should:

1 be able to draw histograms for discrete and continuous data;

2 know that the variance is the mean of all the squared deviations from the mean;

3 know that the standard deviation is another measure of spread and is equal to the square root of the variance;

4 be familiar with the following results:

For raw data

$$\bar{x} = \frac{\sum x}{n}$$

$$\text{variance} = \frac{\sum (x - \bar{x})^2}{n}$$

or $\quad \dfrac{\sum x^2}{n} - \bar{x}^2$

For frequency distributions

$$\bar{x} = \frac{\sum fx}{\sum f}$$

$$\text{variance} = \frac{\sum f(x - \bar{x})^2}{\sum f}$$

or $\quad \dfrac{\sum fx^2}{\sum f} - \bar{x}^2$

5 know that:

(a) if each value is multiplied by a constant a, then the standard deviation and the mean are also multiplied by a,

(b) if each value is increased by adding on a constant b, then the standard deviation is unchanged, but the mean is increased by b.

1 Living with uncertainty

.3 Probability models

1.3.1 Order from chaos

Statistics and probability might appear to have applications only in the social sciences and not in the natural, physical world. The quotations below give an indication that probability is also profoundly important in the physical and biological sciences.

Gott würfelt nicht.
(God does not play dice.)

Albert Einstein

Whence comes all that order
and beauty we see in the world?

Isaac Newton

In current theories about the behaviour of small particles, of the origin of the universe and of life on our planet (and elsewhere!) the idea of chance looms large. Richard Feynman, one of the greatest theoretical physicists of this century, wrote:

> ... *what we are proposing is that there is probability all the way back: that in the fundamental laws of physics there are odds.*

Richard Feynman, *The Character of Physical Law* (MIT Press, 1977)

The emergence of ideas of chance into basic physical laws started with the kinetic theory of gases in the nineteenth century and continued in the twentieth century with the development of quantum mechanics.

In general, quantum mechanics does not predict a single definite result for an observation. Instead, it predicts a number of different possible outcomes and tells us how likely each of these is.

Stephen Hawking, *A Brief History of Time* (Bantam Press, 1988)

Chance also plays a large part in biology.

The essence of life is statistical improbability on a colossal scale.

Richard Dawkins, *The Blind Watchmaker* (Longman, 1986)

Ideas of probability are fundamental to our understanding of the nature of life, of evolution and of the creation and behaviour of matter.

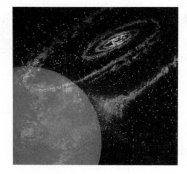

In the nineteenth century, James Clerk Maxwell (in Cambridge) and Ludwig Boltzmann (in Austria) first introduced the ideas of randomness and chance events into the laws of physics with the kinetic theory of gases. They pictured a gas as a vast collection of individual molecules, rushing around chaotically in different directions and at different speeds, colliding with each other and with the walls of the container.

A simple experiment on gases which involves basic ideas of probability is to take a jar containing two gases which are distinguishable (for example by colour). The gases are initially separated by a barrier.

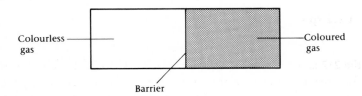

The barrier is removed and the gases mix freely. There will soon be molecules of each gas in each half of the jar. To understand why this happens consider a simplified situation in which there are only four molecules.

Each molecule moves around the jar in a random fashion; sometimes it will be in the left half of the jar and sometimes in the right. The possible distributions are shown in the following table.

No. of molecules on left	No. of molecules on right
4	0
3	1
2	2
1	3
0	4

To assess the probabilities of the five possible distributions it is helpful to 'label' the molecules. There is only one distribution with all molecules on the left:

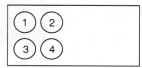

You are not interested in the exact position of a molecule, only in whether it is on the left or the right

whereas there are four cases of a 1:3 split.

 .3A

1 Illustrate the four cases of the 1:3 split.

2 How many cases are there for a 2:2 split?

3 With four molecules, how many different cases are there altogether?

4 Write down the probabilities of:

(a) a 1:3 split;

(b) all four molecules on one side of the box and none in the other;

(c) a 2:2 split.

Though the 2:2 split is the most likely, you will see that each of the others is possible. In a real experiment with a very large number of molecules, although all conceivable states are possible, you can show by a similar argument that each side is likely to contain roughly equal numbers of each type of molecule.

Despite the continuous motion of each molecule, the overall state remains roughly constant. The system is said to be in **dynamic equilibrium**.

The ideas of probability and statistics are now firmly embedded in all kinds of scientific study. In turn, some of the greatest scientists, by applying these ideas, have furthered our understanding of probability and statistics.

The outcome of events in real life is often unpredictable. When a coin is tossed, heads and tails occur at random. No one can yet predict whether the act of conception will produce a male or a female. Although the motion of individual gas molecules is random, the distribution of large numbers of molecules can be described and predicted by physical laws.

In the beginning ...
how the heavens
and earth rose out
of chaos.

Milton

In all these cases, although the outcome of individual events is random, the accumulation of large numbers of similar events produces patterns. Over many trials, a coin will tend to fall as many times on one side as on the other side, and about half the number of babies born are girls.

In order to assess the significance of data objectively, you need to construct **probability models** for the circumstances which generate the data. In this chapter you will learn how to construct probability models for some simple cases.

An example is considered in the following situation.

 .3B

When a piece of toast drops to the floor, it usually lands buttered-side down

(Murphy's law)

1 Does the evidence in the cartoon prove Murphy's law?

2 Would Murphy's law be proved if 70 out of 100 pieces landed butter-side down?

1.3.2 Making probability models

When a measurement or experiment is repeated a number of times, you can record for each outcome:

the **frequency** : how often it occurs
the **relative frequency** : the frequency divided by the number of trials

Although outcomes occur randomly, the relative frequency appears to become close to a fixed number, between 0 and 1, as the number of trials increases. This number, the **probability**, gives a measure of the likelihood of a particular outcome at each trial.

Likelihood	impossible	certain
Probability	0	1

Sometimes you can calculate a value for the probability by arguing that there is a set of outcomes which are 'equally likely'. Often in statistics it is not possible to do this, and you can only propose values for probabilities based on relative frequencies or past experience.

The outcome of statistical enquiries or experiments often produces numerical data. For example, when a die is thrown, the outcome is a number from 1 to 6; a traffic survey produces a number of vehicles per minute; weather data produce the number of millimetres of rainfall per day; a survey of family size might be used to investigate the number of children per family, or annual income. In all these cases, the outcome is a variable which has a set of possible values.

The value which the variable takes for any particular throw of a die, or vehicle count, or day's rainfall, and so on, is essentially random: you cannot predict with certainty what its value will be. These variables are therefore called **random variables**.

Random variable	Set of possible values
Score on a die	1, 2, 3, 4, 5, 6
Number of vehicles per minute	0, 1, 2, ...
Rainfall in millimetres	Any positive real number
etc. ...	...

It is useful to denote a random variable by a capital letter, for example X, and the particular values it can take by lower case letters, for example $x_1, x_2, x_3, \ldots, x_n$. So if a random variable, S, is the score on a die, the particular values it can take are $s = 1, 2, 3, 4, 5, 6$.

Example 1

Two dice are thrown and the number of sixes counted. Calculate and list the probabilities of obtaining 0, 1 and 2 sixes.

Solution
Assume the dice are fair $\Rightarrow P(\text{six}) = \frac{1}{6}$.

Let X be the number of sixes ($x = 0$, 1 or 2).

$$P(x = 0) = \left(\frac{5}{6}\right)^2 = \frac{25}{36}$$

Two possible outcomes occur for one six: (six, no six)   or   (no six, six):

$$P(x = 1) = \frac{1}{6} \cdot \frac{5}{6} + \frac{5}{6} \cdot \frac{1}{6} = \frac{10}{36}$$

Only one outcome leads to $x = 2$ (two sixes):

$$P(x = 2) = P(\text{six, six}) = \left(\frac{1}{6}\right)^2 = \frac{1}{36}$$

x	0	1	2
$P(X = x)$	$\frac{25}{36}$	$\frac{10}{36}$	$\frac{1}{36}$

The list or table above is called the **probability distribution** for the random variable X. In general, the probability distribution for a random variable is a statement (or table) which assigns probabilities to the possible values of the variable.

Sometimes probabilities are assigned by arguing that the possible outcomes are equally likely. But in other cases, you may need to estimate the probabilities from relative frequencies, or from past experience.

Note that, since the probability distribution gives the probability of every possible outcome, the sum of the probabilities must be 1 (one of the events *must* happen).

> For any probability distribution, the sum of the probabilities must equal 1.

Example 2

A family with two children is chosen at random. The random variable X stands for the number of boys. Assume each child is equally likely to be a boy or girl.

(a) Write down the probability distribution for the random variable.

(b) Draw a graph of the probability distribution.

Solution

(a) Considering the sex of the children (youngest followed by eldest) gives a set of four equally likely outcomes $\{(B, B) \ (B, G) \ (G, B) \ (G, G)\}$

Only one of the four possible outcomes gives two boys, so

$$P(x = 2) = \tfrac{1}{4}$$

Two possible outcomes result in just one boy in the family, so

$$P(x = 1) = \tfrac{2}{4}$$

By a similar argument

$$P(x = 0) = \tfrac{1}{4}$$

x	0	1	2
$P(X = x)$	0.25	0.5	0.25

Notice that the three possible values for X are *not* equally likely and that the sum of the probabilities equals 1. The most likely number of boys is 1.

(b) As X can only take discrete values, the most appropriate form of graph is a **stick graph**.

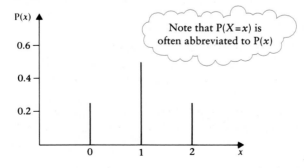

Note that $P(X=x)$ is often abbreviated to $P(x)$

There are two fundamentally different types of distribution of quantitative data: continuous and discrete. Similarly, there are the same two types of probability model.

The time taken for a telephone call is a **continuous** random variable. The duration of a call can theoretically take any real number value (within reasonable limits for telephone calls). On the other hand, many variables are **discrete**. They cannot be said to vary continuously. For example, the number of children in a family must be a whole number.

Other examples are:

Discrete	Continuous
The number of children in a family	Weight
The number of cracked eggs in a box of 6	Height
The number of kittens in a litter	Reaction time

1.3 Exercise 1

For each of the following random variables, either calculate its probability distribution or estimate it using relative frequencies calculated from the data given. Check also that the sum of the probabilities in each distribution is 1.

1 S = score obtained throwing an unbiased die.

2 X = number of children in a family chosen from the following population.

Number of children x	0	1	2	3	4 or over
Number of families f	123	179	457	88	45

3 S = score when a coin is tossed, counting 0 for a head and 1 for a tail.

4 Y = value of a playing card cut from a pack, counting 1 for an ace, and 10 for a ten, jack, queen or king.

5 T = duration of a telephone call.

Duration (min) t	0–1	1–2	2–3	3 or over
Number of calls f	230	420	480	358

6 X = positive difference of the scores showing on two dice (so that $(6, 2)$ would score 4, as would $(2, 6)$).

7 H = the number of heads when three coins are thrown.

1.3.3 The mean and variance of a random variable

In section 1.2, you used the *mean* as a representative value for a set of data. For a sample of values of a variable X you calculated this using the formula

$$\bar{x} = \frac{\sum fx}{n}$$

Σ stands for 'the sum of'

where f is the frequency of the value x, and n is the total number of values. As the frequency f divided by the total number of values n is the relative frequency, you can rewrite this formula using relative frequencies.

$$\bar{x} = \sum \left(\frac{f}{n}\right)x$$

So to calculate the mean, you multiply the values of x by their relative frequencies, and sum over all values of x.

Example 3
Using relative frequencies, calculate the mean of the following data set: 1, 1, 2, 3, 3, 3, 3, 3, 4, 4.

Solution

x	1	2	3	4	
f	2	1	5	2	$n = 10$
$\dfrac{f}{n}$	0.2	0.1	0.5	0.2	

$$\text{Mean} = \sum \left(\frac{f}{n}\right)x$$

$$= 0.2 \times 1 + 0.1 \times 2 + 0.5 \times 3 + 0.2 \times 4$$

$$= 2.7$$

Suppose you are to be 'banker' in the following game. You ask the player to select a card at random from a special yellow pack. You pay out £y, where y is the number on the card selected. The full pack is reshuffled after each game. The mean winnings per game is given by the formula

$$\bar{y} = \sum \left(\frac{f}{n}\right)y$$

There are 40 yellow cards in the pack and the constitution of the pack is as follows.

Score on card (y)	1	2	3	4
Number of cards (f)	16	12	8	4

◆ .3c

1 You play the game 400 times. How much would you expect to pay out? What would be a reasonable amount to charge for each game?

2 Out of 1000 games, you would expect, 'on average', 400 £1 payouts, 300 £2 payouts, 200 £3 payouts and 100 £4 payouts.

y	1	2	3	4	
f	400	300	200	100	$n = 1000$
$\dfrac{f}{n}$	0.4	0.3	0.2	0.1	

Achieving this precise result is, of course, unlikely, but it is the distribution you might 'expect' from the probability distribution. Work out the mean of these winnings.

The 'expected relative frequencies' are simply the probabilities. So this mean value is simply the sum of the values of Y multiplied by their probabilities.

$$\text{Mean} = \sum y\,P(y)$$

The mean represents the average winnings from a game. It is called the **mean of the random variable Y**, and is often denoted by the Greek letter μ ('mu'). To break even in the long run, you should charge this amount per game.

3 A pack of blue cards is made up as follows.

Score on card	1	2	3	4
Number of cards	10	20	10	0

(a) Write down the probability distribution for B, the score on a card selected from this pack.

(b) Calculate the mean μ of the random variable B.

For any discrete random variable X, the mean is defined as

$$\mu = \sum x\,P(x)$$

This means that to find the mean of a discrete random variable, you multiply the values of X by their probabilities, and add. Compare the formulas for sample distributions and probability distributions.

Real world	Mathematical model
Sample distributions	Probability distributions
$\bar{x} = \sum \left(\dfrac{f}{n}\right) x$	$\mu = \sum x \, \mathrm{P}(x)$

For probability distributions, the relative frequencies are replaced by the probabilities. For large samples, relative frequency and probability are likely to be close, and get closer as the sample size gets larger and larger.

The ideas used to calculate the mean of a random variable from its probability distribution can also be applied to the variance.

The variance of a frequency distribution can be redefined in terms of relative frequency.

$$\text{Variance} = \frac{\sum fx^2}{n} - \bar{x}^2$$

$$= \sum \left(\frac{f}{n}\right) x^2 - \bar{x}^2$$

Replacing relative frequency with probability gives a formula for the variance of the random variable. The symbol σ^2 ('sigma squared') is used to denote this variance to distinguish it from the sample variance which is given the symbol s^2. So the *standard deviation* of the population is σ and of a sample is s.

Real world	Mathematical model
Sample distributions	Probability distributions
$s^2 = \sum \left(\dfrac{f}{n}\right) x^2 - \bar{x}^2$	$\sigma^2 = \sum x^2 \, \mathrm{P}(x) - \mu^2$

Example 4

Calculate (a) the mean and (b) the standard deviation of the number of boys in a family of two children.

Solution

(a) The mean

n	0	1	2
P(n)	0.25	0.5	0.25

$$\mu = \sum n\,\mathrm{P}(n)$$

$$= 0 \times 0.25 + 1 \times 0.5 + 2 \times 0.25$$

$$= 1$$

Using this probability model, you can predict that for a large sample of families with two children, the mean number of boys per family will be approximately 1.

(b) The standard deviation

$$\sigma^2 = \sum n^2\,\mathrm{P}(n) - \mu^2$$

$$= (0^2 \times 0.25 + 1^2 \times 0.5 + 2^2 \times 0.25) - 1^2$$

$$= 1.5 - 1 = 0.5$$

$$\sigma = 0.707$$

According to this probability model, you can predict that for a large sample of families with two children, the standard deviation of the number of boys will be approximately 0.707.

Example 5

At a fund-raising charity event a game consists of rolling three regular six-sided dice. Each die has two yellow, two blue and two red faces. If all three faces show the same colour then you pay out a prize of £1. If two faces are the same colour, you pay 10p. How much should you charge per turn so that you can expect to make a profit for the charity?

Solution

$$\mathrm{P(red)} = \mathrm{P(blue)} = \mathrm{P(yellow)} = \tfrac{1}{3}$$

$$\mathrm{P(all\ the\ same\ colour)} = \mathrm{P(all\ red)} + \mathrm{P(all\ blue)} + \mathrm{P(all\ yellow)}$$

$$= \left(\tfrac{1}{3}\right)^3 + \left(\tfrac{1}{3}\right)^3 + \left(\tfrac{1}{3}\right)^3 = \tfrac{1}{9}$$

$$\mathrm{P(two\ the\ same\ colour)} = \mathrm{P(two\ reds)} + \mathrm{P(two\ blues)} + \mathrm{P(two\ yellows)}$$

Two reds can be obtained as follows:

$$R\,R\,(Y \text{ or } B) \quad \text{or} \quad R\,(Y \text{ or } B)\,R \quad \text{or} \quad (Y \text{ or } B)\,R\,R$$

So, P(two reds) $= 3 \times \frac{1}{3} \times \frac{1}{3} \times \frac{2}{3} = \frac{2}{9}$

Similarly, P(two yellows) $=$ P(two blues) $= \frac{2}{9}$

So P(two the same colour) $= \frac{6}{9}$

Let $X =$ amount paid out per game (in pence). X takes values in the set $\{0, 10, 100\}$.

x	0	10	100
$P(x)$	$\frac{2}{9}$	$\frac{6}{9}$	$\frac{1}{9}$

Mean of $X = 0 \times \frac{2}{9} + 10 \times \frac{6}{9} + 100 \times \frac{1}{9}$

$= \frac{160}{9} = 17\frac{7}{9}$ pence

Since on average you would pay out $17\frac{7}{9}$ pence per game, if you charge anything greater than this you can expect to make a profit. If you charged 20p a game you would make an average profit of $2\frac{2}{9}$ p per game.

Working through calculations for mean and variance a few times should give you a 'feel' for the meaning of these important statistical formulas. However, to save time spent on laborious 'number-crunching', you may already have been tempted to see if the statistical function keys of your calculator will work out means and variances for random variables, just as they did for data. The answer is that they can! All that is required is for probabilities to be entered instead of frequencies.

1.3 Exercise 2

For questions 1, 2, 3 in this exercise you should calculate the mean and variance *without* using the statistical functions on your calculator.

1 The random variable D has the value obtained from a single roll of an unbiased die. Write down the probability distribution for D, and calculate the mean and the variance.

2 There are five coins in a bag, one 50p coin, two 20p coins and two 10p coins. One coin is withdrawn at random. Calculate the mean value of the amount withdrawn and the variance.

3 Calculate the mean and variance of the score for each of the spinners shown below.

(a)
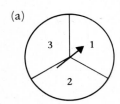

(b)
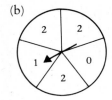

(c)
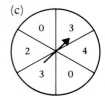

4 A card is withdrawn at random from a pack of playing cards. Counting 1 for an ace and 10 for a jack, queen or king, calculate the mean and variance of the value of the card withdrawn.

5 I walk to work two days in five, cycle two days in five, and take the bus one day in five. The walk takes 45 minutes, cycling takes 20 minutes and the bus 15 minutes. Define a random variable to model this situation, and hence calculate the mean time for my journey.

6 (a)

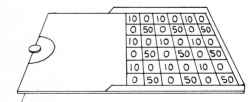

In a game of 'shove ha'penny', a player pushes a penny to land on the grid shown. Assume that the penny lands at random inside the frame, and the amount scored is the amount in pence shown in the square containing the centre of the coin. Work out the expected gain.

(b) Suppose that, to win, the coin must land entirely inside a square, and that the side of each square is twice the diameter of the coin. By considering the area of the square within which the centre must lie for the coin to land entirely in the square, work out the probability that this happens. Deduce what the expected gain is now.

7 For a probability model, the variance is defined by

$$\sum (x - \mu)^2 \, P(x) \quad \text{where} \quad \sum P(x) = 1 \quad \text{and} \quad \mu = \sum x \, P(x)$$

Write out the algebraic proof that the variance can be written as

$$\sum x^2 \, P(x) - \mu^2$$

After working through section 1.3 you should:

1 understand the terms **random variable** and **probability distribution;**

2 be able to construct simple probability models;

3 appreciate the difference between **discrete** and **continuous** random variables;

4 be able to calculate the **mean** and **variance** of a discrete random variable and understand their significance.

1 Living with uncertainty

.4 More probability models

1.4.1 Compound events

In using probability models it is often necessary to consider outcomes of events which are combinations of simpler events. These are called **compound events**.

> If two events are such that *the occurrence of one does not affect the probability of the other occurring*, they are called **independent events**.
>
> The probability of two independent events *both* occurring can be found by multiplying their individual probabilities.

Example 1
Three coins are tossed. What is the probability of obtaining three tails?

Solution
The tosses are independent events and so

$$P(T\ T\ T) = P(T) \times P(T) \times P(T)$$
$$= 0.5 \times 0.5 \times 0.5$$
$$= 0.125$$

Example 2
Suppose that 20% of cars fail the Department of Transport (or MOT) test on steering and 30% on brakes. What is the probability of a randomly chosen car passing on both counts?

Solution
Assuming the events 'failing on steering' and 'failing on brakes' are independent, then

$$P(\text{passing on brakes } and \text{ on steering}) = 0.8 \times 0.7$$
$$= 0.56$$

In practice, you might expect the events not to be independent. It is likely that of those cars that fail the brake test, a higher proportion than average also fail the steering test. If this is true, the answer calculated on the assumption of independence will be an underestimate.

In the examples above you looked at the compound event 'A and B'. If A and B are independent events then P(A and B) = P(A) × P(B). In many situations you might be interested in the event that 'A or B' happens. This is considered below.

 .4A

Two people are playing 'snap' with two special packs of cards. One has a yellow pack (16 ones, 12 twos, 8 threes and 4 fours) and one has a red pack (10 each of ones, twos, threes and fours). The packs are well shuffled and each plays the top card simultaneously.

1 There are 40 cards in each pack. What is the total number of pairs of cards which could be played?

2 (a) How many of these are 'double ones', that is a one from the yellow pack and a one from the red pack?

 (b) How many are:

  (i) double twos, (ii) double threes, (iii) double fours?

 (c) How many are doubles (i.e. double anything)?

For equally likely outcomes, the probability of an event is

$$\frac{\text{the number of outcomes which correspond to the event}}{\text{the total number of possible outcomes}}$$

So the probability of a double one is

$$\frac{\text{the number of possible 'double ones'}}{\text{the total number of pairs}}$$

3 Use this principle and your answers from question 2 to work out the probability of:

 (a) a double one, (b) a double two, (c) a double.

The probability distributions for the two packs are as follows.

Yellow pack					Red pack				
Number	1	2	3	4	Number	1	2	3	4
Probability	0.4	0.3	0.2	0.1	Probability	0.25	0.25	0.25	0.25

4 Work out the probabilities in question 3 directly from the probability distributions.

5 A blue pack has 10 ones, 20 twos, 10 threes and no fours. Working directly from the probability distributions, calculate the probability of a 'snap' if a yellow pack is played against a blue pack.

The following example is solved by counting cases and demonstrates a general rule for adding probabilities in such cases.

Example 3

A card is selected from an ordinary pack. What is the probability that the card is either an ace or a diamond?

Solution

There are 52 possible cards that chould be chosen; 4 of these are aces, 13 are diamonds.

There are only 16 cards which are either aces or diamonds because the ace of diamonds is counted in both the 4 aces and the 13 diamonds.

$$P(\text{ace } or \text{ diamond}) = \frac{4 + 13 - 1}{52} = \frac{4}{13}$$

This solution can be written as

$$P(\text{ace } or \text{ diamond}) = \frac{4}{52} + \frac{13}{52} - \frac{1}{52}$$

$$= P(\text{ace}) + P(\text{diamond}) - P(\text{both ace } and \text{ diamond})$$

This is a particular example of the **addition law**.

> For any two events A and B, the probability of either A or B or both occurring is
>
> $$P(A \text{ } or \text{ } B) = P(A) + P(B) - P(A \text{ } and \text{ } B)$$

As a further illustration, consider the MOT test of example 2. A car fails the test if it fails on *either* brakes or steering *or* both.

$$P(\text{fails on brakes or steering}) = 0.3 + 0.2 - 0.3 \times 0.2$$

$$= 0.44$$

The addition law is especially simple when events A and B are **mutually exclusive**, i.e. both cannot occur, because then $P(A \text{ } and \text{ } B) = 0$.

.4в

Consider whether the following pairs of events are mutually exclusive and whether they are independent.

(a) The weather is fine; I walk to work.

(b) I cut an ace; you cut a king.

(c) Dan's Delight wins next Saturday's 2:30 race at Newbury; Andy's Nag wins next Saturday's 2:30 race at Newbury.

(d) Dan's Delight wins next Saturday's 2:30 race at Newbury; Andy's Nag wins next Saturday's 3:15 race at Newbury.

(e) Mrs Smith has toothache today; Mr Smith has toothache today.

(f) Mrs Smith has a cold today; Mr Smith has a cold today.

You can use the addition law to find out the probability of an event *not* occurring from the probability of its occurring. In the example of the MOT test considered earlier, the probability of a pass on steering and brakes was found to be 0.56, and the probability of a fail was shown to be 0.44. The events 'pass MOT test' and 'fail MOT test' are mutually exclusive: since one of the events *must* occur, the sum of their probabilities must be 1. So

$$P(\text{fail test}) = 1 - P(\text{pass test})$$
$$= 1 - 0.56$$
$$= 0.44$$

In general, given an event A and its opposite A',

$$P(A') = 1 - P(A)$$

where $P(A')$ is the probability that A does *not* occur.

This is often a useful problem-solving tool for working out probabilities; if you cannot work out the probability of an event directly, see if you can work out the probability of the opposite event, then subtract this from 1.

Example 4

Three coins are tossed. What is the probability of at least one head?

Solution

There are lots of ways of getting at least one head. But the only way of getting the opposite event, namely no head at all, is to toss three tails.

$$P(T\ T\ T) = 0.5 \times 0.5 \times 0.5 = 0.125$$

$$P(\text{at least 1 head}) = 1 - P(\text{no head})$$

$$= 1 - P(T\ T\ T) = 0.875$$

Example 5

I travel by bus and train on my journey to work. The probability that the bus is late is 0.1 and (independently) the probability that the train is late is 0.05. Calculate the probability that:

(a) the bus and train are late,

(b) either the bus or the train is late.

Solution

(a) $P(\text{bus and train late}) = P(\text{bus late}) \times P(\text{train late})$

$$= 0.1 \times 0.05 = 0.005$$

(b) $P(\text{bus or train late}) = 1 - P(\text{bus and train on time})$

$$= 1 - 0.9 \times 0.95 = 0.145$$

1.4 Exercise 1

1 In a board game two dice are rolled. Work out the probability of:

(a) a double six,   (b) at least one six,   (c) only one six.

2 A card is selected from a pack of ordinary playing cards. What is the probability that it is:

(a) a red ace,   (b) a six or a seven,   (c) either an ace or a queen?

3 A card is selected from an ordinary pack of 52 cards. What is the probability that it is:

(a) a heart or a six,   (b) a heart or a spade?

4 In a small factory, there are two machines for doing the same job. One is under repair for 10% of the time and the other for 5%. What is the probability of both being out of action at the same time? (Assume independence.)

5 A car manufacturer sends 50 cars of a new model on a test run. The following petrol consumptions are recorded.

Litres km^{-1}	0.120–0.124	0.124–0.128	0.128–0.132	0.132–0.136	0.136–0.140
No. of cars	5	11	16	12	6

A consumer organisation buys two cars of this type and tests them under similar conditions. Estimate the probability that both use more than 0.136 litres km^{-1}. (State any assumptions you make.)

6 Each packet of a breakfast cereal contains a plastic soldier. Equal numbers of 12 different models are used. What is the probability of buying two packets in a supermarket and finding Hannibal in both? (State any assumptions you make.)

7 Under normal working, 8% of the articles being mass-produced in a factory are substandard. If a sample of 2 is checked every half hour, what proportions of the samples would you expect to consist of (a) 2 good articles, (b) 2 substandard articles? (State any assumptions you make.)

1.4.2 Tree diagrams

When analysing the probabilities of a combination of events, a **tree diagram** often helps.

Example 6
A student's assessment consists of three tests, of which he must pass at least two to continue with the course. He estimates that the probabilities of passing the tests are 0.7, 0.8 and 0.9 respectively. Calculate the probability that he will be able to stay on the course.

Solution
You can represent the situation with a tree diagram (see overleaf).

Assume independence at each test (i.e. the probability of passing the test is not influenced by what happens at the previous test). To find the probability of a particular sequence of events, you *multiply* the probabilities on the branches.

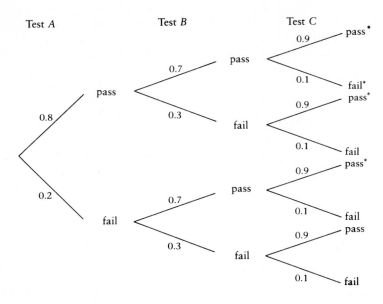

For example, P(passes A, fails B, passes C) = $0.8 \times 0.3 \times 0.9$
$= 0.216$

To obtain the probability of continuing with the course, you should *add* the probabilities on the branches representing 'one or no failed tests'. These are marked with a star on the tree diagram. The answer required is therefore

$$0.8 \times 0.7 \times 0.9 + 0.8 \times 0.7 \times 0.1 + 0.8 \times 0.3 \times 0.9 + 0.2 \times 0.7 \times 0.9$$
$$= 0.902$$

The probabilities can be added here because the combined events are mutually exclusive and cannot occur together.

▶ 1.4 **Tasksheet E1 – The Hardy–Weinberg law (page 301)**

1.4 **Exercise 2**

1 For example 6, work out the probability distribution of the random variable F = number of fails.

2 Trish selects a card at random from a pack of playing cards, and replaces it. She repeats this three times.

   (a) Calculate the probability of her getting:

      (i) three hearts,   (ii) three cards of the same suit.

   (b) Suppose she selects the three cards without replacement. Re-calculate the probabilities for (a).

3 Assuming that the probability of a female birth is approximately 0.49, construct a tree diagram to show the possible outcomes of the sexes of children in a family with three children. Hence find the probability of:

(a) exactly one girl,

(b) at least one girl,

(c) at least one child of each sex.

4 A company has four external telephone lines. Assuming the probability is $\frac{2}{3}$ that any one is in use at any instant, calculate the probability that:

(a) at least one line is free,

(b) at least two lines are free.

Have you assumed independence? If so, is this justified?

5 A bag contains 5 white and 7 black beads; another contains 3 white and 9 black beads. One bead is taken from the first bag and placed in the second. After thorough mixing, one bead is then taken from the second bag and placed in the first bag. What is the probability that there are 5 white beads in the first bag at the end?

1.4.3 The binostat

The diagram shows a binostat. It is like a pinball machine; balls are fed in at the top, fall through a triangular grid and collect in a series of slots. The picture shows the distribution in the slots after a number of balls have passed through the grid.

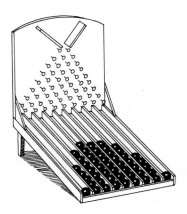

The picture shows that more balls collect in the central slots than in the outside slots. Why do you think this happens?

To examine what is going on in more detail, consider the following simple binostat.

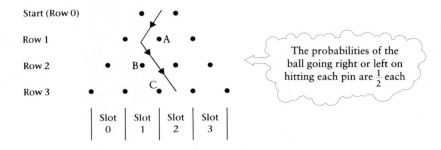

The probabilities of the ball going right or left on hitting each pin are $\frac{1}{2}$ each

The rows and slots have been labelled for reference. You will see later that it is helpful to label the slots starting with 0 rather than 1.

The arrow shows *one* possible route for a ball which ends up in slot 2. The ball hits the pin at A and goes through the gap on the left (as you look at the diagram). At B it hits the pin and goes through the gap on the right; at C it goes right again, ending up in slot number 2.

 .4c

1 Find how many different routes the ball could take to slot 2. What is the probability of each route? Deduce the probability of a ball falling into slot 2.

2 Repeat the calculation of question 1 for slots 0, 1 and 3, and hence write down the probability distribution of the random variable X, where X = slot number.

3 Use the result of question 2 to predict the expected frequencies in each slot when 400 balls are used.

4 This is a binostat with two rows. By considering the number of routes to slots 0, 1 and 2, find the probability distribution of X = slot number.

Calculate the expected number of balls in each slot when 400 balls are used.

For a larger number of rows, you need a way of calculating the number of routes to each slot. Consider this binostat with four rows.

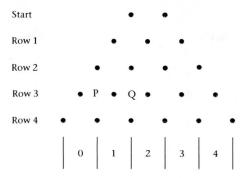

5 Find the probability of taking any particular route through this binostat.

To find how many routes there are to, for example, slot 1, you can use the fact that all routes to this slot pass through *either* P *or* Q (see diagram).

6 By writing down the number of routes to points P and Q, deduce how many routes there are to slot 1 and hence the probability of a ball falling into this slot.

7 Repeat the argument for the other slots and hence write down the probability distribution for $X =$ slot number in this case.

The results obtained above can be summarised as follows.

(a) The number of routes to each position or slot is given by the following triangle, where each number is the sum of the numbers in the previous row immediately to the left and to the right.

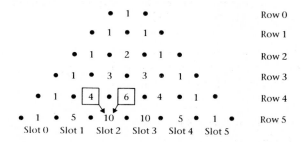

(b) For a binostat with n rows (not counting the first row of pins), there are 2^n equally likely paths and the probability of a ball following one particular path is $\dfrac{1}{2^n}$.

You can use the results of (a) and (b) to find the probability distribution for a ball's final position.

You may already recognise this triangle of numbers from previous work. It is known as **Pascal's triangle**, after the French mathematician Blaise Pascal (1623–1663), whose deeply held religious beliefs did not hold him back from a study of the calculus of chance inspired by his interest in gambling!

The sort of probability distribution you found for the binostat occurs quite often. Before finding the circumstances in which it arises, you will need a generalised interpretation of the numbers in Pascal's triangle.

Consider this three-row binostat.

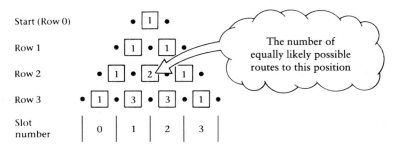

Notice that the 'slot number' just gives the number of times the ball is deflected to the right in its path to the slot. So, for example, to get to slot 2, the ball must be deflected twice to the right (and hence once to the left) out of the total of three deflections. So the number of routes to slot 2 is simply the number of ways of choosing two deflections out of three to be 'right', i.e. L R R, R L R and R R L.

Similarly, the entry '10' in slot 2 of row 5 gives the number of ways of choosing 2 'right' deflections out of 5. It could equally give the number of ways of getting 2 heads from 5 tosses, or choosing 2 presents from 5 presents, or more generally choosing 2 things from 5.

This number is written as $\binom{5}{2}$. You can now use Pascal's triangle to work out similar probability distributions.

Example 7

A coin is tossed. Find the number of ways, and hence the probability, of getting:

(a) exactly two heads from three tosses;

(b) exactly two tails from six tosses.

Solution

(a) There are $\binom{3}{2} = 3$ ways of choosing two heads from three tosses, namely HHT, HTH and THH. As there is a total of eight (2^3) possible outcomes, the probability is

$$P\,(2\text{ heads}) = 3 \times \frac{1}{2^3} = \frac{3}{8}$$

(b) Six tosses have $2^6 = 64$ possible equally likely outcomes.

Two tails can occur $\binom{6}{2}$ ways, which is obtained as row 6, slot 2 of the triangle.

$$\boxed{\text{Slot 2}}$$

$\boxed{\text{Row 6}}$ 1   6   ⑮   20   15   6   1

$$\Rightarrow \binom{6}{2} = 15$$

$$\Rightarrow P\,(2\text{ tails}) = 15 \times \tfrac{1}{64} = \tfrac{15}{64}$$

1.4 Exercise 3

1 Extend the triangle as necessary to work out:

(a) the number of ways of choosing 4 objects from 7 like objects;

(b) $\binom{7}{5}$ (c) $\binom{6}{4}$ (d) $\binom{5}{2}$ (e) $\binom{2}{1}$

(f) $\binom{7}{3}$ (g) $\binom{5}{4}$ (h) $\binom{5}{5}$

2 A coin is tossed 7 times. In how many ways can you get exactly:

(a) 2 heads   (b) 5 tails?

Explain your answers. What does this tell you about Pascal's triangle?

3 A pack of playing cards (without jokers) is cut eight times. What is the probability of cutting a red card on six occasions?

4 Assuming that boy and girl births are equally likely, what is the probability that a family of four children will contain three or more girls?

5 In a nuclear reaction, a free neutron has an equal chance of being absorbed or colliding to produce a fission. What is the probability that out of five free neutrons:

(a) all will be absorbed;

(b) all but two are absorbed?

6 A bag contains equal numbers of white and red marbles. Ten players in turn
draw a marble from the bag and replace it. What is the probability that
precisely five players draw a white marble?

1.4.4 The binomial probability model

So far, you have modelled the probabilities for repetitions (or **trials**) of an event
with two possible outcomes (for example head or tail, boy or girl, etc.) which are
assumed to be equally likely to occur. You have found that the probability of r
outcomes from n trials is

number of choices of r from n × probability of each choice

$$= \binom{n}{r} \times \frac{1}{2^n}$$

Before generalising this model you need to consider situations where the
probability at each *trial* is not equal to 0.5. This is equivalent to a binostat which
is not properly balanced, so, for example, the probability of deflecting to the left
is greater than to the right. The distribution of balls in the slots becomes
'skewed', i.e. there are more balls in the left-hand slots than in the right.
This is explored further below.

 .4D

A binostat with three rows is tilted so that for each deflection there is a
probability of 0.6 of the ball going left (and hence 0.4 of going right).

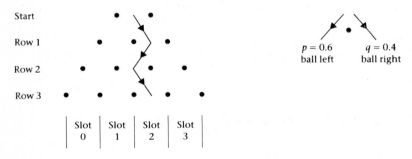

1 Calculate the probability of a ball taking the route shown above to slot 2.
What assumption are you making when you multiply the probabilities for
each deflection?

2 Calculate the probability of a ball falling into slot 2 by any other route.

3 Calculate the probability of a ball falling into slot 2.

4 Repeat the calculation for slots 0, 1 and 3 and hence find the probability distribution of X = slot number.

5 Calculate the expected frequencies if 500 balls are sent down this binostat.

6 Calculate the probability distribution for 5 rows, with $p = 0.6$ as before.

7 Calculate the probability distribution for X with $p = 0.2$ and 3 rows.

You can now generalise the probability model to all situations when:

- there are n repetitions or trials of an event, the outcomes of which are *independent*;
- the probability of a particular outcome is fixed;
- you are counting the number of times this outcome occurs.

The probability distribution for the random variable R is found by:

(a) working out the probability of a sequence containing r occurrences out of n,

(b) then multiplying by the number of ways of getting this outcome,

namely $\binom{n}{r}$.

Probability models of this type occur frequently enough to merit a name of their own. They are called **binomial** probability models.

Example 8
Three fair dice are thrown. What is the probability of throwing two sixes?

Solution
The probability of, for example,

$$\underset{\text{(six)}}{\frac{1}{6}} \times \underset{\text{(no six)}}{\frac{5}{6}} \times \underset{\text{(six)}}{\frac{1}{6}}$$

is

So the probability of two sixes is $\binom{3}{2} \times \frac{1}{6} \times \frac{5}{6} \times \frac{1}{6} = \frac{5}{72}$.

Example 9
On average 90% of seeds from a particular packet germinate. If you plant ten seeds in a row, what is the probability of eight or more germinating?

Solution
The probability of, say, the first eight germinating and the last two dying is

$$0.9 \times 0.9 \times \ldots \times 0.9 \times 0.1 \times 0.1 = (0.9)^8 (0.1)^2$$

Extending Pascal's triangle to row 10 shows that the number of ways of getting exactly eight germinations is

$$\binom{10}{8} = 45$$

So the probability of eight germinations is

$$45 \times (0.9)^8 (0.1)^2 = 0.1937 \quad \text{(to 4 s.f.)}$$

Similarly, the probability of nine germinations is

$$10 \times (0.9)^9 \times 0.1 = 0.3874$$

and of all the ten germinating is

$$1 \times (0.9)^{10} = 0.3486$$

So the total probability of eight or more is

$$0.1937 + 0.3874 + 0.3486 = 0.93 \quad \text{(to 2 s.f.)}$$

You should note that a number of assumptions are made in the calculation above.

(a) The seeds must be of uniform quality so that the probability of *each* seed germinating is 0.9.

(b) The probability of germination must be independent of both the soil conditions at the planting site and the weather after planting.

Neither of these assumptions will be precisely true. However, in practice, the binomial model will be a reasonable approximation unless the assumptions are grossly contravened, for example by planting the seeds just before a heavy frost.

When forming probability models of your own, or when making calculations to solve problems, you *must* be conscious of the assumptions you are making and should convince yourself that they are reasonable and realistic ones to make.

The binomial probability distribution can be summarised as follows.

Given n trials of an event, the probability of r occurrences of an outcome which has a probability p of occurring at each trial is

$$\binom{n}{r} p^r (1 - p)^{n-r}$$

assuming that the trials are independent.

You can now model the toast-dropping experiment considered in 1.3B on pages 44 and 45.

On the assumption that the outcomes of 'butter up' and 'butter down' are equally likely, the probability of seven slices out of ten landing 'butter down' is

$$\binom{10}{7}(0.5)^7(0.5)^3 = 0.117$$

The full probability distribution for the random variable R, the 'number of "butter down" slices out of ten' is given below.

r	0	1	2	3	4	5	6	7	8	9	10
$P(R = r)$	0.001	0.010	0.044	0.117	0.205	0.246	0.205	0.117	0.044	0.010	0.001

$$P(R = r) = \binom{10}{r} 0.5^r 0.5^{10-r}$$

Notice that no single result in itself has a high probability.

No matter what the probability is for a single slice landing 'butter-side down', getting *exactly* seven slices out of ten 'butter down' will have a fairly low probability, and so considering the probability of this event does not help to decide about Murphy's law.

The probability of an event such as 'seven or more butter-side down' is a much more discriminating test of the proposed model and so you should always consider the probability of events such as 'seven *or more*' when testing a model, rather than P(seven exactly).

From the table the probability of seven or more slices landing butter-side down is $0.117 + 0.044 + 0.010 + 0.001 = 0.172$.

So, on the assumption that Murphy's law is incorrect, you can expect a result of seven or more 'butter down' slices out of ten on about one in six occasions. This is quite often, and so the result is not very significant evidence in favour of Murphy's law.

Calculating the likelihood of getting 70 or more out of 100 'butter down', given an equal chance of landing either way, is explored in Chapter 2. The probability of this result is about 0.001, and observing such an event *would* be strong evidence in support of Murphy's law.

1.4 Exercise 4

1 Four dice are thrown. Calculate the probability distribution for S, the number of sixes thrown.

2 'Eight out of ten prefer Wizzo to Wow' is the sort of claim advertisements sometimes make. It could be based on one sample of only ten people!

  (a) Assume that Wizzo is no better or worse than Wow. Work out the probability that out of a random sample of ten people who were offered the choice, eight or more prefer Wizzo to Wow.

  (b) Assume Wizzo is in fact preferred by 80% of people. Work out the probability that out of a random sample of ten people, eight or more prefer Wizzo to Wow.

3 Birth statistics show that 51% of babies born in Britain are male. Use this to calculate the probability that a family of four children will contain three or more girls.

4 Boat Race statistics to date show that Oxford have won on 54% of occasions. Use a binomial model to calculate the probability that Cambridge win three times in a period of five years. Do you think the model is appropriate in this case? Explain.

5 (a) Poker dice have six faces marked ace, king, queen, jack, 10 and 9. What is the probability of throwing three or more aces with five dice?

  (b) A player gets three or more aces three times out of four throws. Calculate the probability of this event.

6 A cricket captain wins the toss nine times out of ten. Investigate how lucky this is.

7 Weather statistics for Blackpool in July suggest that it rains one day in three. The Wilsons take a week's holiday there in July, and it rains on six days out of seven. Use a binomial model to estimate how unlucky this is. Is the model appropriate?

8 In a test of a new recipe for a popular soft drink, eight people sampled a glass of new and a glass of original. Out of these, seven preferred the new flavour, and one the original. How strong is this evidence that the new recipe is in fact better?

9 A rare plant is difficult to grow. Each seed has a 20% chance of germinating.

  (a) If I plant five seeds, what chance is there that at least one will germinate?

  (b) Investigate how many seeds I should plant to get a 90% chance of at least one germination.

After working through section 1.4 you should:

1 understand the term **mutually exclusive** as applied to events, and appreciate when it is appropriate to add probabilities;

2 understand when two events are statistically **independent** and when it is appropriate to multiply probabilities;

3 be able to use **tree diagrams** to analyse the probability of compound events;

4 know how to apply **binomial models** to appropriate situations;

5 know that, if the random variable R is the number of occurrences (r) of an event in n independent trials, then

$$P(R = r) = \binom{n}{r} p^r q^{n-r}$$

where p is the probability of the event, and $q = 1 - p$.

1 Living with uncertainty

.5 An introduction to sampling

1.5.1 Random samples

The following are three particular examples of sampling:

- road-testing a vehicle, perhaps to assess its safety characteristics in a collision;

- surveying opinions by direct questioning – market research perhaps;

- taking a 'taster' from a vat of wine.

A central problem of statistics is how to use information from a **sample** to infer whatever one can about the **parent population** from which the sample is taken.

There are several reasons why you might wish to sample a parent population rather than test every member of the population.

(a) There would be little point in a car manufacturer collision-testing every car produced. There would be no cars left to sell! Some items need to be 'tested to destruction' to see how strong or safe they are. Motorcycle helmets, climbers' ropes and steel for building bridges are some examples.

(b) If you wanted people's opinions about something, for example which party they would vote for if there were a general election tomorrow, it would be very costly and time-consuming to interview every voter in the country.

When you next read about a survey in a newspaper look to see what size of sample the results are based on.

(c) Wine tasters sample just a small mouthful of wine to judge its quality. Sampling from a large vat of wine enables the quality of hundreds of bottles to be ascertained.

A 'good' sample should:

(i) be representative of the parent population;
(ii) enable you to find out what you want to know about the parent population.

The following two problems involve particular sampling procedures which are *not* good!

.5A

1 At a particular railway station the trains run hourly in each direction. However, when a traveller arrives at a random time at this station, the next train is five times more likely to be eastbound than westbound. Explain this curious result.

2 A mythical king decides to choose between his daughter's various suitors and boost the palace renovation fund by asking each of his prospective sons-in-law to contribute as many gold coins as they could to the fund.

The coins are marked with the suitors' names and are placed by the princess in a couple of urns. The king then chooses at random an urn and a coin from that urn.

The princess' favourite suitor is very poor and can only contribute one coin to the thousands that are collected.

How could the princess legitimately improve her favourite's chances and what precisely would his chances then be?

Sampling procedures such as these are **biased**. The 'next train' is not likely to be representative of all the trains and the apparently random method of selecting a coin proves to be similarly flawed.

When attempting to draw conclusions on the basis of a particular sample it is vital to consider whether the method of selecting the sample is likely to have introduced bias.

To enable reliable information to be obtained about a population from a sample, it is important to be careful about *how* the sample is chosen.

In the following questions you are asked to take samples from a population of the heights of 300 sixth-formers – the heights are listed on the datasheet on page 84. In order to estimate the mean height for the group, two different **sampling procedures** are employed:

A start anywhere on the page and select the next five numbers in that column;

B start anywhere on the page and select the next five numbers across the page.

Although the heights listed on the datasheet form a fairly small group, this will be used as an example of a *population* from which *samples* can be selected.

 .5B

1 Take a sample of five heights anywhere on the datasheet using procedure A. Record the five sample values and calculate the mean height for this sample.

Now repeat, using procedure B. You now have two different estimates of the population mean height.

2 The population mean height for the entire group of 300 sixth-formers is actually 167.4 cm.

How close were your sample estimates?

3 What criticisms do you have of the sampling procedures used in this experiment? How could they be improved?

An important requirement of a sample is that every member of the population has an equal chance of being selected. The sample members are **selected at random**.

1.5 **Exercise 1**

In each of the following examples, decide what bias, if any, the sampling procedure has introduced.

1 George Anderson is an accountant for a large company and works on the third floor of a twelve-storey building. He frequently has to visit the computer room on the tenth floor and travels up and down using one of the lifts. He often grumbles about the lifts and says, 'When I'm on the third floor waiting to go up, the first lift that comes is usually going down, whereas when I want to come back down again the first lift to arrive is usually going up'.

2 To obtain information about diseases amongst the elderly, everyone in a large residential home is given a thorough health check.

3 In the US Presidential Election in 1948, a major telephone opinion poll predicted a victory of the Republican, Dewey, over the Democrat, Truman.

4 A headmistress is asked to prepare a report for the school governors on the reasons for absences from school: illness, interviews, truancy and so on. Part of the report is based upon a full investigation of all absences during a week in November.

1.5.2 Sample size

Ensuring that the sample members are selected at random is not the only requirement of a good sample. Sample size is also important − not much information can be obtained from a sample of one, for example! It should be clear that the more information you obtain, the better able you are to make inferences about the population.

 .5c

1 Using random numbers, select ten samples of size 5 from the sample of students' heights on the datasheet on page 84. Calculate the mean of each sample and the mean and variance of the ten sample means. (Help on how you might select a random sample is provided in the solutions to 1.5B.)

2 Repeat question 1 for samples of size 10.

3 Compare and comment on the mean and the variance of the sample means for samples of size 5 and 10.

4 (a) Which size of sample produced better estimates of the population mean (167.4 cm)?

(b) Which distribution of sample means was least variable? Comment on how the difference in spread of the two sets of sample means affects your ability to infer results from a particular sample mean.

Larger samples are **more likely** to give reliable information about a population. This conclusion has an element of common sense about it. A sample of 10 is **likely** to be better than a sample of 5.

The following histograms show possible distributions of samples of size 5 and 10 taken from the students' heights on the datasheet on page 84.

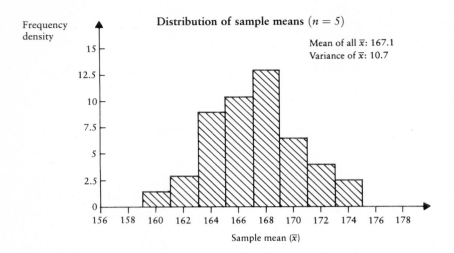

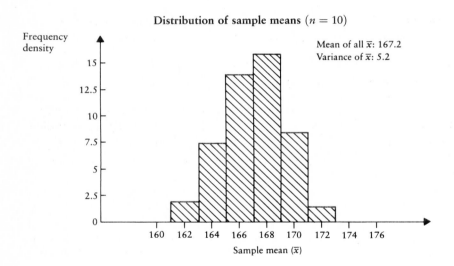

Although each distribution has a mean which is very close to that of the whole population (167.4 cm), the distribution for samples of size 10 has a very much reduced variance than that of the distribution of samples of 5. This implies that a sample mean from a sample of size 10 is *more likely* to be close to the true population mean than one from a sample of size 5. It is clear that this effect will be even more pronounced for a sample of size 20.

A more interesting problem is how large the sample needs to be to give reliable information about the population. Public opinion polls, for example, always state sample size as well as the method used to select the sample. The sample size is generally up to about 10 000 people.

When studying reports of sampling procedures you must consider both whether the sample has been chosen in a random way and whether the sample is sufficiently large for any results to be significant.

Canvassing 'everyone' is so costly and time-consuming that sampling is a widespread technique, despite the inevitable problems.

> The sample should be selected at random. Any hint of possible bias should be avoided.
>
> The sample must be large enough to provide sufficiently accurate information about the population.

The concepts relating to sampling techniques and the inference of results from samples will be developed and made more precise in later chapters.

1.5.3 Testing claims based on sample evidence

Using the ideas of this section, you can investigate some of the claims typically made in television and newspaper advertising. Suppose, for example, a television commercial states that 8 out of 10 dogs prefer Wolfit dog food. The claim is based upon a particular test in which 8 out of 10 dogs chose Wolfit when given a choice between Wolfit and another dog food.

The manufacturer hopes that you will infer that 80% of dogs prefer Wolfit!

The evidence here is based on a single sample of 10 dogs – it may not even be a representative sample of all dogs. Even if only 50% of dogs prefer Wolfit, there is a chance that as many as 8 out of 10 would choose it in a random trial. In this section you will study whether the result of this trial does at least indicate that there is some preference for Wolfit amongst dogs.

Following the advertisement, a complaint is made by rival dog food manufacturers that the commercial is misleading. They say that 8 out of 10 dogs choosing Wolfit would not be an unusual occurrence if it is assumed that dogs have no particular preference for Wolfit. The assumption that dogs have no preference for either dog food implies that they will choose either one or the other at random. The probability of choosing Wolfit is 0.5 on the basis of this assumption. The probability of 8 or more dogs out of 10 choosing Wolfit can be obtained from the binomial distribution.

The probability that exactly 8 choose Wolfit is

$$\binom{10}{8}\left(\frac{1}{2}\right)^8\left(\frac{1}{2}\right)^2 = \frac{45}{1024}$$

If R is the number choosing Wolfit, then the full probability distribution is

r	0	1	2	3	4	5	6	7	8	9	10
$P(R=r)$	$\frac{1}{1024}$	$\frac{10}{1024}$	$\frac{45}{1024}$	$\frac{120}{1024}$	$\frac{210}{1024}$	$\frac{252}{1024}$	$\frac{210}{1024}$	$\frac{120}{1024}$	$\frac{45}{1024}$	$\frac{10}{1024}$	$\frac{1}{1024}$

The result '8 or more out of 10' is only likely to occur in about 5% of all samples of 10 dogs. This is not very likely and suggests that the assumption made by the rival manufacturers is probably wrong. It appears likely that more than 50% of dogs would indeed choose Wolfit.

As a further example, the article below is reprinted from the *Southampton Guardian*.

You throw out monorail idea

By Mark Hodson

COUNCIL plans for a £20m futuristic monorail through the centre of Southampton have been given a thumbs down from city residents.

According to a Guardian readers' survey, 90 per cent of people do not want the new 'Metro 2000' system, and almost half would prefer to see the return of trams to the city.

Of those responding, 10 per cent said they want the monorail, 48 per cent want the trams back and 42 per cent said neither idea was worth taking up.

The Metro 2000 would join 13 central stations with electrically-driven remote controlled modules carrying up to 20 people at a time.

The proposals are not yet council policy, but are being used as the basis for discussions with local groups.

A report summarising views of local people will be compiled later this year, and the council is now keen to gauge public response before then.

Tory leader Cllr Norman Best, who has branded the monorail "a gimmick", said the council should think again in the light of the results of our poll.

"These figures do not surprise me at all," he said. "When all these people have taken the trouble to write in, they should be listened to. I am convinced the majority of people in Southampton do not want this monorail, but would prefer to see the return of the trams."

Council leader Alan Whitehead wrote in his introduction to the plans: "I am aware that such an innovation may fundamentally change the face of the city. An understanding and agreement across the city of exactly where we are going and what steps we need to take to get there will immensely strengthen the hand of whoever is charged with taking such decisions."

He says the scheme has met with an enthusiastic response from developers who he hopes will put up the £20m needed.

There will be a public meeting on June 1 when council officers will answer questions about the details of the plans.

WHAT YOU SAY:

● "A definite NO to the city-wrecking, crazy idea of a monorail, which would benefit no-one," said J Gubb, Bedford Place.

● "I am against the monorail, trams and any other gimmicks by aspiring Westminster residents. Surely the priority must be to improve existing services," said S Hunter, Radstock Road.

● "Trams would add to noise pollution. A monorail would be much more exciting and would attract visitors to the city," said M Buckle of Rushington Lane.

● "A monorail is a ridiculous idea. It would completely ruin the appearance of the city. The supporting structures would certainly look awful, and the noise for those people working in adjoining buildings would be unbearable," said Mrs J Draper of Chilworth.

● "Bring back the trams. They are cheap to ride, cheap to run and efficient as transport can be," said Alfred Hole of Peach Road.

● Our poll attracted 48 replies.

.5D

1 (a) Which people would you expect to be in favour of a monorail in the centre of a city?

   (b) How many replied and of those who replied, how many wanted:

   (i) the monorail,   (ii) the trams,   (iii) neither?

2 How do you think the monorail 'poll' was carried out? Would this method introduce bias in the sample? Suggest a better method. What do you understand the word 'bias' to mean?

The article uses the views from a sample of Southampton residents to judge the general support, or lack of support, for the monorail idea. Such sampling is widely used for purposes as varied as market research on proposed new products, establishing views about changes in public services, quality control in manufacturing processes and judging public opinion before elections.

In any sampling procedure it is important that the way the poll is carried out should not introduce bias. For example, a poll conducted by telephone would automatically exclude approximately one fifth of the population. This could be a crucial omission.

The second important consideration for any sampling procedure is connected with the sample size. How reasonable is it to infer from a sample size of only 48 that the majority of the inhabitants of Southampton are opposed to the monorail? Is it possible that the citizens are divided roughly equally on this issue and that the sample result occurred simply by chance?

Again, the probability that such a result could have occurred simply by chance can be calculated using the binomial distribution. If you assume that 50% of the population are in favour of the monorail, the probability that a random sample of 48 shows only 5 or fewer in favour would be

$$\binom{48}{5}\left(\frac{1}{2}\right)^5\left(\frac{1}{2}\right)^{43} + \binom{48}{4}\left(\frac{1}{2}\right)^4\left(\frac{1}{2}\right)^{44} + \ldots + \binom{48}{0}\left(\frac{1}{2}\right)^0\left(\frac{1}{2}\right)^{48}$$

This would not be easy to calculate!

A computer can be used to **simulate** a poll several times and you can then see from the **simulation** how likely particular occurrences appear to be.

A computer simulation can help you to test conjectures based upon results from a particular sample. You should use the following procedure.

- First make an assumption about the parent population to enable you to simulate the taking of samples. You might, for example, assume that 50% of the population support a particular measure such as the construction of a monorail.

- Next, simulate the selection of a large number of samples of the same size as the actual sample.

- From the distribution of the simulated samples, use the actual sample to judge the reasonableness of the original assumption.

The result of a simulation, where 100 samples of size 48 were taken, is shown below.

Distribution of simulated samples

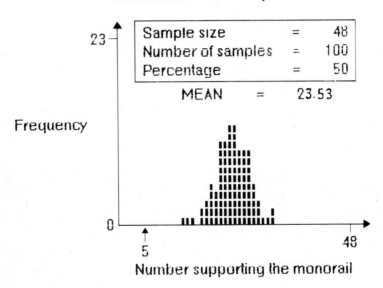

Number supporting the monorail

.5E

1 Do you think the initial assumption of 50% supporting the monorail is likely, considering the simulation result?

2 Comment on the results of the poll in the newspaper article in the light of the evidence provided by the simulation.

3 Suppose that the 48 randomly selected *Southampton Guardian* respondents had contained 22 people in favour of the monorail. What conclusion would you reach in this case?

Remember that you must *always* consider how the original data in any sample are collected. If the method of collection is suspect and likely to lead to distorted results, then no amount of analysis of the data will correct matters. Poor data collection will undermine any survey.

1.5 Exercise 2

1 A person claims that he can predict which way a coin will land, either heads or tails. In eight throws he gets it right on six occasions.

Calculate, on the basis of a binomial model, the probability of:

(a) getting six correct out of eight;

(b) getting six or more correct out of eight.

Do you think the result supports his claim? Explain your answer.

2 A blind tasting is organised to see if people can tell the difference between two different brands of orange juice. They have ten 'tastes'. On each occasion they have to say whether it is juice A or juice B.

On how many occasions would you expect them to get it right before you were reasonably convinced that they could actually tell the difference?

After working through section 1.5 you should:

1 appreciate the need for **sampling** and for ensuring that the sampling procedure does not introduce **bias**;

2 know how to check **significance** either by simulation or, when appropriate, by using the binomial distribution;

3 be aware that as the sample size increases, the distribution of the sample mean becomes increasingly clustered around the true value of the population mean.

Datasheet

These data are the heights in centimetres of 300 sixth-formers. The data have been listed so that each row of ten figures across the page consists of five boys' heights followed by the heights of five girls.

170.1	172.2	179.3	176.4	168.9	168.1	154.8	157.0	164.8	165.3
178.1	181.1	180.4	178.3	179.6	160.3	157.7	151.5	157.0	159.3
176.6	175.0	170.5	181.2	168.5	158.6	153.0	155.5	170.5	159.4
178.8	172.4	163.6	167.0	176.3	155.4	157.4	160.4	165.7	161.2
173.3	179.4	177.9	165.2	172.5	157.3	164.1	160.7	160.1	156.3
175.3	186.1	176.6	169.6	174.1	164.4	153.8	160.2	163.0	157.6
165.9	162.7	166.2	168.7	163.7	168.8	154.6	173.8	155.3	159.9
171.4	170.0	181.5	181.0	176.6	158.7	168.3	159.8	154.9	155.7
184.3	175.1	188.0	181.4	171.7	167.1	150.5	152.9	165.3	154.2
175.9	173.0	173.0	175.0	178.1	159.5	160.3	160.9	179.6	167.3
175.0	162.8	178.4	163.7	163.7	162.9	175.6	165.4	165.6	162.1
169.0	163.6	167.9	164.9	181.9	155.7	152.0	141.1	152.0	168.8
167.1	174.1	172.0	180.1	176.7	150.2	164.6	158.3	156.2	170.1
159.9	160.2	173.7	173.7	169.4	157.0	156.9	166.2	156.8	163.2
168.5	170.0	176.3	166.2	163.4	164.2	171.2	164.1	168.3	160.0
167.8	171.0	179.9	177.2	183.8	169.3	166.3	162.5	168.9	153.2
179.7	167.4	172.7	175.8	168.7	162.3	172.3	171.9	159.1	164.7
179.0	177.6	160.8	186.7	182.3	155.9	166.0	162.8	163.8	157.4
171.3	162.2	173.3	170.0	184.9	157.0	155.0	171.8	164.8	162.5
165.2	173.1	180.2	175.1	168.8	161.1	159.4	159.2	162.2	156.7
178.2	171.8	175.2	178.0	173.9	171.8	166.0	166.9	162.7	157.2
163.7	189.1	175.1	171.0	171.1	156.2	166.5	164.4	154.7	156.3
182.6	173.7	168.8	183.3	170.3	164.7	162.3	175.7	160.0	176.4
167.9	179.4	171.2	170.6	175.5	172.9	156.6	162.9	153.7	160.8
171.0	174.8	176.1	172.9	170.5	167.3	146.4	164.5	159.1	170.4
174.8	178.4	180.9	177.2	163.3	150.4	157.3	168.3	156.8	169.4
170.6	185.9	173.2	179.5	179.7	163.6	155.1	152.9	166.7	156.8
175.6	172.2	178.9	164.9	172.0	153.7	166.7	160.0	163.7	158.9
178.8	182.0	160.5	183.6	163.6	150.3	179.3	158.0	161.5	164.6
172.3	169.6	182.9	168.2	159.9	161.7	153.9	158.5	165.5	161.1

Living with uncertainty

.6E Further probability

1.6.1 Conditional probability

Colour blindness is a defect of vision reducing the ability to distinguish between colours. In the principal type there is an inability to distinguish between colours in the red/yellow/green range, for example, between red and yellow or between yellow and green.

Because males are more likely to be colour blind than females, the probability of colour blindness is **conditional** on a person's sex.

 .6A

The probability of colour blindness in the adult population is 0.03, but males are more prone to the condition than females and the probability among males is 0.05.

1 Out of a population of 1000 'typical' adults, how many would you expect in each of the categories:

(a) male and colour blind;   (b) male and not colour blind;

(c) female and colour blind;   (d) female and not colour blind?

2 Let $P(C\,|\,M)$ stand for the *conditional* probability of colour blindness given that the subject is male. What is the value of $P(C\,|\,M)$?

3 Interpret and find the value of $P(C'\,|\,F)$, where C' is the event 'not C' (i.e. the event C does *not* occur), and F is the event that the subject is female.

4

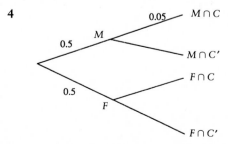

Copy and complete the tree diagram, giving the probabilities at each tip.

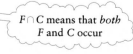

$F \cap C$ means that *both* F and C occur

5 Verify that

$$P(C \mid M) = \frac{P(M \cap C)}{P(M)}$$

6 Write similar formulas for:

(a) $P(C' \mid M)$ (b) $P(C \mid F)$ (c) $P(C' \mid F)$

7 Find a formula for $P(C)$ in terms of conditional probabilities.

The conditional probability $P(B \mid A)$ is the probability that event B will happen given that event A happens.

$$P(B \mid A) = \frac{P(A \cap B)}{P(A)}$$

Note that the branches of a two-stage tree diagram may be labelled as shown.

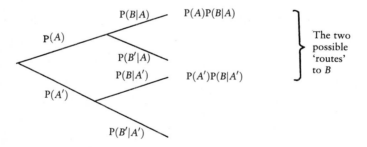

From the diagram you can see that

$$P(B) = P(A) P(B \mid A) + P(A') P(B \mid A')$$

and $P(B') = P(A) P(B' \mid A) + P(A') P(B' \mid A')$.

If you consider only the topmost branch you find that

$$P(A \text{ and } B) = P(A \cap B) = P(A) P(B \mid A)$$

Similarly, considering the other branches of the tree diagram,

$$P(A \cap B') = P(A) P(B' \mid A), \quad P(A' \cap B) = P(A') P(B \mid A')$$

and $P(A' \cap B') = P(A') P(B' \mid A')$.

Example 1

The events A and B are such that $P(A) = \frac{1}{2}$, $P(A' \mid B) = \frac{1}{3}$ and $P(A \cup B) = \frac{3}{5}$. Find $P(B)$.

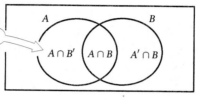

$A \cup B$ means that *either* A or B *or both* occur

Solution

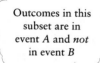

Outcomes in this subset are in event A and *not* in event B

$A \cap B'$ $A \cap B$ $A' \cap B$

You will see from the diagram that

$$P(A \cup B) = P(A \cap B) + P(A \cap B') + P(A' \cap B)$$

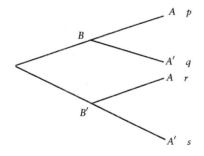

The tree diagram has tips labelled p, q, r and s. From the result above,

$$P(A \cup B) = p + q + r$$
$$P(A) = p + r$$
$$P(A' \cap B) = q$$

From the information given,

$$p + q + r = \tfrac{3}{5}$$
$$p \quad\ + r = \tfrac{1}{2}$$
$$q \quad\ = \tfrac{3}{5} - \tfrac{1}{2} = \tfrac{1}{10}$$

So $P(B) \times \frac{1}{3} = P(B)\,P(A' \mid B) = P(A' \cap B) = \frac{1}{10}$ and hence $P(B) = \frac{3}{10}$.

The idea of a conditional probability helps to redefine *independence* of events. A and B are independent if the probability of B occurring does not depend on whether A occurs.

> The events A and B are independent if
>
> $P(B \mid A) = P(B)$

This definition leads to the familiar result given and used in section 1.4.1, that $P(A \cap B) = P(A)\,P(B)$. This can be shown as follows: events A and B are independent, so

$$P(B \mid A) = P(B)$$
$$\Rightarrow \ P(A)\,P(B \mid A) = P(A)\,P(B)$$
$$\Rightarrow \quad P(A \cap B) = P(A)\,P(B)$$

$P(A \ or \ B)$

Example 2

Given that events A and B are independent, that $P(A \cup B) = \frac{5}{8}$ and that $P(A \cap B') = \frac{7}{24}$, calculate:

(a) $P(B)$ (b) $P(A)$ (c) $P(A \cap B)$ (d) $P(A' \cup B')$

Solution

$P(not \ A \ or \ not \ B)$

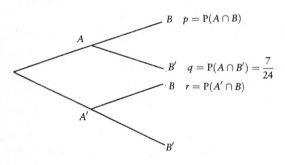

$B \quad p = P(A \cap B)$

A

$B' \quad q = P(A \cap B') = \dfrac{7}{24}$

$B \quad r = P(A' \cap B)$

A'

B'

(a) $P(A \cup B) = \frac{5}{8}$

$p + \frac{7}{24} + r = \frac{5}{8}$

$P(B) = p + r = \frac{5}{8} - \frac{7}{24} = \frac{1}{3}$

Because of the independence of A and B, $P(B \mid A) = P(B \mid A') = P(B)$. The branches of the tree may be labelled as shown.

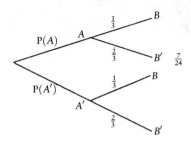

(b) $P(A) \times \frac{2}{3} = \frac{7}{24}$

$\quad\quad P(A) = \frac{7}{16}$

(c) $P(A \cap B) = P(A) \times P(B) = \frac{7}{16} \times \frac{1}{3} = \frac{7}{48}$

(d) $P(A' \cup B') = P[(A \cap B)'] = 1 - P(A \cap B) = \frac{41}{48}$

1.6 Exercise 1

1 State conditions on probabilities associated with the events A and B such that A and B:

(a) are independent,   (b) are mutually exclusive.

2 Simplify the expressions:

(a) $P(A) + P(A')$ (b) $P(A \mid B) + P(A' \mid B)$

(c) $P(A' \mid B) P(B)$ (d) $P(A \cup B) + P(B') P(A' \mid B')$

3 The probability that a blue-eyed person is left-handed is $\frac{1}{7}$. The probability that a left-handed person is blue-eyed is $\frac{1}{3}$. The probability that a person has neither of these characteristics is $\frac{4}{5}$. What is the probability that a person has both?

4 (a) Two events A and B are such that

$\quad\quad P(A) = \frac{1}{2}, \quad\quad P(B) = \frac{1}{3}, \quad\quad P(A \mid B) = \frac{1}{4}$

Evaluate:

(i) $P(A \cap B)$ (ii) $P(A \cup B)$ (iii) $P(A' \cap B')$

(b) Another event C is such that A and C are independent and

$\quad\quad P(A \cap C) = \frac{1}{12}, \quad\quad P(B \cup C) = \frac{1}{2}$

Show that B and C are mutually exclusive.

▶ 1.6 **Tasksheet E1 – Sampling without replacement (page 303)**

1.6.2 Bayes' theorem

Some of the most interesting work in probability theory has been in the resolution of paradoxes – problems having two apparently contradictory solutions. A famous one is sometimes called the 'Three Prisoners' paradox; it proceeds as follows.

The president of Vinovia has decreed that of three political prisoners, *A*, *B* and *C*, two will be executed as an example to others. The jailer is to choose two at random, not revealing which until the morning of the execution.

Some time before this, the prisoners are all in solitary confinement and *A* asks the jailer to name one of the others to be executed. The jailer reasons that since *A* cannot communicate with the other prisoners and since he knows that at least one of *B* and *C* is to be executed there can be no harm in this. He tells *A*, '*B* is to be executed'.

Before the jailer spoke, *A* knew that his survival was one of three equally likely events and therefore had probability $\frac{1}{3}$. Now, however, *A* reasons that the survivor will be either *C* or himself and so his chances have improved to $\frac{1}{2}$. Is *A* correct, or was the jailer right in assuming that the information he gave was of no use to *A*?

The paradox can be resolved by methods already met in this section, and it would be a pity not to give you the opportunity to try. A neat solution uses a theorem named after the eighteenth-century mathematician, Thomas Bayes, and will be given later. The theorem is introduced by an example.

Example 3

An automated blood pressure machine is being tested. Members of the public, about 20% of whom have high blood pressure (hypertension), try it out and are then seen by a doctor. She finds that 80% of those with hypertension and 10% of those with normal blood pressure have been diagnosed as hypertensive by the machine. How useful is the machine?

Solution

The probabilities of the various compound events may be illustrated using a tree.

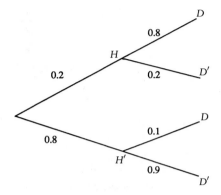

H – person has hypertension

D – machine diagnoses hypertension

One probability the doctor wants to find is that of correct positive diagnosis, i.e. $P(H \mid D)$. She calculates this as follows.

$$P(H \cap D) = P(H) \times P(D \mid H) = 0.2 \times 0.8 = 0.16$$

$$P(D) = P(H \cap D) + P(H' \cap D) = 0.16 + 0.08 = 0.24$$

$$\text{So } P(H \mid D) = \frac{P(H \cap D)}{P(D)} = \frac{0.16}{0.24} \approx 0.67$$

The doctor also calculates the probability of a correct negative diagnosis, i.e. $P(H' \mid D')$.

$$P(H' \cap D') = P(H') \times P(D' \mid H') = 0.8 \times 0.9 = 0.72$$

$$P(D') = P(H \cap D') + P(H' \cap D') = 0.04 + 0.72 = 0.76$$

$$\text{So } P(H' \mid D') = \frac{P(H' \cap D')}{P(D')} = \frac{0.72}{0.76} \approx 0.95$$

The machine is a good tool for initial screening. If it does not find you hypertensive then you can be reasonably confident that your blood pressure is normal. If it diagnoses hypertension, then you should consult your doctor for further tests.

In the solution above, $P(H \cap D)$ was expressed both as

$$P(H) \times P(D \mid H) \quad \text{and as} \quad P(D) \times P(H \mid D)$$

The equality of these two expressions is one statement of **Bayes' theorem**. It is more often used in the form

$$P(D \mid H) = \frac{P(D) \times P(H \mid D)}{P(H)}$$

The denominator is often calculated with the help of a tree diagram. Sometimes the whole calculation can be managed without a diagram, using conditional probabilities, in which case the statement would take the form

Bayes' theorem

$$P(A \mid B) = \frac{P(A) \times P(B \mid A)}{P(A) \times P(B \mid A) + P(A') \times P(B \mid A')}$$

You are now in a position to tackle the 'Three Prisoners' paradox using Bayes' theorem.

Let A denote the event that A is to be executed and similarly for B and C. Then initially,

$$P(A) = P(B) = P(C) = \tfrac{2}{3}$$

After receiving the jailer's information, A calculated the probability

$$P(A \mid B) = \frac{P(A \cap B)}{P(B)} = \frac{1/3}{2/3} = \frac{1}{2}$$

However, he should have calculated $P(A \mid S_B)$, where S_B is the event that the jailer *says* that B is to be executed. S_B is not the same as B. Since the jailer knows which two prisoners are to be executed, $P(S_B) = P(S_C) = \tfrac{1}{2}$ by symmetry.

Then

$$P(A \mid S_B) = \frac{P(A) \times P(S_B \mid A)}{P(S_B)} = \frac{\tfrac{2}{3} \times \tfrac{1}{2}}{\tfrac{1}{2}} = \frac{2}{3}$$

The jailer was correct. The probability of A's execution has not been changed.

 .6B

1 Explain why $P(S_B \mid A) = \tfrac{1}{2}$, and find $P(S_B \mid A')$.

2 Calculate $P(S_B)$ as $P(A) \times P(S_B \mid A) + P(A') \times P(S_B \mid A')$.

Example 4

A mail-order firm recruits all its agents through newspaper advertisements, in both the 'tabloid' and the 'broadsheet' press. The firm receives three times as many applications through the tabloid press as through the broadsheet press. Furthermore, applicants reached through the tabloid press are three times as likely to become active as those reached via the broadsheet press.

Find the probability that a randomly selected active agent takes a tabloid newspaper.

Solution

Using the notation

$$T - \text{reached via a tabloid}, \qquad A - \text{active},$$

$$P(T\,|\,A) = \frac{P(T)\,P(A\,|\,T)}{P(T)\,P(A\,|\,T) + P(T')\,P(A\,|\,T')}$$

$$= \frac{0.75 \times 0.75}{0.75 \times 0.75 + 0.25 \times 0.25}$$

$$= 0.9$$

1.6 Exercise 2

1 Of a library of 100 books, 60 are non-fiction and 40 are fiction. Of the non-fiction books, 40 are hardbacks. Of the fiction books, 10 are hardbacks. A book selected at random from the library is found to be hardback. What is the probability that it is a work of fiction?

2 It is estimated that one quarter of the drivers on the road between 11 p.m. and midnight have been drinking during the evening. If a driver has not been drinking, the probability that he will have an accident at that time of night is 0.004%; if he has been drinking, the probability of an accident goes up to 0.2%. What is the probability that a car selected at random at that time of night will be involved in an accident?

A policeman on the beat at 11:30 p.m. sees a car run into a lamppost and jumps to the conclusion that the driver has been drinking. What is the probability that he is right?

1.6.3 Further applications of Bayes' theorem

The words **prior** and **posterior** (or the Latin phrases 'a priori' and 'a posteriori') are often used in probability theory to describe the probability of an event before and after another event upon which it is conditional. In the formula

$$P(A\,|\,B) = \frac{P(A) \times P(B\,|\,A)}{P(B)}$$

the prior probability of A is $P(A)$ and the posterior probability (after the event B has occurred) is $P(A\,|\,B)$.

Another illustration of the use of these words is given in the following example, which shows a typical 'real-life' application of Bayes' theorem as part of a decision-making process.

Example 5

A broker is offered a consignment of fruit from South America at a favourable price. Before he can import it into the EU and make a good profit he needs a licence. Unfortunately, the granting of a licence takes a long time and is by no means certain. If he delays, the deal may fall through. To help him make a decision he could seek the services of a consultant. The consultant is not infallible but usually makes a correct assessment. Her track record on similar assessments is shown in the table.

Assessment	Licence granted	Licence denied	Decision referred
Favourable	80	10	5
Unfavourable	20	40	20

(In 80 out of 100 cases when a licence has been granted, the consultant's decision has been favourable, and so on.)

Based on previous experience, the prior probabilities are

licence granted 0.6;   denied 0.3;   referred 0.1

What would be the posterior probabilities following a favourable decision by the consultant?

Solution

The abbreviations used are

G granted; D denied; R referred; F favourable

Care must be taken in interpreting the table. The probabilities needed are, for example, $P(F\,|\,D)$, the probability of a favourable decision having been given when a licence is denied.

$$P(F\,|\,D) = \frac{10}{10 + 40} = 0.2$$

Similarly, $P(F\,|\,G) = 0.8$ and $P(F\,|\,R) = 0.2$

So, $P(G\,|\,F) = \dfrac{P(G)\,P(F\,|\,G)}{P(G)\,P(F\,|\,G) + P(D)\,P(F\,|\,D) + P(R)\,P(F\,|\,R)}$

$$= \frac{0.6 \times 0.8}{(0.6 \times 0.8) + (0.3 \times 0.2) + (0.1 \times 0.2)}$$

$$= \frac{6}{7} \approx 0.86$$

1.6 Exercise 3

1 Find the other two posterior probabilities in Example 5 above, and check that the sum of all three probabilities is 1.

2 The marketing director of the Sudso corporation thinks that the probability that New Sudso is better than Kleenrite is 0.9. Because he lacks confidence in his intuition he arranges a hasty survey. The market research company can only manage a small sample over a short period and will only claim 80% reliability; i.e. there is a probability of 0.2 that their conclusion will be incorrect.

Find the probability that New Sudso will prove better than Kleenrite if their survey predicts this.

3 An electronics company has bought a batch of resistors from a manufacturer. The company knows that all the resistors are produced on one of two machines, A and B. 10% of the output of A and 20% of the output of B are defective. The manufacturer has guaranteed that 70% of the batches come from A and 30% from B. Three resistors chosen randomly from the batch are all satisfactory.

(a) If the batch came from A, find the probability that three randomly chosen resistors will be satisfactory.

(b) Find the probability that the batch came from A.

4 A mining company assesses the chances of finding minerals in a certain area as follows

low grade spar (L) 0.5;   high grade spar (H) 0.25;

high grade spar with viable metallic ore (M) 0.25

If a detailed geological survey is made, the findings will be good (G) or poor (G') with probabilities as shown in this table.

Mineral	Survey result	
	G	G'
L	0.2	0.8
H	0.5	0.5
M	0.9	0.1

To decide whether or not to commission a survey, the company needs the six posterior probabilities conditional on the survey. Calculate these probabilities.

5 You assess the probability of an event E as being in the range given by $0.5 < P(E) < 0.7$. If E happens, then F is 90% certain to happen. Otherwise the probability of F is only 0.2.

Given that F happens, what is the chance of E?

Comment on your answer:

(a) in strictly mathematical terms;

(b) in terms of a possible application.

After working through section 1.6 you should:

1 be able to use tree diagrams as an aid and illustration in situations involving several probabilities and stages;

2 know the definition of a **conditional probability**;

3 be able to construct and use formulas such as

$$P(B) = P(A)\,P(B\,|\,A) + P(A')\,P(B\,|\,A')$$

$$P(A \cap B) = P(A)\,P(B\,|\,A);$$

4 given **prior probabilities** and relevant conditional probabilities, be able to find **posterior probabilities**, using the generalised form of Bayes' theorem.

1 Living with uncertainty

Miscellaneous exercise 1

1 A student investigates the effect of a fertiliser on the growth of seedlings and records the following results.

Heights of seedlings

with fertiliser						without fertiliser

```
              4   4 | 2 |
        3   3   2   2 | 2 | 2
    1   1   1   1   0 | 2 | 0   0
    9   9   8   8   8 | 1 | 8
            6   6   6 | 1 | 6   7   7
                      | 1 | 4   5   5   5
                    2 | 1 | 2   2   3
                      | 1 | 0   1   1   1
                      | 0 | 8
```

Key: $1\,|\,4$ means $14\,\text{cm}$

Find the median and the upper and lower quartiles of the heights for both sets of data. Represent the data by drawing two separate box plots.

2 The time taken for 120 runners to complete a cross-country race is given in the table.

Time taken (min)	20–	25–	30–	35–	40–60
Number of runners	10	25	55	15	15

(a) Represent the data by a histogram and calculate the mean (m) and standard deviation (s) of the finishing times.

(b) What proportion of the runners took longer than $m + s$ minutes?

(c) Use your histogram to estimate the median finishing time.

3 The mean weight of the eight forwards in a rugby team is 82 kg and the standard deviation of the weights is 5 kg. A forward of weight 90 kg is dropped from the team and replaced by one weighing 85 kg. Calculate the mean weight and the standard deviation of the weight of the eight forwards after this change.

4 (a) Prove that $\sum (x - \bar{x})^2 = \sum x^2 - n\bar{x}^2$.

   (b) 50 apples of class A have a mean weight of 210 grams and a standard deviation of 15 grams. 60 apples of class B have mean weight 180 grams and standard deviation 25 grams. All 110 apples are mixed together. Calculate the mean and standard deviation of the mixed batch.

5 A weighing machine recording the weight of sugar in 2 kg bags was noted as recording every weight as 0.2 kg more than it should have been. At the end of a quality audit the mean weight of 250 bags of sugar as recorded by the machine was 2.15 kg; the recorded standard deviation was 0.05 kg. Write down the correct mean and standard deviation of the weights of the 250 bags.

6 The scores of a hundred students on a mathematics examination have a mean of 55 marks and standard deviation of 12 marks.

   (a) If 5 marks are added to each score, calculate the new mean and standard deviation for the group.

   (b) If each mark is multiplied by 1.8, calculate the new mean and standard deviation.

   (c) If the marks are scaled by doubling and then adding 5 to each, calculate the new mean and standard deviation.

7 The probability of my car failing to start in the morning is 0.2.

   (a) Calculate the probability that, during a given working week (Monday to Friday):

   (i) my car starts on the first three days but not on the last two;
   (ii) it only starts on three days during the week.

   (b) List the probability distribution of the number of days (N) on which it starts. Calculate the mean and the standard deviation of N.

8 A market gardener sows a large number of seeds, some of which are old seeds from last year's batch. 80% of the new seeds and 40% of the old seeds germinate. 30% of the seeds are from last year's batch, the remainder are this year's.

   (a) Draw a tree diagram to illustrate this information and calculate the percentage of seeds which germinate.

   (b) Of the seeds that germinate, what percentage of them are last year's seeds?

   (c) What percentage of the seeds which fail to germinate are this year's seeds?

9 A student spent several weeks collecting data on the time taken for letters to be delivered. She recorded the number of working days between the date on the post mark and the delivery date for each letter. From her analysis she devised the following probability model.

Number of working days since posting	Probability of letter being delivered First class	Second class
1	0.8	0.1
2	0.1	0.55
3	0.05	0.3
4	0.03	0.04
5	0.02	0.01

(a) Show that the mean and standard deviation of the delivery time for second class mail are 2.31 days and 0.74 days, respectively.

(b) Calculate the mean and standard deviation of the delivery times for first class mail. Compare the delivery times for first and second class letters.

10 One of the pioneers of probability theory was Blaise Pascal (1623–62). Other mathematicians were fond of sending him questions. One such was:

Is it worth betting that in 24 throws of two dice there will be at least one double 6?

What would you advise? Give your reasons.

11 Looking back at weather records gives these probabilities.

P(rain today) = 40%

P(rain tomorrow) = 50%

P(rain today and tomorrow) = 30%

Given that it rains today, what is the probability that it will rain tomorrow?

12 There are two urns, the first of which contains 3 black beads and 4 white beads. The second urn contains 5 black beads and 4 white beads. An urn is chosen at random (each with probability $\frac{1}{2}$) and a bead is chosen at random from that urn.

(a) Draw a tree diagram for this situation.

Give the appropriate probability expressions to each branch of the tree.

(b) Calculate the probability that the bead drawn is black.

13 Two boxes, A and B, contain beads. Box A contains 3 red beads and 2 white ones. Box B contains 2 red and 4 white beads.

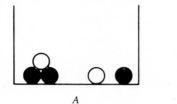
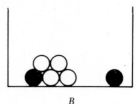

A

B

One bead is selected at random from A and put into B. Then a bead is taken at random from B and put into A.

What is the probability that A now contains 4 red beads?

14 The manager of a firm running 10 taxis assesses the life of a car battery as follows.

Life (months)	20	22	24	26	28	30
Probability	0.1	0.2	0.2	0.3	0.15	0.05

How much should he expect to spend on batteries per year, if they cost £37 each?

15 For every 1000 tickets sold for a monthly lottery, there are 20 prizes of 10 jiks, 6 prizes of 25 jiks and 1 prize of 100 jiks.

(a) If Rick buys 1 ticket (costing 1 jik) each month, how much will he expect to lose on average in a year?

(b) Calculate the probability that:
   (i) he will win at least one prize next year;
   (ii) he will win more than 10 jiks in the first two months of next year.

16 A box contains N beads, of which a are white. If three beads are drawn in succession, what is the probability that they are all white:

(a) if after each draw the bead is replaced;

(b) if beads are not replaced?

17 If a box contains N beads, of which a are red and the others blue, what is the probability of obtaining one bead of each colour in two successive drawings from the box:

(a) with replacement,

(b) without replacement?

18 A company has three external telephone lines. Assuming the probability is $\frac{3}{5}$ that any one is in use at any instant, calculate the probability that:

(a) at least one line is free;

(b) exactly two lines are free.

Have you assumed independence? If so, is this justified?

19 (a) A wholesaler receives a large consignment of pressure-cookers and tests four. Find the probability that this sample contains:

   (i) one or more defectives if 2% of the whole batch are defective,

  (ii) no defectives if 12% of the batch are defective.

Give your answers to 2 significant figures.

(b) The consignment is accepted if the sample contains no defective cooker or if the sample contains exactly one defective and a second sample of four contains no defective items. Find the probability of acceptance if 2% of the whole batch are defective.

20 A test paper contains five multiple choice questions, in each of which one answer has to be chosen from four alternatives. Four correct answers are required to pass the test. Find the probability of passing if guessing is used for each question.

The Normal distribution

.1 An important distribution

2.1.1 Introduction

Variability is an important feature of life − without it there would be little call for a study of probability and statistics! Standing on any busy street corner you cannot fail to notice the immense variety in the human form. In this chapter you will consider whether there are patterns in such variability and whether or not you can describe the patterns mathematically.

 .1A

1 Suppose you were asked to sample the heights of adult males and draw a frequency distribution. Jot down the rough shape of the frequency distribution you would expect.

Why would you expect to get the shape you have drawn?

2 The frequency distribution for the weights of 100 2p coins is shown.

Weight in grams	Frequency
6.80−	1
6.85−	1
6.90−	0
6.95−	5
7.00−	10
7.05−	19
7.10−	19
7.15−	24
7.20−	11
7.25−	4
7.30−	4
7.35−	0
7.40−	2
Total	100

(a) Show that the mean weight is 7.14 grams and the standard deviation is 0.10 grams.

(b) The frequency distribution is shown below.

Weights of 100 2p coins

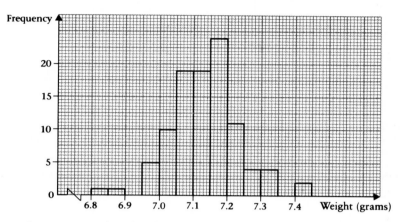

Show, using either this diagram or the frequency table, that there are *approximately* 70% of the observations within ±1 standard deviation of the mean and *approximately* 95% within ±2 standard deviations of the mean.

There are very many examples of random variables whose distributions have the same general shape and properties as the one above. The distribution is often described as being '**bell-shaped**'.

● The frequency distribution is approximately symmetrical.

● Most of the values are grouped around the mean.

● Values a long way from the mean are not very likely.

The weights of 2p coins have a distribution which is approximately symmetrical about the mean value. Roughly 70% of observations lie within ±1 standard deviation (s.d.) of the mean and about 95% within ±2 s.d. It is very rare to find values more than, for example, 3 s.d. from the mean. These properties are common for the distributions of many (*but not all*) random variables. This might lead you to suspect that there is, or might be, a common underlying distribution for various physical situations. If there is, then perhaps it is possible to find a suitable mathematical model to describe it.

To take this idea further, first consider a technique for **standardising** data, the importance of which will become apparent as you proceed through the text.

2.1.2 Standardising data

A group of students sat examinations in both mathematics and economics.

The class results were are follows.

The mathematics scores had mean 54 and standard deviation 4.8.

The economics scores had mean 68 and standard deviation 8.0.

Suppose Debbie scored 64 for mathematics and 78 for economics. Which was the better result?

In comparing two examination scores, working out how far each is above or below the mean takes account of the difference in means, but not the difference in spread. To take account of this, you can measure the distance from the mean in **units of standard deviation**. So, for Debbie,

- her mathematics score was $\dfrac{(64-54)}{4.8} = 2.08$ standard deviations above the mean;

- her economics score was $\dfrac{(78-68)}{8.0} = 1.25$ standard deviations above the mean.

These results, 2.08 and 1.25, are called the **standardised** scores, and give a simple method of comparison. The higher the standardised score, the better the (relative) examination performance.

Standardised data is often denoted by the variable Z. (It is sometimes referred to as the z-score.) It is conventional to use capital letters for random variables and lower case letters for their values.

> Suppose a data set has mean $\bar{x}$ and standard deviation s. The standardised value of an observation x is z, where
>
> $$z = \frac{x - \bar{x}}{s}$$

 .1B

Suppose eight competitors in a school quiz programme have scores of 9, 9, 10, 12, 14, 16, 16 and 18.

1 Show that the mean score is 13 and the standard deviation is 3.28 (to 3 s.f.).

The standardised form of the score of 9 is $\dfrac{9-13}{3.28} = -1.22$ (to 3 s.f.).

This means that a score of 9 is 1.22 standard deviation units *below* the mean.

2 Copy and complete the set of standardised scores below.

Original score	9	9	10	12	14	16	16	18
Standardised score	−1.22	−1.22						

3 Show that the mean of the standardised scores for the data set is 0.00, and the standard deviation is 1.00 (to 3 s.f.).

The calculations could be performed conveniently on a computer spreadsheet or with a statistics package on the computer. You might like to try this, or you could write a short program to do the job for you on a programmable calculator or computer.

4 Investigate other small data sets and comment on your findings.

A standardised data set has a mean of 0 and a standard deviation of 1.

2.1 Exercise 1

1 Standardise:

(a) a score of 6 from a population of mean 8 and standard deviation 2;

(b) a score of 1.45 from a population of mean 2.3 and standard deviation 0.3;

(c) a score of 3.4 from a population of mean 0 and standard deviation 3.4;

(d) a score of x from a population of mean m and standard deviation d.

2 (a) By calculating the standardised scores, compare the results of the following students in mathematics and economics. The results for the full entry of students in mathematics had a mean of 54 and a standard deviation of 4.8. For economics, there was a mean of 68 and a standard deviation of 8.

	Mathematics	Economics
Karen	58	71
Alex	41	41
Melanie	54	68
Chris	20	25

   (b) Cindy did equally well in economics and mathematics. If she scored 64 marks in mathematics, what was her economics mark?

   (c) Mark obtained the same mark in each subject, and his performances were equally good. What marks did he get?

3 A population of men has a mean height of 5 ft 8 in and standard deviation 2.8 inches. A population of women has a mean height of 5 ft 6 in and standard deviation 2.4 inches.

   (a) Which is taller (relative to his or her own population), a 5 ft 7 in man or a 5 ft 5 in woman?

   (b) What woman's height, to the nearest inch, is equivalent to that of a 6 ft man?

4 Prove that, for any standardised data set, the mean is zero and the standard deviation is one.

2.1.3 Considering the area

All standardised data sets have mean 0 and variance 1. To make comparisons between data sets even more meaningful you can also make the area under the graph of each distribution the same.

You should recall that, for a histogram,

$$\text{height of a block} = \text{frequency density} = \frac{\text{frequency}}{\text{width of interval}}$$

For example, consider the data below for the weights of 100 2p coins.

Weight (g)	6.8–7.0	7.0–7.1	7.1–7.2	7.2–7.3	7.3–7.5
Frequency	8	29	46	12	5

The histogram is illustrated opposite. The area of each block represents frequency in the corresponding interval, i.e. 8, 29, 46, 12 and 5. The total area of all the blocks represents the frequency or total number of values, i.e. 100.

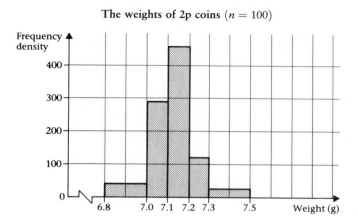

The weights of 2p coins ($n = 100$)

The area of a frequency density histogram is dependent on the total frequency. Since this is different in each case, each histogram will have a different area.

To make the area independent of total frequency, consider the **relative frequency** in each class, which is simply the frequency for each class divided by the total frequency.

$$\text{Relative frequency} = \frac{\text{frequency for the class}}{\text{total frequency}}$$

The height of each block on the histogram now becomes:

$$\text{height} = \frac{\text{relative frequency}}{\text{width of interval}} = \text{relative frequency density}$$

The **relative frequency density histogram** for the coins can now be drawn using the data given below.

Weight (g)	6.8–7.0	7.0–7.1	7.1–7.2	7.2–7.3	7.3–7.5
Frequency	8	29	46	12	5
Relative frequency	0.08	0.29	0.46	0.12	0.05
Relative frequency density	0.4	2.9	4.6	1.2	0.25

Height of block

$$\frac{\text{Relative}}{\text{frequency}} = \frac{\text{frequency}}{\text{total frequency}} = \frac{8}{100}$$

$$\frac{\text{Relative frequency}}{\text{density}} = \frac{\text{relative frequency}}{\text{width of block}} = \frac{0.46}{0.1} = 4.6$$

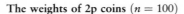

The weights of 2p coins ($n = 100$)

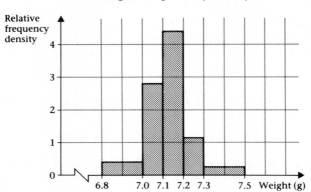

.1c

1 (a) What is the total relative frequency?

(b) What is the total area of the histogram?

2 Draw the relative frequency density histogram for the data provided below. Confirm that the total area is 1.

Times taken for 10 oscillations of a pendulum, initial angle 45°

$n = 100$ mean = 15.07   standard deviation = 0.066

15.11	15.17	15.12	15.01	15.17	15.08	15.02	15.07
15.04	14.99	15.07	15.00	15.11	14.97	15.07	15.06
15.13	15.00	15.06	15.18	15.05	15.05	15.11	15.10
15.12	15.15	15.08	15.15	15.14	15.09	15.09	15.13
15.09	14.98	15.13	15.02	15.01	15.11	15.12	15.09
15.13	15.10	14.90	14.95	15.03	15.05	15.03	15.10
15.07	15.12	14.97	15.13	15.09	15.17	15.07	15.02
15.11	14.98	15.06	15.05	15.05	15.07	15.07	15.03
15.02	14.98	15.05	14.98	15.12	15.01	15.12	15.09
15.11	15.06	15.05	15.14	15.01	15.17	15.03	15.18
15.12	14.99	15.20	15.05	14.91	15.04	15.06	14.99
15.15	15.02	15.28	15.01	15.13	15.11	15.09	15.20
15.10	15.01	15.02	14.99				

A relative frequency density histogram has a total area of 1.

2.1.4 The 'Normal' curve

You have seen that many, *but not all*, data sets have an approximately bell-shaped histogram. This has been observed and noted by many mathematicians, among them Carl Friedrich Gauss (1777–1855) and Abraham de Moivre (1667–1754).

Gauss noted that 'errors' in scientific measurement produced the bell-shaped histogram. He hypothesised that measurements which are subject to accidental or random effects will always produce a histogram of this shape.

The histogram below illustrates a very large data set where the data are grouped into small block widths. The data represents the mass (kg) of new-born babies.

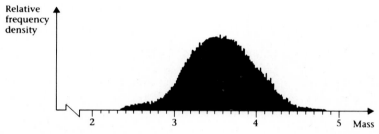

The histogram has a fairly smooth bell shape and it is natural to draw a smooth curve through the tops of the blocks, ironing out the bumps.

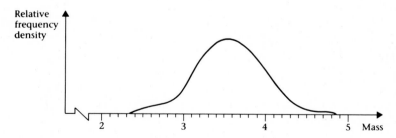

You can model this curve approximately with the graph of a symmetrical function.

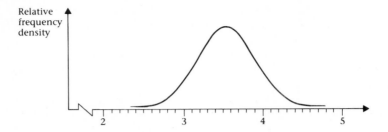

The sketch above shows the bell-shaped distribution which has provided the skeleton shape for many distributions. A mathematical model for such distributions was developed by de Moivre and by Pierre-Simon Laplace (1749–1827). It was upon this model that Gauss, de Moivre and Laplace based their theory of errors. For this reason, the bell-shaped curve is sometimes called the 'Gaussian error curve'. It is more commonly known as the **Normal curve**.

Many (but not all) distributions which occur in statistics turn out to be Normal distributions.

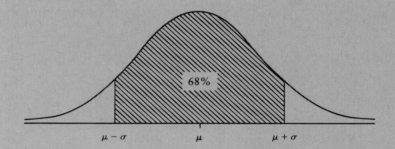

The distribution shown here has mean μ and standard deviation σ. About 68% of the area under the curve lies within $\pm\sigma$ of μ.

When a data set has been standardised, the particular Normal curve which models the data takes on a number of important properties. The Normal curve for standardised data is called the **Standard Normal curve.**

The Standard Normal distribution has mean 0 and standard deviation 1.

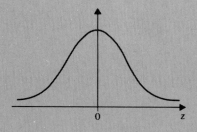

The area under the curve is 1.

To make full use of this mathematical model to describe data sets you need to find an expression for the function involved.

 .1D

1 Using a graph plotter or otherwise, plot the graphs of functions of the form

$$f(x) = k\,e^{-ax^2}$$

taking different values of a (with $k = 1$) and then different values of k (with $a = 1$). Hence show that functions of this form have the same basic *shape* as the Normal curve.

It can be shown that the value of a we require is $a = \frac{1}{2}$, so that

$$f(x) = k\,e^{-\frac{1}{2}x^2}$$

2 What other important *area* property should the function possess? How does this help in finding the required value of k?

Sketches of the graph of f for various values of k are shown below.

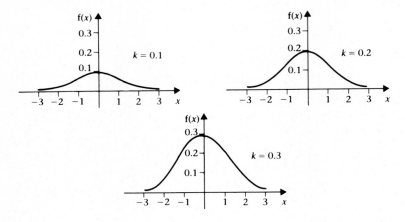

Each curve has the correct shape. It is necessary for the area under the curve to equal 1, and it can be shown that this is true with a value of k of approximately 0.4. The exact value of k is in fact $\dfrac{1}{\sqrt{(2\pi)}}$.

The equation of the Standard Normal curve is

$$f(x) = \frac{1}{\sqrt{(2\pi)}}\, e^{-\frac{1}{2}x^2}.$$

As the data are standardised, a Standard Normal random variable has mean 0 and standard deviation 1.

After working through section 2.1 you should:

1 know how to standardise a data set;

2 know that standardised data have mean 0 and standard deviation 1;

3 know that a **relative frequency density histogram** has a total area of 1;

4 appreciate that the **Normal** distribution is often a good model for real data sets. You should remember, however, that even if the distribution *is* bell-shaped the Normal curve will only be an *approximate* fit. The fit should be good enough to obtain useful information from the use of a Normal model.

5 know that the mathematical description for the **Standard Normal function**, f(x), is

$$f(x) = \frac{1}{\sqrt{(2\pi)}} \, e^{-\frac{1}{2}x^2}$$

6 know that the area under the Standard Normal curve is 1;

7 know that the Standard Normal distribution has mean 0 and standard deviation 1.

2 The Normal distribution

.2 Applying the Normal distribution

2.2.1 Area and probability

You have seen how the Normal curve can be used as a model for the distribution of a number of continuous variables. The following example shows how you can use this information.

Example 1

Over a long period of time a farmer notes that the eggs produced by his chickens have a mean weight of 60 g, and a standard deviation of 15 g. If eggs are classified by weight and small eggs are those having a weight of less than 45 g, then what proportion of his eggs:

(a) will be classified as small;

(b) will have a weight of between 60 g and 75 g?

Solution

(a) *Assume* that the distribution of the weight of the eggs is Normal, having mean 60 g and standard deviation 15 g.

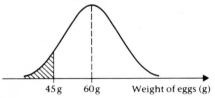

45 g is 1 standard deviation below this mean. You know that roughly 68% of the weights will be within ±1 standard deviation of the mean.

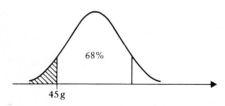

From the diagram you can see that about 16% of his eggs will be small.

(b) If approximately 68% of the weights lie within ±1 standard deviation of the mean, then by using the symmetry property of the curve, approximately 34% of the weights will lie between the mean (60 g) and 1 standard deviation above the mean (75 g).

You saw in Chapter 1 that relative frequency provides an estimate of probability.

The standardised Normal function, which you have used to model data sets, is also known as the **Normal probability density function.**

With relative frequency density histograms, the area of a block represents the relative frequency of occurrence of the values in the particular interval.

For the Normal distribution, the area shaded is the probability of obtaining a value of x between a and b.

$$\text{Area} = \mathrm{P}(a \le x \le b)$$

$$= \frac{1}{\sqrt{(2\pi)}} \int_a^b e^{-\frac{1}{2}x^2}\, \mathrm{d}x$$

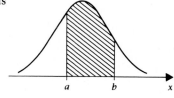

It is not possible to integrate $e^{-\frac{1}{2}x^2}$ exactly and so you need to resort to numerical methods – the trapezium rule, for example. Your calculator may be able to perform numerical integration and so you could use it to find the areas directly. Use one or other method to complete the questions below.

 .2A

1 Copy and complete the table, which gives the approximate area under $f(x) = \dfrac{1}{\sqrt{(2\pi)}}\, e^{-\frac{1}{2}x^2}$ between the limits a and b as shown.

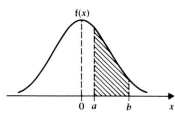

a	b	Area
0	1	
1	2	
2	3	

2 Use the symmetry property of the curve to write down the areas enclosed between ± 1, ± 2, ± 3 standard deviations of the mean.

3 For the Standard Normal curve write down estimates of the probability of obtaining a value of x which is:

(a) between ± 1 standard deviation of the mean;

(b) more than 2 standard deviations above the mean;

(c) more than 3 standard deviations above the mean. (Be careful how you calculate this!)

2.2.2 Tables for the Standard Normal function

There are many possible ways in which you can obtain areas under the curve. You could use your calculator to evaluate the required integral. For example,

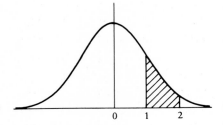

$$\frac{1}{\sqrt{(2\pi)}} \int_1^2 e^{-\frac{1}{2}x^2} \, dx = 0.1359$$

Other calculators will find the area under Normal curves as part of their standard statistical procedures.

Another possibility is to use tables of the area under the Standard Normal curve.

Using numerical methods, accurate tables have been constructed for the area under the Normal curve. A typical table is shown opposite.

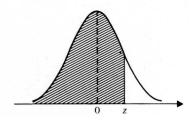

The table gives the area to the left of (or below) any given z value. This is best illustrated with a diagram. z is the number of standard deviation units from the mean value.

From the table you can see that the area to the left of $z = 2$ is 0.977 (to 3 s.f.).

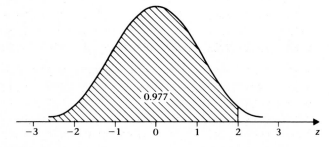

The unshaded area to the right of $z = 2$ is $1 - 0.977 = 0.023$.

z	.00	.01	.02	.03	.04	.05	.06	.07	.08	.09
.0	.5000	.5040	.5080	.5120	.5160	.5199	.5239	.5279	.5319	.5359
.1	.5398	.5438	.5478	.5517	.5557	.5596	.5636	.5675	.5714	.5753
.2	.5793	.5832	.5871	.5910	.5948	.5987	.6026	.6064	.6103	.6141
.3	.6179	.6217	.6255	.6293	.6331	.6368	.6406	.6443	.6480	.6517
.4	.6554	.6591	.6628	.6664	.6700	.6736	.6772	.6808	.6844	.6879
.5	.6915	.6950	.6985	.7019	.7054	.7088	.7123	.7157	.7190	.7224
.6	.7257	.7291	.7324	.7357	.7389	.7422	.7454	.7486	.7517	.7549
.7	.7580	.7611	.7642	.7673	.7704	.7734	.7764	.7794	.7823	.7852
.8	.7881	.7910	.7939	.7967	.7995	.8023	.8051	.8078	.8106	.8133
.9	.8159	.8186	.8212	.8238	.8264	.8289	.8315	.8340	.8365	.8389
1.0	.8413	.8438	.8461	.8485	.8508	.8531	.8554	.8577	.8599	.8621
1.1	.8643	.8665	.8686	.8708	.8729	.8749	.8770	.8790	.8810	.8830
1.2	.8849	.8869	.8888	.8907	.8925	.8944	.8962	.8980	.8997	.9015
1.3	.9032	.9049	.9066	.9082	.9099	.9115	.9131	.9147	.9162	.9177
1.4	.9192	.9207	.9222	.9236	.9251	.9265	.9279	.9292	.9306	.9319
1.5	.9332	.9345	.9357	.9370	.9382	.9394	.9406	.9418	.9429	.9441
1.6	.9452	.9463	.9474	.9484	.9495	.9505	.9515	.9525	.9535	.9545
1.7	.9554	.9564	.9573	.9582	.9591	.9599	.9608	.9616	.9625	.9633
1.8	.9641	.9649	.9656	.9664	.9671	.9678	.9686	.9693	.9699	.9706
1.9	.9713	.9719	.9726	.9732	.9738	.9744	.9750	.9756	.9761	.9767
2.0	.9772	.9778	.9783	.9788	.9793	.9798	.9803	.9808	.9812	.9817
2.1	.9821	.9826	.9830	.9834	.9838	.9842	.9846	.9850	.9854	.9857
2.2	.9861	.9864	.9868	.9871	.9875	.9878	.9881	.9884	.9887	.9890
2.3	.9893	.9896	.9898	.9901	.9904	.9906	.9909	.9911	.9913	.9916
2.4	.9918	.9920	.9922	.9925	.9927	.9929	.9931	.9932	.9934	.9936
2.5	.9938	.9940	.9941	.9943	.9945	.9946	.9948	.9949	.9951	.9952
2.6	.9953	.9955	.9956	.9957	.9959	.9960	.9961	.9962	.9963	.9964
2.7	.9965	.9966	.9967	.9968	.9969	.9970	.9971	.9972	.9973	.9974
2.8	.9974	.9975	.9976	.9977	.9977	.9978	.9979	.9979	.9980	.9981
2.9	.9981	.9982	.9982	.9983	.9984	.9984	.9985	.9985	.9986	.9986
3.0	.9987	.9987	.9987	.9988	.9988	.9989	.9989	.9989	.9990	.9990
3.1	.9990	.9991	.9991	.9991	.9992	.9992	.9992	.9992	.9993	.9993
3.2	.9993	.9993	.9994	.9994	.9994	.9994	.9994	.9995	.9995	.9995
3.3	.9995	.9995	.9995	.9996	.9996	.9996	.9996	.9996	.9996	.9997
3.4	.9997	.9997	.9997	.9997	.9997	.9997	.9997	.9997	.9997	.9998

Joint Matriculation Board

It is convenient to have a shorthand notation for the area under the curve up to a given standardised value z.

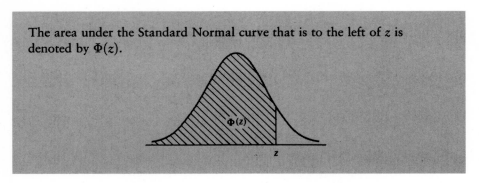

The area under the Standard Normal curve that is to the left of z is denoted by $\Phi(z)$.

When solving problems using the Normal curve you should *always* start with a sketch to help you see exactly what is required.

Example 2

Find the area under the Standard Normal curve:

(a) between 1 and 2 standard deviations above the mean;

(b) more than 2 standard deviations above the mean;

(c) more than 1 standard deviation below the mean;

(d) between $-\frac{1}{2}$ and $+1$ standard deviation from the mean.

Solution

(a)

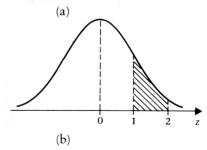

The area to the left of $z = 1$ is 0.8413

The area to the left of $z = 2$ is 0.9772

The shaded area $= 0.9772 - 0.8413$

$$= 0.136 \quad \text{(to 3 s.f.)}$$

(b)

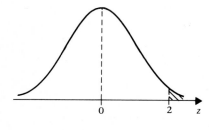

The area up to $z = 2$ is $\Phi(2) = 0.9772$

The area beyond $z = 2$ is $1 - 0.9772 = 0.0228$

since the total area under the curve has to be 1

(c)

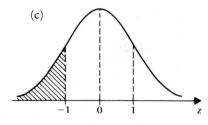

Using the symmetry property of the curve,

$$\Phi(-1) = 1 - \Phi(+1)$$
$$= 1 - 0.841$$
$$= 0.159$$

(d)

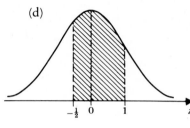

The required area is

$$\text{(area up to } z = 1) - \text{(area up to } z = -\tfrac{1}{2})$$
$$= \Phi(1) - \Phi(-\tfrac{1}{2})$$

Now $\Phi(-0.5) = 1 - \Phi(0.5)$ (by symmetry)

$$= 1 - 0.6915$$
$$= 0.3085$$

and $\Phi(1) = 0.8413$

The shaded area $= 0.8413 - 0.3085$

$$= 0.533$$

It is sometimes necessary to **interpolate** between values in the table. For example, if you need to know $\Phi(1.437)$, you will find that it is not in the table provided. Its value can be found *approximately*, however, by taking $\frac{7}{10}$ of the interval between $\Phi(1.43)$ and $\Phi(1.44)$.

$$\Phi(1.437) = \Phi(1.43) + \tfrac{7}{10}[\Phi(1.44) - \Phi(1.43)]$$
$$= 0.9236 + \tfrac{7}{10}(0.9251 - 0.9236)$$
$$= 0.9246$$

Similarly, you can work 'backwards' in the table. Suppose that $\Phi(z) = 0.90$. From the table,

$$\left. \begin{array}{l} \Phi(1.28) = 0.8997 \\ \Phi(1.29) = 0.9015 \end{array} \right\} \Rightarrow 1.28 < z < 1.29$$

A difference of 0.0018; 0.9000 is $\frac{3}{18}$ of the difference between the values given.

$$z = 1.28 + \tfrac{3}{18} \times 0.01 \approx 1.282$$

Usually it is not useful to work to this accuracy, but it may be appropriate in some situations.

2.2 Exercise 1

In each of the examples below, if you are in any doubt about which calculation to make, you should draw a sketch which shows the relevant area.

1 Using the table of areas under the Standard Normal curve or otherwise, find:

(a) the area between $z = 1$ and $z = 1.5$

(b) the area above:

(i) $z = 1.5$ (ii) $z = -2$

(c) the area below:

(i) $z = 1.62$ (ii) $z = 1.47$ (iii) $z = -1.6$

(d) the area enclosed between:

(i) $z = 1.42$ and $z = 1.84$ (ii) $z = -1$ and $z = 1.5$
(iii) $z = -0.5$ and $z = -1.5$

2 Find the area enclosed between:

(a) ± 1 standard deviation of the mean (between $z = 1$ and $z = -1$)

(b) ± 2 standard deviations of the mean

(c) ± 3 standard deviations of the mean

3 Find the value of z for which the area to the left of z is:

(a) 0.8888   (b) 0.670   (c) 0.9332

(d) 0.484   (e) 0.1251

4 Find the value of z for which the area to the right of z is:

(a) 0.9357   (b) 0.881   (c) 0.2206

(d) 0.3632   (e) 0.5279

2.2.3 Other Normal distributions

In section 2.1 of this chapter you saw that any Normal curve can be reduced to the Standard Normal curve by standardising the variable. It is therefore possible to use the Standard Normal curve to solve problems for any Normally distributed variable. For example, figures from the Office for National Statistics show that the mean height of British women (over 16 years) is 160.9 cm and the standard deviation is 6 cm. How would you find the proportion of British women over 166 cm tall?

Always start by illustrating the problem with a sketch.

Note that 166 is about 1 s.d. above the mean.

Assuming that the heights are Normally distributed, approximately 68% of the population are within ±1 s.d. of the mean.

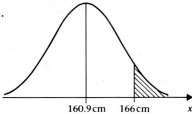

Therefore, about 34% of women will have a height of between 160.9 cm (the mean height) and 166 cm.

So 16% (i.e. 50% − 34%) of women have a height greater than 166 cm.

You can tackle the problem more precisely in the following way.

First consider the distribution of female heights. The mean height is given as 160.9 cm and the standard deviation is 6 cm. Assume that the distribution of heights is approximately Normal.

To find the proportion of women taller than 166 cm you need to find the area to the right of that value. In order to use the Standard Normal tables, first convert the variable X to a **standardised Normal variable**, Z.

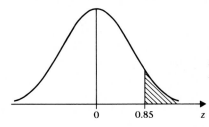

$$z = \frac{166 - 160.9}{6} = \frac{5.1}{6} = 0.85$$

So 166 cm is 0.85 standard deviations above the mean value.

The area to the left of $z = 0.85$ is 0.8023 (from tables).

So about 80.2% of women are shorter than 166 cm. It follows that just less than 20% of women will be taller than 166 cm. This should compare reasonably well with your earlier estimate.

If a variable X has a distribution which is modelled by a Normal function, and X has mean μ and standard deviation σ, then

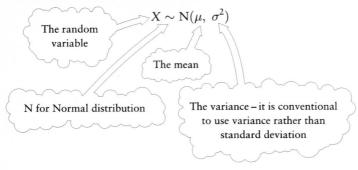

$$X \sim N(\mu, \sigma^2)$$

The random variable

The mean

N for Normal distribution

The variance – it is conventional to use variance rather than standard deviation

This is a standard notation and is a convenient way of providing the essential information about the distribution of the random variable.

> To show that a random variable X has a Normal distribution with mean μ and standard deviation σ, you can write
>
> $$X \sim N(\mu, \sigma^2)$$

Example 3

The length of life (in months) of a certain hair-drier is approximately Normally distributed with mean 90 months and standard deviation 15 months.

(a) Each drier is sold with a 5-year guarantee. What proportion of driers fail before the guarantee expires?

(b) The manufacturer decides to change the length of the guarantee so that no more than 1% of driers fail during the guaranteed period. How long should he make the guarantee?

Solution

(a) Let X = length of life of a drier.
Then $X \sim N(90, 15^2)$

5 years is 60 months.

$$z = \frac{60 - 90}{15} = -2.0$$

$$P(X < 60) = \Phi(-2.0)$$
$$= 1 - \Phi(2.0)$$
$$= 1 - 0.9772$$
$$= 0.0228$$

So 2.28% of driers will fail during the guarantee period.

(b)

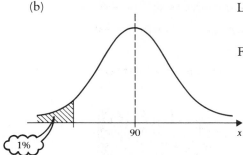

90

x

1%

Let the length of guarantee be t months.

You require $P(X < t) = 0.01$

First find z where $\Phi(z) = 0.01$

$$\Rightarrow z = -2.33$$
$$\text{(from tables)}$$

$$\Rightarrow -2.33 = \frac{x - 90}{15}$$

$$\Rightarrow x = 55.05 \text{ months}$$

The manufacturer should give a guarantee of 55 months, or 4 years 7 months.

2.2 Exercise 2

In each of the following questions, assume that the variable is Normally distributed.

1 The mean IQ of a large number of children aged 12 years is 100 and the standard deviation of the distribution is 15. What percentage of children have an IQ of 132 or more?

2 A machine turns out bolts of mean diameter 1.5 cm and standard deviation 0.01 cm. If bolts measuring over 1.52 cm are rejected as oversize, what proportion are rejected in this way?

3 A machine is used to package sugar in 1 kg bags. The standard deviation is 0.0025 kg. To which mean value should the machine be set so that at least 97% of the bags are over 1 kg in mass?

4 Flour is sold in packets marked 1.5 kg. The average mass is 1.53 kg. What should be the maximum value of the standard deviation to ensure that no more than 1 packet in 200 is underweight?

5 An examiner who regularly assigns 10% As, 20% Bs, 40% Cs, 20% Ds and 10% Es sets an examination in which the average mark is 68. The borderline between Cs and Bs is 78. What is the standard deviation?

6 The mean lifespan for a species of locust is 28 days. If the probability of a locust surviving longer than 31 days is 0.25, estimate the standard deviation of the lifespan.

7 Simply More Pure margarine is sold in tubs with a mean of 500 g and standard deviation 4 g. What proportion of tubs will weigh between 498.5 g and 500.5 g?

8 The heights of girls in a particular year group have mean 154.2 cm and standard deviation 5.1 cm. What percentage of the girls are between 150 cm and 155 cm tall?

9 The results of an examination were approximately Normally distributed. 10% of the candidates had more than 70 marks and 20% had fewer than 35 marks. Find the mean and standard deviation.

After working through section 2.2 you should:

1 know that, for observations that can be modelled with a Normal distribution, about 68% of all observations lie within ±1 standard deviation of the mean and about 95% are within 2 standard deviations;

2 know how to use tables of the area under the **Standard Normal curve**;

3 know how to solve problems for Normal variables by converting to standardised variables (z-scores) and using approximate (order of magnitude) as well as precise methods;

4 know the notation for a Normal variable X, i.e.

$$X \sim N(\mu, \sigma^2)$$

where μ is the mean value of X and σ is the standard deviation of X.

2 The Normal distribution

.3 From binomial to Normal

2.3.1 Binomial to Normal

In Chapter 1 you met the binomial distribution, an important model for a *discrete* random variable under certain conditions. For example, the binomial probability distribution for the number of heads when 30 coins are thrown is shown below.

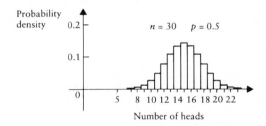

Here the probability of, for example, 20 heads is represented by the area of the block above 20, as shown below.

$$P(X = 20) = \binom{30}{20}\left(\frac{1}{2}\right)^{20}\left(\frac{1}{2}\right)^{10}$$

$$= 0.028 \quad \text{(to 2 s.f.)}$$

Area = 0.028
Width = 1
Height = 0.028

It is difficult to calculate the probabilities of some events using the binomial model.

Example 1

(a) A box contains 60 dice. A prize of a car is offered to anyone who obtains 30 or more sixes on turning out the dice from the box. Is it worth paying 10p for a turn?

(b) Would it be worth paying 10p if the prize were £10 for 20 or more sixes?

Solution

(a) Let X be the random variable: 'the number of sixes obtained'. Then X has a binomial probability distribution. The probability of 'success' at any given trial is $\frac{1}{6}$, and there are 60 trials ($p = \frac{1}{6}, n = 60$). The probability of winning the car is

$$P(X = 30) + P(X = 31) + \ldots + P(X = 60)$$

$$P(X = 30) = \binom{60}{30}\left(\frac{1}{6}\right)^{30}\left(\frac{5}{6}\right)^{30} \approx 2 \times 10^{-9}.$$ The other probabilities are even less likely and the total probability of winning the car is actually less than 10^{-8}.

Winning once in 10^8 turns would cost you $10^8 \times 10$p or £10 million. It would be much better to buy a car!

(b) Obtaining 20 or more sixes is slightly more likely.

$$P(X = 20, 21, 22, \ldots, 60) = \binom{60}{20}\left(\frac{1}{6}\right)^{20}\left(\frac{5}{6}\right)^{40} + \binom{60}{21}\left(\frac{1}{6}\right)^{21}\left(\frac{5}{6}\right)^{39} \ldots$$

$$\approx 0.001$$

Winning £10 once in every 1000 goes would cost you £100 so, again, it does not seem worth having a turn.

Working out the probability in (b) above is of course possible in principle, but in practice it is extremely tedious. Fortunately, it is possible to obtain an approximate result using the Normal distribution as an approximation to the binomial distribution. For example, consider the following situation.

If the probability of being left-handed is found to be 0.1, what is the probability that there will be 60 left-handed children in a school of 500 children?

Let X be the number of left-handed children.
X will have binomial distribution with $p = 0.1$, $n = 500$.
It is convenient to write this as

$$X \sim B(500,\ 0.1)$$

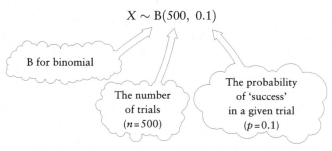

B for binomial

The number of trials ($n = 500$)

The probability of 'success' in a given trial ($p = 0.1$)

The probability of there being *exactly* 60 left-handers is

$$\binom{500}{60}(0.1)^{60}(0.9)^{440}$$

To work out $\binom{500}{60}$ you would need a very large number of rows of Pascal's triangle and the numbers would be too large for a calculator. It would be even more difficult to calculate the probability of 60 *or more*.

$$P(60 \text{ or more}) = P(60) + P(61) + P(62) + \ldots + P(500)$$

The similarity with the Normal distribution may provide an alternative basis for the calculation, since using Normal tables to obtain probabilities is relatively easy.

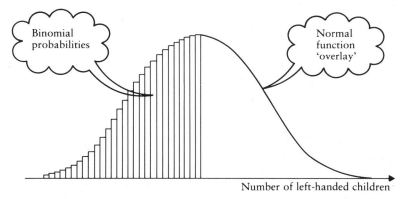

Binomial probabilities

Normal function 'overlay'

Number of left-handed children

The distribution looks very close to the bell-shaped Normal distribution. In order to obtain the right Normal curve to describe this situation you need to know the mean and variance of the binomial distribution $B(500, 0.1)$.

If a binomial variable is to be modelled by a Normal variable then the Normal variable must have the same mean and the same variance. Expressions for the mean and variance of $X \sim B(n, p)$ are given below. (A neat way of proving these results can be found in Chapter 3.)

The mean of $B(n, p)$ is np.
The variance $B(n, p)$ is $np(1 - p) = npq$, where $q = 1 - p$.

A binomial model and its Normal approximation should have the same mean and the same variance. If

$$X \sim B(n, p)$$

is approximated by

$$Y \sim N(\mu, \sigma^2)$$

then $\mu = np$, and $\sigma^2 = npq$.

You can use this information to solve the original problem. It can be done approximately as follows.

The number of left-handed children $X \sim B(500, 0.1)$.
A Normal variable Y with mean $= np = 50$ and standard deviation $= \sqrt{(npq)} \approx 6.7$ would model this distribution.

60 is about $1\frac{1}{2}$ standard deviations above the mean, i.e. the standardised value is approximately 1.5.

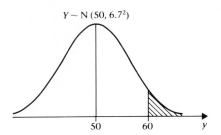

$$\Phi(1.5) = 0.9332 \quad \text{(from tables)}$$

So there is only about a 7% probability that there will be more than 60 left-handed children in the school.

2.3.2 More detailed considerations

Although there are obvious similarities between some binomial distributions and the Normal curve, there are complications, not least of which is the fact that the Normal distribution models a *continuous* variable, while the binomial distribution is for a *discrete* variable. The approximation of the binomial by the Normal is only a good approximation under certain conditions. The graphs of a number of binomial distributions are shown, and these illustrate the conditions for an effective approximation.

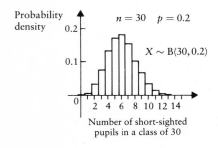

With $p = 0.2$ and $n = 30$ the distribution is still slightly skewed and not symmetric.

With $n = 40$ and $p = 0.3$ the distribution looks symmetric and may be modelled approximately by a Normal probability model.

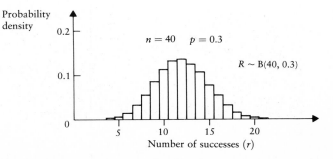

The effect of increasing n when $p = 0.3$ is shown in the three diagrams below.

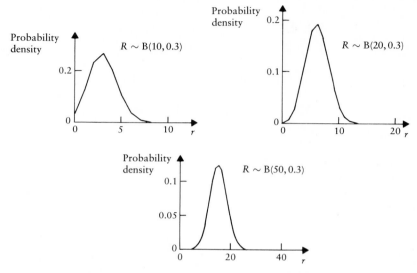

You can see that the distribution looks more like the Normal probability density function as n increases in value. When $p = 0.5$ the binomial distribution is symmetric and will be approximated effectively for smaller values of n.

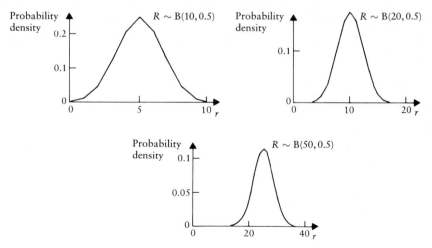

The binomial distribution is bell-shaped for values of p close to $\frac{1}{2}$, even for quite low values of n.

Even for p not close to $\frac{1}{2}$ the binomial distribution is bell-shaped for larger values of n.

You have seen that in certain situations, although the binomial distribution really applies, it is often more convenient to use the Normal distribution as an approximation. This is particularly true when n is large and the calculation of binomial probabilities would be very tedious. This approach is illustrated in the following example.

Suppose a student takes a test composed of 48 multiple-choice questions. Each question has 4 possible answers of which only one is correct. The student is unable to answer any of the questions, so she guesses. Find the probability that she will obtain a pass mark by getting 20 or more correct answers.

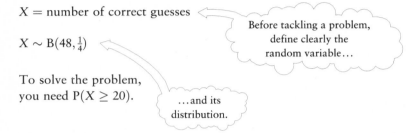

X = number of correct guesses

$X \sim B(48, \frac{1}{4})$

Before tackling a problem, define clearly the random variable...

To solve the problem, you need $P(X \geq 20)$.

...and its distribution.

To find the required probability (of 20 *or more* correct guesses) you must take into account the fact that you are using a continuous distribution (Normal) as an approximation to a discrete distribution (binomial). The diagram below shows the right-hand side of the correct binomial distribution.

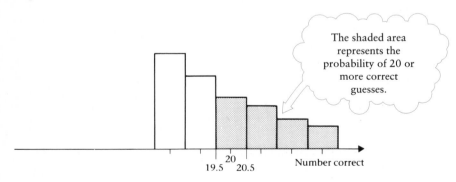

The shaded area represents the probability of 20 or more correct guesses.

On the binomial model,

$$P(X \geq 20) = P(X = 20) + P(X = 21) + \ldots + P(X = 48).$$

This probability is represented by the shaded columns on the distribution.

The Normal distribution used as a model for the distribution of X must have the same mean ($np = 48 \times \frac{1}{4} = 12$) and variance ($npq = 48 \times \frac{1}{4} \times \frac{3}{4} = 9$).

Therefore, you can model the distribution of X (i.e. $B(48, \frac{1}{4})$) with the distribution of a Normal random variable, Y, where $Y \sim N(12, 9)$, i.e. $Y \sim N(12, 9)$ approximately models $X \sim B(48, \frac{1}{4})$.

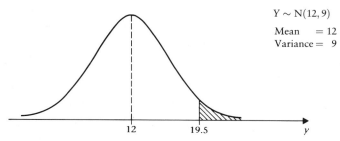

$Y \sim N(12, 9)$

Mean $= 12$
Variance $= 9$

When $X \sim B(48, \frac{1}{4})$ then $P(X \geq 20)$ is approximately the same as $P(Y > 19.5)$ when $Y \sim N(12, 9)$.

The probability for $X \geq 20$ is therefore the area to the right of 19.5 on the appropriate Normal distribution. The relevant area is shaded on the diagram above.

The standardised value, z, is given by $\quad z = \dfrac{y - \mu}{\sigma}$

For $y = 19.5$

$$z = \frac{19.5 - 12}{3} = 2.5$$

The area to the *left* of z is

$$\Phi(2.5) = 0.994 \quad \text{(to 3 s.f.)}$$

The area to the *right* of $z = 2.5$ is

$$1 - 0.994 = 0.006$$

The probability of a pass using guesswork alone is therefore less than 1%.

Example 2
Find the probability that *between* 25 and 30 of the next 50 births at a hospital will be of girls.

Solution
Let $X =$ number of girls in 50 births.
Assume that the births of boys
and of girls are equally likely.
$X \sim B(50, \frac{1}{2})$ and you need to find
$P(25 < X < 30)$.

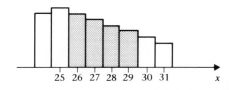

The variable $Y \sim N(25, 3.54^2)$ is an appropriate model for the distribution of X.

You require $P(25.5 < Y < 29.5)$.

Standardising, $z_1 = \dfrac{29.5 - 25}{3.54} = 1.27$

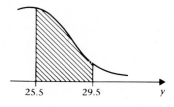

$z_2 = \dfrac{25.5 - 25}{3.54} = 0.14$

$P(25 < X < 30) = \Phi(1.27) - \Phi(0.14)$

$= 0.8980 - 0.5557$

$= 0.342 \quad$ (to 3 s.f.)

It is interesting to compare this result with that obtained using the binomial model itself.

$$P(25 < X < 30) = \binom{50}{26}\left(\frac{1}{2}\right)^{50} + \binom{50}{27}\left(\frac{1}{2}\right)^{50} + \ldots + \binom{50}{29}\left(\frac{1}{2}\right)^{50}$$

$$= 0.343$$

which gives very good agreement with the (approximate) Normal model.

2.3 Exercise 1

1 A coin is tossed a number of times. Using an appropriate Normal approximation, calculate approximately the probability of:

(a) 52 or more heads in 100 tosses,

(b) 520 or more heads in 1000 tosses,

(c) 5200 or more heads in 10 000 tosses.

2 From experience, an employer finds that he has to reject 30% of applicants as unsatisfactory for employment as machine operatives. What is the probability that after interviewing 200 applicants he will find at least 150 who are suitable for work in his new factory?

3 Thirty dice are thrown. Calculate the probability of obtaining exactly 5 ones, using:

(a) a binomial model,   (b) a Normal approximation.

4 It is known that 2% of all light bulbs are faulty. What is the probability that there will be more than 20 faulty bulbs in a consignment of 1000?

5 15% of the biscuits produced by a particular machine are misshapen. What is the probability that out of a batch of 1000 biscuits:

(a) fewer than 130 are misshapen;

(b) between 140 and 155 exclusive are misshapen?

6 A gardener sows 75 sunflower seeds in his allotment. The packet states that 80% of the seeds will germinate. What is the probability that more than 65 seeds will germinate?

7 In Eastfork, 24% of the population have blood type Y. If 250 blood donors are taken at random what is the probability that fewer than 55 will be of blood type Y?

8 A coin is biased so that the probability that it will land heads up is $\frac{3}{5}$. The coin is thrown 160 times. Find the probability that there will be *between* 90 and 100 heads.

9 In 1984, 11% of households in Britain owned a microwave oven. If a random sample of 200 householders were interviewed, work out the probability that:

(a) fewer than 20 owned a microwave oven;

(b) between 20 and 30 households owned a microwave oven.

10 18.6% of boys and 18.9% of girls leaving school in 1987 had at least one A level.

(a) Calculate the probability of finding, in a random sample of 250 men who left school in 1987, more than 50 who have at least one A level.

(b) If 300 girls (who left school in 1987) were interviewed, find the probability that between 50 and 60 had at least one A level.

After working through section 2.3 you should:

1 understand that the Normal distribution can be used as a model for the binomial in some circumstances and that this provides an easy way of estimating binomial probabilities;

2 know that the Normal distribution is a good approximation to $B(n, p)$ if p is close to $\frac{1}{2}$ and that if p is not very close to $\frac{1}{2}$, large values of n are necessary before a Normal distribution can closely fit the particular binomial model;

3 know that if $X \sim B(n, p)$ then

$$\text{mean of } X = np, \qquad \text{variance of } X = npq$$

4 know that if $B(n, p)$ is approximated by $N(\mu, \sigma^2)$, then

$$\mu = np, \qquad \sigma^2 = npq$$

5 be able to use the Normal approximation to the binomial distribution to solve problems.

The Normal distribution

.4 Sampling distribution of the mean

2.4.1 Sample and population

This section develops some of the ideas of sampling from a population which you met briefly in Chapter 1, and shows how the Normal probability model plays a crucial role in the mathematical theory of sampling, with huge practical implications.

For example, suppose a manufacturer of slot machines decides to check for invalid coins by incorporating a weighing device into each machine. Checking coins is not straightforward since there is considerable variation in the weights of genuine coins. The problem is to decide what weight *range* the machines should accept.

It is not possible to weigh all the coins in circulation in an attempt to find acceptable weight limits. Taking a sample of coins is possible but the problem is how to relate information from the sample to the population. This is explored in 2.4A.

 .4A

> You can explore some of the properties of samples by taking samples of size 2 from a population of weights of 200 coins, given below.
>
> For the weights of coins, you can assume that the *parent population* (of all 2p coins) is approximately Normal, and its mean and variance are known (mean = 7.13, variance = 0.01).
>
> 1 Use two-figure random numbers to take at least 50 samples of size 2 from the population given below. Calculate the mean of each sample and record your results. (The coins can be selected more than once.)
>
> 2 Draw a histogram to illustrate the distribution of the sample means.
>
> 3 Calculate the mean and variance of the distribution of the sample means.

4 Comment on the similarities and differences between the parent population and the distribution of the sample means.

Weights of 100 2p coins (grams)

7.15	7.08	7.09	7.05	7.33
7.05	7.09	7.12	7.18	7.19
7.08	7.09	7.09	7.20	7.07
7.12	7.11	7.26	6.86	7.14
6.80	7.11	6.99	7.05	7.11
7.27	6.97	7.40	7.12	7.44
7.17	7.17	7.05	7.18	7.13
7.11	7.19	7.16	7.04	7.15
7.11	7.01	7.21	7.02	7.05
7.03	7.22	7.30	7.18	7.14
7.08	7.06	7.30	7.12	7.04
7.11	7.16	7.07	7.22	7.18
7.24	7.20	7.09	7.13	7.11
6.95	7.01	7.18	7.23	7.16
7.00	7.08	7.03	7.04	7.18
7.17	7.12	7.14	7.13	7.18
7.19	7.07	6.98	7.22	7.15
7.34	7.18	7.21	7.06	7.24
6.98	7.25	7.19	7.29	7.17
7.20	7.04	7.17	7.19	7.11

It is clear that there is a large number of possible samples which may be selected from a population. If, for each sample, the mean is calculated and the distribution of mean values is plotted, you obtain the **sampling distribution of the mean**.

It is noticeable that the distribution of the sample means is more tightly clustered around the mean than is the parent population. This is borne out by the fact that its variance is smaller than the variance of the parent population.

You could explore this idea by taking further samples with increasing sample size. Doing so would show that increasing the sample size decreases the variance of the sampling distribution of the mean. In fact, if the parent population has variance σ^2 then it may be shown that the variance of the distribution of the sample mean is $\dfrac{\sigma^2}{n}$. This important result is extensively used in the work that follows (its *proof* is beyond the scope of this book).

The distribution of the sample mean is Normal.

The mean of the distribution of the sample mean is equal to the mean of the parent population.

The larger the sample size, the more tightly clustered around its mean is the distribution (i.e. the smaller is the variance of the distribution of the sample mean).

If the population variance is σ^2 and samples of size n are taken, then the distribution of the sample mean of these samples will have variance $\dfrac{\sigma^2}{n}$.

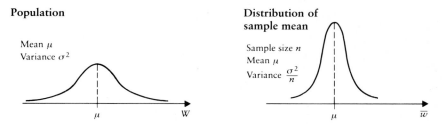

Population

Mean μ
Variance σ^2

Distribution of sample mean

Sample size n
Mean μ
Variance $\dfrac{\sigma^2}{n}$

These results show how the distribution of the sample mean is related to that of its parent population; they are central to the development of sampling theory.

It is now possible to consider in a little more detail how an acceptable weight interval for the coin machine in 2.4A might be chosen.

Assume that the distribution of all 2p coins in circulation is Normal with mean 7.13 g and variance $0.01\,\text{g}^2$.

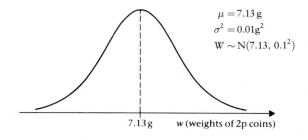

$\mu = 7.13\,\text{g}$
$\sigma^2 = 0.01\text{g}^2$
$W \sim N(7.13,\ 0.1^2)$

7.13 g w (weights of 2p coins)

Suppose the machine is fed 5 coins, each 2p, and records the mean weight.

The distribution of the mean weight of samples of 5 coins will:

- be Normal

- have mean $\mu = 7.13\,\text{g}$

- have variance $\dfrac{\sigma^2}{n} = \dfrac{0.01}{5}$

  $= 0.002$

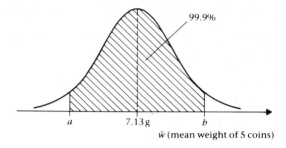

Suppose the acceptance limits a and b are such that the machine accepts 99.9% of all batches of 5 coins.

The limits to include 99.9% of all coins will be very close to 3 standard deviations either side of the mean.

The standard deviation of the distribution of sample means is

$$\sqrt{0.002} = 0.0447$$

Therefore the limits are $7.13 \pm 3 \times 0.0447 = 7.13 \pm 0.134$.

So the machine should be set to accept batches of coins of mean weight between 7.00 g and 7.26 g.

2.4.2 The Central Limit Theorem

Up to now you have been sampling from a parent population which you know is Normal.

However, the ideas and results of 2.4.1 extend to other distributions because of a remarkable result, the **Central Limit Theorem**, which can be illustrated, but not proved, here.

The Central Limit Theorem states that, when sampling from a population,

- the distribution of the sample mean is approximately Normal if the sample size is large enough;
- the mean of the distribution of the sample mean is equal to the population mean;
- the variance of the distribution of the sample mean is the variance of the parent population divided by the sample size.

The Central Limit Theorem is crucial to work on sampling. It enables you to make predictions about the distribution of the sample mean even if you know nothing about the distribution of the parent population. In addition, you can be confident that the mean of the sample is close to the population mean, provided the sample is large enough.

The process of obtaining information about a population based on evidence from a sample is considered in the next section.

Example 1
The mean weight of trout in a fish farm is 980 g and the standard deviation is 100 g. What is the probability that a catch of 10 trout will have a mean weight per fish of more than 1050 g?

Solution
Assume that the weight of the population (of all fish in the farm) is $N(980, 100^2)$.

Parent population

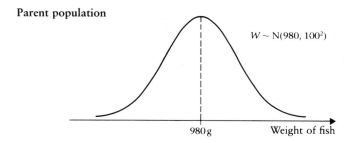

$W \sim N(980, 100^2)$

980 g   Weight of fish

The catch of 10 fish is a sample of size $n = 10$. The mean weight of samples of 10:

- is distributed Normally;
- has a mean of 980 g;
- has a variance of $\dfrac{100^2}{10} = 1000 = 31.6^2$.

Distribution of the sample mean
$(n = 10)$

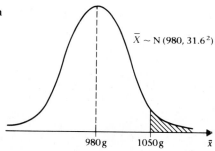

$\bar{X} \sim N(980, 31.6^2)$

980 g   1050 g $\bar{x}$

The probability of obtaining a sample of 10 having a mean weight per fish greater than 1050 g is represented by the shaded area on the sketch of the distribution.

Standardising the weight of 1050 g gives

$$z = \frac{1050 - 980}{\sqrt{1000}} = 2.21$$

$$P(Z > 2.21) = 1 - \Phi(2.21)$$

$$= 1 - 0.9864 \quad \text{(from Normal tables – see page 117)}$$

$$= 0.0136$$

So the probability of obtaining a sample mean weight greater than 1050 g is 0.0136.

i.e. about 1.4% of all samples of 10 will have a mean weight per fish greater than 1050 kg.

Example 2
Screws are produced with a mean length of 4 cm and standard deviation 0.2 cm. How large a sample should be taken to be 95% certain that the mean of the sample will be within 0.1 cm of the population mean length?

Solution
Let the required sample size be n.

Population

$$\sigma^2 = 0.2^2$$
$$\mu = 4.0$$

Distribution of sample means (size n)

$$\text{Variance} = \frac{\sigma^2}{n} = \frac{0.2^2}{n}$$
$$\text{Mean} = 4.0$$

4.0 l(cm)   3.9   4.0   4.1 $\bar{l}$(cm)

So $L \sim N(4.0, 0.2^2)$ and $\bar{L} \sim N\left(4.0, \frac{0.2^2}{n}\right)$

You require

$$P(3.9 < \bar{L} < 4.1) = 0.95$$

This is represented by the shaded area shown.

Consider the upper end of the distribution of sample means.

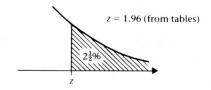

$$1.96 = \frac{4.1 - 4.0}{0.2/\sqrt{n}}$$

$$\Rightarrow \sqrt{n} = \frac{1.96 \times 0.2}{0.1}$$

$$n = 15.4 \quad \text{(to 3 s.f.)}$$

To be 95% certain of a sample with mean screw length between 3.9 and 4.1 cm you should take 16 screws.

2.4 Exercise 1

1 The girls of sixth-form age in a large town have a mean height of 166 cm and standard deviation 6 cm.

In one school there is a mathematics group with 5 girls. What is the probability that the mean height of this group is in the interval (162 cm, 170 cm)?

There are 8 girls in an English group. What is the probability that the mean height of the English group lies in the interval (162 cm, 170 cm)?

2 The mean weight of trout in a fish farm is 980 g. The standard deviation of the weights is 120 g.

If 10 fish are caught at random what is the probability that the mean weight of the catch is in the intervals:

(a) (970 g, 1010 g)   (b) (950 g, 1030 g)   (c) (940 g, 1040 g)?

3 Boys aged 13 in a large town have a mean height of 162 cm and standard deviation 3.5 cm.

What size sample of boys must be taken to be 95% certain that the mean height of the sample will be in the intervals:

(a) 160.5 cm to 163.5 cm   (b) 161 cm to 163 cm?

4 The mean length of a mass-produced metal rod is 7.3 cm. The standard deviation of the lengths is 0.078 cm.

What size sample must be taken to be 95% certain that the mean length of the sample will be in the intervals:

(a) (7.27 cm, 7.33 cm)   (b) (7.29 cm, 7.31 cm)?

5 A packaging machine produces packets of butter with a mean weight of 250 g and standard deviation 5 g. If 10 packets are chosen at random and weighed, what is the probability that they will have a mean weight of more than 253 kg?

6 The length of a particular species of worm is Normally distributed with mean 5.6 cm and standard deviation 0.4 cm.

(a) What is the probability that a worm chosen at random is longer than 5.7 cm?

(b) Find the probability that the mean length of a sample of 12 worms is greater than 5.7 cm.

After working through section 2.4 you should:

1 understand that the mean of a sample will have its own distribution, the **sampling distribution of the mean**;

2 know the Central Limit Theorem, which states that, when sampling from a population,

- the distribution of the sample mean is approximately Normal if the sample size is large enough;
- the mean of the distribution of the sample mean is equal to the population mean;
- the variance of the distribution of the sample mean is the variance of the parent population divided by the sample size.

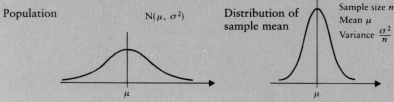

Population $N(\mu, \sigma^2)$ Distribution of sample mean   Sample size n Mean μ Variance $\frac{\sigma^2}{n}$

μ μ

2 The Normal distribution

.5 Estimating with confidence

2.5.1 The standard error

Estimating the pollution of river water is typical of many statistical procedures: you cannot measure the whole population, so you use information from samples to make estimates of the properties of the population.

Suppose regular checks of a water supply are made to ensure that the degree of pollution is within acceptable limits. One measure of pollution is the degree of acidity, or pH value, of the water. Liquids which are 'neutral', that is neither acid nor alkali, have a pH value of 7; a pH value of less than 7 indicates an acid; a pH greater than 7 indicates an alkali. EU recommendations specify that safe drinking water should have a pH of between 6.5 and 8.5. To investigate the level of pollution in a local river, three groups takes samples of water from the river as follows.

- In Clean Valley, an environmental group claims that the mean pH is 8.6. Their evidence is based on five random samples of river water.

- The members of class 5 from Clean Valley Primary School decide to check the water as part of a pollution project. They collect twenty-five jars of water from the river and calculate a mean pH of 8.5.

- The Clean Valley Water Authority, in an effort to clear its name, selects a random sample of one hundred test-tubes of water, and claims, after testing these, that the mean pH is 8.3.

In section 2.4 you saw that the distribution of sample means has the same mean as the population. So, if class 5 continued taking samples of 25 jars of water, you would expect all their various values for the mean pH to average out at the actual mean pH of the river. The single mean value they obtained is therefore called an **unbiased estimator** of the population mean. You have also seen that the larger the sample size, the more tightly clustered is the distribution of sample means. An estimate based upon a sample mean is therefore more reliable when the sample size is large.

The mean pH values for the water from Clean Valley, as calculated by two of the groups, fall within EU guidelines, although the value obtained by the environmental group lies outside the recommended range. This value was based on a smaller sample (5 measurements) and is therefore less reliable.

> An **unbiased estimator** is one for which the mean of its distribution (i.e. the mean of all possible values of the estimator) is equal to the population value it is estimating.
>
> The sample mean is an unbiased estimator of the population mean.

Confidence in how close an estimate is to the actual population mean depends upon the **variability** of the sample mean. For example, suppose you had the evidence of a number of samples, which gave mean values tightly bunched between 7.5 and 8.5, as shown below.

pH levels of 12 water samples

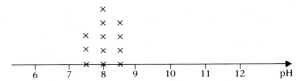

Another batch of samples might produce mean values like this:

pH levels of 12 water samples

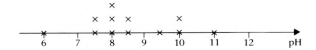

Confidence is increased when there is less variation in the sample mean values. The first batch clearly has less variability and forms a firmer basis on which to predict the population mean. This suggests that you might use the variance of the sample mean values as a **measure of confidence**.

In section 2.4 you saw that the variance of the distribution of the sample mean is equal to the variance of the population divided by the sample size.

$$\text{Variance of } \bar{x} = \frac{\sigma^2}{n}$$

Suppose you know from past experience that the variance of the pH of Clean Valley water is 0.5. Then, for the environmentalists' sample,

$$n = 5, \qquad \text{variance of } \bar{x} = \frac{0.5}{5} = 0.1$$

It is standard practice when reporting an estimate such as this to state the size of the sample and its standard deviation. The standard deviation of $\bar{x}$ is called the **standard error** (s.e.).

The standard deviation of the distribution of the sample mean ($\bar{x}$) is called the standard error (of the mean).

$$\text{s.e.} = \frac{\sigma}{\sqrt{n}}$$

For the environmentalists' data,

$$\bar{x} = 8.6 \quad (n = 5, \text{ s.e.} = 0.32)$$

For Clean Valley Primary School,

$$n = 25, \quad \text{variance of } \bar{x} = \frac{0.5}{n} = 0.02$$

$$\bar{x} = 8.5 \quad (n = 25, \quad \text{s.e.} = \sqrt{0.02} = 0.141)$$

For Clean Valley Water Authority,

$$n = 100, \quad \text{variance of } \bar{x} = \frac{0.5}{n} = 0.005$$

$$\bar{x} = 8.3 \quad (n = 100, \quad \text{s.e.} = \sqrt{0.005} = 0.071)$$

The smaller the standard error of the sample mean, the less variability you can expect in samples, and so the more confidence you can have in your estimate of the population mean.

2.5 Exercise 1

1 Calculate the standard error of the sample mean $\bar{x}$ for a sample of size n from a population of variance σ^2, when:

(a) $n = 25$, $\sigma^2 = 4$ (b) $n = 100$, $\sigma^2 = 0.9$

2 The following sets of data come from a population whose standard deviation is 2 units. Find $\bar{x}$, n and s.e. for each sample.

(a) 6.0, 7.4, 4.3, 4.6, 5.5, 5.6

(b) 7.3, 6.4, 6.5, 6.8, 5.9, 6.7, 5.0, 8.1, 6.5, 5.0, 6.8, 5.2, 5.9, 8.4, 7.7, 7.1, 7.2, 5.8, 8.9, 7.8

3 Rain falling through clean air is known to have a pH of 5.7 (a little more acidic than most drinking water). Water samples from 40 rainfalls are analysed for pH. The mean pH value of the sample is 3.7. Assuming that the population standard deviation is 0.5, express the result for the sample in $\bar{x}$ (n, s.e.) form. Do you think there is evidence of excess acid in the rain?

2.5.2 Confidence intervals

Stating the size of the sample and the standard error of the mean is one way of expressing how confident you are in your estimate of a population mean, but it is not very 'user-friendly'.

You can express the degree of confidence in your estimate in a more precise way by using an **interval estimate**. The idea is similar to that of tolerance. For example, if a 15 mm panel pin is manufactured to within a tolerance of 1 mm, you could give the length of the pin as

$$15 \text{ mm} \pm 1 \text{ mm}$$

meaning that all pins have lengths (in millimetres) which lie in the interval (14, 16). If about half the pins have lengths within $\frac{1}{2}$ mm of 15 mm, then you could say that the interval (14.5, 15.5) contains about 50% of the population of pins.

You can use the sample data to construct an interval estimate for the population mean. For example, suppose that in a certain population of adults, height is distributed Normally with a variance of 25 cm^2. The mean height (μ) is unknown. A random sample of 100 adults has mean height 175 cm. What can you say about the mean height of the whole population of adults?

It is clear that a 'point' estimate of the population mean would have to be 175 cm. However, it would be very unlikely that this *was* the mean. It is better to try to estimate a *range* of possible values which you are confident contains the true value.

You know from section 2.4 that the mean of samples ($n = 100$) from $N(\mu, \sigma^2)$ will:

- be Normally distributed;
- have mean value μ;
- have variance $\dfrac{\sigma^2}{n}$.

Population distribution   **Sample mean distribution**

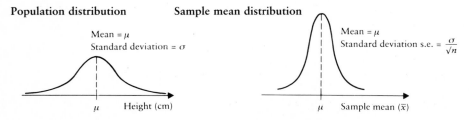

Mean = μ
Standard deviation = σ

μ Height (cm)

Mean = μ
Standard deviation s.e. = $\dfrac{\sigma}{\sqrt{n}}$

μ Sample mean ($\bar{x}$)

You know, for example, that 68% of sample mean values are within 1 s.e. of the mean value.

When you take a sample, you can be 68% **confident** of getting a value of $\bar{x}$ for the sample which lies in the range $\mu \pm 1$ s.e.

You can write this as

$$P(\mu - 1\,\text{s.e.} < \bar{x} < \mu + 1\,\text{s.e.}) = 0.68$$

The inequality can be rearranged to give

$$P(\bar{x} - 1\,\text{s.e.} < \mu < \bar{x} + 1\,\text{s.e.}) = 0.68$$

Since 1 s.e. $= \dfrac{\sigma}{\sqrt{n}} = 0.5$ and $\bar{x} = 175$ cm then you are 68% confident that the interval

$$(175 - 0.5) \text{ to } (175 + 0.5) \qquad \text{i.e. } (174.5, 175.5)$$

contains the true population mean.

The range of values 174.5 to 175.5 is called a **68% confidence interval for the mean.**

Approximately 95% of sample means fall within two standard errors of the population mean (the figure taken from the Normal tables is in fact 95.4%). To be *more* confident of providing an interval estimate that contains the true population mean, you would simply quote a wider confidence interval. An approximate 95% confidence interval for the mean would be $\bar{x} \pm 2$ s.e.

$$175 \pm (2 \times 0.5) \quad \text{or} \quad (174, 176)$$

Example 1
The water in a particular lake is known to have pH values with variance 0.5^2.

Environmentalists obtain ten samples of water from the lake and test them. The mean pH of the samples is 8.2.

Obtain an approximate 95% confidence interval for the true population mean pH for the lake.

Solution
Approximately 95% of values of $\bar{x}$ lie within 2 s.e. of the true mean (μ).

So $P(\mu - 2\,\text{s.e.} < \bar{x} < \mu + 2\,\text{s.e.}) = 0.95$

$\Rightarrow P(\bar{x} - 2\,\text{s.e.} < \mu < \bar{x} + 2\,\text{s.e.}) = 0.95$

Now $\bar{x} = 8.2$,   s.e. $= \dfrac{\sigma}{\sqrt{n}} = \dfrac{0.5}{\sqrt{10}} = 0.158$, so

$$8.2 - 2 \times 0.158 < \mu < 8.2 + 2 \times 0.158$$

$$7.88 < \mu < 8.52$$

You can be 95% confident that the interval $(7.88, 8.52)$ contains the population mean μ.

For the Normal distribution, 68% and 95% are approximate figures for confidence given by considering a *whole* number of standard deviations from the sample mean. In practice, confidence intervals are based on 90% and 95% and sometimes 99% confidence. To do this you need to calculate the correct multiples of the standard error which give these percentages, using the Standard Normal curve.

For example, to find the correct multiple for a 90% confidence interval, proceed as follows.

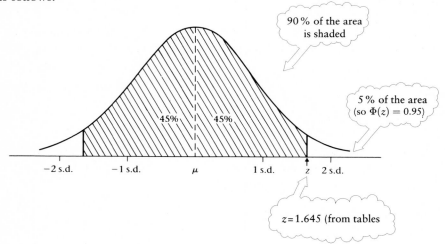

The 90% confidence interval for μ is $(\bar{x} - 1.645 \text{ s.e.}, \bar{x} + 1.645 \text{ s.e.})$.

Similarly, using tables you find that:

- the 95% confidence interval for μ is $\bar{x} \pm 1.96$ s.e.

- the 99% confidence interval for μ is $\bar{x} \pm 2.58$ s.e.

(This is because $\Phi(1.96) = 0.975$ and $\Phi(2.58) = 0.995$;
you need 'tails' with 2.5% or 0.5% of the area, respectively.)

2.5 Exercise 2

1 Children from Clean Valley Primary School collect twenty-five samples of river water. The mean pH of the twenty-five samples is 8.15. The water authority collects one hundred samples with a mean pH of 7.8.

Assume that the variance of pH values for the river is known to be 0.5. Calculate 68% and 95% confidence intervals for the mean pH from:

(a) the primary school results,

(b) the water authority results.

2 A sample of size 9 is drawn from a Normal population with standard deviation 10. The sample mean is 20. Calculate 90%, 95% and 99% confidence intervals for the population mean.

3 Suppose the sample in question 2 was of size 25 (rather than 9). Would the calculated confidence intervals be larger or smaller? Calculate them and verify your prediction.

4 Find a 95% confidence interval for a population mean μ, given a population variance σ^2, sample size n and sample mean $\bar{x}$, where:

(a) $n = 36$, $\bar{x} = 13.1$, $\sigma^2 = 2.42$

(b) $n = 64$, $\bar{x} = 2.65$, $\sigma^2 = 0.234$

(c) $n = 28$, $\bar{x} = 205$, $\sigma^2 = 83.5$

5 Find a 90% confidence interval for a population mean μ given a population variance of σ^2 and a sample of size n with sample mean $\bar{y}$, where:

(a) $n = 125$, $\bar{y} = 0.13$, $\sigma^2 = 0.042$

(b) $n = 60$, $\bar{y} = 20.9$, $\sigma^2 = 3.34$

(c) $n = 55$, $\bar{y} = 845$, $\sigma^2 = 145$

6 A doctor calculates that the mean waiting time for 50 patients is 26 minutes. If the population variance is 6 minutes^2, calculate a 95% confidence interval for the mean waiting time at the surgery.

7 The standard deviation of systolic blood pressure for a population of females is known to be 9.5. The systolic blood pressures of ten women are given below:

$$120 \quad 134 \quad 128 \quad 116 \quad 120 \quad 132 \quad 85 \quad 98 \quad 125 \quad 113$$

Assuming this is a random sample, construct a 90% confidence interval for the mean systolic blood pressure for this population.

8 A random sample of n measurements is selected from a Normal population with unknown mean μ and standard deviation $\sigma = 10$. Calculate the width of a 95% confidence interval for μ when:

(a) $n = 100$ (b) $n = 200$ (c) $n = 400$

Calculate the size of the sample required to give a 95% confidence interval of width 1.

2.5.3 Estimating a population variance

Suppose that to each member of the world's population you assign -1 if the person is male and $+1$ if female. Assuming that there are approximately equal numbers of males and females in the world, the distribution of these values has (approximately) $\mu = 0$ and $\sigma^2 = 1$.

A sample of size 2 from this population is shown. The sample mean is 0 and the sample variance is 1.

There are four equally likely samples of size 2:

[male, male], [male, female], [female, male], [female, female]

and so samples of size 2 have the following probability distribution.

Sample	$(-1, -1)$	$(-1, 1)$	$(1, 1)$
Probability	$\frac{1}{4}$	$\frac{1}{2}$	$\frac{1}{4}$
Sample mean, $\bar{x}$	-1	0	1
Sample variance	0	1	0

.5A

1 Show that the variance of the population (*all* males and females in the world) equals 1 (i.e. $\sigma^2 = 1$).

2 Show that the variance of the sample of 2 illustrated opposite is 1.

3 Explain the other entries in the table opposite.

4 Calculate a similar table for samples of size 3.

5 For both $n = 2$ and $n = 3$, show that $\bar{x}$ is an unbiased estimator of μ.

The distribution of the sample variances is as shown.

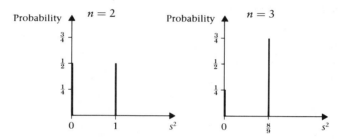

Although the population variance is 1, these distributions have means of $\frac{1}{2}$ and $\frac{2}{3}$ respectively. So, unlike the distribution of sample means, the mean of the distribution of sample variances does *not* equal the population variance. Consequently, the sample variance is not an unbiased estimator of population variance.

> The sample variance is a **biased** estimator of the population variance.

It is straightforward (but perhaps tedious) to repeat the calculations of this section for samples of size 4, 5, 6, ... The results, however, are striking.

n	2	3	4	5	6	7	...
Mean of the distribution of s^2	$\frac{1}{2}$	$\frac{2}{3}$	$\frac{3}{4}$	$\frac{4}{5}$	$\frac{5}{6}$	$\frac{6}{7}$	...

As the sample size increases, s^2 looks increasingly good as an estimator for σ^2 (which is equal to 1). However, for small n, it looks as if you should use $\left(\dfrac{n}{n-1}\right)s^2$ as an estimator for σ^2. (Check that you agree with this observation.)

Remarkably, this result holds generally, not just for the special distribution considered in this section.

> If s^2 is the sample variance of a sample of size n then
>
> $\left(\dfrac{n}{n-1}\right)s^2$ is an unbiased estimator of the population variance.

On calculators, σ_n usually stands for the *sample* standard deviation s, and σ_{n-1} stands for its unbiased estimator $s\sqrt{\left(\dfrac{n}{n-1}\right)}$. So the quantity $\left(\dfrac{n}{n-1}\right)s^2$ is obtained on many calculators by pressing the σ_{n-1} key (instead of σ_n) and then squaring. For large samples, the difference between σ_{n-1} and σ_n is small and usually masked by the fact that s^2 varies considerably.

A rigorous demonstration that $\left(\dfrac{n}{n-1}\right)s^2$ is an unbiased estimator of σ^2 is beyond the scope of this book. The result is studied further on tasksheet E1.

▶ 2.5 **Tasksheet E1 – Boxes of matches (page 305)**

2.5 **Exercise 3**

1 Use the relevant formulas and the statistical functions on your calculator to calculate the sample variance and $\left(\dfrac{n}{n-1}\right)s^2$ for each of the following samples.

(a) The heights of eight students in metres:

   1.54,   1.66,   1.62,   1.68,   1.65,   1.63,   1.67,   1.65

(b) The speeds of ten cars entering a village in $km\,h^{-1}$:

   45,   40,   49,   53,   48,   57,   50,   60,   47,   56

2 Calculate s^2 for each of the following samples. Hence write down an estimate of the population variance.

(a) The sizes of men's shoes sold in one weeks in a shoe shop:

Size	39	40	41	42	43	44	45	46
Pairs sold	1	6	13	20	25	14	7	1

(b) The lifetimes in minutes of twenty batteries:

Lifetime (min)	0–60	60–90	90–120	120–150	150–180	180–210	210–240
Number of batteries	1	0	1	5	7	4	2

3 An inspector of weights and measures selects at random six bags of flour from a consignment and finds the weights in kilograms to be 1.502, 1.499, 1.506, 1.497, 1.501, 1.503. Find unbiased estimates for the mean and variance of the weights of the bags in this entire consignment of flour.

2.5.4 Populations with unknown variance

So far, to calculate confidence intervals, you have assumed:

- that you know the standard deviation of the population (so that you can work out the standard error of the sample mean);
- that the distribution of the sample mean is Normal.

In the examples you have considered so far, the variance of the population was known. In practice you would usually not know the population variance and it would be necessary to find an estimate for it.

 .5B

Suppose you conduct clinical trials for a drug company and are testing a drug to see how effective it is. For 29 patients with the same disease, you measure the remission time (the number of days' relief from symptoms after taking the drug). These remission times in days are as follows:

5, 12, 7, 24, 1, 23, 20, 23, 15, 20, 5, 13, 15, 16, 9,

2, 13, 34, 21, 19, 12, 2, 13, 12, 10, 3, 4, 6, 35

1 From these data, can you calculate the standard error of the mean remission time?

2 Do you know the population standard deviation in this case? What could you use instead?

3 Do you think the distribution of remission time is likely to be Normal? Is the distribution of *mean* remission time Normal?

The population variance is often not known when calculating confidence intervals from samples. In this case you can use the sample standard deviation to estimate the population standard deviation.

You will recall that there are *two* possible estimators for the population variance: the sample variance itself, s^2, and $\dfrac{ns^2}{(n-1)}$.

There is a variety of notations for these values. It is conventional to denote them by s_n^2 and s_{n-1}^2, respectively.

> s_n^2 is the variance of the sample of n data values.
>
> $s_{n-1}^2 = \dfrac{n}{n-1} s_n^2$ is an unbiased estimator for σ^2.

s_n^2 is biased, whereas s_{n-1}^2 is unbiased. However, when n is large, the difference between these two estimators becomes insignificant and for large samples (for example $n > 25$) you can use the variance of the sample as your estimate of the population variance.

Using the biased estimator s_n^2 for σ^2 you can obtain the 95% confidence limits for the mean remission time (see 2.5B) as follows.

$$n = 29 \quad \bar{x} = 13.59 \quad s_n^2 = 8.826^2 \quad s_{n-1}^2 = 8.982^2$$

95% confidence interval $\left(13.59 - 1.96\left(\dfrac{8.826}{\sqrt{29}} \right), 13.59 + 1.96\left(\dfrac{8.826}{\sqrt{29}} \right) \right)$

$$= (10.38, 16.80)$$

Using the unbiased estimator s_{n-1}^2 you obtain

95% confidence interval $\left(13.59 - 1.96\left(\dfrac{8.982}{\sqrt{29}} \right), 13.59 + 1.96\left(\dfrac{8.982}{\sqrt{29}} \right) \right)$

$$= (10.32, 16.86)$$

In this case, with the sample size $n = 29$, the confidence interval is not very different in either case. You should, however, always make clear which estimator you are using, and where you use the biased estimator s_n^2, state *why* you are doing so.

Throughout this chapter, s_{n-1}^2 is used to estimate the population variance, on the grounds that it is unbiased.

Example 2

A random sample of 15 visitors to the York Viking Museum showed that they had waited the following times (in minutes) to get in.

$$19, \quad 28, \quad 34, \quad 10, \quad 27, \quad 31, \quad 25, \quad 37, \quad 54, \quad 27, \quad 54, \quad 8, \quad 17, \quad 24, \quad 21$$

Estimate a 95% confidence interval for the mean waiting time.

Solution

Working in minutes, the sample has mean 27.73.

The variance of the sample values is 165.3.

An unbiased estimate of the population variance (s_{n-1}^2) is $\dfrac{15}{14} \times 165.3 = 177.1$

An estimate of the standard error is $\dfrac{\sqrt{177.1}}{\sqrt{15}} = 3.44$

The 95% confidence interval for waiting times is 27.73 ± 1.96 s.e. minutes, i.e. $(21.0, 34.5)$ minutes.

Notice that these results apply even when the parent population does *not* have a Normal distribution – an important consequence of the Central Limit Theorem.

2.5 Exercise 4

1 Calculate an approximate 95% confidence interval for the population mean using the following sample data.

(a) $n = 36$, $\bar{x} = 10$, sample variance $= 4$

(b) $n = 100$, $\bar{x} = 20$, sample variance $= 9$

(c) $n = 5$, $\bar{x} = 20$, $s_n^2 = 0.01$

Give a reason why your answer to part (c) may be unreliable.

2 In an alpine skiing competition, the times taken by 59 of the competitors to complete the course gave a mean of 1 minute 54 seconds. The standard deviation of the sample was 4.1 seconds. Calculate a 90% confidence interval for the mean time to complete the course.

3 A population of small fish was sampled, giving the following age distribution.

Age (years)	1	2	3	4	5	6	7	8	9
Frequency	0	80	345	243	124	56	34	6	3

Find an approximate 95% confidence interval for the mean age of this population of fish. Write down in your own words how you would explain the meaning of this interval to a local fisherman not versed in the art of statistics.

4 (a) Calculate a 90% confidence interval for the population mean based on a sample with $n = 10$, $\bar{x} = 10$ and $s_n = 4$.

(b) Why is the interval not reliable in this case?

2.5.5 Estimating a population proportion

One important area of application of some of the ideas encountered in this chapter is that of trying to find out how the population would vote in an election. Newspapers and television companies often engage professional organisations (such as Mori or Gallup) to conduct an opinion poll for them. The poll is of a carefully selected random sample of the population. Your earlier work has been about obtaining information on a population *mean* from a sample. Most opinion polls set out to tackle another problem – what **proportion** (or percentage) of the population will vote for a particular party.

For example, suppose that a survey of 400 randomly selected adults shows that 120 will vote Conservative at the next general election. To obtain a 95% confidence interval for the proportion of the population which will vote Conservative, you can proceed as follows.

Let p be the proportion of the population who will vote Conservative. Although p is not known, an estimate would be $\frac{120}{400} = 0.3$. You need a confidence interval for this estimate.

Let X be the number of people in a sample who will vote Conservative.

A member of the population chosen at random has probability p of voting Conservative. As the population is very large, this probability is (virtually) the same for each member of the sample independently of the voting intentions of other members of the sample.

The distribution of X is therefore binomial with 400 trials and probability of success p, i.e.

$$X \sim B(400, p)$$

$$\text{Mean } (X) = np = 400p$$

$$\text{Variance } (X) = np(1 - p) = 400p(1 - p)$$

For large samples ($n = 400$ here) you can approximate this distribution with a Normal distribution having the same mean and variance. So,

$$X \sim N(400p, 400p(1 - p))$$

For 95% of samples,

$$400p - 1.96\sqrt{(400p(1 - p))} < X < 400p + 1.96\sqrt{(400p(1 - p))} \quad \text{①}$$

$$\Rightarrow \frac{X}{400} - 1.96\sqrt{\left(\frac{p(1 - p)}{400}\right)} < p < \frac{X}{400} + 1.96\sqrt{\left(\frac{p(1 - p)}{400}\right)} \quad \text{②}$$

.5c

Carefully show how inequality ② can be deduced from inequality ①.

The interval you have obtained is the 95% confidence interval for p, the proportion of the population which will vote Conservative.

Unfortunately, the expression cannot be evaluated as you cannot work out $\sqrt{\left(\dfrac{p(1-p)}{400}\right)}$ because p is not known! Since you have a large sample, however, you can take the sample value $\dfrac{x}{400} = 0.3$ as an estimate of p. So, approximately,

$$0.3 - 1.96\sqrt{\left(\frac{0.3 \times 0.7}{400}\right)} < p < 0.3 + 1.96\sqrt{\left(\frac{0.3 \times 0.7}{400}\right)}$$

You can be 95% confident that between 25.5% and 34.5% of the population will vote Conservative. In general,

if p_s is the proportion in a sample of size n, the 95% confidence interval for the population is

$$p_s - 1.96\sqrt{\left(\frac{p_s(1-p_s)}{n}\right)} < p < p_s + 1.96\sqrt{\left(\frac{p_s(1-p_s)}{n}\right)}$$

Example 3
A school of 300 pupils has 42 who are left-handed. Obtain a 95% confidence interval for the proportion of the population (p) who are left-handed.

Solution
The proportion of left-handed pupils in the school $= \dfrac{42}{300} = 0.14$

A 95% confidence interval for the population proportion (p) is

$$0.14 - 1.96\sqrt{\left(\frac{0.14 \times 0.86}{300}\right)} < p < 0.14 + 1.96\sqrt{\left(\frac{0.14 \times 0.86}{300}\right)}$$

$0.10 < p < 0.18$ (to 2 s.f.)   i.e. between 10% and 18%.

2.5 Exercise 5

1 The extract is from an article in the *Daily Telegraph* of 5 April 1996. Read the article and answer the questions.

LATEST GALLUP SNAPSHOT

If there were a General Election tomorrow, which party would you support?

	Early Mar	**Now**	Change
Labour	57¹/₂	**55¹/₂**	−2
Conservative	23	**26**	+3
Lib Democrats	16	**15¹/₂**	−¹/₂
Other	3¹/₂	**3**	−¹/₂
Lab lead	34¹/₂	**29¹/₂**	−5

The figures are based on a sample of 1,119 electors interviewed between Mar 27 and April 1 in 100 districts across Great Britain.

MARCH GALLUP 9000

If there were a General Election tomorrow, which party would you support?

	1992 Election	Jan	Feb	**Mar**	Change
Lab	35·2	55·6	55·4	**57·3**	+1·9
Con	42·8	23·1	25·4	**23·9**	−1·5
L Dem	18·3	16·8	14·9	**15·1**	+0·2
Other	3·7	4·4	4·4	**3·7**	−0·7
Lab lead	−7·6	32·5	30·0	**33·4**	+3·4

The figures are based on 10,284 interviews conducted face-to-face between Feb 29 and April 2 in more than 350 districts across Great Britain.

THE GOVERNMENT

Do you approve or disapprove of the Government's record to date?

	1992 Election	Feb	**Mar**	Change
Approve	29·4	14·4	**13·3**	−1·1
Disapp	57·0	74·7	**75·3**	+0·6

THE LEADERS

Who would make the best Prime Minister, Mr Major, Mr Blair or Mr Ashdown?

	1992 Election	Feb	**Mar**	Change
*Blair	27·7	38·2	**41·8**	+3·6
Major	39·1	18·3	**17·8**	−0·5
Ashdown	17·1	14·9	**13·9**	−1·0

*1992 election figure refers to Mr Kinnock

THE FEEL GOOD FACTOR

How do you think the financial situation of your household will change over the next 12 months?

	1992 Election	Jan	Feb	**Mar**	Change
Get a lot/ a little better	28·9	20·5	19·7	**19·5**	−0·2
Get a little/ a lot worse	16·3	26·3	28·7	**29·4**	+0·7
Difference	+12·6	−5·8	−9·0	**−9·9**	−0·9

ECONOMIC COMPETENCE

With Britain in economic difficulties, which party do you think could handle the problem best − the Conservatives or Labour?

	1992 Election	Jan	Feb	**Mar**	Change
Labour	38·0	45·4	44·6	**46·9**	+2·3
Conservative	44·6	22·8	24·1	**22·8**	−1·3
Lab advantage	−6·6	22·6	20·5	**24·1**	+3·6

The Gallup 9000 survey is large enough for its findings to be reported to one decimal place. In the case of the smaller snapshot survey, the findings are reported to the nearest whole or half number.
Those who refused to answer any questions or replied 'don't know' have been excluded from the above percentages. In the March Gallup 9000 the total was 15·5 per cent; in the latest snapshot survey it was 14½ per cent.

The Gallup sample was based on 10 284 interviews.

(a) Calculate 95% confidence intervals for the proportions of the population in March 1996 who thought that:

    (i) Mr Major   (ii) Mr Blair

was the best person to be Prime Minister.

(b) In the main part of the report (the second table), 57.3% of the population said they would vote Labour. Calculate a 90% confidence interval for the population proportion.

(c) The 'snapshot' figures (the first table) are based on a sample of only 1119 people. $55\frac{1}{2}$% said they would vote Labour. Find a 99% confidence interval for the population proportion who will vote Labour.

(d) The author states that for the Gallup 9000 poll it is acceptable to report the percentages correct to 1 decimal place. Confirm that this is so.

2 The newspaper cutting shows the results of a poll of 750 travellers on British Rail following a bomb scare at a London main-line station.

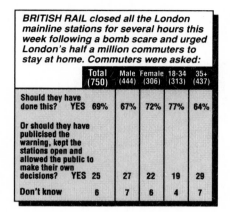

	Total (750)	Male (444)	Female (306)	18-34 (313)	35+ (437)
Should they have done this? YES	69%	67%	72%	77%	64%
Or should they have publicised the warning, kept the stations open and allowed the public to make their own decisions? YES	25	27	22	19	29
Don't know	6	7	6	4	7

Evening Standard

(a) Calculate 95% confidence limits for the proportion of:

(i) male   (ii) female

travellers who felt British Rail were correct in advising passengers to stay at home.

(b) Calculate a 90% confidence interval for the proportion of 18–34-year-olds who felt they should have let passengers make up their own minds.

3 A local council conducts a quick poll and discovers that about 50% of people would support a new shopping complex. In order to estimate this proportion more accurately (to within ±2%) it decides to have a second poll of size n. Calculate n for:

(a) 90% confidence   (b) 95% confidence

After working through section 2.5 you should:

1 appreciate that any statistic taken from a sample will have its own distribution and may be used to estimate measures for the whole population;

2 know what the terms **biased** and **unbiased estimators** mean;

3 know that the sample mean is an unbiased estimator of the population mean;

4 know that, for a sample size n, the sample variance s^2 is a biased estimator of the population variance but $\dfrac{ns^2}{n-1}$ is unbiased;

5 understand that the standard error of the sample mean gives a measure of how close the sample mean is likely to be to the population mean;

6 understand the idea of a **confidence interval** for the population mean, and be able to construct 90%, 95% and 99% confidence intervals from a sample of a population with known variance;

7 know how to construct confidence intervals for the mean of a population when the variance is not necessarily known, using a large sample;

8 be able to calculate approximate confidence intervals for a population proportion based on a large sample;

9 know that if the proportion in a sample of size n is p_s then a 95% confidence interval for the population proportion is

$$\left(p_s - 1.96\sqrt{\left(\frac{p_s(1-p_s)}{n} \right)}, p_s + 1.96\sqrt{\left(\frac{p_s(1-p_s)}{n} \right)} \right)$$

2 The Normal distribution

Miscellaneous exercise 2

1 The mean annual rainfall at a weather station is 850 mm with standard deviation 100 mm. If the rainfall records over a large number of years fit the Normal model closely, what is the probability that in a particular year the rainfall will not exceed 1000 mm?

2 The blood pressures of adult males in England are Normally distributed, with mean 125 and standard deviation 8. What proportion of the male population has dangerously high blood pressure if the danger level is 140?

3 The mean life of the African locust is 28 days. If the probability of a locust surviving longer than 31 days is 0.25, estimate the standard deviation of the lifespan (assuming a Normal distribution).

4 A certain make of battery has a mean life of 26 months, and the makers guarantee to pay compensation to anyone whose battery does not last two years. In fact the firm pays compensation for $\frac{1}{2}$% of the batteries sold. Assuming that the battery life has a Normal distribution, find the standard deviation of the battery life. How many batteries per thousand will last longer than 27 months?

5 A 200-page book averages 500 words to a page. If the number of words per page has an approximately Normal distribution with standard deviation 30 words, estimate the number of pages on which you would expect to find:

(a) more than 520 words,

(b) between 500 and 520 words inclusive,

(c) fewer than 450 words.

6 A fair coin is tossed 100 times. Use the Normal approximation to the binomial distribution to find the probability of getting more than 54 heads. Repeat the calculation to find the probabilities of:

(a) more than 540 heads in 1000 tosses,

(b) more than 5400 heads in 10 000 tosses.

7 In the course of a game, a fair die is thrown 180 times. What is the probability that there will be fewer than 24 sixes?

8 An airline regularly books 320 passengers for an aeroplane with 295 seats. If the probability that any particular passenger will not turn up is $\frac{1}{10}$, what is the probability that more than 295 passengers actually arrive?

If the airline offers 100 such flights in a year, on average how many times will it be overbooked?

9 A school makes 500 entries for a particular examination, and usually has a 90% pass rate. Assuming that each entry has a $\frac{9}{10}$ chance of a pass, what is the probability that fewer than 440 passes are recorded?

10 30% of the population of Ruritania are left-handed. If a random sample of 200 people is taken, what is the probability that fewer than 50 will be left-handed?

11 In a particular constituency, 23 000 people propose to vote Labour and 17 000 Conservative, in a straight fight. On the eve of the poll, 200 voters chosen at random are asked their intentions, and answer truthfully. What is the probability that the sample will indicate:

(a) a tie,

(b) a Conservative victory?

12 A playing card is drawn from a standard pack of 52 (with no jokers). Its suit is noted and it is replaced. The pack is shuffled and a card is drawn again. If a total of 50 cards are drawn, find the probability that:

(a) more than 30 are black,

(b) fewer than 9 clubs are drawn.

13 The length of a particular species of insect is Normally distributed with mean length 4.6 mm and standard deviation 0.2 mm.

(a) Calculate the probability that one of these insects selected at random will have a length greater than 4.75 mm.

(b) Find the probability that a sample of 20 of the insects will have a mean length of less than 4.5 mm.

14 61 blue cars are observed in a count of 200 passing a certain point on a country road. Give 95% confidence limits for the proportion of blue cars passing that point.

15 (a) A survey showed that, out of a sample of 250 viewers, 75 watched the Cup Final on television last year. Estimate 95% confidence limits for the proportion of TV viewers in the whole country who watched the Cup Final.

   (b) What should you do to the sample size to halve the length of the confidence interval?

16 65 out of a sample of 100 randomly selected adults were able to drive. Calculate a 95% confidence interval for the proportion of drivers in the population.

17 A random sample of 50 crates of apples was selected and the number of apples in each crate counted. The mean number of apples per crate in this sample was found to be 40 and the standard deviation 0.5. Calculate a 95% confidence interval for the mean number of apples per crate.

18 In an experiment, 40 values for the acceleration due to gravity, g, were measured. The mean value was $9.80 \, \mathrm{m \, s^{-2}}$ and the standard deviation $0.20 \, \mathrm{m \, s^{-2}}$. Calculate a 90% confidence interval for the value of g.

19 The mean weight of a random sample of 20 male college students was found to be 68.0 kg and the standard deviation of the weights was 5.3 kg. Calculate a 95% confidence interval for the mean weight of the male students at the college.

20 Ten measurements of the resistance (in ohms) of a piece of wire are taken. The results are:

$$24, \quad 26, \quad 21, \quad 22, \quad 23, \quad 25, \quad 26, \quad 21, \quad 23, \quad 25$$

Assuming that measurements of the resistance of the wire would be Normally distributed, calculate a 90% confidence interval for the resistance of the wire.

3 Probability models for data

.1 Goodness of fit: the chi-squared test

3.1.1 Deterministic and probabilistic models

Some mathematical models are **deterministic** in nature. They provide exact information which can be used to predict future behaviour. For example, the path of a cricket ball can be modelled by equations of motion based on the laws of Newtonian mechanics. Various assumptions will be made. For example, you can treat the ball as a particle and so ignore spin; you can ignore frictional forces, or perhaps model them in some way (for example, as being proportional to the speed of the ball); and so on. Once the assumptions are made clear, however, the equation of motion which is produced by the mathematical model can be used to predict such things as time of flight, maximum height and range.

The Newtonian model of the solar system is regarded as a good model because predictions of events such as eclipses can be made with extreme accuracy. The 'goodness of fit' of any model can be assessed by considering how well the predictions fit in with actual events.

Statistical data are not deterministic in nature, but are subject to random variation so that you cannot predict future values with certainty. However, one of the themes of Chapter 1, *Living with uncertainty*, was that long-term relative frequencies of events closely match predictable patterns, i.e. there is 'order from chaos'.

For example, although the path a ball takes through a binostat is unpredictable, when the experiment is repeated with a large number of balls, the relative frequencies of the balls exhibit a pattern which can be modelled mathematically.

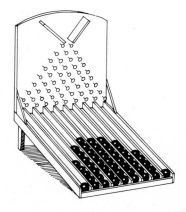

Although the values of statistical data can never be predicted with certainty, you can model relative frequencies with probabilities. You can then use the resulting **probability models** to make predictions and inferences. These will not have the exactness of a deterministic model, but their degree of uncertainty can be measured.

.1A

Which of the following situations are more likely to be successfully modelled with a deterministic mathematical model and which with a probabilistic mathematical model?

(a)   the number of matches in a matchbox

(b)   the amount the pound in your pocket will be worth in five years' time

(c)   the flight of a space probe to the planet Mars

(d)   the result of the next general election

(e)   the rate of a nuclear reaction

(f)   whether a new baby is a boy or girl

It is relatively easy to evaluate the appropriateness of a deterministic model: you can see if its predictions turn out to be true! With a probabilistic model, this is not so easy since it deals with uncertainties.

 .1B

Suppose a woman has five daughters and is expecting a sixth child. She might predict from her experiences so far that the next one will also be a daughter. On the other hand, she sees roughly equal numbers of men and women walking the streets, and this might suggest that there is an equal chance of her next child being a boy or a girl.

1 Are babies equally likely to be male or female?

Do you think that the sex of a first child affects that of a second? How could you find out?

2 The following table of data concerns 100 families.

	Boy first	Girl first
Boy second	31	21
Girl second	22	26

Do these data affect your answers to questions 1?

Provided you make a number of assumptions, you can **model** this situation. Suppose that:

• a baby is equally likely to be a boy or girl;

• the sex of the second child is independent of that of the first.

3 Using these assumptions, show that the probability of each of the events (boy first, boy second), (boy first, girl second), (girl first, girl second) and (girl first, boy second) is 0.25.

One you have established the probability model above, you can deduce the **expected frequencies** for each of the events by multiplying the probabilities (0.25 in each case) by the total number of families (100).

	Boy first	Girl first
Boy second	25	25
Girl second	25	25

Notice that these frequencies are 'expected' in the sense that they are predicted by the probability model. They are what you might 'expect' the frequencies observed to be 'close to', although you would certainly not expect to get these exact values. (The probability of obtaining any particular set of frequencies is very small.)

The closer the 'observed frequencies' of the data are to the 'expected frequencies' of the probability model, the more likely it is that the assumptions of the model are correct. This idea is considered in the activity which follows, where you investigate a model for random sequences and compare it with observed results.

 .1c

1 (a) As quickly as you can, write down a sequence of zeros and ones which you believe to be random. Record 101 numbers.

(b) Consider the string of numbers in pairs and record the observed frequencies of the four pairs (0, 0), (0, 1), (1, 0) and (1, 1) in your sequence. For example, the sequence

   0 1 0 0 1 0

generates the pairs (0, 1), (1, 0), (0, 0), (0, 1) and (1, 0) and gives

Pair	(0, 0)	(0, 1)	(1, 0)	(1, 1)
Frequency	1	2	2	0

(c) Assuming the sequence was random, what are the probabilities of obtaining each of the number pairs (0, 0), (1, 0), (0, 1) and (1, 1)? Hence write down the expected frequencies of each pair in a sequence of 101 zeros and ones picked at random.

(d) Compare the observed and the expected frequencies. Do you think your sequence *is* a random sequence?

Statistical problems are often simulated using the random number generator on a computer or calculator. Doing this begs the question of whether the numbers generated are truly random.

2 (a) Repeat question 1 using the random number facility on your calculator. You will need to consider how to use the random number generated to produce a sequence of zeros and ones. One way of doing this would be to treat each digit as a member of the sequence, counting 0–4 as a zero, and 5–9 as a one.

(b) (i) Is the calculator 'better' than you are at generating random sequences?

(ii) How can you tell?

Example 1
Two dice are thrown and the positive difference between their scores recorded. Calculate the expected frequencies for the difference in 600 such throws.

Solution
The table lists all the possible number pairs and the difference each produces.

		First die					
		1	2	3	4	5	6
	1	0	1	2	3	4	5
	2	1	0	1	2	3	4
Second	3	2	1	0	1	2	3
die	4	3	2	1	0	1	2
	5	4	3	2	1	0	1
	6	5	4	3	2	1	0

From this table, you can count the number of ways differences can occur and hence obtain the associated probabilities as shown in the next table.

Difference	0	1	2	3	4	5
Number of ways	6	10	8	6	4	2
Probability	$\frac{3}{18}$	$\frac{5}{18}$	$\frac{4}{18}$	$\frac{3}{18}$	$\frac{2}{18}$	$\frac{1}{18}$
Expected frequency	100	167	133	100	67	33

$\frac{3}{18} \times 600 =$ expected frequency
$= 100$

3.1.2 How good is the model?

Suppose you have proposed a probability model and deduced expected frequencies. You could compare these with observed data. But how close should you *expect* these to be? How 'good' is the fit?

A measure of 'goodness of fit' which will give some idea of how far the observed frequencies are from the expected frequencies, and whether the discrepancy is 'reasonable', is introduced below.

  .1D

If you wanted to check whether a die is biased towards scoring a six or a one, you could throw it, for example 1200 times, and record the number of ones, sixes and other scores.

Suppose you obtained the results below for dice A, B, C and D (which was thrown only 600 times).

Die A	1	6	Other	Die B	1	6	Other
Observed	182	238	780	Observed	201	199	800
Expected	200	200	800	Expected	200	200	800

Die C	1	6	Other	Die D	1	6	Other
Observed	220	218	762	Observed	120	118	362
Expected	200	200	800	Expected	100	100	400

1 Explain why the expected frequencies for an unbiased die would be 200 ones, 200 sixes and 800 other scores for 1200 throws.

2 Which of the dice A, B, C and D appear to be biased?

A measure of 'goodness of fit' is needed which confirms an intuitive idea of how biased the dice appear to be.

3 One possibility would be to calculate the deviation (+ or −) between **observed** and **expected** frequency for each category, or cell, and then sum these.

(a) Calculate this for die A.

(b) Why is it not a satisfactory measure?

4 To improve the measure used in question 3, you could square the deviations, then add. You could write this measure as

$$\sum (\text{observed} - \text{expected})^2$$

where the sum is across all the categories or cells.

(a) Calculate $\sum (\text{observed} - \text{expected})^2$ for each die.

(b) Compare the results for die C and die D. Why is this measure not satisfactory?

(c) Compare the results for die A and die C. Why is this measure not satisfactory?

A better measure is to divide the squared differences in each cell *by the expected frequency for that cell*. This gives the statistic

$$\sum \frac{(\text{observed} - \text{expected})^2}{\text{expected}}$$

For die A, this works out as

$$\frac{(182 - 200)^2}{200} + \frac{(238 - 200)^2}{200} + \frac{(780 - 800)^2}{800} = 9.34$$

This '**goodness of fit**' statistic is usually denoted by X^2. (The reason for this choice of symbol will become apparent later.)

5 (a) Calculate X^2 for the dice B, C and D.

(b) List all four dice in order of increasing value of X^2.

The larger the value of X^2 obtained, the further the observed frequencies deviate from the expected frequencies for an unbiased die, and hence the more likely it is that the die is biased.

The X^2 results for the dice A, B, C and D should confirm your intuition about which are more likely to be biased.

A suitable measure of goodness of fit is obtained by dividing the square of the difference between each observed and expected frequency by the expected frequency and then adding together the results.

The 'goodness of fit' test statistic, X^2, is defined by

$$X^2 = \sum \frac{(O - E)^2}{E}$$

O stands for 'Observed frequency'
E stands for 'Expected frequency'

3.1 Exercise 1

1 (a) Calculate X^2 for the following birth data

	Boy first	Girl first
Boy second	31	21
Girl second	22	26

(i) assuming $P(\text{boy}) = P(\text{girl}) = 0.5$;

(ii) assuming $P(\text{boy}) = 0.513$.

(b) Which model in (a) gives the closer fit?

2 Before you can start a game of 'snakes and ladders', you need to throw a six. The following data are for the number of throws taken to get the six you need to start the game.

Number of throws to get a six	1	2	3	4	5	6 or more	
Frequency	25	24	23	22	15	91	Total = 200

Let N be the number of throws until a six is obtained.

(a) Using a tree diagram or otherwise, show that

(i) $P(N = 1) = \frac{1}{6}$

(ii) $P(N = 2) = \left(\frac{5}{6}\right)\left(\frac{1}{6}\right)$

(iii) $P(N = 3) = \left(\frac{5}{6}\right)^2\left(\frac{1}{6}\right)$

(b) Deduce the probability distribution for N and calculate the expected frequencies corresponding to the observed frequencies.

(c) Calculate X^2 for the given data.

3 At the local library, the number of books loaned on each day of a particular week were

Monday	Tuesday	Wednesday	Thursday	Friday	Saturday
200	290	250	285	265	270

Calculate X^2 on the basis of a probability model which assumes that books are equally likely to be borrowed on any day.

4 Three coins were tossed 800 times and the number of heads recorded. The following data were obtained.

Number of heads	0	1	2	3
Frequency	78	255	341	126

(a) Construct a probability model for this situation and calculate the expected frequencies.

(b) Calculate X^2 for the data.

3.1.3 The chi-squared distribution

You have now met a statistic, X^2, for measuring the 'goodness of fit' of a probability model when applied to data.

$$X^2 = \sum \frac{(O - E)^2}{E}$$

O stands for observed frequency
E stands for expected frequency

Thus for die A (in 3.1D on page 168), assuming it is unbiased, you calculated X^2 as 9.34 for the following data.

Die A	1	6	Other
Observed	182	238	780
Expected	200	200	800

Similarly, for dice B, C and D, the X^2 values were 0.01, 5.42 and 10.85 respectively. These values suggest that die D is the most likely to be biased, whereas the results for die B seem almost too good to be true!

The data for die A shown above refer to a single data collection of 1200 throws, and the value of $X^2 = 9.34$ is specific to this data collection. If the same die was thrown 1200 times again then you would almost certainly obtain a different set of results and therefore a different value of X^2 for die A. Clearly, X^2 will be different for every data collection – it will have its own distribution of values. The greater X^2 is, the worse is the fit of the model to the data. The question you need to answer is: how high does X^2 have to be before you should become unhappy with the fit of the probability model to the data?

To answer this question you need to consider the *distribution* of X^2 which, fortunately, can be modelled mathematically. It can be approximated by one of a family of distributions known as the **chi-squared (χ^2) distributions**, written $\chi^2(1)$, $\chi^2(2)$, $\chi^2(3)$ and so on. (χ (chi) is the Greek letter x: hence the use of X^2 in the 'goodness of fit' statistic.)

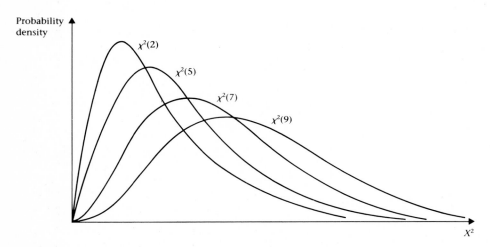

The n of $\chi^2(n)$ is known as the number of **degrees of freedom** and is often denoted by the Greek letter ν (nu). It is calculated as follows for die D.

Score	1	6	Other
Frequency	120	118	362

Once the frequencies for score 1 and score 6 are known, the frequency of the other scores is fixed as $600 - (120 + 118)$, so the relevant χ^2 distribution has two degrees of freedom ($\nu = 2$).

The actual mathematical function for $\chi^2(\nu)$ is complicated. In practice, as in the case of the Normal distribution, all you need to know is how the area is distributed.

A typical table of χ^2 probabilities is illustrated opposite.

The tabulated value is χ^2_p, where $P(X^2 > \chi^2_p) = p$, when X^2 has a χ^2 distribution with ν degrees of freedom.

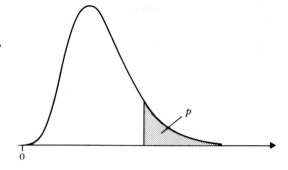

p		.1	.05	.025	.01	.005	.001
$\nu =$	1	2.71	3.84	5.02	6.63	7.88	10.83
	2	4.61	5.99	7.38	9.21	10.60	13.81
	3	6.25	7.81	9.35	11.34	12.84	16.27
	4	7.78	9.49	11.14	13.28	14.86	18.47
	5	9.24	11.07	12.83	15.09	16.75	20.52
	6	10.64	12.59	14.45	16.81	18.55	22.46
	7	12.02	14.07	16.01	18.48	20.28	24.32
	8	13.36	15.51	17.53	20.09	21.95	26.12
	9	14.68	16.92	19.02	21.67	23.59	27.88
	10	15.99	18.31	20.48	23.21	25.19	29.59
	12	18.55	21.03	23.34	26.22	28.30	32.91
	14	21.06	23.68	26.12	29.14	31.32	36.12
	16	23.54	26.30	28.85	32.00	34.27	39.25
	18	25.99	28.87	31.53	34.81	37.16	42.31
	20	28.41	31.41	34.17	37.57	40.00	45.31
	25	34.38	37.65	40.65	44.31	46.93	52.62
	30	40.26	43.77	46.98	50.89	53.67	59.70
	40	51.81	55.76	59.34	63.69	66.77	73.40
	50	63.17	67.50	71.42	76.15	79.49	86.66
	60	74.40	79.08	83.30	88.38	91.95	99.61
	100	118.5	124.3	129.6	135.8	140.2	149.4

Joint Matriculation Board

.1ᴇ

1 Find the value 18.55 in the table on page 173. Find also:

(a) the value of $\chi^2(12)$ which has 1% of the area to the right;

(b) the value of $\chi^2(5)$ which has 5% of the area to the right.

2 X^2 has a χ^2 distribution with five degrees of freedom.

(a) What is the probability that X^2 is greater than 12.83?

(b) In what percentage of samples does X^2 exceed 11.07?

3 X^2 has a χ^2 distribution with ten degrees of freedom.

(a) X^2 exceeds the value a in 5% of samples. Find a.

(b) There is a 2.5% probability of X^2 exceeding the value b. Find b.

You are now in a position to make some judgement on each of the dice considered on page 168. For die A the observed data led to an X^2 value of 9.34. There are only two degrees of freedom, so consider $\chi^2(2)$.

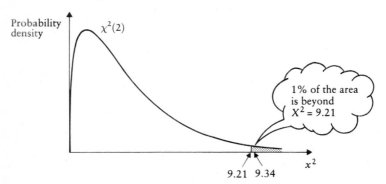

A value of X^2 greater than 9.21 would occur in fewer than 1% of cases. This suggests that the model used for die A (that of an unbiased die) is *not* a good fit to the real data. The difference between the expected and observed frequencies is high, and such a high value for X^2 would occur in fewer than 1% of cases by chance alone. There is strong evidence to suggest that A is biased.

You could consider each of the other dice in the same way.

3.1.4 Testing a model: the chi-squared test

In a project to investigate the distribution of the number of girls in families, the following data were obtained for families having three children.

Number of girls	0	1	2	3	
Number of families	9	17	21	4	Total = 51 families

A binomial probability model, with $p = 0.5$ and $n = 3$, is proposed for the numbers of girls in families of size three. The *model* is used as a basis for calculating the *expected frequencies*.

$$P(\text{2 girls}) = \binom{3}{2}\left(\frac{1}{2}\right)^2\left(\frac{1}{2}\right) = \frac{3}{8}$$

Number of girls	0	1	2	3	
Probability	$\frac{1}{8}$	$\frac{3}{8}$	$\frac{3}{8}$	$\frac{1}{8}$	
Expected frequency in 51 families	6.38	19.13	19.13	6.38	$\frac{1}{8} \times 51$

$$X^2 = \sum \frac{(O-E)^2}{E}$$
$$= \frac{(9-6.38)^2}{6.38} + \frac{(17-19.13)^2}{19.13} + \frac{(21-19.13)^2}{19.13} + \frac{(4-6.38)^2}{6.38}$$
$$= 2.38$$

There are four **cells** in the table. In this case, the number of degrees of freedom is $4 - 1 = 3$. From tables of $\chi^2(3)$, the 5% (or 0.05) value of X^2 is 7.81. The value obtained (2.38) is well below this value and so is not unusual. This suggests good agreement between the model and the real data. The result is said to be **not significant**.

If you obtain a value for X^2 greater than 7.81, then the difference between the values predicted by the model and those actually observed (the real data) would have been greater than would have been expected by chance variation alone. The model seems inappropriate for the data. In such a case, the result is described as **significant at the 5% level**.

A word of warning here – the χ^2 test as described above should only be used if the expected frequency of a cell is 5 or more. Otherwise, groups/cells must be combined. The total frequency should also be 50 or more.

The χ^2 test should only be used if

- the expected frequency of each cell is 5 *or more*;
- the total frequency is 50 *or more*.

Deciding on the correct number of degrees of freedom is crucial in choosing the appropriate χ^2 distribution with which to test the model.

The number of degrees of freedom is the number of **independent** cells used to calculate the value of X^2. This is equal to the number of cells minus the number of **constraints**. For example, in a die experiment where you record ones, sixes and other scores in 120 throws, you might obtain

Score	1	6	Others	
Frequency	25	18	77	Total = 120

Here, there are three cells and one constraint (that the total is 120). Therefore there are $3 - 1 = 2$ degrees of freedom.

Further constraints on the observed frequencies are considered in 3.1F below.

 .1F

The following data for the distribution of girls in 51 families of three children were considered earlier.

Number of girls	0	1	2	3
Number of families	9	17	21	4

If you assume that boys and girls are equally likely to be born ($p = 0.5$), then the binomial model gives a value of $X^2 = 2.38$.

Instead, you could *use the data* to estimate the proportion of girls and then model the data with a binomial distribution using this estimate for p.

1 (a) Show that the total number of girls in this sample is 71.

   (b) Show that the proportion of girls in the sample is 0.464.

   (c) Using this value as an estimate of p, the proportion of girls in the population, complete the binomial probability distribution and the expected frequencies in the table opposite.

Number of girls per family	0	1	2	3
Probability	0.154	0.400		
Expected frequency	7.85	20.4		

2 (a) Calculate the value of X^2 for the model above.

(b) Confirm that this is lower than the value obtained by taking $p = 0.5$. Why do you think this is?

There is now an extra constraint on the observed frequencies. Not only does the total observed frequency have to be 51; in addition, the total number of girls must be 71, to give the estimated probability of 0.464.

3 Given these two constraints and the first two observed frequencies of 9 and 17, deduce that the other two observed frequencies *must* be 21 and 4 respectively.

By estimating the proportion (p) from the observed frequencies, an extra constraint has been added to the observed frequencies – you are now using the constraints '71 girls among 51 families' as opposed to just '51 families'. The number of degrees of freedom is therefore reduced by one. There are four cells and two constraints, giving $4 - 2 = 2$ degrees of freedom. The correct distribution for X^2 in this case is $\chi^2(2)$.

$$\text{Number of degrees of freedom} = \text{number of cells} - \text{number of constraints}$$

Since the total frequency is fixed, this is always a constraint. In addition, each time the data are used to estimate a parameter for the model (such as p in the binomial model), this adds another constraint and reduces the number of degrees of freedom by one. For example, suppose you had collected the following data on the number of girls in 100 families of size four.

Number of girls	0	1	2	3	4	
Number of families	5	24	37	30	4	Total $= 100$

If you were to compare these data with the frequencies expected on the basis of using $B(4, \frac{1}{2})$ for the number of girls in each family, then the number of degrees of freedom (ν) is:

Number of cells $- 1 = 4$

If, instead, you were to use $B(4, p)$ with p calculated from the data as $\frac{204}{400} = 0.51$, then there would be the extra constraint that the mean of the model must equal the mean of the data, and

$$\nu = 5 - 2 = 3$$

3.1 Exercise 2

1 Six samples of 180 men under the age of forty were selected randomly from a large population to test the hypothesis that one-sixth of men have black hair. The numbers observed were 40, 35, 30, 28, 25 and 20. Is there evidence against the hypothesis?

2 According to Mendel's theory of genetics, the number of peas of a certain variety which fall into the classifications round and yellow, wrinkled and yellow, round and green, and wrinkled and green should be in the ratio $9:3:3:1$. Suppose that for 100 such peas, 55, 20, 16 and 9 were in these respective classes. Do these results agree with Mendelian theory?

3 Imported peaches come in boxes each holding six peaches. A batch of 100 boxes in a supermarket revealed the following distribution of imperfect fruit amongst the boxes.

No. of imperfect peaches in box	0	1	2	3	4	5	6
Frequency	49	24	14	9	3	1	0

Use the data to estimate the proportion of imperfect peaches. Use this to calculate the expected frequency of boxes out of 100 with 0, 1, 2, and 3 or more imperfect peaches (assume statistical independence). Then conduct a χ^2 goodness of fit test on these four cells, and test the model.

4 Four coins are tossed 100 times and the number of heads (H) counted each time. The results were as follows.

No. of heads (H)	0	1	2	3	4
Frequency	5	21	32	34	8

(a) Test the data against the model $H \sim B(4, \frac{1}{2})$.

(b) Estimate p (the probability of obtaining a head when a coin is thrown) from the data. Test the data against the model $H \sim B(4, p)$.

Comment on your results in (a) and (b).

3.1.5 Contingency tables

In the remainder of this chapter, you will be looking at a range of probability models which can be used to model data. The χ^2 goodness of fit test can be used as a check to see if a model is appropriate, or to see if the assumptions behind a model are reasonable.

This section considers a particularly common and useful application of χ^2 which tests the **independence** of two characteristics.

Here are some data on voting intentions for a council election in a small rural community. They are classified according to the age of the voters. There were only two candidates, one Labour and one Conservative. 'Don't knows' were discounted.

	Age (years) 18–25	26–40	41–60	60+	Total
Will vote Labour	5	27	13	21	66
Will vote Conservative	14	35	47	56	152
Total	19	62	60	77	218

This sort of two-way table is called a **contingency table**.

A total of 66 out of 218 intend to vote Labour and 152 out of 218 intend to vote Conservative. *Assuming that age does not affect voting intention*, you would expect the following frequencies in the 18–25 category.

Will vote Labour	$19 \times \frac{66}{218} = 5.8$
Will vote Conservative	$19 \times \frac{152}{218} = 13.2$
	Total $= 19$

.1G

1 Calculate expected frequencies for the remaining age categories and hence complete the following table of expected frequencies.

	18–25	26–40	41–60	60+	Total
Will vote Labour	5.8				66
Will vote Conservative	13.2				152
Total	19	62	60	77	218

2 Calculate $X^2 = \sum \dfrac{(O - E)^2}{E}$ for the eight cells of the table.

In determining the expected frequencies, both the row totals (to determine the overall proportion of Labour/Conservative voters) and the column totals (to calculate the expected frequencies in each age category) have been used. So these are fixed constraints on the observed frequencies in this table.

	18–25	26–40	41–60	60+	Total
Will vote Labour					66
Will vote Conservative					152
Total	19	62	60	77	218

3 In this case, once three observed frequencies are known, the others are determined by the row and column totals. Therefore, $\nu = 3$.

Complete the χ^2 test and comment on whether voting intention is related to age.

You can generalise to find a rule for the number of degrees of freedom in this sort of test. The row and column totals are fixed in determining the model. Suppose you had a four by five table, as opposite.

Observed table of values

	A	B	C	D	E	Total
i						fixed
ii						fixed
iii						fixed
iv						fixed
Total	fixed	fixed	fixed	fixed	fixed	

There are only three **free entries** in each column; the fourth entry is fixed so that the total for the column agrees with the observed data. Similarly each row has only four full entries, as the row total must agree with the observed data. In this 4×5 contingency table there will be $3 \times 4 = 12$ free entries, so that the table has 12 degrees of freedom. This result may be generalised:

> In an $m \times n$ contingency table there will be $(m-1)(n-1)$ degrees of freedom.

The χ^2 distribution is used to test the calculated value of X^2 for the data. Conditions on its use are that the *expected frequency* of each cell must be five or more and that the *total frequency* should be at least 50. Under such conditions, χ^2 satisfactorily models the distribution of the difference measure, X^2. However, the approximation is less good when there is only one degree of freedom. This is always the case for 2×2 contingency tables. A correction to improve the fit, known as **Yates's correction**, is sometimes used to improve the situation. However, this correction will be ignored here.

Example 2
In a trial, 120 out of 200 women can distinguish margarine from butter, whereas 108 out of 200 men can tell the difference. Does this trial provide evidence of a gender-related difference in taste discrimination?

Solution
The data can be expressed in a 2×2 contingency table.

	Men	Women	Total
Can tell	108	120	228
Cannot tell	92	80	172
Total	200	200	400

A model based on the assumption that there is no difference in the ability of men and women to distinguish between butter and margarine would lead to the following expected frequencies:

	Men	Women	
Can tell	114	114	228
Cannot tell	86	86	172
Total	200	200	400

$\frac{228}{400}$ can tell the difference. You would expect that $\frac{228}{400}$ of the 200 women to be able to do so i.e. $\frac{228}{400} \times 200 = 114$

Calculating the difference measure,

$$X^2 = \sum \frac{(O - E)^2}{E}$$

$$X^2 = \frac{(108 - 114)^2}{114} + \frac{(120 - 114)^2}{114} + \frac{(92 - 86)^2}{86} + \frac{(80 - 86)^2}{86}$$

$$X^2 = 1.47 \quad \text{with one degree of freedom}$$

As this value does not exceed the $\chi^2(1)$ value of 2.71, then the difference between the observed values and those of the model is *not* significant at the 10% level.

There is insufficient evidence (from the data) that ability to distinguish between margarine and butter is gender-related.

3.1 Exercise 3

1 The following data compare performances of candidates in the sociology honours degree at two colleges.

	Grade				
	1	2	3	4	Total
College A	6	66	114	56	242
College B	5	40	86	49	180

Is there a significant difference in grades awarded?

2 In a hospital survey, staff were asked whether they were satisfied or dissatisfied in their work. Results were as follows.

	Satisfied	Not satisfied	Total
Doctors	50	20	70
Nurses	30	30	60
Ancillary staff	12	48	60
Total	92	98	190

What evidence do these data provide that job satisfaction is related to the type of job?

3 In a clinical trial of a drug for arthritis, 200 patients received treatment with the drug, and a control group of 200 received treatment with a seemingly identical placebo (which is non-active). After a period of time, patients were asked if their condition had improved. The results were as follows.

	Drug	Placebo
Improved	119	72
Not improved	81	128

Consider a χ^2 test to decide if these results give evidence (significant at the 1% level) that the drug is effective in improving the condition.

4 As part of the National Child Development Study, a report recorded the numbers of boys and girls aged 7 who had had a temper tantrum in the previous three months.

	Yes	No
Boys	1209	2849
Girls	1064	2863

Do these figures indicate a significant difference in behaviour between boys and girls?

After working through section 3.1 you should:

1 understand the difference between a deterministic and a probabilistic model and know when each is appropriate;

2 understand the terms **observed** and **expected frequencies,** and be able to calculate expected frequencies from a probability model;

3 be able to calculate the 'goodness of fit' statistic

$$X^2 = \sum \frac{(O - E)^2}{E}$$

4 know that the goodness of fit statistic X^2 has a distribution which can be modelled by one of the chi-squared functions;

5 know the conditions under which the χ^2 test may be applied;

6 know how to find areas under the χ^2 distribution using probability tables, and interpret these results in terms of probability;

7 understand what is meant by **significance level** as applied to problems involving fitting probability models;

8 be able to apply a χ^2 goodness of fit test to test probability models for data, including contingency tables;

9 know how to work out the number of degrees of freedom by considering the number of constraints on the observed frequencies;

10 know that an $m \times n$ contingency table has $(m - 1)(n - 1)$ degrees of freedom.

3 Probability models for data

.2 Distributions for counting cases

3.2.1 The geometric distribution

Most people's lives follow a fairly routine pattern, although chance events do affect things. Nevertheless, an order emerges from the 'chaos' of random events. Some of the emerging pattern may be modelled by random variables and the probability distributions which describe their behaviour.

For example, the number of girls in a family with four children is a random variable, X, which can take any of the values $X = 0$, 1, 2, 3 or 4. You should be aware that, with appropriate assumptions, X has a binomial probability distribution.

In Chapter 1, *Living with uncertainty*, you considered the binomial distribution in some detail, and Chapter 2, *The Normal distribution*, was based entirely on one important probability distribution for a continuous random variable which is important for much of statistics.

All the distributions considered in this section apply to random variables which *count* events and therefore take whole number values 0, 1, 2 and so on. The situations which they can be used to model will be compared and contrasted.

For example, on one day a midwife delivers eight boys in a row before the first girl is born. How rare is this event?

First you must clearly define a random variable. In this case, let X be the number of births *up to and including* the first girl; so X takes the values $\{1, 2, 3 \ldots\}$.

The random variable X does have a number of properties in common with a binomial variable. It is a discrete variable; there is a constant probability of the event occurring at each trial; and there is independence between trials. However, there is *not a fixed number of trials* (the value of n in the binomial distribution).

The probability distribution for X is considered in 3.2A below.

3 .2A

What is the probability of there being eight or more births until the first female is born?

Let X be the number of births until the first female birth, so $X = \{1, 2, 3 \ldots\}$.

In Britain, it is slightly more likely that a baby is a boy. From census data, you can estimate the probability of a girl as 0.487 and of a boy as 0.513.

If you count the number of births until a girl, the possible events are G ($X = 1$), BG ($X = 2$), BBG ($X = 3$), BBBG, . . . These can be illustrated by a tree diagram.

1 Draw a tree diagram to illustrate the outcomes. What assumptions do you need to make when drawing the tree diagram?

2 Use the tree diagram to write down the probability that the first female birth occurs at:

(a) the first delivery (i.e. $X = 1$),

(b) the second delivery (i.e. $X = 2$),

(c) the fifth delivery ($X = 5$),

(d) the nth delivery ($X = n$).

3 Use your answers to question 2 to complete the probability distribution for X, the number of children up to and including the first girl, for values of X up to 7. (Round the probabilities to 3 significant figures.)

4 Calculate the probability of seven or more boys being born before the first girl.

5 For a series of independent trials, let p be the probability that a chosen outcome occurs on any one particular trial. Let X be the number of trials needed to obtain the chosen outcome.

If $q = 1 - p$, show that:

(a) $P(X = 1) = p$

(b) $P(X = 3) = q^2 p$

(c) $P(X = n) = q^{n-1} p$

Notice that the sequence of probabilities p, qp, $q^2 p$, $q^3 p$, . . . forms a geometric series with common ratio q.

> If the random variable X counts the number of **independent trials** until the occurrence of an event whose probability is p, then X has a geometric distribution.
>
> The **geometric distribution**, abbreviated to $G(p)$, is defined in the following way.
>
> $$P(X = r) = q^{r-1}p \quad \text{where } r = 1, 2, 3, \ldots$$

A cautionary note: you have been counting the number of trials up to and including the occurrence of the event itself, so that the lowest possible value of X is 1 (i.e. the event occurs at the first trial). Defined in this way, X cannot take the value 0. In some treatments of the geometric distribution, X is defined slightly differently, being the number of trials *before* the occurrence of the event. If X is defined in this way, its lowest possible value will be 0 (if the event occurs at the first trial, there are no trials *before* the occurrence).

Thus, you need to take care over how X is defined, both in the problems and exercises which follow, and elsewhere.

Example 1

To start a game of 'snakes and ladders', you need to throw a six. Calculate the probability that it takes more than 6 throws to get a six.

Define the distribution

Solution

Let X be the number of throws taken to get a six. Then $X \sim G\left(\frac{1}{6}\right)$.

X takes the values $\{1, 2, 3, \ldots\}$.

$$P(X > 6) = 1 - P(X \leq 6)$$

$$= 1 - [P(X = 1) + \ldots + P(X = 6)]$$

$$= 1 - [\tfrac{1}{6} + \left(\tfrac{5}{6}\right)\tfrac{1}{6} + \left(\tfrac{5}{6}\right)^2 \tfrac{1}{6} + \ldots + \left(\tfrac{5}{6}\right)^6 \tfrac{1}{6}]$$

$$= 0.335$$

The probability that it takes more than 6 throws is 0.335.

Alternatively,

$$P(6 \text{ 'non-sixes'}) = \left(\tfrac{5}{6}\right)^6 = 0.335$$

The distribution of X is illustrated.

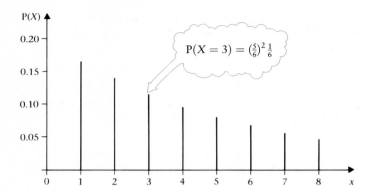

$$P(X = 3) = \left(\tfrac{5}{6}\right)^2 \tfrac{1}{6}$$

3.2 Exercise 1

1 X has a geometric distribution with $p = 0.2$. Calculate:

(a) $P(X = 3)$ (b) $P(X < 3)$ (c) $P(X \geq 3)$

2 I have a key ring on which there are four keys, all of the same type. To get into my office I select a key at random.

(a) If it is a wrong key then I choose another at random from the remaining three. Calculate the probability that I try:

(i) two keys,   (ii) all four keys.

(b) If, instead, I simply keep choosing at random from all four keys until I get the correct one, calculate the probability that I try:

(i) two keys,   (ii) more than two keys.

(c) Which strategy is better for getting into my room? Why?

3 Suppose that each time you take a driving test you have a probability of 0.4 of passing. What is the probability that you:

(a) pass the test on the third attempt;

(b) need at least six attempts to pass?

4 From a table of single-digit random numbers, what is the probability that:

(a) you select five digits and you still do not have a zero;

(b) you need to select more than twenty digits to obtain your first zero?

3.2.2 The binomial distribution revisited

On a particular morning, there are ten babies in the maternity ward at a local hospital. Only one of them is a boy. Just how likely an event is this?

 .2B

1 Identify the random variable in the situation described above and an appropriate binomial distribution to model it.

2 Discuss the differences between the binomial and the geometric distributions by considering the conditions under which each applies.

To calculate binomial probabilities in Chapter 1, you used Pascal's triangle to work out $\binom{n}{r}$, the number of ways of choosing r objects from n. When n gets large, using Pascal's triangle is cumbersome. Even though you can use the Normal approximation to the binomial when n is large, the following formula for evaluating $\binom{n}{r}$ is useful.

$$\binom{n}{r} = \frac{n!}{r!(n-r)!} \qquad \text{where } n! = n(n-1)(n-2)\ldots 1 \\ \text{and} \quad 0! = 1$$

$\binom{n}{r}$ is sometimes written as ^nC_r or $_nC_r$.

If $X \sim B(n, p)$, then:

$$P(X = r) = \binom{n}{r} p^r q^{n-r} \qquad r = 0, 1, 2, \ldots, n$$

$$P(X = r) = \frac{n!}{r!(n-r)!} p^r q^{n-r}$$

Example 2

Approximately 20% of the pupils at a primary school are vegetarians. Seven of the pupils are to visit another school and have lunch there. Calculate the probability that, in addition to normal requirements, the school will need to provide:

(a) three vegetarian lunches,   (b) at least one vegetarian lunch.

Solution

Let X be the number of vegetarians on the visit.

Specify the random variable

$$X \sim B(7, 0.20)$$

Specify its probability distribution

(a) $P(X = 3) = \binom{7}{3}(0.2)^3(0.8)^4 = \left(\frac{7!}{3!\,4!}\right)(0.2)^3(0.8)^4$

$$= 0.115$$

$=35$

(b) $P(X \geq 1) = 1 - P(X = 0) = 1 - 0.8^7 = 0.79$

▶ 3.2 **Tasksheet E1 – Programming the binomial (page 308)**

3.2 **Exercise 2**

1 In a series of five matches between two teams, calculate the probability that one team wins the toss:

(a) on exactly three occasions, (b) on three or more occasions

2 If $X \sim B(8, \frac{2}{3})$, find the most likely value of X.

3 Six people, selected at random, sample two brands of orange squash, brands A and B. If five of them say they prefer brand B, do you think this is sufficient evidence for an advertiser to say, 'Most people prefer brand B'? Explain.

4 In a multiple choice test where there are only three alternatives to each of the twenty questions, a student randomly guesses each answer. If fifteen is the pass mark for the test, calculate the probability that he passes.

5 A coin is tossed eight times. What is the probability that there will be more tails on the first four throws than on the last four?

3.2.3 The Poisson distribution

A small company handles emergency medical deliveries by motor cycle. On average, it receives four delivery requests in a 12-hour period. When it gets more than four emergency requests, it has to pass on the work to another company. The company wishes to know the probability of this happening to enable them to evaluate their employment policy.

Let X be the number of emergency calls in a 12-hour period.

Theoretically, X can take any whole number value, although large numbers will be very unlikely. The distribution could not be binomial as it has the possibility of infinitely many outcomes. The distribution is not geometric as it is not waiting for an event to happen. The nature of the distribution of X is explored in 3.2c which follows.

 .2c

It is possible to find *approximate* binomial models which describe the demands on the emergency system.

On average, requests for deliveries are made four times in a 12-hour period. Assume that in each hour no more than one request can be made. So for each hour,

$$P(\text{request}) \quad = \tfrac{1}{3}$$
$$P(\text{no request}) = \tfrac{2}{3}$$

and the total number of requests in 12 hours will be $B(12, \tfrac{1}{3})$.

1 (a) Show that this model has the correct mean.

(b) Complete the probability distribution of X.

X	0	1	2	3	4	5	6	7	8	9	10	11	12
$P(X = x)$	?	0.046	0.127	0.212	?	0.191	0.111	0.048	?	0.003	0	0	0

This model is not very realistic since there could be more than one request in any one hour. Suppose you assumed that no more than one request is made in each 15-minute interval.

2 (a) For any 15-minute interval, calculate P(request).

(b) Define a binomial distribution of X using the assumption that no more than one request is made in each 15-minute interval.

There could still be more than one request made in a 15-minute interval although this is less likely than when intervals of an hour are considered. Suppose you consider one-minute intervals.

3 Given that no more than one request is made in any one minute, find a binomial model for X.

4 Take intervals of 6 seconds ($\tfrac{1}{10}$ minute) and define the binomial distribution for X.

You could continue this process of considering smaller and smaller intervals of time and assuming at most one event in each interval. The smaller the interval you choose, the more realistic will be the binomial model obtained.

This is equivalent to taking a series of binomial distributions $B(n, p)$, where the mean np is constant (equal to 4) but n increases and p decreases. The probabilities associated with each of the distributions you have defined for X are summarised in the table.

X	$B(12, \frac{1}{3})$	$B(48, \frac{1}{12})$	$B(720, \frac{1}{180})$	$B(7200, \frac{1}{1800})$
0	0.008	0.015	0.018	0.018
1	0.046	0.067	0.073	0.073
2	0.127	0.143	0.146	0.147
3	0.212	0.199	0.196	0.195
4	0.238	0.204	0.196	0.195
5	0.191	0.163	0.157	0.156
6	0.111	0.106	0.104	0.104
7	0.048	0.058	0.060	0.060
8	0.015	0.027	0.030	0.030
9	0.003	0.011	0.013	0.013
10	0.000	0.004	0.005	0.005

From the table, you can see that these distributions seem to tend to a limiting distribution, which can be assumed to be the true distribution of X.

5 For each distribution, show that $np = 4$.

The correct probability distribution for X, for which the binomial models above are approximations, is given by the formula

$$P(X = r) = \frac{e^{-4}4^r}{r!}$$

6 What is the significance of the 4 in this expression?

This result is justified in 3.2 tasksheet E2 (page 310).

7 Confirm that this formula gives the same probability distribution (to 3 s.f.) as $B(7200, \frac{1}{1800})$ above.

8 Calculate the probability of four or more requests using the probability distribution

$$P(X = r) = \frac{e^{-4}4^r}{r!} \quad \text{where } r = 0, 1, 2, 3, \ldots$$

The correct probability distribution for this type of situation is called the **Poisson distribution**, after the French statistician, Siméon Denis Poisson (1781–1840).

X is said to have a Poisson distribution with mean λ if

$$P(X = r) = \frac{e^{-\lambda}\lambda^r}{r!} \quad \text{for } r = 0, 1, 2, 3, \ldots$$

This is written as

$$X \sim P(\lambda)$$

(λ is the Greek letter l, pronounced 'lambda'.)

Poisson derived his probability distribution by considering what happens to the binomial distribution when n increases and np is kept fixed.

The mean of the binomial distribution $B(n, p)$ is np. As it is np that determines the particular Poisson distribution $P(\lambda)$, then it is likely that λ will be the mean of the Poisson. This result will be proved in section 3.4 (3.4 tasksheet E2, page 313), where the means of the various distributions are considered.

3.2 Tasksheet E2 – From binomial to Poisson (page 310)

Example 3

Cars arrive at a petrol station at an average rate of two cars every 10 minutes. For a given 10-minute period, calculate the probability that:

(a) exactly three cars arrive;   (b) two or more cars arrive.

Solution

(a) Let X be the number of cars arriving in a 10-minute period.

$$X \sim P(2) \text{ (i.e. } \lambda = 2)$$

$$P(X = 3) = \frac{e^{-2}2^3}{3!}$$

$$= 0.180$$

Define the random variable.

Define its distribution.

(b) $P(X \geq 2) = 1 - P(X < 2)$

$$= 1 - [P(X = 0) + P(X = 1)]$$

$$= 1 - \left[e^{-2} + \frac{e^{-2}2^1}{1!}\right]$$

$$= 0.594$$

3.2 Exercise 3

In each question, assume statistical independence. Comment on this assumption in each context.

1 Over a period of time it was shown that a particular daily paper had on average 1.4 misprints per page.

Calculate:

(a) the probability of finding no misprints on a page;

(b) the probability of finding a page with two or more misprints.

2 On average, 2% of goods on a production line are found to be defective. A random sample of 100 items is taken from production.

(a) What is the mean number of defective goods in a sample of 100?

(b) Use a suitable binomial model to find the probability of:
   (i) no defective items in the batch,
   (ii) at least one defective item in the batch.

(c) Repeat the calculations in (b) using the Poisson distribution to approximate the binomial probabilities.

3 If $X \sim P(5)$, calculate:

(a) $P(X = 0)$ (b) $P(X = 2)$ (c) $P(X \geq 2)$

4 On average, customers arrive at a supermarket check-out till at the rate of 2.4 per minute. A queue begins to develop if more than three people arrive in a given minute. Use a Poisson model to find the probability that a queue develops.

5 A Geiger counter records α-particles striking a sensor. If the average rate is 0.6 particles a second, calculate the probabilities of 0, 1, 2, and 3 or more particles striking the sensor within a one-second interval.

6 Cars travelling randomly along a road at an average rate of two a minute arrive at a level crossing. If the crossing gates are closed for a minute to allow a train to pass, what is the probability that more than two cars will be held up?

7 On average I get 30 letters a week (Monday to Saturday). Would you expect a Poisson probability model to be a suitable way of finding the probabilities of getting various numbers of letters in each day's mail? On this assumption, calculate the probability that on a particular day I shall receive fewer than three letters.

8 Telephone calls coming in to a switchboard follow a Poisson probability model with an average rate of three a minute. Find the probability that in a given minute there will be five or more calls.

After studying section 3.2 you should:

1 be familiar with the geometric, binomial and Poisson distributions and the situations they describe;

2 be able to calculate the probabilities of events described by these distributions.

3 Probability models for data

.3 Selecting and testing the models

3.3.1 Choosing a suitable model

A basketball player counts the number of shots he takes to score a basket. He records the following data.

Shots taken	Frequency
1	14
2	11
3	7
4	6
5	3
6	2
7	0
8	1

 .3A

1 (a) Of the models you have considered for counting cases, which do you think is the most suitable here? Consider carefully the reasons for your choice.

   (b) What assumptions need to be made for your chosen model to be suitable?

2 For each variable, suggest whether the binomial, Poisson or geometric are likely to be suitable models. State assumptions you need to make and define the model where possible.

   (a) The number of sixes obtained when five dice are thrown.

   (b) The number of throws needed until you obtain a six on a die.

   (c) The number of boys in families of four children.

   (d) The number of clicks made by a geiger counter in a five-second interval.

   (e) The number of home matches a team plays until they score a goal.

3.3 Exercise 1

1 A survey of 300 families with five children produced the following results for the number of boys (X) in the family.

Number of boys (X)	Number of families
0	7
1	37
2	82
3	104
4	54
5	16
Total	300

(a) Explain why these data might be modelled by a binomial distribution and state the assumptions necessary to use $X \sim B(5, \frac{1}{2})$ as a model.

(b) Use the chi-squared distribution to test $X \sim B(5, \frac{1}{2})$.

(c) Use the data to estimate p, the probability of a male birth, and test $X \sim B(5, p)$. Take care over the number of degrees of freedom for the χ^2 test.

(d) Which of the two models best fits this data set? Give a reason for your choice.

2 Four drawing pins are thrown into the air and the number (N) landing point up is counted.

(a) Explain why N has a binomial distribution.

The four pins are thrown 300 times with the following results.

Number landing point up (N)	Frequency
0	10
1	48
2	120
3	86
4	36

(b) (i) Calculate the mean number landing point up and hence obtain an estimate of p, the probability that a pin lands point up.

(ii) Use the χ^2 test to assess the suitability of $N \sim B(4, p)$ as a model for the data.

3.3.2 The geometric distribution as a model

You may have considered the geometric distribution as a suitable model for the basketball data.

Shots taken	Frequency
1	14
2	11
3	7
4	6
5	3
6	2
7	0
8	1

The geometric distribution, $G(p)$, depends only on the probability p of the event. Since you have no prior information on which to base a value for p, it must be obtained from the data. Remember that this provides a *constraint* which reduces the number of degrees of freedom by one when you conduct the χ^2 test.

Set up a model

The data show that the player scored 44 baskets out of 126 shots.

An estimate of the probability of scoring a basket is

$$P(\text{scoring a basket}) = \tfrac{44}{126}$$

$$= 0.349$$

Suppose that $X \sim G(0.349)$ where X is the number of shots needed to score a basket.

The probability distribution and expected frequencies are as follows.

x	$P(x)$	Expected frequency
1	0.349	15.4
2	0.227	10.0
3	0.148	6.5
4	0.096	4.2
5	0.063	2.8
6	0.041	1.8
7	0.027	1.2
≥ 8	0.049	2.2

| Analyse the problem | To apply a chi-squared test, you need to ensure that the cells have *expected frequencies of at least five* to ensure that X^2 has approximately a χ^2 distribution. You can do this by combining the cells as indicated to obtain the following. |

x	Observed frequencies	Expected frequencies
1	14	15.4
2	11	10.0
3	7	6.5
4 or 5	9	7.0
6 or more	3	5.1

$$X^2 = \sum \frac{(O-E)^2}{E} = \frac{(14-15.4)^2}{15.4} + \frac{(11-10.0)^2}{10.0} + \cdots$$

$$X^2 = 1.7 \quad \text{(to 2 s.f.)}$$

There are five cells on which the calculation of X^2 is based. However, there are *two* constraints — the total number of baskets must be 44, and the probability ($p = 0.349$) has been estimated from the data. There are therefore $5 - 2 = 3$ degrees of freedom.

Testing X^2 with three degrees of freedom, $X^2 > 7.81$ in 5% of samples (from tables). Since $1.7 < 7.81$, the proposed model is not rejected at the 5% level.

| Interpret /validate | The geometric distribution with $p = 0.349$ is a reasonably good model for the data given. |

The activity which follows is a data collection exercise in which you consider two different geometric models as possible models for the data.

 .3B

You will need a calculator or tables for obtaining random numbers.

Random digits $(0, 1, 2, \ldots, 9)$ are produced so that each has an equal probability of occurrence. Count the number of digits that occur up to the occurrence of the first zero. This is called the **run length**.

1, 3, 9, 7, 0	five digits needed to get zero
3, 6, 0	three digits needed
0	one digit needed

1 Use your random number generator and count the digits generated up to and including the first zero. Repeat about 200 times and complete the table.

Length of run (L)	1	2	3	4	. . .
Number of runs					

2 State the assumptions necessary to use $L \sim G(\frac{1}{10})$ as a model here. Why does $p = \frac{1}{10}$?

3 Set up and test the $G(\frac{1}{10})$ model against your data. Take care to combine groups as necessary when using the χ^2 test. This, of course, has an effect on the number of degrees of freedom for the test.

4 Use the data to calculate an estimate of p, where p is the probability of obtaining a run of length one.

5 Set up and test an alternative model $G(p)$. Which of the two models is better for your data? Why?

6 Calculate the mean run length for your data.

3.3.3 Fitting a Poisson distribution to data

There are many situations where you can identify an event which is occurring randomly and independently in time (or space), but with a fixed average number of occurrences per unit interval of time (or space).

Randomly occurring event	Unit of time or space
A case of appendicitis is diagnosed	A day in hospital
A geiger counter clicks	A 5-second interval
A telephone rings	A 15-minute interval
A water flea is found	A jar of pond water

Examples of this kind are called **Poisson processes**, and in so far as they fit the conditions above, they can be modelled effectively by the Poisson distribution.

Example 1
After a nuclear accident, the number of cases of thyroid disease in babies born in the vicinity was eleven. The average for an equivalent period in the same vicinity was three. Model the situation with a Poisson distribution, stating the assumptions behind the model. Does this provide evidence that the nuclear accident increased the risk of thyroid disease?

Solution

Let X be the number of occurrences of thyroid disease in babies.
Then X is a Poisson variable with mean 3, assuming that:

- the same vicinity and length of period are considered;
- thyroid disease occurs randomly in babies;
- incidences of thyroid disease in babies occur independently.

On the basis of the model,

$$P(X \geq 11) = 1 - P(X \leq 10)$$

$$P(X \leq 10) = P(0) + P(1) + \ldots + P(10)$$

$$= e^{-3} + 3e^{-3} + \frac{3^2 e^{-3}}{2!} + \ldots + \frac{3^{10} e^{-3}}{10!}$$

$$= 0.9997$$

$$\Rightarrow P(X \geq 11) = 0.0003$$

It is therefore extremely unlikely that this number of cases of thyroid disease in babies would have occurred by chance.

Of course, this in itself does not prove that the nuclear accident caused the increase in thyroid disease in babies – there may have been other factors present. However, it does suggest that a possible connection is worth further investigation.

One feature of the data which appears to conform to the Poisson model is that the mean for the data appears to be roughly equal in value to the variance. This is confirmed mathematically later, but is a useful rough test to apply to data which you think might be effectively modelled by the Poisson distribution.

If X is a random variable with a Poisson probability distribution,

$$\text{Mean}(X) = \text{Variance}(X)$$

3.3 Exercise 2

1 The numbers of people arriving at a post office queue in each of 60 consecutive one-minute intervals are summarised in the table.

Number of arrivals (X)	0	1	2	3	4	5
Number of one minutes (f)	15	19	19	5	1	1

(a) Calculate the mean and variance of the number of people arriving in a one-minute interval.

(b) Explain why the Poisson model might be considered a suitable model for the data.

2 Pityriasis rosea is a skin disorder which has never been shown to be infectious. The number of cases reported in each of 100 consecutive weeks in a particular town was recorded. The data are summarised in the table.

Number of cases (X)	0	1	2	3	4	5	6	7
Number of weeks (f)	31	34	22	8	3	1	0	1

(a) Justify the use of a Poisson model for these data.

(b) Obtain the 'expected' frequencies based on a suitable Poisson probability model.

(c) Conduct a χ^2 goodness of fit test to assess the suitability of the model chosen.

3 The following data refer to the numbers of water fleas present in 50 samples of pond water.

Number of water fleas	2	3	4	5	6	7	8	9	10	11	12	13	14	15	16
Number of samples	1	1	2	2	2	6	7	4	5	7	3	5	3	1	1

(a) Find the mean and variance of the data.

(b) Fit a Poisson distribution to the data and test using the chi-squared distribution.

4 Over a number of months in the Second World War, 576 squares of territory with $\frac{1}{2}$ km sides were observed, and many flying bomb hits were recorded. The table gives the number of squares in which r hits were recorded:

r	0	1	2	3	4	5
Frequency	229	211	93	35	7	1

Calculate the frequencies which would be expected from a Poisson model having the same mean as these data, and compare these with the observed frequencies.

Conduct a χ^2 goodness of fit test on the data.

5 A statistician, Ladislaus von Bortkiewicz, published a pamphlet in 1898 which provided one of the most famous examples of data which seem to have a Poisson distribution. The number of men killed by horse kicks each year was recorded for each of the fourteen corps in the Prussian army from 1875 to 1894. The data are summarised below.

Men killed (X)	0	1	2	3	4	5+	Total
Observed frequency	144	91	32	11	2	0	280

(a) Using the sample mean as an estimate of λ, calculate the expected frequencies on the basis of a Poisson model having this mean.

(b) Compare the observed and expected frequencies and comment on whether you think the Poisson distribution you have used is a good fit for the data.

(c) Conduct a χ^2 goodness of fit test on the model and comment on your findings.

After studying section 3.3 you should:

1 be able to choose a suitable probability model for counting cases data;

2 be able to set up and test a chosen model;

3 know how to calculate the number of degrees of freedom when modelling with the binomial, geometric and Poisson distributions;

4 know that the mean and variance for data having a Poisson distribution are approximately equal;

5 be able to make simple inferences on the basis of a chosen model.

3 Probability models for data

.4 Forming new variables

3.4.1 Combining random variables

So far, the situations you have studied have each involved a single variable together with its associated probability distribution. There are many interesting situations where **combining** random variables arises in some way. The chapter begins by considering **discrete random variables** and later extends the results to **continuous variables**.

As an illustration, consider a game which has two options.

Option 1: Two dice are thrown and you win 1p for each point. Your score is the *total* score showing on the two dice.

Option 2: A single die is thrown and you win 1p per point, your score being double that shown on the die.

The entry price is the same for both games. Which would you choose to play and why?

It is clear that the mean winnings on the two games will be the same. However, the probability distributions for the two games are very different.

For option 1, the score X can take values from 2 to 12. The probabilities of the extreme scores are

$$P(X = 2) = \tfrac{1}{6} \times \tfrac{1}{6} = \tfrac{1}{36}$$
$$P(X = 12) = \tfrac{1}{36}$$

You could work out the probabilities for each value of X and the distribution would be:

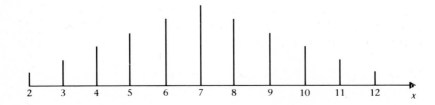

For option 2, all scores are equally likely. The only possible values of X are 2, 4, 6, 8, 10 and 12 and the distribution is as follows.

You *cannot* alter your expected winnings by your choice of game. Option 2 offers you a greater chance of winning a large amount but, at the same time, a greater chance of winning only a small amount.

The methods developed in this section will enable you to analyse this problem in greater detail, and you will have a chance to come back to it later on.

Many situations involve combining random variables. For example, the total weight of passengers on an aircraft is a random variable (with its own mean and variance) made up of a sum of independent random variables, each having its own mean and variance. How is the mean related to the means of the individual variables? How are the variances related? You can start to consider this important problem in 3.4A below, which develops some useful results for your later work.

 .4A

The probability distributions for two packs of cards are shown below. Y is the score on a card from the yellow pack:

y	1	2	3	4	Mean $= 2$
$P(Y = y)$	0.4	0.3	0.2	0.1	Variance $= 1$

For a blue pack, the distribution is

b	1	2	3	Mean $= 2$
$P(B = b)$	0.25	0.50	0.25	Variance $= 0.5$

A game consists of selecting a card at random from the yellow pack and noting its score (Y). A second card is then selected from the blue pack (B) and the total score ($Y + B$) recorded.

All possible totals ($Y + B$) are shown in the table.

		Score on blue card		
		1	2	3
Score on	1	2	3	4
yellow card	2	3	4	5
	3	4	5	6
	4	5	6	7

The probability of obtaining a score of 3 is

$$P(3) = P(1, 2) + P(2, 1)$$

$$= 0.4 \times 0.5 + 0.3 \times 0.25$$

$$= 0.275$$

1 (a) Show that $P(5) = 0.20$ and complete the probability distribution for the total score $Y + B$.

Score $Y + B$	Probability
2	
3	0.275
4	
5	0.20
6	0.10
7	

   (b) Find the mean and variance of $Y + B$. How are the mean and variance of $Y + B$ related to those of Y and B?

2 Write down the probability distributions for the new variables $2B$ and $3Y$. In each case, calculate the mean and variance and show how they are related to the means and variances of B and Y respectively.

You have considered combining random variables in two ways:

- adding two (or more) together, for example, $Y + B$;
- multiplying by a constant, for example, $2Y$, $5B$, and so on.

The examples of 3.4A should lead you to *conjecture* the following results:

$$\text{Mean}\,(X + Y) = \text{mean}\,(X) + \text{mean}\,(Y)$$
$$\text{Variance}\,(X + Y) = \text{variance}\,(X) + \text{variance}\,(Y)$$
$$\text{Mean}\,(aX) = a \times \text{mean}\,(X)$$
$$\text{Variance}\,(aX) = a^2 \times \text{variance}\,(X)$$

You should note that the variables you have combined have been *independent* and *discrete*. The results obtained above can be proved for all independent random variables, as you will see later (on 3.4 tasksheet E1).

Example 1

In a game using two spinners, the score is counted as the total of the score on each spinner. The probability distributions for the two spinners are:

Spinner 1

Score	1	2	3
Probability	$\frac{1}{2}$	$\frac{1}{4}$	$\frac{1}{4}$

Spinner 2

Score	2	4
Probability	$\frac{1}{4}$	$\frac{3}{4}$

It costs 20p to have a go and you win five times the total score on the two spinners in pence.

(a) Calculate the probability of a score of five.

(b) What is the most likely score?

(c) Calculate your expected winnings per turn.

Solution

(a) $P(\text{total} = 5) = P(1, 4) + P(3, 2)$

$\qquad\qquad\qquad = \frac{1}{2} \times \frac{3}{4} + \frac{1}{4} \times \frac{1}{4}$ (the events are independent)

$\qquad\qquad\qquad = \frac{7}{16}$

(b) The most likely score is five. The most likely outcome is a one on spinner 1 with a four on spinner 2.

$\qquad P(1, 4) = \frac{1}{2} \times \frac{3}{4} = \frac{3}{8}$

(c) Let S_1 and S_2 be the scores on the two spinners.

Expected winnings $= (5 \times \text{mean score}) - 20$

Expected score $\quad = \text{mean}\,(S_1 + S_2)$

$\qquad\qquad\qquad = \text{mean}(S_1) + \text{mean}(S_2)$

$\text{Mean}(S_1) = \frac{7}{4}, \quad \text{mean}(S_2) = \frac{14}{4}$

$\Rightarrow \text{Mean}\,(S_1 + S_2) = \frac{7}{4} + \frac{14}{4} = \frac{21}{4}$

The winnings are $\dfrac{5 \times 21}{4} - 20 = 6.25\text{p}$

You would expect to win an average of 6.25 pence per game.

3 .4B

1 Use these ideas and results to analyse the dice game described on page 204.

New random variables may also be formed by subtraction. If A and B are random variables, then $A - B$ is also a random variable.

2 (a) List the probability distribution for $(A - B)$ where A and B have probability distributions as follows.

a	0	1	2
P(a)	0.2	0.6	0.2

b	1	2
P(b)	0.5	0.5

(b) Confirm that:

(i) $\text{mean}(A - B) = \text{mean}(A) - \text{mean}(B)$

(ii) $\text{variance}(A - B) = \text{variance}(A) + \text{variance}(B)$

The earlier results on combining random variables can be simply extended.

For independent random variables, X and Y,

$$\text{Mean}\,(X \pm Y) = \text{mean}(X) \pm \text{mean}(Y)$$

$$\text{Variance}\,(X \pm Y) = \text{variance}(X) + \text{variance}(Y)$$

Example 2

Independent random variables A, B and C have the following means and variances.

	A	B	C
Mean	4	2	3
Variance	2	1	2

Write down the mean and variance of:

(a) $2A - B$ (b) $A + B - C$ (c) $2A + 2B - 3C$

Solution

(a) $\text{Mean}(2A - B) = 2\,\text{mean}(A) - \text{mean}(B)$
$$= 6$$
$\text{Variance}(2A - B) = 2^2\text{variance}(A) + \text{variance}(B)$
$$= 9$$

(b) $\text{Mean}(A + B - C) = 4 + 2 - 3 = 3$
$\text{Variance}(A + B - C) = 2 + 1 + 2 = 5$

(c) $\text{Mean}(2A + 2B - 3C) = 2 \times 4 + 2 \times 2 - 3 \times 3 = 3$
$\text{Variance}(2A + 2B - 3C) = 2^2 \times 2 + 2^2 \times 1 + 3^2 \times 2 = 30$

3.4 Exercise 1

1 A board game uses a cuboid roller with square cross-section to determine how many places forward a player moves. The four rectangular faces are numbered 1, 2, 5 and 8.

(a) If X is the score obtained by rolling the cuboid, find:
(i) mean(X),   (ii) variance(X).

(b) If, during the game, a player lands on a yellow square, the next score on the roller is doubled. Find the mean and variance of the doubled scores.

(c) If, during the game, a player lands on a red square, the next score on the roller is trebled. Find the mean and variance of the trebled scores.

(d) Write down the mean and variance of the total score obtained when two identical rollers are used together.

2 (a) A cubical die has its faces numbered 1, 2, 2, 3, 3 and 4. If X is the score obtained by rolling the die, find the mean and variance of the scores.

(b) A second die has its faces numbered 2, 4, 4, 6, 6 and 8. What are the mean and variance of the scores?

(c) Write down the mean and variance of the total score when both dice are rolled.

3 If X and Y are independent random single-digit numbers from 1 to 9 inclusive, calculate the variance of:

(a) X (b) $2X$ (c) $X + Y$ (d) $2X - Y$

4 An ordinary die is thrown once and X is the score obtained. Calculate the mean of X and show that the variance of X is $\frac{35}{12}$.

5 Each of the variables X_1, X_2, X_3 independently takes values from the set $\{-1, 0, 1\}$ with probabilities 0.2, 0.6, 0.2 respectively; the variable Y is defined to be the median of X_1, X_2, X_3.

(a) Show that $P(Y = -1) = 0.104$ and deduce $P(Y = 1)$ and $P(Y = 0)$.

(b) Calculate the mean and variance of Y.

3.4.2 Combining Poisson variables

For Poisson variables, the following result can be proved, although we do not do so here. (γ is the Greek letter g, 'gamma'.)

> If X and Y are independently distributed Poisson variables having means λ and γ respectively, then $X + Y$ is also a Poisson variable.
>
> $$X + Y \sim P(\lambda + \gamma)$$

Example 3

Cars stopping at a roadside garage come from either the north-bound or south-bound traffic. On average, there are three cars from the south-bound lane in a 15-minute interval and 1.6 cars from the north-bound lane every 15 minutes. The number of arrivals has a Poisson distribution in both cases.

Calculate the probability that:

(a) no cars arrive from the north-bound lane in a 15-minute interval;

(b) more than two cars arrive in a 15-minute interval.

Solution

(a) Let the number of cars stopping from the north-bound lane be N.

$$N \sim P(1.6) \qquad P(N = 0) = e^{-1.6} = 0.202$$

(b) The total number of cars stopping is $T = N + S$

$$T \sim P(3 + 1.6) \quad \text{or} \quad T \sim P(4.6)$$

$$P(T > 2) = 1 - P(T = 0, 1, 2)$$

$$= 1 - \left(e^{-4.6} + 4.6e^{-4.6} + \frac{4.6^2 e^{-4.6}}{2!} \right)$$

$$= 1 - e^{-4.6}\left(1 + 4.6 + \frac{4.6^2}{2} \right) = 0.837$$

3.4 Exercise 2

1 A and B are random variables having means μ_A and μ_B and variances σ_A^2 and σ_B^2 respectively.

Write down the mean and variance of the variables:

(a) $A + B$

(b) $2A$

(c) $3A - B$

2 X and Y have independent Poisson distributions, where

$$X \sim P(4) \quad \text{and} \quad Y \sim P(3)$$

(a) Write down the mean of $X + Y$.

(b) Calculate the probability that $X + Y < 4$.

3 An executive has two telephones on her desk which receive calls independently. The number of calls received by each telephone has a Poisson distribution with, on average, 3 calls per five-minute interval on one and 2 calls per five-minute interval on the other.

(a) Write down the mean and variance of the *total* number of calls received in a five-minute interval.

(b) If the distribution of the total number of calls is also Poisson, find the probability that the number of calls received in any five-minute interval is

(i) 0,   (ii) more than 2.

4 Cars arrive at a garage for petrol from either the north-bound or the south-bound carriageway. There are on average 3 cars every five minutes travelling north and 1.8 cars every five minutes travelling south.

(a) Calculate the probability that:

(i) no cars   (ii) more than 2 cars

arrive at the garage in a particular five-minute interval.

(b) Calculate the probability that exactly 5 cars arrive in a ten-minute interval.

3.4.3 Expectation

The **expected value**, or **expectation**, of a random variable (X) is the mean value of the variable. It is written $E[X]$.

$$\text{Mean}(X) = \sum_i x_i P(x_i) = E[X]$$

$$\text{Mean}(2X) = \sum_i 2x_i P(x_i) = E[2X]$$

$$\text{Mean}(X^2) = \sum_i x_i^2 P(x_i) = E[X^2]$$

So the result $\quad \text{Mean}(X + Y) = \text{mean}(X) + \text{mean}(Y) \quad$ obtained earlier can therefore be written

$$E[X + Y] = E[X] + E[Y]$$

Example 4
The probability distribution of X is given below.

x	1	2
$P(X = x)$	0.2	0.8

(a) Find the expected value of X^3.

(b) Find the expected value of $2X^2$.

Solution

(a) X^3 can take the values 1^3 and 2^3 with probabilities 0.2 and 0.8 respectively.

$$E[X^3] = 1^3 \times 0.2 + 2^3 \times 0.8$$

$$= 6.6$$

(b) $E[2X^2] = 2 \times 1^2 \times 0.2 + 2 \times 2^2 \times 0.8$

$$= 6.8$$

A convenient shorthand for the variance is $V[X]$. The variance may be defined in terms of expectations as follows.

$$V[X] = \sum_i x_i^2 P(x_i) - \mu^2$$

But $\sum_i x_i^2 P(x_i) = E[X^2]$ and $\mu = E[X]$

So,

$$V[X] = E[X^2] - (E[X])^2$$

 .4c

Show that:

(a) $E[aX] = aE[X]$

(b) $V[aX] = a^2 V[X]$

The results of section 3.4.1 may be written using this new notation as follows.

$$E[X \pm Y] = E[X] \pm E[Y]$$
$$V[X \pm Y] = V[X] + V[Y]$$
$$E[aX] = a \times E[X]$$
$$V[aX] = a^2 \times V[X]$$

Example 5

Two random variables X and Y are such that $E(X) = V(X) = 1$, $E(Y) = 3$ and $V(Y) = 2$. Find:

(a) $E(X - Y)$ (b) $V(3X - 2Y)$

Solution

(a) $E(X - Y) = E(X) - E(Y) = -2$

(b) $V(3X - 2Y) = V(3X) + V(2Y)$
$$= 3^2 V(X) + 2^2 V(Y)$$
$$= 17$$

Although a full and general proof of these results is a little tricky, an outline of how to proceed is given on tasksheet E1.

3.4 **Tasksheet E1 – Combining random variables (page 311)**

3.4.4 The mean and variance of $B(n, p)$ – a proof

The results of the previous sections can be used to prove results for the mean and variance of a binomial random variable. A binomial variable occurs when you are considering the total number of times a given event occurs in n independent trials. For example, the trial might be the throwing of a coin and the outcome might be the occurrence of a head. The total number of heads occurring when, for example, four coins are thrown would be a binomial random variable taking values of 0, 1, 2, 3 or 4.

Suppose the outcome of a particular trial occurs with probability p and does not occur with probability $(1 - p)$ or q.

There are 0 or 1 occurrences in a given trial.

Let X be the number of occurrences in a trial. X takes values in $\{0, 1\}$. The probability distribution for X is

x	0	1
$P(X = x)$	q	p

First, obtain the mean and variance of X. Using 'expectation' notation,

$$E[X] = 0 \times q + 1 \times p = p$$

$$V[X] = E[X^2] - (E[X])^2$$

$$= (0^2 \times q + 1^2 \times p) - p^2$$

$$= p - p^2$$

$$= p(1 - p)$$

$$= pq, \quad \text{since } q = 1 - p$$

Now, for n trials, define the binomial variable R, where

$$R = X_1 + X_2 + \ldots + X_n \quad \text{and} \quad R \sim B(n, p)$$

$$\Rightarrow E[R] = E[X_1 + X_2 + \ldots + X_n]$$

$$= E[X_1] + E[X_2] + \ldots + E[X_n] \qquad ①$$

$$= E[X] + E[X] + \ldots + E[X] \qquad ②$$

$$= n \times E[X]$$

$$= np$$

(Note that line ① uses the result $E(X_1 + X_2) = E(X_1) + E(X_2)$ proved earlier (see 3.4 tasksheet E1, page 311). Line ② uses the fact that each X_i has the same probability distribution as X.)

Also, for the variance $V[R]$,

$$V[R] = V[X_1 + X_2 + \ldots + X_n]$$
$$= V[X_1] + V[X_2] + \ldots + V[X_n]$$
$$= V[X] + V[X] + \ldots + V[X]$$
$$= nV[X]$$
$$= npq$$

If $R \sim B(n, p)$ then

$$E[R] = np$$
$$V[R] = npq$$

▷ 3.4 Tasksheet E2 – Some proofs (page 313)

After working through section 3.4 you should:

1 know that random variables may be combined to give composite variables;

2 understand the term **expectation** as applied to random variables and be familiar with the notation of expectation;

3 know that for *independent* random variables:

(a) $E(X \pm Y) = E(X) \pm E(Y)$

(b) $V(X \pm Y) = V(X) + V(Y)$

4 be able to obtain the formulas for the mean and variance of a binomial random variable.

3

Probability models for data

.5 Continuous random variables

3.5.1 The Normal probability density function

Chapter 3 has concentrated on **discrete** random variables and some of the important probability models associated with them. There are, of course, models for **continuous** random variables, the single most important being the Normal probability model which you considered earlier. It would be worth looking at an example as a reminder before considering other continuous probability distributions.

 .5A

A machine is set to deliver sugar into bags. The weight of sugar it delivers is Normally distributed, having a mean of 1.1 kg and standard deviation 0.1 kg.

1 *Approximately* what proportion of bags marked 1 kg will be underweight?

2 Confirm your answer to 1 by calculating this proportion using Normal tables (page 396).

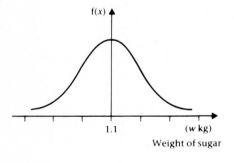

The graph of this distribution is called the **Normal probability density function**.

If X is a continuous random variable, the probability that X takes a value between a and b is given by the area under the probability density function for X, between $X = a$ and $X = b$. This is usually calculated by direct integration in the case of simple functions, or by using tables which give the area in the two important cases of the Normal distribution and the chi-squared distribution (see pages 396 and 398).

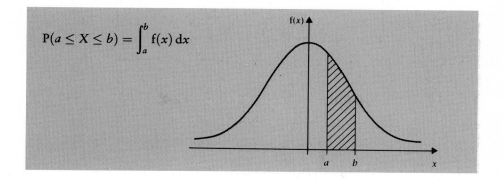

$$P(a \leq X \leq b) = \int_a^b f(x)\,dx$$

Example 1

A certain manufacturer claims that there are 64 g of real fruit in every 100 g of their jam. The actual weight of fruit in the jam is distributed Normally, having a mean weight of 68 g and standard deviation 1.6 g. Calculate the proportion of 100 g measures of jam which contain:

(a) more than 70 g of fruit,

(b) less than 64 g of fruit.

Solution

Let the weight of fruit in 100 g of jam be W g. Then $W \sim N(68, 1.6^2)$.

(a)

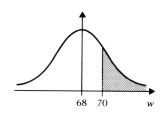

$$z = \frac{70 - 68}{1.6} = 1.25$$

$$P(W > 70) = 1 - \Phi(1.25)$$

$$= 1 - 0.8944$$

$$= 0.106 \quad (\text{to 3 s.f.})$$

So 10.6% of the 100 g measures will contain more than 70 g of fruit.

(b)

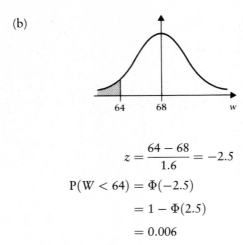

$$z = \frac{64 - 68}{1.6} = -2.5$$

$$P(W < 64) = \Phi(-2.5)$$

$$= 1 - \Phi(2.5)$$

$$= 0.006$$

0.6% of the 100 g measures will contain less than 64 g of fruit.

3.5 Exercise 1

1 My journey to work takes 20 minutes on average, with a standard deviation of 5 minutes. The journey time may be considered to be Normally distributed. If I take longer than 26 minutes, I am late. Calculate the probability of my being late.

2 The length of time that a particular make of light bulb lasts is distributed Normally, having mean 2000 hours and standard deviation 50 hours. Calculate the probability that a particular light bulb will last:

(a) longer than 1970 hours,

(b) between 2050 and 2080 hours.

3 The mean survival period for daisies after being sprayed with a weed killer is 20 days. The survival time is Normally distributed. If a quarter of the daisies are still surviving after 23 days, calculate an estimate for the standard deviation of the survival time.

4 In a certain country, the heights of adult males have mean 170 cm and standard deviation 10 cm, and the heights of adult females have mean 160 cm and standard deviation 8 cm; for each sex the distribution of heights approximates closely to a Normal probability model. On the hypothesis that height is not a factor in selecting a mate, calculate the probability that a husband and wife selected at random are both taller than 164 cm.

3.5.2 General probability density functions

A general probability density function f(x) must have the following properties.

- f(x) ≥ 0   for all x
- The total area under the curve f(x) must be 1.

f(x) ≥ 0 for all x because f(x) determines *probabilities* which *must* always be greater than or equal to 0 (and less than or equal to 1).

The total area under the graph of f(x), $\int_{-\infty}^{\infty} f(x)\, dx$, represents the probability that one of the X values occurs. Since the probability is 1 that *some* value will occur, $\int_{-\infty}^{\infty} f(x)\, dx$ *must* equal 1.

Example 2

A probability density function f(x) is defined as follows.

$$f(x) = \begin{cases} \dfrac{k}{x^2} & \text{for } 1 \le x \le 6 \\ 0 & \text{for all other } x \end{cases}$$

Find the value of k.

Solution

$$\int_1^6 f(x)\, dx = 1, \quad \text{so} \int_1^6 \frac{k}{x^2}\, dx = 1$$

$$\Rightarrow k \int_1^6 \frac{1}{x^2}\, dx = 1$$

$$\Rightarrow k \left[-\frac{1}{x} \right]_1^6 = 1$$

$$\Rightarrow k \left[\left(-\frac{1}{6} \right) - \left(-\frac{1}{1} \right) \right] = 1$$

$$\Rightarrow \frac{5}{6} k = 1$$

$$\Rightarrow \quad k = \frac{6}{5} = 1.2$$

Example 3

The incubation period, X days, for a particular infection is modelled by the probability density function $f(x)$, where $f(x)$ is defined as follows.

$$f(x) = \tfrac{1}{144}(36 - x^2) \qquad \text{for } 0 \leq x \leq 6$$

What is the probability that you will catch the infection during the second day?

Solution

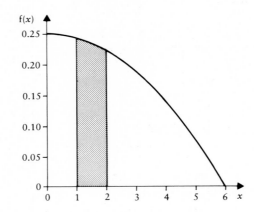

$$P(1 \leq X \leq 2) = \int_1^2 f(x)\,dx$$

$$= \int_1^2 \tfrac{1}{144}(36 - x^2)\,dx$$

$$= \tfrac{1}{144}\left[36x - \tfrac{1}{3}x^3\right]_1^2$$

$$= \tfrac{1}{144}\left[\left(72 - \tfrac{8}{3}\right) - \left(36 - \tfrac{1}{3}\right)\right]$$

$$= 0.23 \qquad \text{(to 2 s.f.)}$$

The probability that you will become infected on the second day is 0.23.

3.5 Exercise 2

In each of the examples, $f(x)$ refers to a probability density function.

1

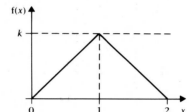

(a) Define the possible values of X.

(b) Show that the area under the graph of $f(x)$ is 1.

(c) Find:

    (i) $P(X \geq 1)$

    (ii) $P(X \geq \frac{1}{2})$

    (iii) $P(\frac{1}{2} \leq X \leq 2)$

    (iv) $P(X \leq 3)$

2 (a) Find k.

   (b) Find:

      (i) $P(X \geq 1.5)$

      (ii) $P(X \leq 0.5)$

      (iii) $P(0.5 \leq X \leq 1.5)$

3 In a game, a wooden block is propelled with a stick across a flat deck. On each attempt, the distance, X metres, reached by the block lies between 0 and 10 metres, and the variation is measured by the probability density function

$$f(x) = 0.0012x^2(10 - x)$$

Calculate the probability that the block:

(a) travels more than 5 metres;

(b) travels between 1 and 2 metres.

3.5.3 The mean and variance

For a discrete variable X, the mean μ was defined by

$$\mu = \sum_i x_i P(x_i)$$

The analogous form of this definition for a continuous variable X having density function $f(x)$ is

$$\mu = \int x f(x)\, dx$$ where the integral is taken over the whole range of X values.

For the variance, the expression equivalent to

$$\sigma^2 = \sum_i x_i^2 P(x_i) - \mu^2 \qquad \text{(for a discrete variable)}$$

is

$$\sigma^2 = \int x^2 f(x)\,dx - \mu^2 \qquad \text{(for a continuous variable)}$$

> If X is a continuous random variable having a probability function $f(x)$ when $a \le x \le b$,
>
> $$\mu = \int_a^b x f(x)\,dx$$
>
> $$\sigma^2 = \int_a^b x^2 f(x)\,dx - \mu^2$$

Example 4

A probability density function $f(x)$ is defined as follows.

$$f(x) = \begin{cases} k\,e^{2x} & \text{for } 0 \le x \le 1 \\ 0 & \text{otherwise} \end{cases}$$

(a) Find k.

(b) Calculate the mean value of x.

(c) Calculate the median value of x.

Solution

(a) $k \displaystyle\int_0^1 e^{2x}\,dx = 1 \Rightarrow k \left[\dfrac{e^{2x}}{2}\right]_0^1 = 1$

$$k\left(\frac{e^2}{2} - \frac{1}{2}\right) = 1$$

$$k = \frac{2}{e^2 - 1} = 0.313 \quad \text{(to 3 s.f.)}$$

(b) $\mu = \displaystyle\int_0^1 x f(x)\,dx = k \int_0^1 x e^{2x}\,dx$

$$= k\left[\frac{x e^{2x}}{2} - \int \frac{e^{2x}}{2}\,dx\right]_0^1$$

$$= k\left[\frac{x e^{2x}}{2} - \frac{e^{2x}}{4}\right]_0^1$$

$$= 0.657 \quad \text{(to 3 s.f.)}$$

(c) If the median is m then $\displaystyle\int_0^m f(x)\,dx = 0.5$

$$k\int_0^m e^{2x}\,dx = 0.5$$

$$\left[\frac{e^{2x}}{2}\right]_0^m = \frac{0.5}{k}$$

$$\frac{e^{2m}}{2} - \frac{1}{2} = \frac{0.5}{k}$$

$$e^{2m} = 4.195$$

$$2m = \ln(4.195)$$

$$m = 0.717 \text{ (to 3 s.f.)}$$

The area under the graph of $f(x)$ is divided in half by the vertical through $x = m$.

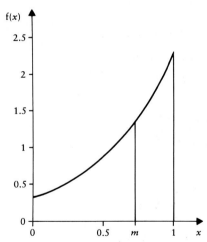

3.5 Exercise 3

1 A random variable X has probability density function $f(x)$, where

$$f(x) = \begin{cases} kx^2 & 0 \le x \le 1 \\ 0 & \text{otherwise} \end{cases}$$

(a) Show that $k = 3$.

(b) Calculate the mean and variance of X.

(c) Find the probability that $X \ge 0.5$.

2 A department store will deliver parcels within a range of 5 and 15 miles. The probability of a delivery being for a distance X miles is given by the probability density function $f(x)$, where

$$f(x) = \begin{cases} \dfrac{k}{x^3} & 5 \leq x \leq 15 \\ 0 & \text{otherwise} \end{cases}$$

(a) Calculate k and sketch a graph of $f(x)$.

(b) Find the mean delivery distance.

(c) Half of all deliveries are for distances of m miles or more. Find m.

3 The distance (X metres) travelled by a wooden block in a game is given by the probability density function $f(x)$, where

$$f(x) = \begin{cases} 0.0012x^2(10 - x) & 0 \leq x \leq 10 \\ 0 & \text{otherwise} \end{cases}$$

Calculate the mean distance travelled.

4 A random variable X has a probability density function $f(x)$, where

$$f(x) = \begin{cases} \dfrac{k}{1 + x} & \text{for } 1 \leq x \leq 2 \\ 0 & \text{otherwise} \end{cases}$$

(a) Show that $k = \dfrac{1}{\ln\left(\frac{3}{2}\right)}$.

(b) Find the median value of X.

(c) Find $P(X > 1.5)$.

5 A random variable X has a probability density function $f(x)$ defined as follows.

$$f(x) = \begin{cases} kx(x - 1) & \text{for } 0 \leq x \leq 1 \\ 0 & \text{otherwise} \end{cases}$$

(a) Find k.

(b) Sketch the graph of $f(x)$. Explain why the median value of x is 0.5.

(c) Find $P(X > 0.75)$.

3.5.4 The exponential distribution

You saw earlier that the Poisson distribution described a discrete variable occurring randomly in time or space. For example, if a computer is programmed to 'bleep' randomly on average once every ten seconds, then bleeps might occur as indicated by the arrows.

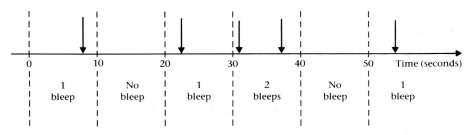

It is interesting to consider how long, on average, you would have to wait for a bleep to occur.

Bleeps occur randomly.

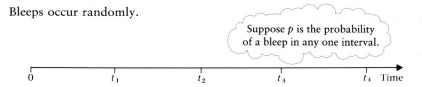

Suppose p is the probability of a bleep in any one interval.

The probability of a bleep in the first time interval is p.
The probability of one in the second but not in the first is $(1 - p)p$ because the bleeps occur independently of each other.

Now $p > (1 - p)p$ and so the first bleep is more likely to occur in the first interval than in the second.

For example, if $p = 0.01$ then

P(bleep in 1st interval) = 0.01

and

P(first bleep in 2nd interval) = $0.99 \times 0.01 = 0.0099$

The first interval is the most likely, the next interval is the second most likely and so on.

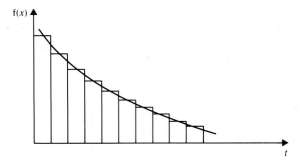

This brings to mind the graph of an exponential function.

The distribution which describes the length of wait between random events is known as the **exponential** (or **negative exponential**) **distribution**.

> If X has an exponential distribution, then its probability density function f(x) is
>
> $$f(x) = \lambda e^{-\lambda x} \qquad \text{for } x \geq 0$$

The distribution is determined by fixing the value of λ. Although it will not be proved here, $\dfrac{1}{\lambda}$ is the mean value of X. (You can prove this for yourself in exercise 4, question 3E below.)

The exponential distribution of a 'waiting time' random variable is closely connected to the geometric distribution for a discrete variable which counts the number of trials until a particular event. In both cases you are waiting for the event to occur. Notice also that if $Y \sim G(p)$, $E[Y] = \dfrac{1}{p}$. This is a similar result to $E[X] = \dfrac{1}{\lambda}$.

3.5 **Exercise 4**

1 A computer bleeps randomly, on average once every second. The probability density function describing the time, T, between bleeps is $f(t) = e^{-t}$.

(a) Sketch $f(t)$.

(b) Shade the areas representing the probability of:
   (i) a bleep in the first second,
   (ii) waiting longer than two seconds for a bleep.

(c) Calculate the probability of each event in (b).

2 People join a particular queue at random. The average time between arrivals is two minutes. The time between arrivals (T minutes) has probability density function $f(t) = 2e^{-2t}$. Calculate the probability that:

(a) one person arrives in the first minute;

(b) the next person arrives between one and two minutes later.

3E X is a random variable with probability density function $f(x)$, where

$$f(x) = \lambda e^{-\lambda x} \quad \text{for } x \geq 0$$

(a) Prove that $E[X] = \dfrac{1}{\lambda}$.

(b) Prove that $V[X] = \dfrac{1}{\lambda^2}$.

3.5.5 Combining Normal random variables

In section 3.4 you considered the possibility of combining discrete variables. You can combine continuous random variables in the same way and, indeed, some most important practical applications arise where Normal variables are combined. Remember that the variables being combined must be *independent* of each other.

A common example is as follows. All passenger lifts have a notice specifying the maximum load and usually state the maximum number of persons that can be carried safely. The maximum number of persons is determined from the maximum load by considering the distribution of the total weight of n adult males. The weight of an adult male is well modelled by a Normal variable, so the manufacturer needs to consider the problem of adding together Normal variables.

When you add independently distributed Normal variables, you need to know the answers to three questions.

(a) How is the sum *distributed*? Is it also a Normal variable?

(b) What is its mean value and how is this related to the original parameters?

(c) What is its variance and how is this related to the original parameters?

Questions (b) and (c) were answered in section 3.4. The results you found there also apply to *continuous* variables.

If $X \sim N(\mu_x, \sigma_x^2)$ and $Y \sim N(\mu_y, \sigma_y^2)$

then

$$E[X \pm Y] = \mu_x \pm \mu_y$$

$$V[X \pm Y] = \sigma_x^2 + \sigma_y^2$$

Although the result is beyond the scope of this book to prove theoretically, it can be shown that the sum or difference of *independent* Normal variables is also Normally distributed: if X and Y are independent Normal random variables, then

$$\left. \begin{array}{l} Z = X + Y \\ M = X - Y \\ P = X + X + Y \\ \text{and so on ...} \end{array} \right\} \quad \text{are also Normal random variables.}$$

These results may be summarised as follows.

A sum or difference of *independent* Normal random variables is also Normally distributed.

If X and Y are independent random variables, where

$$X \sim N(\mu_x, \sigma_x^2) \quad \text{and} \quad Y \sim N(\mu_y, \sigma_y^2)$$

then

$$X + Y \sim N(\mu_x + \mu_y, \sigma_x^2 + \sigma_y^2)$$

and

$$X - Y \sim N(\mu_x - \mu_y, \sigma_x^2 + \sigma_y^2)$$

These results can be used to solve problems like that of the maximum load for a lift. Some simple examples are given.

Example 5
If $X \sim N(10, 2)$ and $Y \sim N(8, 1)$, find $P(X + Y > 20)$.

Solution

Variances are added

$$X + Y \sim N(10 + 8, 2 + 1)$$

$$X + Y \sim N(18, 3)$$

Standardising the value $X + Y = 20$

$$\Rightarrow z = \frac{20 - 18}{\sqrt{3}}$$

$$= 1.15$$

$$\Rightarrow P(X + Y > 20) = 1 - \Phi(1.15)$$

$$= 1 - 0.875$$

$$= 0.125$$

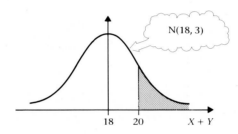

So, in $12\frac{1}{2}\%$ of cases the value of the sum of the two variables will be greater than 20.

Example 6

The length (in centimetres) of a matchbox is a random variable $X \sim N(5, 0.01)$. The length (in centimetres) of matches to go in the box is a random variable, $Y \sim N(4.6, 0.01)$.

What percentage of matches will not fit in the box?

Solution

The matches will not fit if $Y > X$. This condition can be rearranged as $X - Y < 0$.

$$E[X - Y] = 5 - 4.6$$

Add variances

$$= 0.4$$

$$V[X - Y] = 0.01 + 0.01$$

$$= 0.02$$

$$\Rightarrow X - Y \sim N(0.4, 0.02)$$

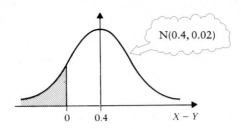

You need to find the shaded area. Standardising in the usual way,

$$z = \frac{0.0 - 0.4}{\sqrt{(0.02)}}$$

$$= -2.83$$

$$P(Z < 0) = \Phi(-2.83)$$

$$= 1 - \Phi(2.83)$$

$$= 0.0023$$

So only about 0.2% of matches will not fit into a randomly selected box.

3.5 Exercise 5

1 A manufacturer of toiletries is producing a special offer pack containing a deodorant spray and a bar of soap. The deodorant spray can has a length (in centimetres) given by the random variable $X \sim N(14, 0.02)$. The soap has a length (in centimetres) given by the random variable $Y \sim N(9, 0.01)$.

Find the probability that the deodorant and soap will not fit a container of length 23.4 cm if they are packed end to end.

2 A bottle of shampoo has a stopper which has length (in centimetres) given by the random variable $X \sim N(3, 0.003)$. The length of the bottle in centimetres, not including the stopper, is given by the random variable $Y \sim N(20, 0.06)$.

What percentage of bottles will not fit on a shelf with a space of 23.5 cm below the next shelf?

3 The thickness in centimetres of an Oatbix is given by a random variable $X \sim N(1.9, 0.01)$. There are twelve Oatbix in a packet. What percentage of boxes that are 24 cm long are too small?

4 A storage cupboard has width X cm, where $X \sim N(79, 1.25)$. What is the probability that five similar cupboards placed side by side will fit along a wall 3.98 m long?

5 The internal diameter (in millimetres) of a nut is a random variable
$X \sim N(10, 0.013)$. The diameter (in millimetres) of a bolt is a random variable
$Y \sim N(9.5, 0.013)$.

(a) If the difference between the two diameters is less than 0.2 mm, the nut
and bolt jam tight. What percentage of nuts and bolts jam?

(b) If the difference between the two diameters is more than 0.75 mm, the nut
and bolt are too loose. What percentage of nuts and bolts are too loose?

6 A small saucepan has an external diameter (in centimetres) given by the
random variable $X \sim N(18, 0.005)$. The saucepan lid has an internal diameter
(in centimetres) given by the random variable $Y \sim N(18.2, 0.005)$.

What percentage of the lids do not fit their saucepans if the gap must never be
less than 0.05 cm?

After studying section 3.5 you should:

1 know what probability density means for a continuous random variable;

2 know how to calculate the mean and variance from a probability density
function;

3 know how to calculate the probability of an event when given the
probability density function of the variable;

4 know and understand that, if $f(x)$ is a probability density function, then:

(a) $f(x) \geq 0$ for all x

(b) $\int f(x)\, dx = 1$

5 be familiar with the exponential and Normal distributions and the sorts
of situation they describe;

6 know how to combine two or more independent Normal variables and
know and be able to use the result

if

$$X \sim N(\mu_x, \sigma_x^2), \quad Y \sim N(\mu_y, \sigma_y^2)$$

then

$$X \pm Y \sim N(\mu_x \pm \mu_y, \sigma_x^2 + \sigma_y^2)$$

3 Probability models for data

Miscellaneous exercise 3

1   The table shows the number of pupils absent from school during one half-term.

	Monday	Tuesday	Wednesday	Thursday	Friday	Total
Number of absentees	46	36	28	38	52	200

(a) Find the expected frequencies if the number of pupils absent was independent of the day of the week.

(b) Conduct a χ^2 test to see if the number of pupils absent is independent of the day of the week.

2   The number of cases of poliomyelitis notified during the years 1937–46 and in the epidemic year, 1947, are given below.

Age group	Number of cases 1937–46	1947
0–14	467	453
15 and over	131	249

Is there any statistical evidence to suggest that the age distribution of cases in the epidemic year, 1947, was significantly different from that of previous years?

3   Examine the following data on the performance of candidates in the Sociology honours degree for two colleges.

College	Grade 1	2	3	4	Total
A	6	66	114	56	242
B	5	40	86	49	180

4   The numbers of home wins, draws and away wins in the four divisions of
the English Football League in the 1982–3 season were

	Division			
	1	2	3	4
Home wins	255	220	297	283
Draws	111	144	137	142
Away wins	96	98	118	127

Do these figures suggest a difference in the pattern of results from one
division to another?

5   A learner driver has constant probability k of passing the driving test at any
attempt.

(a) Find the most probable number of times that he will have to take the
test.

(b) Find the expected value of the number of times that he will have to
take it.

(c) Find the value of k which maximises the probability that he will take it
exactly four times.

(d) Find a formula for the probability that he will have to take it more than
n times.

6   A small firm's switchboard was on duty one day from 8:40 a.m. to 1:10 p.m.
and from 1:40 p.m. to 5:30 p.m. The table below gives the frequency
distribution for telephone calls that were answered during the
100 five-minute intervals that made up the day.

No. of calls	0	1	2	3	4	5	6	7	8 or more
Frequency	5	22	28	24	11	5	4	1	0

(a) Find the mean and standard deviation of these data.

(b) Find the corresponding frequencies that would be predicted by a Poisson
model with equal mean, and test the agreement between observed and
predicted frequencies.

(c) Are there any features of the situation that would cause you to doubt
the suitability of a Poisson model?

7 A piece of electronic equipment has been designed to cause a light to flash at random. The number of flashes per minute produced by the apparatus is recorded for 100 separate one-minute intervals, and the following results are obtained.

Number of flashes	0	1	2	3	4	5	6	7
Frequency	21	20	27	15	8	6	2	1

What probability model is it reasonable to use to describe the data above? Do the results cast any doubt on the randomness of the flash-producing mechanism?

8 It has been suggested that the numbers of goals scored in football matches might be described by a Poisson probability model. On a particular Saturday the numbers of goals scored in 44 matches in the English Football League were

Number of goals	0	1	2	3	4	5	6	7	8	9
Frequency	3	7	8	9	9	4	3	0	0	1

Find the mean number of goals per match, and calculate the frequencies you would expect to get if the theory were correct. Do your results suggest that the Poisson model is a suitable one in this case?

9 A grocer sells raisins and currants in packets with mean net weights 500 g and 250 g, and standard deviations of 20 g and 15 g respectively. Customers shopping at this grocer's use one packet of each in their Christmas cakes. Find the expected value and variance of the total weight of fruit used in their cakes.

10 X and Y are independent Poisson random variables having distributions $P(2)$ and $P(1.2)$ respectively. Calculate the probability that:

(a) X takes a value greater than 2

(b) $X + Y = 1$

(c) $X + 2Y \geq 2$

11E Calculate the mean and standard deviation of $X + Y$, where X and Y are continuous random variables having a uniform distribution over the interval from 0 to b.

Hint: what does the graph of $X + Y$'s probability density function look like?

12 A random variable X has probability density function $f(x)$ defined as follows.

$$f(x) = \begin{cases} \dfrac{k}{x^2} & 1 \le x \le 2 \\ 0 & \text{otherwise} \end{cases}$$

(a) Find k.

(b) Find the mean and variance of X.

13 A mathematical model for the age x years to which a new-born infant will live assigns to this a probability density function

$$f(x) = kx^3(90 - x) \qquad \text{for } 0 < x < 90$$

On this basis, calculate the proportion of the population who would live to be over 80.

14 A probability density function for the life t hours of Luxa light bulbs is

$$f(t) = k \, \exp\left(-\frac{t}{1200}\right) \qquad (t > 0)$$

(a) Find the value of the constant k.

(b) Find the probability that a bulb will last more than 2000 hours.

(c) Find the age beyond which only 10% of Luxa bulbs still work.

15 Gamma ray sources are screened by surrounding them with lead.
A probability model for the depth to which a gamma ray of fixed energy from a given source penetrates the lead is given by the probability density function

$$f(x) = A \, e^{-0.05x} \qquad (x \ge 0)$$

for the distance x mm the gamma ray will penetrate.

Find:

(a) the value of the constant A;

(b) the probability that a gamma ray will penetrate more than 30 mm.

Hence find the proportion of gamma rays from this source that will go straight through a 30-mm-thick shield.

16 Sketch the graph of the function f defined by

$$f(x) = \begin{cases} kx^3(1 - x) & 0 < x < 1 \\ 0 & \text{otherwise} \end{cases}$$

If f is a probability density function for a continuous random variable X, use the fact that $\int_{-\infty}^{\infty} f(x)\,dx = 1$ to find the value of k. Then find the mean and variance of X, and mark the lines $x = \mu - \sigma$ and $x = \mu + \sigma$ on your graph.

Calculate the probability that X lies between $\mu - \sigma$ and $\mu + \sigma$.

17 The continuous random variable X has probability density function f
given by

$$f(x) = \begin{cases} kx^2(1-x) & 0 \le x \le 1 \\ 0 & \text{otherwise} \end{cases}$$

where k is a constant.

(a) Determine the value of k, and sketch the graph of the density function.

(b) Find $E[X]$ and $V[X]$.

(c) Find $P(X < E[X])$.

18 An observer records the time intervals between the passages of successive
vehicles along a motorway. He obtains the following frequency distribution.

Time interval (s)	0–15	15–30	30–45	45–60	60–75	75–90
Frequency	69	25	12	7	5	2

(a) Find the mean of this distribution.

(b) The exponential distribution with parameter λ ($\lambda > 0$) has probability
density function $A\,e^{-\lambda t}$ for $t \ge 0$, where A is a suitable constant whose
value depends on the value of λ. Determine A, and show that the
exponential distribution has mean λ^{-1}.

(c) Suppose that the parameter λ is chosen so as to fit the mean of the
traffic data in the table. Show that it is then predicted that 63.3 passage
times (correct to one decimal place) will lie in the range 0–15 seconds.
Determine the corresponding frequencies for the other ranges of passage
times, and test the agreement between the observed and predicted
frequencies.

19 A psychologist carries out an experiment in which she asks a large number
of subjects to estimate the position of the mid-point of a line. She finds that
nobody is more than 2 cm out to the left (negative) or 3 cm to the right
(positive). She postulates a probability model for the distribution of the
errors, x cm, by means of a probability density function

$$f(x) = \tfrac{6}{125}(2+x)(3-x)$$

where $-2 \le x \le 3$. Verify that this satisfies the condition $\int_{-2}^{3} f(x)\,dx = 1$,
and use the model to calculate the probabilities that a subject selected at
random will

(a) err to the right of the true mid-point

(b) get within 1 cm of the true position.

20 Lengths of fire hose are joined by fitting the 'arm' end of one into the 'sleeve' end of the other. The arms have mean external diameter 89 mm, and the sleeves mean internal diameter 94 mm; each has variance 8 mm^2. Find the probability that the difference in diameter of a pair chosen at random will be less than 1 mm or more than 7 mm.

21 Tent-poles for a frame tent are in three sections, supposedly of length 70 cm, 62 cm and 55 cm. A batch of 50 long sections shows a mean of 70 cm and a standard deviation of 0.4 cm; a batch of 60 mid-sections also has the correct mean, with a standard deviation of 0.35 cm; but a sample of 50 short sections proves to have a mean of only 54.4 cm and a standard deviation of 0.6 cm. How likely is it that a complete pole as sent out by the manufacturer will be more than 2 cm too short?

22 The mass of a particular sweet is a Normal random variable with mean 50 g and standard deviation 3 g. The sweets are packed in boxes, each box containing 15 sweets. The mass of the box is also a Normal variable, having a mean of 120 g and a standard deviation of 5 g. Find the probability that the total mass of a box of sweets:

(a) is greater than 850 g;

(b) is less than 825 g.

Statistics in action

.1 Hypothesis testing

4.1.1 Making a decision: the null hypothesis

The following results were established earlier in the text and will be needed to analyse this problem.

- For $R \sim B(n, p)$

  $$P(R = r) = \binom{n}{r} p^r (1 - p)^{n-r} \quad \text{where} \quad \binom{n}{r} = \frac{n!}{r! \, (n - r)!}$$

  mean $= np$ and variance $= np(1 - p)$

- The Normal approximation to the binomial is often used to estimate probabilities such as $P(R \geq 14)$.

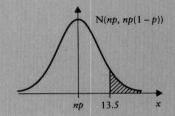

A teacher has a set of loaded dice which are biased in such a way that the probability of any one of these dice showing a six is $\frac{1}{4}$. The loaded dice have become mixed up with a set of ordinary dice so she hands out all the dice to her students and asks them to throw each die sixty times. If a die shows a six on fourteen or more occasions she decides it must be 'loaded'. Otherwise it is classified as 'fair'. The students are then asked to discuss this method of sorting the dice.

 .1A

1 What is the probability that a die is classified as 'loaded' when in fact it is 'fair'?

2 What is the probability that a die is classified as 'fair' when in fact it is 'loaded'?

3 Do you think the teacher should change her threshold for rejecting a die as 'fair' from fourteen to:

(a) thirteen, (b) fifteen, (c) some other value?

Justify your answer.

4 Suppose a die showed a six on just two occasions. How would you interpret such a result?

In the example above, if you start on the assumption that a die is 'fair', then this is called the **null hypothesis**. The **alternative hypothesis** is that the die is 'loaded'.

The conventional shorthand for expressing these hypotheses is:

$H_0 : p = \frac{1}{6}$ (The null hypothesis)

$H_1 : p = \frac{1}{4}$ (The alternative hypothesis)

In this case, you could put a specific value on the alternative hypothesis. This is not always possible.

 .1B

Suppose a student arranges a number of glasses on a table to test whether a friend can tell the difference between 'diet' cola and 'ordinary' cola. (Each glass is filled at random with either 'diet' or 'ordinary' cola.) He asks his friend, who claims to be able to taste the difference, to taste each in turn and identify what is in each glass.

State whether you think the null and alternative hypotheses for this experiment should be

$$H_0 : p = \frac{1}{2} \qquad \qquad H_0 : p = \frac{1}{2}$$
$$\qquad \qquad \text{or} \qquad \qquad$$
$$H_1 : p > \frac{1}{2} \qquad \qquad H_1 : p \neq \frac{1}{2}$$

where p is the probability that the friend makes a correct identification. Justify your answer.

A hypothesis is an assumption about the population from which the data has been sampled.

The null hypothesis (H_0) is the assumption against which the data are initially compared.

If, after comparison, the null hypothesis appears unlikely, it is rejected in favour of the alternative hypothesis (H_1).

4.1.2 Making the wrong decision

A farmer knows from experience that the yield he obtains from a particular type of tomato plant is Normally distributed with a mean of 6.2 kg and standard deviation 1.8 kg. A friend claims to be able to increase the yield of a plant by talking to it. They decide to put this claim to the test. A plant is selected at random and the farmer's friend talks to it for at least half an hour a day during its growing season.

If μ is the yield in kilograms of a tomato plant which has received the treatment, then the null and alternative hypotheses are:

$$H_0 : \mu = 6.2$$

$$H_1 : \mu > 6.2$$

The farmer says that he will be convinced if the plant's yield, X, exceeds 10 kg. His friend disagrees and feels that the farmer should accept the alternative hypothesis if the plant yields more than 9 kg.

> Rejecting H_0 when in fact it is the correct hypothesis is called a **type I error.**
>
> Accepting H_0 when in fact H_1 is the correct hypothesis is called a **type II error.**

$H_0 : X \sim N(6.2, 1.8^2)$ $H_1 : X \sim N(\mu, 1.8^2)$

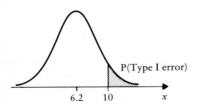

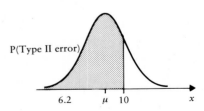

 .1c

1 Calculate the probability of a type I error if H_0 is rejected for $X > 10$.

2 Explain why it is not possible to calculate the probability of a type II error.

3 What would be the probability of a type I error if H_0 is rejected for $X > 9$?

4 If it is decided to reject H_0 for $X > 9$ rather than $X > 10$, will the probability of a type II error increase or decrease?

5 The farmer and his friend agree that a probability of 5% for a type I error is reasonable. For what x is $P(X > x) = 0.05$?

4.1.3 Level of significance

The cornerstone of English law is that a person is assumed innocent until proved guilty. Similarly, a null hypothesis is accepted until there is sufficient evidence to 'prove' it false.

A null hypothesis is rejected in favour of an alternative hypothesis when the observed data (the evidence) fall into a **critical region**. However, there is always a chance of rejecting a null hypothesis when in fact it is correct, just as there is always a chance of convicting an innocent person in a court of law. The probability of a type I error is the **significance level** of the test. Data which fall into the 5% critical region are said to be **significant at the 5% level**.

If the critical region is in just one tail of the distribution, then the test is called a **one-tail test**. If the critical region is split equally between the two tails, then the test is called a **two-tail test**. Whether a test is a one-tail test or a two-tail test depends on the alternative hypothesis.

One-tail test
H_0 : mean $= \mu$
H_1 : mean $> \mu$

The critical region at the 5% level is

$$X > \mu + 1.645\sigma$$

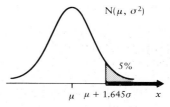

Two-tail test
H_0 : mean $= \mu$
H_1 : mean $\neq \mu$

The critical region at the 5% level is

$$X < \mu - 1.96\sigma \quad \text{or} \quad X > \mu + 1.96\sigma$$

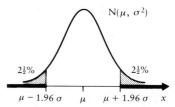

In hypothesis testing, statisticians adopt the following convention to describe the significance of observed data.

- Data which occur in the critical region at the 5% level of significance are called *significant*.

- Data which occur in the critical region at the 1% level of significance are called *very significant*.

- Data which occur in the critical region at the 0.1% level of significance are called *highly significant*.

Example 1

Last year Lisbeth was elected president of the students' union when 40% of members supported her. She claims that her support has increased during her year in office. The college magazine selects 150 students at random for a survey and finds that 75 say they will vote for her this year. Does this provide significant evidence for an increase in her support?

Solution

Assuming that her support is unchanged, if the number of students who support her in a random sample of 150 is r, then $R \sim B(150, 0.4)$.

$H_0 : p = 0.4$
$H_1 : p > 0.4$

Level of significance: 5%

The Normal approximation to the binomial is $X \sim N(60, 36)$.

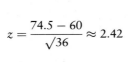

$$z = \frac{74.5 - 60}{\sqrt{36}} \approx 2.42$$

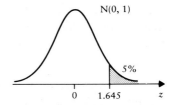

As the result of the survey falls in the critical region, you should reject H_0 and conclude that there has been a significant increase in her support.

The following result was established in Chapter 2, *The Normal distribution*.

> The Central Limit Theorem states that if $X \sim N(\mu, \sigma^2)$ then the distribution of sample means is $\bar{X} \sim N\left(\mu, \frac{\sigma^2}{n}\right)$.

Example 2

You can buy a cup of cola from a drinks machine. The amount dispensed, 300 ml, varies slightly. If X is the amount dispensed in millilitres, then $X \sim N(300, 10^2)$.

The operator samples four cups and accurately measures their contents. If the sample mean is significantly different from the expected value, she resets the machine.

Calculate the 'acceptable' range of values for the sample mean.

Solution

$H_0 : \mu = 300$
$H_1 : \mu \neq 300$

Level of significance: 5%

The distribution of sample means is Normally distributed: $\bar{X} \sim N\left(300, \dfrac{10^2}{4}\right)$

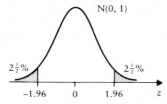

N(0, 1)

$2\frac{1}{2}\%$ $2\frac{1}{2}\%$

−1.96   0   1.96 z

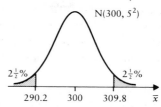

N(300, 5²)

$2\frac{1}{2}\%$ $2\frac{1}{2}\%$

290.2   300   309.8 $\bar{x}$

The region of acceptance is $300 - 1.96 \times 5 < \bar{X} < 300 + 1.96 \times 5$

or $290.3 < \bar{X} < 309.8$

4.1 Exercise 1

1 In a multiple-choice question paper of 120 questions, each with five possible answers, what number of correct answers would lead you to accept that a candidate is *not* answering purely by guesswork? To answer this question, set up appropriate null and alternative hypotheses and test at a 5% significance level.

2 3.141 592 653 589 79 . . . shows the first fourteen decimal places of π. Is there any evidence to suggest that the number of even digits after the decimal point will be significantly different from the number of odd digits when the expansion is continued?

3 The breaking strain of a type of rope is Normally distributed with mean 1300 newtons and standard deviation 40 newtons. A sample of nine lengths gives the following results when tested.

$$1334, \quad 1264, \quad 1284, \quad 1308, \quad 1198,$$

$$1244, \quad 1236, \quad 1204, \quad 1304 \quad \text{(newtons)}$$

Is there significant evidence that the breaking strain is lower than expected, and if so, at what level of significance?

4 A machine produces ball-bearings whose diameters are Normally distributed with mean 3.00 mm and standard deviation 0.05 mm. A random sample of 50 ball-bearings is found to have mean 3.01 mm. Does the machine need adjusting?

5 A farmer grows cabbages under stable greenhouse conditions. Their weights are Normally distributed with mean 0.85 kg and variance 0.04 kg². One year he tries out a new fertiliser and weighs a random sample of 60 cabbages to see if there has been a significant improvement in yield. He finds that the 60 cabbages have a mean weight of 0.91 kg. Would you describe this evidence as 'significant', 'very significant' or 'highly significant'?

4.1.4 Population proportions

Suppose that a proportion, p, of the members of a parent population possess a particular characteristic. As you found earlier in your work on the Normal distribution, if p_s is the proportion of the members of a large random sample of size n which possess the characteristic, then p_s has sampling distribution approximately

$$N\left(p, \frac{p(1-p)}{n}\right)$$

The ideas of significance testing can therefore be applied to population proportions and have particular relevance in the area of opinion polls. The modern importance of opinion polls largely stems from Dr Gallup's successful prediction of the American election in 1936. Although there have been several notable failures since then, such as the incorrect forecasts for the United Kingdom general election of 1992, opinion polls, at least in theory, depend upon mathematical ideas of significance and properties of the Normal distribution. For example, one of the well-known claims for general election opinion polls is that they have a 'margin of error of 3%'. This is based upon the result proved in the next example.

Example 3

The support for a particular political party is approximately 40%. What size of random sample is needed so that you can be 95% certain of predicting the actual support to within 3%?

Solution
For the Normal distribution, 95% of samples are within 1.96 s.d. of the mean.

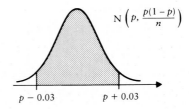

$$N\left(p, \frac{p(1-p)}{n}\right)$$

$p - 0.03 \qquad p + 0.03$

For the required certainty, 1.96 s.d. must correspond to 3%, i.e.

$$1.96\sqrt{\left(\frac{p(1-p)}{n}\right)} = 0.03$$

$$\Rightarrow \quad 1.96\sqrt{\left(\frac{0.4 \times 0.6}{n}\right)} \approx 0.03$$

$$\Rightarrow \qquad\qquad \frac{0.922}{n} \approx 0.0009$$

$$\Rightarrow \qquad\qquad n \approx 1024$$

In practice, you will find that many general election polls have a sample size of approximately 1000 and so 95% of such polls will be accurate to within 3%.

 .1D

> If support for the Liberal Democrats is approximately 20%, what size of sample is needed to predict support for this party to within 3% with 95% certainty?

4.1 Exercise 2

1 In one constituency, 46% of the votes cast were for Labour. Six months later an opinion poll was carried out in the area. 400 people were interviewed and 52% indicated that they would vote Labour. Has there been a significant increase in the Labour vote?

2 A survey of 400 randomly selected adults is held in a particular constituency a month before a general election and 144 indicate that they will vote Conservative. In the election the Conservative candidate polls 33.8% of the votes. Is there a discrepancy between the results of the poll and the election?

3 The manufacturers of Kleenrite claim that 50% of people prefer their product. In a public opinion survey of 200 people, 86 stated a preference for Kleenrite. Does this survey provide significant evidence that the manufacturers are overstating the preference for their product?

After working through section 4.1 you should:

1 understand the terms **null hypothesis** and **alternative hypothesis**;

2 be familiar with the symbols H_0 and H_1;

3 understand the meaning of a **type I error** and a **type II error**;

4 understand what is meant by level of significance;

5 know how to carry out a test of significance;

6 know when to use a **one-tail test** and when to use a **two-tail test**;

7 be able to apply a significance test to a population proportion.

Statistics in action

.2 The Student t-distribution

4.2.1 Large samples

In Chapter 2 you met the result that if $X \sim N(\mu, \sigma^2)$, then, for a sample of size n,

$$\overline{X} \sim N\left(\mu, \frac{\sigma^2}{n}\right).$$

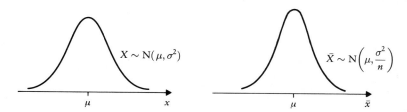

The standardised variable representing the difference between the sample mean and the population mean is

$$z = \frac{\bar{x} - \mu}{\sigma/\sqrt{n}} \qquad \text{where } Z \sim N(0, 1)$$

From the Central Limit Theorem, this standardised variable can be used even when the parent population is not Normally distributed providing the sample size is large.

> If a large sample of size n is taken from a population with mean μ and standard deviation σ, then the distribution of $z = \frac{\bar{x} - \mu}{\sigma/\sqrt{n}}$ is approximately $N(0, 1)$.

In section 4.1 you saw how to set up and test hypotheses against evidence gathered from statistical sampling. This type of testing is often used in research, quality control or to test the outcome of some change in production methods. Suppose, for example, that a market gardener changes to an organic method of growing cucumbers and is concerned that the cucumbers should be about the same size as those he grew in previous years.

Example 1

Before using organic methods, a gardener kept detailed records and found that his cucumbers had a mean length of 35.0 cm. To check the lengths of his organically grown cucumbers, he takes a random sample of 100 and measures their lengths. He finds that the sample mean is $\bar{x} = 34.1$ cm and that $s_{n-1}^2 = 16.0$ cm^2.

Does this constitute evidence of a decrease in length? State carefully any assumptions you make.

Solution

Assume that s_{n-1}^2 is a good estimate of the population variance, i.e. that $\sigma^2 = 16.0$.

Assume that $\overline{X} \sim N\left(35, \dfrac{16}{100}\right)$.

$H_0 : \mu = 35$
$H_1 : \mu < 35$

Level of significance: 5%

$$z = \frac{\bar{x} - \mu}{\sigma/\sqrt{n}} = \frac{34.1 - 35}{\sqrt{(16/100)}} = -2.25$$

H_0 is rejected because $-2.25 < -1.645$. There is significant evidence to support the claim that the organic cucumbers are shorter.

Note: Because of the Central Limit Theorem, it is reasonable to assume that

$$\frac{\bar{x} - \mu}{\sigma/\sqrt{n}} \sim N(0, 1)$$

Similarly, you know that s_{n-1} is an unbiased estimator of σ. However, a particular value of s_{n-1} might differ considerably from σ. As you will soon appreciate, the distribution of $\dfrac{\bar{x} - \mu}{s_{n-1}/\sqrt{n}}$ is *not* Normal, although the difference is small for *large* values of n.

Sometimes it is necessary to use data from a sample to estimate a population variance. In the case of the market gardener's cucumbers, the variance of the parent population was unknown and had to be estimated before the problem could be analysed. The following result, demonstrated in Chapter 2, enables a population variance to be estimated from a sample variance.

$$s_{n-1}^2 = \frac{n}{n-1} s_n^2 \text{ is an } \textit{unbiased} \text{ estimator of } \sigma^2.$$

The error incurred in using the sample variance to estimate σ^2 is small when the sample size is large and the following result can be applied.

For large samples, if $z = \dfrac{\bar{x} - \mu}{s_{n-1}/\sqrt{n}}$ then $Z \sim N(0, 1)$.

Example 2

A biologist is investigating whether the use of chemical sprays by farmers adversely affects wild life. It is known that twenty years ago the mean weight of wood mice was 55.0 g. No information on the variance is available. The biologist catches 50 wood mice and finds that their mean weight $\bar{x} = 53.9$ g and that $s_{n-1}{}^2 = 25.3$ g^2. Is this significant evidence of a decrease in weight?

Solution
$H_0 : \mu = 55.0$
$H_1 : \mu < 55.0$

Level of significance: 5%

Reject H_0 if $z < -1.645$ where $z = \dfrac{\bar{x} - \mu}{s_{n-1}/\sqrt{n}}$

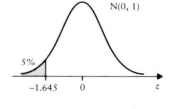

Here $z = \dfrac{53.9 - 55}{\sqrt{(25.3/50)}} = -1.546$

As $-1.546 > -1.645$, H_0 is *not* rejected. The evidence is not significant.

4.2.2 Small samples

In section 4.2.1, dealing with large samples, you saw that the distribution of $\dfrac{\bar{x} - \mu}{s_{n-1}/\sqrt{n}}$ is approximately $N(0, 1)$ even if the parent population is not Normally distributed. However, decisions often have to be made on evidence gathered from small samples. In particular, there are many instances where it is necessary to use a small sample to estimate a population variance.

The statistician William S. Gossett was particularly concerned with finding ways of dealing with decision-making when the only available information came from small samples. He was able to develop results for small samples, but *only* for parent populations which are Normally distributed. For X Normally distributed, with mean μ, Gossett investigated the distribution of $\dfrac{\bar{x} - \mu}{s_{n-1}/\sqrt{n}}$ for small n. He called this new distribution the **t-distribution**. The following activity (4.2A) gives you the opportunity to replicate his work.

.2A

Gossett worked for the Guinness brewery in the early 1900s. It was the policy of the company that employees should not publish under their own name so Gossett adopted the pen-name 'Student' and is now best known by this name. 'Student' was particularly interested in the distribution of the statistic

$$t = \frac{\text{sample mean} - \text{population mean}}{\textbf{estimated} \text{ standard error}} = \frac{\bar{x} - \mu}{s_{n-1}/\sqrt{n}}$$

He investigated the distribution of t by calculating $\bar{x}$ and s_{n-1} (and hence t) for a large number of samples of size $n = 4$. The samples were all picked at random from a Normally distributed population with known mean and variance.

He chose as his parent population one which had been investigated some years previously by the statistician W. R. Macdonnell and published in *Biometrika* in 1901. Macdonnell had shown that the height distribution of 3000 criminals, obtained from the records of Scotland Yard, was in very close agreement with what would be expected from a Normal distribution.

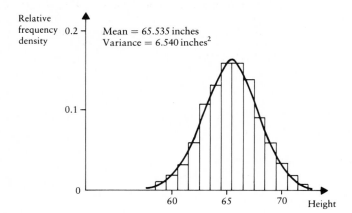

The histogram shows the distribution of the heights of the 3000 criminals (mean 65.535, variance 6.540), while the superimposed curve is that of a Normal random variable with the same mean and variance. The distribution of the heights of the criminals is very well modelled by this Normal random variable.

'Student' wrote down the 3000 heights in random order and, taking each consecutive set of 4 as a sample from the population, he calculated 750 values of t.

1 Suppose the values in one of 'Student's' samples were 62, 63.5, 65 and 62.5 inches. Calculate the values of $\bar{x}$, s_{n-1}^2 and t for this sample.

2 (a) Calculate the value of $z = \dfrac{\bar{x} - \mu}{\sqrt{(\sigma^2/n)}}$ for the sample in question 1.

  (b) Explain why you would expect $Z \sim \mathrm{N}(0, 1)$.

3 In what way would you expect the variance of the distribution of T to differ from that of Z?

The results 'Student' obtained were published in *Biometrika* in 1908 and are shown in the histogram. The **theoretical** *t*-distribution for samples of size 4 is superimposed.

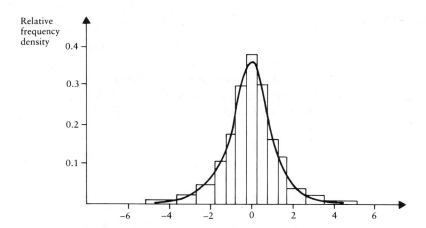

4 What feature of the histogram shows that the distribution is *not* a Standard Normal distribution?

It can be shown that the equation of a *t*-distribution is given by

$$f(t) = c_\nu \left(1 + \frac{t^2}{\nu}\right)^{-(\nu+1)/2}$$

where the parameter $\nu = n - 1$, and c_ν is a constant such that $\displaystyle\int_{-\infty}^{\infty} f(t)\,dt = 1$.

5 (a) Show that when $n = 4$ (i.e. $\nu = 3$) the equation of the *t*-distribution is given by

$$f(t) = c_3 \left(1 + \frac{t^2}{3}\right)^{-2}$$

  (b) Use a numerical method of integration or the substitution $t = \sqrt{3}\tan\theta$ to evaluate $\displaystyle\int_{-\infty}^{\infty} \left(1 + \frac{t^2}{3}\right)^{-2} dt$.

  (c) Hence explain why the constant $c_3 = 0.368$ (to 3 s.f.).

'Student' was unable to prove that a t-distribution has this equation. It was some time later that his friend and colleague, Sir Ronald A. Fisher, supplied a proof and it is for this reason that the t-distribution is sometimes referred to as the 'Student–Fisher distribution'. However, it is usually called simply the '**Student t-distribution**'. The method 'Student' used to investigate areas under the t-distribution was very time-consuming because he did not have access to the sort of computing power taken for granted today.

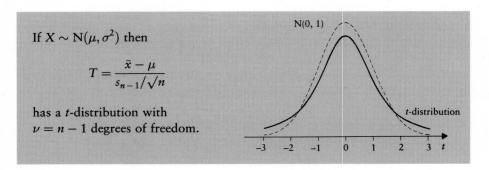

If $X \sim N(\mu, \sigma^2)$ then

$$T = \frac{\bar{x} - \mu}{s_{n-1}/\sqrt{n}}$$

has a t-distribution with $\nu = n - 1$ degrees of freedom.

The random variable

$$T = \frac{\bar{x} - \mu}{s_{n-1}/\sqrt{n}}$$

is the ratio of two random variables, $\overline{X}$ and S_{n-1}. These two random variables are not completely independent as the statistic $\bar{x}$ has to be calculated *before* you calculate s_{n-1}. It is because of this one constraint on the n elements in the sample that the variable S_{n-1} (and hence T) is said to have $n - 1$ degrees of freedom.

Although it is possible to use numerical methods to make accurate probability statements about any t-distribution, the process is tedious and tables of values for the family of t-distributions have therefore been compiled. (These tables can be found at the back of this book on page 399.)

The table opposite gives values of ν in the left-hand column. The values of t corresponding to various probabilities p appear in the body of the table. Note that the table is designed for use in one-tail tests.

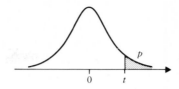

p	0.05	0.025	0.01	0.005	0.001	0.0005
$\nu = 1$	6.31	12.71	31.82	63.66	318.3	636.6
2	2.92	4.30	6.96	9.92		31.6

 .2B

When $\nu = 8$ and $p = 0.025$, you can see from the table on page 399 that $t = 2.31$.

1 Draw a diagram to show this information.

2 Explain carefully what this information tells you about the distribution of sample means.

3 Look at the last line in the *t*-distribution table on page 399. Explain how (and why) these values relate to the corresponding points on the standard Normal distribution.

For practical purposes, the difference between a *t*-distribution and a standard Normal distribution is negligible for values of ν greater than 30.

For sample size $n < 30$, use

$$t = \frac{\bar{x} - \mu}{s_{n-1}/\sqrt{n}}$$

where T has a *t*-distribution with degrees of freedom $\nu = n - 1$

For sample size $n \geq 30$, use

$$z = \frac{\bar{x} - \mu}{s_{n-1}/\sqrt{n}}$$

where $Z \sim N(0, 1)$

For small samples ($n < 30$) it is necessary to assume that X is Normally distributed.

Example 3

It is claimed that a small packet of raisins contains 14.1 g on average. The quality controller at the packing plant rejects a batch if she believes that the average weight of packets in the batch is less than 14.1 g. She selects a random sample of 5 packets from a particular batch and weighs the contents.

x (grams):   12.9   14.7   13.2   13.9   14.0

Is the evidence significant? Should she reject the batch?

Solution

$H_0 : \mu = 14.1$

$H_1 : \mu < 14.1$

Level of significance: 5%

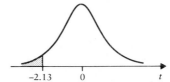

Assume that the weight, X, is Normally distributed. The variance of the population has to be estimated from a small sample and so $\dfrac{\bar{x} - \mu}{s_{n-1}/\sqrt{n}}$ has a t-distribution with 4 degrees of freedom. Reject H_0 if $t \le -2.13$.

The sample gives $\bar{x} = 13.74$ and $s_{n-1} = 0.709$ (to 3 d.p.).

So $t = \dfrac{13.74 - 14.1}{0.709/\sqrt{5}} = -1.135$ (to 3 d.p.)

As $-1.135 > -2.13$, the quality controller should accept H_0 and *not* reject the batch.

4.2 Exercise 1

1 From the table on page 399, find the value of t which would be critical in:

(a) a one-tail test, sample size 6, at the 1% level;

(b) a two-tail test, sample size 15, at the 5% level.

2 To test the effect of an irradiation process on apples, 10 pairs were chosen and one in each pair was irradiated. The pairs were then left in the same conditions and the time before rot set in was noted. The time differences in days for each pair ('treated' − 'untreated') were

x (days):   30,   7,   51,   120,   16,   34,   −8,   −74,   −17,   56

Does the test show a significant difference in the times at the 10% level?

3 It is claimed by the manufacturer that a hearing aid battery lasts for 1000 hours with the hearing aid used at full volume. A random sample of 200 batteries is tested and found to have a mean life of 997 hours with $s_{n-1} = 13$ hours. The tester asserts that the manufacturer's claim is false. Is this fair?

▶ 4.2 **Tasksheet E1 – Plotting *t*-distributions (page 315)**

4.2.3 Confidence intervals

You met the idea of a confidence interval for the mean in Chapter 2, *The Normal distribution*. The *t*-distribution is often used instead of a Normal distribution when calculating a confidence interval if the only available information about a population is provided by the sample itself.

Students on a biology field trip to the Norfolk Broads are asked to investigate the local population of common frogs. During the afternoon they catch just 12 frogs. They weigh them and obtain the following data:

Weight (grams):   85,   125,   95,   160,   95,   70,

110,   105,   115,   50,   140,   145

The students calculate the mean weight as $\bar{x} = 107.9\,\text{g}$, but are not sure how good an estimate this is for the frog population of the area.

They assume that weight has a Normal distribution so that the statistic

$$t = \frac{\bar{x} - \mu}{s_{n-1}/\sqrt{12}}$$

has a *t*-distribution with $\nu = 11$ degrees of freedom.

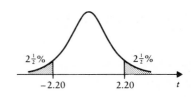

From a *t*-distribution table,

$$P(-2.20 < T < 2.20) = 0.95$$

Another way of looking at this is to say that 95% of samples of size 12 would give a value *t* of the random variable *T* such that

$$-2.20 < t < 2.20$$

A 95% confidence interval for the mean weight can therefore be obtained from

$$-2.2 < \frac{\bar{x} - \mu}{s_{n-1}/\sqrt{12}} < 2.2$$

 .2c

1 Show how this inequality can be rearranged to give

$$\bar{x} - 2.2\left(\frac{s_{n-1}}{\sqrt{12}}\right) < \mu < \bar{x} + 2.2\left(\frac{s_{n-1}}{\sqrt{12}}\right)$$

2 Calculate s_{n-1} for the sample of frogs.

3 Hence show that the 95% confidence interval for the mean weight of the population of frogs is

$$87.7 < \mu < 128.1$$

4 Calculate the 90% confidence interval.

Suppose that a parent population has a Normal distribution and that a small random sample of size n has been obtained. If σ has to be estimated from the data in the sample, then a t-distribution with $n - 1$ degrees of freedom should be used when determining a confidence interval for the population mean μ.

$$\bar{x} - t\left(\frac{s_{n-1}}{\sqrt{n}}\right) < \mu < \bar{x} + t\left(\frac{s_{n-1}}{\sqrt{n}}\right)$$

For example, for a 95% confidence interval, t is the value in the t-distribution which has an area $p = 0.025$ to the right of it.

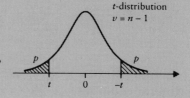

4.2 Exercise 2

1 At a packing station, ten peaches are picked out at random from a large batch of the same variety and are found to have the following weights in grams:

160,   105,   125,   145,   110,   140,   125,   150,   115,   145

(a) Find a 90% confidence interval for the mean.

(b) Find 95% and 99% confidence intervals.

2 Thirty university students volunteer to take part in an investigation into the effect alcohol has on a person's ability to carry out simple tasks. The students are split at random into two groups of fifteen and both groups are asked to perform a test of manual dexterity. However, the members of one group consume a quantity of alcohol half an hour before being tested.

The times taken to complete the test are given in the table.

Without alcohol x (s)	12.2	8.3	14.7	10.7	9.8	12.5	13.2	13.0	9.6	11.3	11.9	10.8	16.2	11.0	10.1
With alcohol y (s)	12.3	14.8	17.2	19.7	10.2	16.7	21.5	9.9	11.7	19.7	19.5	20.0	24.3	13.5	25.9

Calculate 95% confidence intervals for each sample and comment on your findings.

4.2.4 Matched pairs t-test

The technique of **matched pairs testing** is particularly important. You have already met the idea in question 2 of exercise 1. A further example is described below.

A manufacturer claims that a new slimming aid enables you to lose weight without the need to diet. A consumer association doubts the validity of this claim and selects eight volunteers to test it. Each volunteer was weighed before and after a course of treatment.

	A	B	C	D	E	F	G	H
Weight before (kg)	76.3	80.1	77.3	69.5	83.4	72.4	64.0	79.3
Weight after (kg)	75.1	79.5	78.5	68.1	83.3	72.1	62.7	79.0

To see if this provides significant evidence in support of the manufacturer's claim, you can analyse the *change in weight*. However, it is necessary to assume that this variable is Normally distributed.

	A	B	C	D	E	F	G	H
Weight change x (kg)	-1.2	-0.6	$+1.2$	-1.4	-0.1	-0.3	-1.3	-0.3

Assume that X is Normally distributed, $X \sim N(\mu, \sigma^2)$.

$H_0 : \mu = 0$ the treatment makes no difference
$H_1 : \mu < 0$ there has been a decrease in weight

Level of significance: 5%

.2D

1 Calculate $\bar{x}$ and s_{n-1} for the sample of weight changes, and use a t-test to show that the sample does not provide significant evidence in support of the manufacturer's claim.

2 Does this prove that the manufacturer's claim is false?

4.2 Exercise 3

1 Lengths of pipe were buried in soil so that the corrosive effect of the soil on the pipe could be measured. Half the length of each pipe was given a special coating to protect it against corrosion. The following data show the measured corrosion on the coated and uncoated parts in different types of soil.

Soil type	A	B	C	D	E	F	G	H	I
Uncoated	63	42	69	64	79	77	52	85	63
Coated	47	30	73	65	81	71	32	82	51

Carry out a t-test to see if the sample provides very significant evidence (at the 1% level) to support the claim that coating pipes offers some protection against corrosion.

2 A group of trainee managers are given a memory task. The group is then given a course of instruction on how to improve recall. They are then tested again using a similar task.

Their results are shown in the table.

Trainee manager	A	B	C	D	E	F	G	H	I	J	K	L	M	N	O
Score before	11	12	9	7	17	14	13	15	12	16	14	12	13	14	14
Score after	12	11	10	10	16	16	16	19	13	15	18	15	14	14	17

Is the apparent improvement in score significant? (State any assumptions you make.)

3 Two weight-reducing diets, A and B, are to be compared. Ten matched pairs of overweight people are selected and diet A randomly assigned to one of each pair, the other being assigned diet B. At the end of a six-week period the weight losses (in kilograms) are as shown.

Pair	1	2	3	4	5	6	7	8	9	10
Weight loss on diet A	7.5	4.0	3.3	10.5	6.1	8.3	12.1	14.7	9.0	9.8
Weight loss on diet B	10.7	5.3	2.7	13.5	7.3	5.9	15.9	13.7	10.1	6.2

Is there a significant difference in the weight losses?

After working through section 4.2 you should:

1 know that the statistic $t = \dfrac{\bar{x} - \mu}{s_{n-1}/\sqrt{n}}$ has a t-distribution with $\nu = n - 1$ degrees of freedom when $X \sim N(\mu, \sigma^2)$;

2 appreciate the original work of W. S. Gossett ('Student') in investigating the distribution of the random variable T;

3 know how a t-distribution differs from a Standard Normal distribution for small samples;

4 appreciate why a t-distribution can be approximated by a Standard Normal distribution for a sample of size 30 or more;

5 know how to use a t-distribution to test a null hypothesis;

6 know how to use a t-distribution to calculate a confidence interval for a population mean;

7 know how to test for a significant difference using a sample of matched pairs.

4 Statistics in action

.3 Two-sample tests

4.3.1 Testing the equality of two means

In section 4.2 you saw how to test hypotheses about a population mean using a sample drawn from the population. In this section you will be concerned with making comparisons between two population means using two samples, one taken from each of the populations.

For some time, environmentalists have been urging a change from leaded to lead-free petrol. Although motorists are usually keen to be 'green' they might hesitate to change to unleaded if it is expensive to do so. Even if unleaded is a little cheaper they might suspect that leaded petrol will give more miles per gallon.

A company conducts an experiment to investigate how a new lead-free petrol, which does not require an engine conversion, compares with regular four-star. Most of the company's employees have a company car of a particular make and model. A sample of ten of them is selected at random and asked to use four-star petrol for the duration of the trial. Another random sample of ten is asked to use the new unleaded.

For the period of the trial, the twenty employees all calculate their rate of petrol consumption in miles per gallon. The resulting data are as follows.

| Leaded X | 35.4 | 34.5 | 31.6 | 32.4 | 34.8 | 31.7 | 35.4 | 35.3 | 36.6 | 36.0 |
| Unleaded Y | 29.7 | 29.6 | 32.1 | 35.4 | 34.0 | 34.8 | 34.6 | 34.8 | 32.7 | 32.2 |

From the data previously available to the company they decide to assume:

- rates in miles per gallon are Normally distributed;

- the s.d. is 1.8 miles per gallon, for all types of petrol.

So it may be assumed that

$$X \sim N(\mu_X, 1.8^2), \quad Y \sim N(\mu_Y, 1.8^2)$$

The probability distributions for the populations of sample means $\overline{X}$ and $\overline{Y}$ are

$$\overline{X} \sim N\left(\mu_X, \frac{1.8^2}{10}\right), \quad \overline{Y} \sim N\left(\mu_Y, \frac{1.8^2}{10}\right)$$

The means of the particular samples provided are $\bar{x} = 34.37$ and $\bar{y} = 32.99$.

A suitable null hypothesis is that the average rate is the same for both types of petrol.

$$H_0 : \mu_X = \mu_Y$$

A suitable alternative is that the average rate is higher with leaded than with unleaded.

$$H_1 : \mu_X > \mu_Y$$

If the null hypothesis is true and the distributions of X and Y have equal means then you would expect the difference $\bar{x} - \bar{y}$ to be close to zero. What has to be found is how far from zero the difference must be before the null hypothesis is rejected. To carry out a hypothesis test you need to know the distribution of $\overline{X} - \overline{Y}$, and again you should recall the results of earlier work on combining Normal random variables (Chapter 3, section 3.5.5).

If $W \sim N(\mu_W, \sigma_W{}^2)$ and $V \sim N(\mu_V, \sigma_V{}^2)$ are independent, then

$$W - V \sim N(\mu_W - \mu_V, \sigma_W{}^2 + \sigma_V{}^2)$$

That is,

- the difference $W - V$ between two Normally distributed variables W and V is also Normally distributed;
- the mean value of $W - V$ is the **difference** of the means of W and V;
- the variance of $W - V$ is the **sum** of the variances of W and V.

Example 1
W has a Normal distribution with mean 20 and s.d. 3, V has a Normal distribution with mean 15 and s.d. 2. What is the distribution of $W - V$?

Solution
$W - V$ has Normal distribution, with

$$\text{mean } 20 - 15 = 5, \quad \text{variance } 3^2 + 2^2 = 13$$

$$W - V \sim N(5, 13)$$

The hypothesis test to be developed in the next section is based upon the following three assumptions. In the case of large samples, the second and third of these assumptions can be waived. For large samples, sample means are distributed approximately Normally and the variance of the parent population can be estimated with reasonable accuracy.

- A sample is drawn from the first population under consideration and *completely independently* a sample is drawn from the second population.

- Both populations have Normal distributions.

- The variances of both populations are known.

All three assumptions hold in the case of the petrol trial.

You are now in a position to solve the problem of the petrol trial, using the standard procedure.

$H_0 : \mu_X = \mu_Y$

$H_1 : \mu_X > \mu_Y$

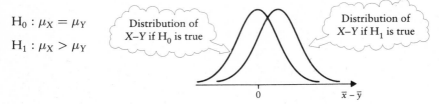

Distribution of X–Y if H_0 is true

Distribution of X–Y if H_1 is true

$X - Y$ has a Normal distribution: $\quad X - Y \sim N\left(\mu_X - \mu_Y, \dfrac{1.8^2}{10} + \dfrac{1.8^2}{10}\right)$

If $z = \dfrac{(\bar{x} - \bar{y}) - (\mu_X - \mu_Y)}{\sqrt{\left(\dfrac{1.8^2}{10} + \dfrac{1.8^2}{10}\right)}}, \quad$ then $Z \sim N(0, 1)$

The company is investigating whether the new petrol gives a lower rate in miles per gallon, so a 5% one-tail test should be applied. H_0 will be rejected at the 5% level if $z > 1.645$.

Assuming H_0, $\quad \mu_X - \mu_Y = 0$, $\bar{x} - \bar{y} = 1.38$ and $\sqrt{\left(\dfrac{1.8^2}{10} + \dfrac{1.8^2}{10}\right)} = 0.805$

So $z = \dfrac{1.38}{0.805} = 1.71$

Since $1.71 > 1.645$, H_0 is rejected at the 5% level. There is evidence that the unleaded petrol gives a lower rate in miles per gallon than the four-star leaded, though the evidence is not strong.

In general, the sizes of the two samples compared need not be equal. The various tests based upon two samples are summarised opposite.

1 Suppose that X is Normally distributed with mean μ_X and variance $\sigma_X{}^2$ and Y is Normally distributed with mean μ_Y and variance $\sigma_Y{}^2$. Then the null hypothesis $H_0 : \mu_X = \mu_Y$ may be tested against any *one* of these three possible alternatives for H_1:

$$\mu_X \neq \mu_Y \quad \text{or} \quad \mu_X > \mu_Y \quad \text{or} \quad \mu_X < \mu_Y$$

2 In the test, assume independent samples of size m for X and of size n for Y. Then the test statistic is

$$z = \frac{\bar{x} - \bar{y}}{\sqrt{\left(\dfrac{\sigma_X{}^2}{m} + \dfrac{\sigma_Y{}^2}{n}\right)}}$$

where $\bar{x}$ is the mean of the sample from X and $\bar{y}$ is the mean of the sample from Y. This value of z is compared with the value in the table of areas under the Standard Normal curve.

The diagrams show when H_0 is rejected (and H_1 accepted) at the 5% level.

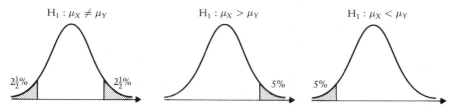

Sometimes you may have to estimate the variance of the parent population from that of the sample.

Example 2
The weights of the first 100 children born in a large city in a given year are recorded and analysed, with these results.

	No. born	Mean weight (kg)	Variance (kg^2)
Boys	44	3.489	0.2675
Girls	56	3.258	0.1473

Does this constitute evidence that in the city the birth weight of boys is greater than that of girls?

Solution
It may be assumed that the 56 girls and 44 boys are independent random samples from Normally distributed populations.

The standard procedure is followed. Samples with means $\bar{b}, \bar{g}$ and variances $s_B{}^2$ and $s_G{}^2$ are taken from the background populations B and G of boys and girls respectively.

$H_0 : \mu_B = \mu_G$

$H_1 : \mu_B > \mu_G$

Level of significance: 5%

$$\overline{B} - \overline{G} \sim N\left(\mu_B - \mu_G, \frac{\sigma_B{}^2}{44} + \frac{\sigma_G{}^2}{56}\right)$$

Since the variances of B and G are not given they can be estimated as $\frac{44}{43}s_B{}^2$ and $\frac{56}{55}s_G{}^2$ respectively, using the formula $\dfrac{ns^2}{n-1}$ for an unbiased estimator for σ^2.

As the sample sizes are large, you can assume that $Z \sim N(0, 1)$ where

$$z = \frac{\bar{b} - \bar{g}}{\sqrt{\left(\dfrac{s_B{}^2}{43} + \dfrac{s_G{}^2}{55}\right)}}$$

H_0 is to be rejected if $z > 1.645$.

$b = 3.489, \quad g = 3.258, \quad s_B{}^2 = 0.2675 \quad \text{and} \quad s_G{}^2 = 0.1473$

So, $\quad z = \dfrac{0.231}{0.0943} = 2.45$

Since $2.45 > 1.645$, H_0 is rejected.

The given data constitute evidence that the birth weight of boys in the city is greater than that of girls.

For sufficiently large samples the distribution of sample means is Normal even when the parent population is not Normally distributed.

Example 3

Glitto and Pufco manufacture Christmas light bulbs. Each company claims that its bulbs have the longest life. In an experiment to investigate whether there is a significant difference in the average lives of the two makes of bulb, 100 bulbs are randomly selected from each production line and tested.

The bulbs in Glitto's sample have a mean life of 798 hours, and Pufco's sample has a mean life of 826 hours. However, Pufco's mean was obtained using a sample of only 98 bulbs, because two were broken after the sample had been taken. It is known that the variance of the life of a Glitto bulb is 7800 hours^2, while for Pufco bulbs the variance is 9000 hours^2. Settle the dispute between Glitto and Pufco.

Solution

Sample means of *large* samples from a parent population with *any* distribution are Normally distributed, by the Central Limit Theorem. In other respects, the requirements for using the standard test apply. Let X and Y be the lives in hours of bulbs made by Glitto and Pufco respectively.

$H_0 : \mu_X = \mu_Y$

$H_1 : \mu_X \neq \mu_Y$

Level of significance: 5%

$$\overline{X} - \overline{Y} \sim N\left(\mu_X - \mu_Y, \frac{\sigma_X^2}{100} + \frac{\sigma_Y^2}{98}\right)$$

$$Z \sim N(0, 1) \text{ where } z = \frac{\bar{x} - \bar{y}}{\sqrt{\left(\dfrac{\sigma_X^2}{100} + \dfrac{\sigma_Y^2}{98}\right)}}$$

H_0 is rejected if $z < -1.96$ or $z > 1.96$.

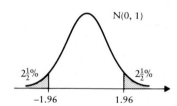

Substituting $\bar{x} = 798, \quad \bar{y} = 826, \quad \sigma_X^2 = 7800, \quad \sigma_Y^2 = 9000$

$$z = \frac{-28}{13.0} = -2.15$$

Since $-2.15 < -1.96$, H_0 is rejected in favour of H_1. There is a significant difference in the average lifetimes of the two makes of bulb.

4.3 Exercise 1

In each of the following examples start by stating suitable null and alternative hypotheses in words before you express them algebraically.

1 The ages at which men married for the first time were recorded for samples of 80 men in country A and 100 men in country B. The mean for A was found to be 24.5 years and that for B was 26.1 years. Previous larger studies found the standard deviations for A and B to be 3.2 and 2.8 years respectively. Is there evidence that men in B marry for the first time later in life than those in A? (Use a 1% significance level.)

2 A company has two models of car in its fleet. A sample of 20 of the first model was found to have an average annual maintenance cost of £540 while a sample of 11 of the second model had an average of £710. National figures show that the standard deviation of annual maintenance costs for the first and second models are £90 and £110 respectively. The company is thinking of changing all its fleet to cars of the first model to save on maintenance costs. Would you advise them to do so? (Use a 5% significance level.) What assumptions did you have to make to carry out this hypothesis test?

3 An educational psychologist suspects a logical thinking test of being biased against girls. She administers the test to a random sample of 50 boys and 50 girls. The average scores are 68.9 for the boys and 61.8 for the girls. It is known that the variance of test scores for boys is 144 whereas the variance for girls is 196. Test whether the psychologist's suspicions are true. (Use a 1% significance level.)

4 A market gardener grows a particular variety of cucumber in two plots. He uses chemical fertilisers and pesticides on the first plot but the cucumbers in the second plot are grown organically.

In a particular year, a sample of 50 cucumbers from the first plot has mean length 36.5 cm and a sample of 50 from the organic plot has mean length 35 cm. Assuming the variance of cucumbers of both types to be $16 \, \text{cm}^2$ test whether using organic methods significantly changes the average length of the cucumbers. (Use a 5% significance level.)

5 The energy (in MJ) expended in 24 hours by 12 men of less than average weight and 10 men of above average weight is shown below.

Underweight	6.1	7.1	10.9	10.1	7.5	8.4	7.6	7.7	8.2	7.9	6.5	7.5
Overweight	12.8	11.9	9.9	10.0	9.7	9.7	9.2	11.7	12.8	8.9		

Previous data show the standard deviation to be $1.20 \, \text{MJ day}^{-1}$ for underweight men and $1.41 \, \text{MJ day}^{-1}$ for overweight men. It is also known that energy consumption has a Normal distribution. Use the data shown above to test whether overweight men expend more energy than underweight men on average. (Use a 5% significance level.)

4.3.2 Confidence intervals

In example 3 it was found that the mean lifetimes of two types of light bulbs were different. A confidence interval for the actual difference can be found using a result from Chapter 2, *The Normal distribution*.

You know that if $X \sim N(\mu, \sigma^2)$ then $P(\mu - 1.96\sigma < X < \mu + 1.96\sigma) = 0.95$.

This inequality can be rearranged to give $P(X - 1.96\sigma < \mu < X + 1.96\sigma) = 0.95$.

You can therefore be 95% confident that an interval $(x - 1.96\sigma, x + 1.96\sigma)$ does in fact contain the mean, μ. This is the **95% confidence interval** for the mean.

A similar result holds for the difference between two means.

If $\bar{X} \sim N\left(\mu_X, \dfrac{\sigma_X^2}{n}\right)$ and $\bar{Y} \sim N\left(\mu_Y, \dfrac{\sigma_Y^2}{m}\right)$ then

$$\bar{X} - \bar{Y} \sim N\left(\mu_X - \mu_Y, \frac{\sigma_X^2}{n} + \frac{\sigma_Y^2}{m}\right)$$

The 95% confidence interval for $\mu_X - \mu_Y$ is

$$\left(\bar{x} - \bar{y} - 1.96\sqrt{\left(\frac{\sigma_X^2}{n} + \frac{\sigma_Y^2}{m}\right)}, \quad \bar{x} - \bar{y} + 1.96\sqrt{\left(\frac{\sigma_X^2}{n} + \frac{\sigma_Y^2}{m}\right)}\right)$$

You can use this result to find a 95% confidence interval for $\mu_X - \mu_Y$ in example 3 on pages 264–5.

$$(\bar{x} - \bar{y}) \pm 1.96\sqrt{\left(\frac{7800}{100} + \frac{9000}{98}\right)} = -28 \pm 25.5$$

The 95% confidence interval is $(-53.5, -2.5)$.

4.3 Exercise 2

1 A sample of size 50 from a Normal distribution with known variance 25 has mean 10.3. A sample of size 72 from a second Normal distribution with known variance 36 has mean 8.2. Construct a 95% confidence interval for the difference between the mean of the first Normal distribution and that of the second.

2 Construct a 95% confidence interval for the difference in daily energy expenditure between underweight and overweight men. Use the data given in question 5 of exercise 1.

3 Use the data given on page 260 to construct a 90% confidence interval for the difference between the mean miles per gallon using leaded petrol and the mean miles per gallon using unleaded petrol.

4 A random sample of 100 low-tar cigarettes of brand A is found to have a mean tar content of 9.9 mg. A random sample of 100 low-tar cigarettes of brand B has a mean tar content of 8.9 mg. Assuming the standard deviation to be 1.6 mg for both brands, find a 99% confidence interval for the difference between the mean tar content of brand A and that of brand B.

4.3.3 The pooled variance estimator

In the pharmaceutical industry, comparisons must often be made between medicines. Suppose a particular pharmaceutical company manufactures two treatments, A and B, for diverticulosis, a disorder of the alimentary canal. With the co-operation of local hospitals, a statistician from the company randomly selects a sample of 15 patients who are receiving treatment A and another sample of 15 patients receiving B.

The experiment consists of administering a marker pellet to each patient and measuring the time taken for the pellet to pass through the alimentary canal. Three of the patients receiving treatment B either do not keep their appointments on the days on which the experiment is conducted or do not record the time, reducing the second sample size to 12. The data which result from the experiment are as follows.

Treatment	Time in hours														
A	44	51	52	55	60	62	66	68	69	71	71	76	82	91	108
B	52	64	68	74	79	83	84	88	95	97	101	116			

It would be reasonable to assume that the times for the two treatments are Normally distributed. However, the two-sample test developed in this chapter cannot be applied to these results because of the small sample sizes and the fact that the population variances are unknown.

By analogy with the methods used in section 4.2, you might think of applying the *t*-test with the samples being used to estimate the population variances. The only examples considered in this chapter will be ones where the two samples can be assumed to come from populations with a **common variance**. In such cases, the variance is estimated using a particular combination of the sample variances. The general method will be illustrated using the example of the two treatments for diverticulosis.

For the actual data provided:

- treatment A: sample mean = 68.4; sample variance $s_A{}^2 = 253.3$
- treatment B: sample mean = 83.4; sample variance $s_B{}^2 = 285.1$

It is important to be clear that $s_A{}^2$, $s_B{}^2$ are the actual variances of the sample data provided − they are *not* estimates of the population variances $\sigma_A{}^2$ or $\sigma_B{}^2$.

However, suppose that the two *populations* from which the times for A and B have been sampled *both* have variance σ^2. Possible *unbiased estimators* for σ^2 are $\frac{15}{14}s_A{}^2$ and $\frac{12}{11}s_B{}^2$. Either of these estimators could be used but it is more reliable to use a combination of both $s_A{}^2$ and $s_B{}^2$. The **pooled variance estimator** is based upon the weighted average of $s_A{}^2$ and $s_B{}^2$, the weightings depending upon the number of measurements in each sample.

$15s_A{}^2 + 12s_B{}^2$ has mean $14\sigma^2 + 11\sigma^2$ and so a suitable unbiased estimator is

$$\frac{15s_A{}^2 + 12s_B{}^2}{25}$$

This is derived by noting that the distribution of $\frac{15}{14}s_A{}^2$ has mean σ^2 and so the distribution of $15s_A{}^2$ has mean $14\sigma^2$. Similarly, the distribution of $12s_B{}^2$ has mean $11\sigma^2$ and so $15s_A{}^2 + 12s_B{}^2$ has mean $14\sigma^2 + 11\sigma^2 = 25\sigma^2$.

$\dfrac{15s_A{}^2 + 12s_B{}^2}{25}$ is therefore an unbiased estimator for σ^2.

In general, the pooled variance estimator is calculated as follows.

> Suppose $X \sim N(\mu_X, \sigma^2)$ and $Y \sim N(\mu_Y, \sigma^2)$. Suppose further that a sample of X of size n_X has variance $s_X{}^2$ and a sample of Y of size n_Y has variance $s_Y{}^2$. The pooled variance estimator for σ^2 is the unbiased estimator
>
> $$\frac{n_X s_X{}^2 + n_Y s_Y{}^2}{n_X + n_Y - 2}$$

 .3A

1 For the samples of times for treatments A and B given earlier, find three separate unbiased estimators for the population variance using:

(a) sample A only,

(b) sample B only,

(c) a pooled estimator.

2 Explain why the three estimates are different. In what sense is the pooled estimate likely to be the 'best' of the three estimates?

4.3.4 Two-sample *t*-tests

Suppose that in advance of the experiment considered in section 4.3.3, the statistician thinks that treatment A is more effective than B, which would be shown by the marker pellets taking less time to pass through the alimentary canal. The significance test is then

$H_0 : \mu_A = \mu_B$
$H_1 : \mu_A < \mu_B$

Level of significance: 5%

The samples are such that: $\bar{a} = 68.4$; $s_A{}^2 = 253.31$

$$\bar{b} = 83.42;\quad s_B{}^2 = 285.08$$

If $A \sim N(\mu_A, \sigma^2)$, then $\bar{A} \sim N\left(\mu_A, \frac{\sigma^2}{15}\right)$. Similarly, $\bar{B} \sim N\left(\mu_B, \frac{\sigma^2}{12}\right)$ and so $\bar{A} - \bar{B} \sim N\left(\mu_A - \mu_B, \left(\frac{1}{15} + \frac{1}{12}\right)\sigma^2\right)$.

The test statistic $\dfrac{\bar{a} - \bar{b}}{\sigma\sqrt{\left(\frac{1}{15} + \frac{1}{12}\right)}}$ has a Standard Normal distribution. However, since σ is unknown it must be replaced by the sample estimate, s. Then, as in section 4.2,

$$\frac{\bar{a} - \bar{b}}{s\sqrt{\left(\frac{1}{15} + \frac{1}{12}\right)}}$$

has a *t*-distribution. It can be proved that the number of degrees of freedom is $(15 - 1) + (12 - 1) = 25$.

 .3B

Complete the significance test for the two treatments. Carefully state your conclusion.

Suppose two small samples of sizes n_1 and n_2 have mean values $\bar{x}_1$ and $\bar{x}_2$. If it is reasonable to assume that the two populations are Normal and have the same variance, then an appropriate statistic to test for the equality of the means of the two populations is

$$t = \frac{\bar{x}_1 - \bar{x}_2}{s\sqrt{\left(\dfrac{1}{n_1} + \dfrac{1}{n_2}\right)}}$$

where s^2 is the pooled sample variance and t has a *t*-distribution with $n_1 + n_2 - 2$ degrees of freedom.

Example 4

A biologist wishes to find out if the habitat of a particular small animal affects its weight. Traps are set by the side of a lake and near the top of a hill. The biologist suspects that those animals by the lakeside will weigh more. The weights of the animals, in grams, are as follows.

| Lakeside | 25.7 | 27.3 | 28.5 | 29.6 | 30.2 | 30.4 | 31.6 |
| Hilltop | 24.2 | 24.6 | 27.3 | 28.2 | 28.9 | | |

Does the habitat affect the weights of the animals? Use the data to test the biologist's suspicion.

Solution

Assume the lakeside weights have a distribution $X \sim N(\mu_X, \sigma^2)$.

Assume the hilltop weights have a distribution $Y \sim N(\mu_Y, \sigma^2)$.

$H_0 : \mu_X = \mu_Y$
$H_1 : \mu_X > \mu_Y$

The biologist carries out a one-tail test at the 5% level.

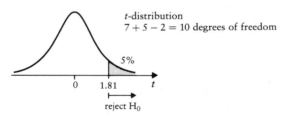

Lakeside: $\bar{x} = 29.04$; $s_X^2 = 3.51$; $n_X = 7$

Hilltop: $\bar{y} = 26.64$; $s_Y^2 = 3.62$; $n_Y = 5$

The pooled variance estimate of σ^2 is

$$\frac{7 \times 3.51 + 5 \times 3.62}{7 + 5 - 2} \approx 4.267$$

Then $t = \dfrac{29.04 - 26.64}{\sqrt{4.267}\sqrt{\left(\frac{1}{7} + \frac{1}{5}\right)}}$

$$\approx 1.98$$

As $1.98 > 1.81$, H_0 is rejected in favour of H_1. There is significant evidence that the lakeside animals are heavier.

4.3 Exercise 3

1 In an experiment to determine the relative effectiveness of two diet plans, six
   people were assigned to plan A and eight to plan B. The weight losses (in
   kilograms) were as shown.

   Plan A: $\quad \bar{x}_A = 3.3; \quad s_A{}^2 = 1.2; \quad n_A = 6$

   Plan B: $\quad \bar{x}_B = 4.1; \quad s_B{}^2 = 1.7; \quad n_B = 8$

   (a) Assuming that the population variances are equal, find the pooled estimate
       for this common variance.

   (b) Conduct a two-tail t-test to see if there is a significant difference in the
       mean weight losses for the two diets.

2 During a particular fishing holiday, trout caught in two rivers, the Arn and the
   Bate, had the following lengths in centimetres.

Arn	27.5	26.1	26.4	27.1		
Bate	25.6	24.3	24.9	25.7	26.0	26.8

   (a) Assuming that both populations of trout have the same variance, find a
       pooled estimate of this variance.

   (b) Is there significant evidence that trout from the Arn have a greater average
       length than those from the Bate?

3 A metallurgist wishes to determine if there is a significant difference in the
   amount of an impurity in silver purified by two different processes. For ten
   samples, she obtained the following percentages of impurity.

Process 1	3.4	2.7	2.5	3.8		
Process 2	3.7	3.5	4.0	3.4	3.4	3.0

   What should she conclude?

4 The times taken (in minutes) for two children to complete an arcade game are
   as shown.

Alex	2.10	2.22	2.15	2.10	2.17		
Jackie	2.11	2.03	2.08	2.04	2.08	2.14	2.11

   How significant is the evidence that the two differ in ability at the game?

NB In these questions, samples sizes have been kept small to illustrate the
    techniques simply; in practice, larger samples would be desirable.

After working through section 4.3 you should:

1 be able to apply a significance test of the hypothesis that the means of two populations are equal, against any one of the three possible alternative hypotheses;

2 know that a test using a Normally distributed statistic can be made if:

- the samples are independent,
- the parent populations are Normally distributed,
- the variance of the parent populations are known,

and understand why the latter two conditions may be waived in the case of large samples;

3 know that for smaller samples a test using a t-distribution can be made if:

- the samples are independent,
- the parent populations are Normally distributed,
- the parent populations have the same (unknown) variance;

4 be able to find confidence intervals for the difference between two means.

Statistics in action

.4 Non-parametric tests

4.4.1 The sign test

Hypotheses have so far been tested either against a binomial distribution or against a Normal distribution. However, it is not always reasonable to assume that a distribution is Normal. For example, in a traffic survey where the lengths of time between cars passing a certain point on a main road are recorded, it is found that the times vary from 0.1 to 15.8 seconds, with 'most' being between 2 and 6 seconds.

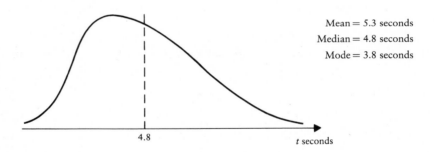

Mean = 5.3 seconds
Median = 4.8 seconds
Mode = 3.8 seconds

The researcher wants to carry out a quick check to see if the average time between cars is the same on a different day of the week. She chooses the median as her measure of average, measures a random sample of 36 time gaps between cars and marks a '+' if a gap is greater than 4.8 seconds and a '−' if it is less. Her results are:

$$+ - + - + - + + - + - - + + - + + -$$
$$- + + - + - + + + - + + - + + - + +$$

Her hypotheses are

H_0 : median = 4.8
H_1 : median ≠ 4.8

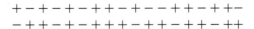

use
a two-tail test

Level of significance: 5%

.4A

1 If r is the number of plus signs, why is it reasonable for her to assume that $R \sim B(36, \frac{1}{2})$?

2 Does her sample provide significant evidence in support of the alternative hypothesis?

3 In theory, why is there zero probability that a gap is precisely equal to the median value?

4 In practice, why are you likely to find that some data items are equal to the median?

The type of test used by the researcher is called the **sign test**. The major advantage of the sign test is that no assumptions need to be made regarding the 'shape' of the population distribution. The test is said to be **non-parametric**.

- The sign test can be used when the null hypothesis is that a population *median* has a particular value.

- Measurements are recorded as being *above* the median (+) or as being *below* the median (−).

- The plus and minus signs are assumed to occur with equal probability so that the number of pluses, R, has distribution $B(n, \frac{1}{2})$.

- For a Normal distribution (or any symmetrical distribution), the mean and median are equal. The sign test can therefore be used to test a null hypothesis about the mean of a Normal distribution without the need for any assumption about the variance.

- If a sample value is *equal* to the assumed median, then that value is ignored and the sample size is reduced.

Example 1
The times that secretaries stay at one branch of a firm have been found to have a median value of 42 months. From another branch, a sample of times (in months) are

$$36, \quad 15, \quad 42, \quad 60, \quad 10, \quad 20, \quad 39, \quad 40, \quad 14$$

Is this significant evidence that the median time at the second firm is less than 42 months?

Solution

H_0 : median $= 42$

H_1 : median < 42

Level of significance: 5%

The signs are $- - 0 + - - - -$

Then, discarding the zero, $R \sim B(8, \frac{1}{2})$ with $r = 1$,

$$P(R \leq 1) = (\tfrac{1}{2})^8 + 8(\tfrac{1}{2})^8 \approx 0.035$$

H_0 is rejected at the 5% level. There is significant evidence that the length of time secretaries stay at the second branch is shorter.

4.4 Exercise 1

1

> **BRITAIN'S** 8 million-plus children aged five to sixteen get an average £1.82 a week, an 8 per cent increase on last year with inflation now at 4.5 per cent. Scottish children get £2.07 a week, while those in London and the South average about £1.79.

Guardian, 3 March 1992; Source: Gallup

A sample of 20 children from a village in Suffolk showed that their weekly pocket money was

60p, £1.20, £3, £2.40, £1, £1, £4.20, £3.50, £2, 70p, £1.50, £2.30, £3.50, £5, £6.50, £1.60, £2.80, £2, £2.50, 50p

Does the sample reveal a significant difference from what was found by the Gallup poll? State your null and alternative hypotheses together with any assumptions you make.

2 The average (median) life of the African locust is 28 days in the wild. A school breeds 14 locusts as part of a biology course and notes how long each survives in captivity. The results are

12, 17, 22, 22, 23, 23, 23, 24, 25, 25, 28, 30, 37, 38 (days)

What conclusions (if any) can be drawn from these results?

3 A maker claims that a particular computer game improves hand–eye co-ordination. To test this, a student selects ten fellow students at random, all of whom say they do not usually play the game.

She asks them to perform a standard hand–eye co-ordination task and gives each a score according to how well they perform. They then spend every lunch hour for a week playing the computer game. The following week they are tested again for co-ordination to see if they have improved.

The results are

Student	A	B	C	D	E	F	G	H	I	J
First score	56	87	32	80	76	56	49	69	61	51
Second score	58	87	52	85	71	60	72	71	70	57
Improvement	+2	0	+20	+5	−5	+4	+23	+2	+9	+6

Write down null and alternative hypotheses and use the sign test to decide if there is significant evidence to support the maker's claim.

4.4.2 The Wilcoxon signed-rank test

For each of the hypothesis tests considered earlier, it is necessary either to assume that the population distribution is known or that the sample size is sufficiently large that the Central Limit Theorem can be applied. In the two-sample t-test, for example, you must assume that both parent populations are Normal and that they have the same variance.

The sign test considered in section 4.4.1 is an example of a non-parametric test. It can be applied irrespective of the 'shape' of the population distribution.

A non-parametric test is one which does *not* assume any knowledge of the distribution involved. Many such tests concentrate on the median of an unknown distribution.

The sign test ignores the magnitudes of the differences from the median. It is a weak test, but it does provide some objective evidence to support fairly clear conclusions. In 1945, Frank Wilcoxon refined the test for roughly symmetrical distributions by taking these magnitudes into account. This test is known as the **Wilcoxon signed-rank test** or the **T test**. As an example of this procedure, consider the data on the locusts bred in captivity.

Lifetime (days): 12, 17, 22, 22, 23, 23, 23, 24, 25, 28, 30, 31, 37, 38

Consider, at the 5% level, the hypotheses

H_0 : median = 28

H_1 : median ≠ 28

The signed differences from the median, in ascending order of magnitude (ignoring sign), are as shown. The sample value equal to the median has been ignored.

2, 3, −3, −4, −5, −5, −5, −6, −6, 9, 10, −11, −16

These 13 differences are then assigned ranks from 1 to 13. When two or more sample values have equal magnitude they are given the average of the relevant ranks. In the case of the locusts the ranks are as shown.

Difference	2	3	−3	−4	−5	−5	−5	−6	−6	9	10	−11	−16
Rank	1	2.5	2.5	4	6	6	6	8.5	8.5	10	11	12	13

The sum of the ranks corresponding to positive differences is then

$$1 + 2.5 + 10 + 11 = 24.5$$

The sum of the ranks corresponding to negative differences is

$$2.5 + 4 + 6 + 6 + 6 + 8.5 + 8.5 + 12 + 13 = 66.5$$

The smaller of the two sums is called T. In this case, $T = 24.5$.

Wilcoxon showed how to calculate the probabilities of each value of T. Critical values of T for various sample sizes and significance levels are given in a table at the back of this book on page 400.

.4B

1 Explain how you would expect the size of T to provide evidence for or against the null hypothesis.

2 Complete the hypothesis test for the locusts.

The Wilcoxon signed-rank test can be used to test for a median of a roughly symmetrical distribution.

1 Calculate the signed differences from the median.

2 Discard any zero value and, ignoring sign, rank the remaining differences in order of magnitude. Assign the average rank to any values which are equal in magnitude.

3 Calculate T, the smaller of the sums of 'positive' ranks or 'negative' ranks.

4 Compare your value of T with that given in a table of critical values of T for various sample sizes. Reject H_0 if T is *smaller* than the appropriate critical value.

4.4 Exercise 2

1 The ages (in years) of first offenders for violent crime is believed to have a median of 24. A prison officer finds that the ages for 12 recently committed first offenders are

    23,   27,   28,   20,   26,   26,   24,   17,   38,   24,   33,   39

Do these data provide significant evidence that the median is greater than 24?

2 For students at a sixth-form college, the median mark on a standardised aptitude test is expected to be approximately 60. A teacher has a group of seven new students whose marks are

    48,   70,   18,   20,   53,   47,   76

Do these scores provide significant evidence that the new entry has a lower median score than 60?

3 For ten days, an executive timed her journey to and from work. On eight days, travelling to work took longer than returning home by 8, 3, 2, 4, 6, 5, 6 and 7 minutes. On the remaining two days the journey to work was shorter by 1 and 4 minutes. Is there significant evidence for a difference in journey times to and from work?

After working through section 4.4 you should:

1 know what is meant by a **non-parametric test**;

2 appreciate why it is sometimes necessary to apply a non-parametric test;

3 be able to test a population median by using either the **sign test** or the **Wilcoxon signed-rank test**.

Statistics in action

.5 Correlation and regression

4.5.1 Bivariate distributions

Up to now you have concentrated on populations of a single variable, such as height or mass. Sometimes it is interesting to study the relationships between a pair of variables, in which case a **bivariate distribution** is involved. For example, each adult in the country has a height X cm and a mass of Y kg; the ordered pair (X, Y) is said to have a bivariate distribution.

Example 1

Display graphically the following data, of mass and foot area, recorded for a sample of 20 South American snails of the species *Biomphalaria glabrata*.

Mass (g), X	0.64	0.21	0.85	0.53	0.18	0.06	0.20	0.07	0.01	0.05
Foot area (mm²), Y	29	16	35	25	20	7	13	7	3	10

Mass (g), X	0.02	0.01	0.21	0.81	0.53	0.18	0.06	0.20	0.07	0.01
Foot area (mm²), Y	4	1	16	35	25	20	7	13	7	1

Solution

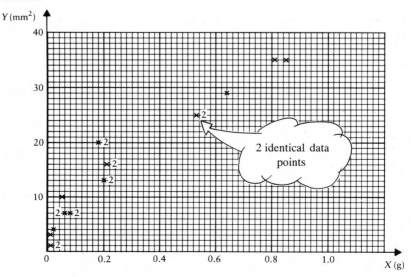

2 identical data points

The graph of a bivariate distribution such as the one in example 1 is called a **scatter plot**.

The points in the scatter plot lie close to a straight line; there is an approximate linear relationship between the variables. In such a case the variables are said to be **positively correlated**.

 .5A

Other possibilities are illustrated by these scatter plots.

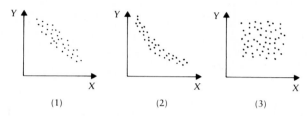

How would you describe the relationship between X and Y in these three cases?

The object of this section is to determine when it is reasonable to use a linear approximation for the relationship between two variables and, when it is, to find the equation of the **line of best fit**. Using the methods developed you will be able to describe precisely the relation between the variables in a given sample from a bivariate distribution. When the relation may be taken as linear you will be able to make predictions based on the linear relationship.

Ideally, you should seek an objective numerical measure for the degree of correlation between two variables; this idea is explored below.

 .5B

1 Draw scatter plots for each of the samples P, Q and R. By inspection of the graphs, comment on the correlation between X and Y in each case.

Sample P

X	17	19	20	22	25	26	28	29	31	33	33	35
Y	8.4	8.6	7.8	7.2	7.1	6.1	6.5	5.8	5.4	4.8	4.2	4.8

Sample Q

X	13	14	17	18	18	18	21	22	22	23	26	26
Y	7.7	6.1	9.2	7.9	10.4	11.3	11.7	13.0	14.9	13.9	14.8	15.8

Sample R

X	24	28	31	33	34	35	35	38	41	43	48	49
Y	3.5	4.5	2.8	2.9	3.4	2.0	5.0	3.8	4.4	2.9	4.3	3.5

The object of this activity is to investigate a measure for correlation. The method you will use considers the distribution of the points of a scatter plot with respect to new axes through the central point $(\bar{x}, \bar{y})$.

The diagram shows the scatter plot for a sample of positively correlated variables. Question 2 refers to this diagram.

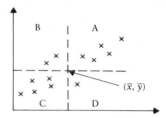

2 (a) In which of the quadrants A, B, C, D do most of the points lie?

(b) If a point (x, y) is in quadrant A, what is the sign of:

(i) $x - \bar{x}$ (the 'moment about the new y-axis'),

(ii) $y - \bar{y}$ (the 'moment about the new x-axis'),

(iii) $(x - \bar{x})(y - \bar{y})$ (the 'product moment')?

Now answer the same questions (i), (ii) and (iii) when (x, y) lies in quadrants B, C, D respectively.

(c) Explain why $\sum_i (x_i - \bar{x})(y_i - \bar{y})$ is a measure of correlation.

3 For each of the samples P, Q and R, find $\bar{x}$, $\bar{y}$ and, on the scatter plot, draw axes parallel to the original axes through the point $(\bar{x}, \bar{y})$.

4 In each of the three cases calculate $\sum_i (x_i - \bar{x})(y_i - \bar{y})$ and explain the significance of the three results.

The statistic often used in this situation is the **covariance**, defined as follows.

If a sample $\{(x_1, y_1), (x_2, y_2), \ldots, (x_n, y_n)\}$ taken from the bivariate distribution (X, Y) has sample mean $(\bar{x}, \bar{y})$, then

$$\text{Cov}(X, Y) = \frac{1}{n} \sum_{1}^{n} (x_i - \bar{x})(y_i - \bar{y})$$

is called the **sample covariance** between X and Y.

5 Why do you think the factor $\dfrac{1}{n}$ is introduced?

4.5.2 The product moment correlation coefficient

A sample covariance close to zero indicates that there is no correlation between the variables. A 'large' positive covariance indicates a positive correlation and a 'large' negative covariance a negative correlation. (How large depends on the sizes of the variables and their variances.)

Example 2
Heights X in a bivariate distribution (X, Y) are at present recorded in metres. What would be the effect on a sample covariance if they were recorded in centimetres?

Solution
Any height in metres, X_i, would be replaced in the calculation by a height in centimetres, $100X_i$. The covariance would change from

$$\frac{1}{n} \sum (x_i - \bar{x})(y_i - \bar{y}) \quad \text{to} \quad \frac{1}{n} \sum (100x_i - 100\bar{x})(y_i - \bar{y})$$

The latter expression may be written as $\dfrac{100}{n} \sum (x_i - \bar{x})(y_i - \bar{y})$, showing that the sample covariance has increased by a factor of 100.

 .5c

1 What happens to $\text{Cov}(X, Y)$ if all the values of X are multiplied by 5 and all the values of Y multiplied by 4?

As you might expect, a subjective assessment of 'largeness' is not acceptable. Sample covariances must be standardised to give an objective statistical measure. This is achieved by dividing the covariance by the product of the sample standard deviations, s_X and s_Y. The new measure of correlation is called **Pearson's product moment coefficient** and is denoted by r.

2 What happens to r if all the values of X are multiplied by 5 and all the values of Y multiplied by 4?

The standard measure of correlation is called Pearson's product moment correlation coefficient and is denoted by r.

It is found by dividing the sample covariance by the product of the sample standard deviations of X and Y, i.e.

$$r = \frac{\text{Cov}(X, Y)}{s_X s_Y}$$

In calculating r it is useful to note that

$$\text{Cov}(x, y) = \frac{1}{n} \sum (x_i - \bar{x})(y_i - \bar{y})$$

$$\sum \bar{x}\,\bar{y} = \bar{x}\,\bar{y} + \bar{x}\,\bar{y} + \dots = n\bar{x}\,\bar{y}$$

$$= \frac{1}{n} \left(\sum x_i y_i - \bar{y} \sum x_i - \bar{x} \sum y_i + n\bar{x}\bar{y} \right)$$

$$= \frac{1}{n} \left(\sum x_i y_i - n\bar{x}\bar{y} - n\bar{x}\bar{y} + n\bar{x}\bar{y} \right)$$

$$= \frac{1}{n} \left(\sum x_i y_i - n\bar{x}\bar{y} \right)$$

since $\sum y_i = n\bar{y}$

Hence,

$$r = \frac{\text{Cov}(X, Y)}{s_X s_Y} = \frac{\frac{1}{n} \left(\sum x_i y_i - n\bar{x}\bar{y} \right)}{\sqrt{\left[\frac{1}{n} \left(\sum x_i^2 - n\bar{x}^2 \right) \frac{1}{n} \left(\sum y_i^2 - n\bar{y}^2 \right) \right]}}$$

$$= \frac{\sum x_i y_i - n\bar{x}\bar{y}}{\sqrt{\left[\left(\sum x_i^2 - n\bar{x}^2 \right) \left(\sum y_i^2 - n\bar{y}^2 \right) \right]}}$$

Example 3

Find the Pearson correlation coefficient for the bivariate distribution in example 1.

Mass (g), X	0.64	0.21	0.85	0.53	0.18	0.06	0.20	0.07	0.01	0.05
Foot area (mm²), Y	29	16	35	25	20	7	13	7	3	10

Mass (g), X	0.02	0.01	0.21	0.81	0.53	0.18	0.06	0.20	0.07	0.01
Foot area (mm²), Y	4	1	16	35	25	20	7	13	7	1

Solution

From the data,

$$\sum x_i y_i = 124.73, \qquad \sum x_i^2 = 2.6032, \qquad \sum y_i^2 = 6514$$

$$\bar{x} = 0.245, \qquad \bar{y} = 14.7, \qquad n = 20$$

Hence,

$$r = \frac{124.73 - 20 \times 0.245 \times 14.7}{\sqrt{[(2.6032 - 20 \times 0.245^2)(6514 - 20 \times 14.7^2)]}}$$

$$= \frac{52.7}{\sqrt{(1.4027 \times 2192.2)}} = 0.95$$

It may be proved algebraically that r always lies between -1 and $+1$. One method of demonstrating this result is given in question 6E of exercise 1. Statements about meanings of covariances including vague ideas of 'largeness' can now be replaced by more precise expressions in terms of the standardised statistic.

If $r \approx 1$, there is strong positive correlation.

If $r \approx -1$, there is strong negative correlation.

If $r \approx 0$, X and Y are uncorrelated.

When $r \approx 1$ you will expect points (x, y) to lie close to a line with positive gradient; when $r \approx -1$ the same applies except that the gradient is negative. Thus, in example 1, the fact that the points lie very close to a straight line is signified by the closeness of r (which is 0.95) to 1.

Correlation coefficients are eagerly calculated by researchers in many fields ranging from social science to agriculture. Generally, they are attempting to prove that a change in one thing leads to a change in another – for example, that increasing unemployment has caused an increase in crime.

In fact, a result $r \approx 1$ or $r \approx -1$ may be interpreted in any one of three ways. If, for example, Y increases as X increases,

- the increase in X may have caused the increase in Y, or vice versa;
- the two increases may have a common cause; or
- the increases may be causally unrelated.

Since these three categories exhaust all the possibilities it is reasonable to conclude that, on its own, a result $r \approx 1$ or $r \approx -1$ gives no information about **causation**.

To be fair to scientific researchers, they are well aware of this and would not attempt to base conclusions just on the value of a correlation coefficient.

 .5D

1 In which of the three categories would you place the connection between weight and height?

2 In the 1980s there was a steady increase in the student population of Sheffield. In the same town, there was also a steady increase in cases of thefts of cars. Into which of the categories above would you place this example?

4.5 **Exercise 1**

1 The sea and air temperatures on a Florida beach were recorded at midday each Monday for 10 weeks. The data were as follows.

Sea X (°C)	19	22	18	19	21	22	18	18	17	16
Air Y (°C)	29	34	27	29	33	35	28	27	26	25

(a) Plot these data on a scatter plot.

(b) Calculate r and comment on the result.

2 Plot the following sets of data on a scatter plot, marking set 1 with crosses and set 2 with points.

Set 1

X	1	4	5	7
Y	11	5	3	−1

Set 2

X	0	2	5	6
Y	20	12	0	−4

Calculate r for each set and comment on the values.

3 An investigation is carried out to see if there is a positive correlation between mathematical ability and verbal reasoning ability. The following data show (maths score, verbal reasoning score) for 14 twelve-year-olds.

$$(15, 18), \quad (19, 18), \quad (23, 19), \quad (19, 22), \quad (18, 21), \quad (26, 22), \quad (22, 25),$$
$$(22, 17), \quad (23, 17), \quad (32, 26), \quad (28, 29), \quad (29, 23), \quad (28, 24), \quad (27, 23)$$

(a) Calculate r.

(b) Do you think the two scores are positively correlated?

4 The period, T seconds, was recorded for seven pendulums of different lengths, l cm, with the following results.

l (cm)	10	20	30	40	50	60	70
T (s)	0.63	0.90	1.10	1.27	1.42	1.56	1.68

(a) Calculate r for the data.

(b) Draw a scatter plot.

(c) Do you think the relationship between l and T is linear?

5 Draw a scatter plot of the four points

$$(1, 1), \quad (1, 3), \quad (3, 1), \quad (3, 3)$$

Calculate r and explain its value.

6E (a) Explain why, for real numbers a and b,

$$a^2 + b^2 \geq 2ab$$

(b) Show (in the same way) that if the numbers x_i and y_i are real,

(i) $(x_1^2 + x_2^2)(y_1^2 + y_2^2) \geq (x_1 y_1 + x_2 y_2)^2$

(ii) $(x_1^2 + x_2^2 + x_3^2)(y_1^2 + y_2^2 + y_3^2) \geq (x_1 y_1 + x_2 y_2 + x_3 y_3)^2$

(c) Generalise the results in part (b) and hence show that

$$[\text{Cov}\,(X, Y)]^2 \leq s_X^2 s_Y^2$$

and so explain why $-1 \leq r \leq 1$.

4.5.3 A line of best fit

Once you have established the likelihood of a linear relationship between two variables you may need to find the equation of the line involved.

The technique used to determine mathematically the equation of a line of best fit is called **regression**. Often, in collecting data from a bivariate distribution, the x-data are thought of as being under the control of the experimenter and hence independently chosen. On the other hand, the y-values will then depend on these x-values. Because y is then the dependent variable you will usually want to estimate values of y for given values of x. Hence, the equation you usually require is found by 'regressing Y on X', taking the x-values as in the data and working out the difference between theoretical and observed values of y.

Suppose that you have evidence of a linear relationship $y = a + bx$.

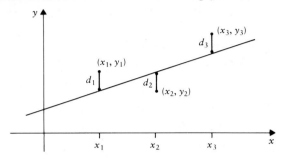

If the points (x_i, y_i) were exactly on the line you would expect

$$y_1 = a + bx_1, \quad y_2 = a + bx_2, \ldots$$

The difference between a value of y in the data set and its expected value is the deviation

$$d_i = y_i - (a + bx_i), \quad i = 1, 2, \ldots, n$$

The technique involves choosing a and b in such a way as to minimise $\sum_{1}^{n} d_i^2$.

It is not helpful to minimise $\sum d_i$, as the positive and negative values of d would tend to cancel each other out.

The technique of minimising $\sum d_i^2$ is called **least squares regression**.

The line of best fit for the regression of Y on X is mathematically defined as the line $y = a + bx$ for which $\sum_{1}^{n} (y_i - (a + bx_i))^2$ is minimum. From this definition, the following result can be derived. (A derivation is provided as an appendix on page 394.)

The equation of the line of best fit for the regression of Y on X is $y = \hat{a} + \hat{b}x$ where

$$\hat{b} = \frac{\text{Cov}(X, Y)}{\text{Var}(X)} \quad \text{and} \quad \hat{a} = \bar{y} - \hat{b}\bar{x}$$

This equation enables you to calculate the expected value of y for a given value of x.

The expressions $\hat{a}$ and $\hat{b}$ are read as 'a hat' and 'b hat'.

Example 4

(a) For the distribution of example 1, find the equation of the line of best fit for the regression of Y on X.

Mass (g), X	0.64	0.21	0.85	0.53	0.18	0.06	0.20	0.07	0.01	0.05
Foot area (mm²), Y	29	16	35	25	20	7	13	7	3	10

Mass (g), X	0.02	0.01	0.21	0.81	0.53	0.18	0.06	0.20	0.07	0.01
Foot area (mm²), Y	4	1	16	35	25	20	7	13	7	1

(b) Hence predict the foot area of a snail of mass 0.40 g.

Solution

(a) In example 3, it was found that

$$\sum x_i y_i = 124.73, \quad \sum x_i^2 = 2.6032,$$

$$\bar{x} = 0.245, \quad \bar{y} = 14.7, \quad n = 20, \quad r = 0.95$$

Hence,

$$\hat{b} = \frac{124.73 - 20 \times 0.245 \times 14.7}{2.6032 - 20 \times (0.245)^2} = \frac{52.7}{1.40} = 37.6$$

$$\hat{a} = 14.7 - 37.6 \times 0.245 = 5.50$$

The equation of the line of best fit is

$$y = 5.50 + 37.6x$$

(b) When $x = 0.40$ the expected value of y is

$$5.50 + 37.6 \times 0.40 = 20.5$$

You would expect the foot area to be about 20 mm².

Some calculators enable you to find $\hat{a}$ and $\hat{b}$ with very little effort. You should find how to use your calculator for least squares regression lines and check the solution of example 4.

4.5 Exercise 2

1 It is thought that reaction time correlates strongly with heart rate. Eleven surgeons take varying amounts of a drug affecting the heart rate to test this conjecture. The resulting data were as follows.

Heart rate x (beats/min)	134	133	132	123	118	110	98	90	84	80	80
Reaction time y (ms)	438	455	467	505	531	557	541	562	591	603	617

(a) Is there a strong correlation between Y and X?

(b) Show the data on a scatter plot.

(c) Find the equation of the Y on X least squares regression line.

(d) Draw the line on your scatter plot.

(e) Predict the reaction time of a surgeon whose heart rate is 95 beats/min.

(f) You are asked to predict the reaction time of a surgeon whose heart rate is 60 beats/min. Comment on this request.

2 A tomato grower uses different amounts of fertiliser in each of twelve experimental beds, which are otherwise identical. The following data result.

Amount of fertiliser x (g)	10	12	14	16	18	20	22	24	26	28	30	32
Yield of tomatoes y (kg)	2	2	2	3	4	3	4	3	5	6	7	9

(a) Calculate the product moment correlation coefficient r.

(b) Find the equation of the regression line $y = \hat{a} + \hat{b}x$.

(c) Is it appropriate to use the line to model the data?

4.5.4 Regressing X on Y

As noted earlier, it is usual for x to be the independent variable and y the dependent variable. Sometimes, though, there is no clearly independent variable and you may want to use regression to calculate expected values of x for given values of y. To find the equation of the line of best fit for regression of X on Y you must minimise the sum of squares of differences between each x-value and its expected value if $x = c + dy$.

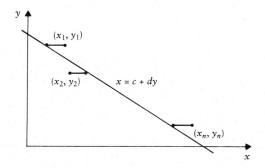

By symmetry with the result for regression of Y on X, the required equation is $x = \hat{c} + \hat{d}y$, where

$$\hat{d} = \frac{\text{Cov}(X, Y)}{\text{Var}(Y)} \quad \text{and} \quad \hat{c} = \bar{x} - \hat{d}\bar{y}$$

4.5 Exercise 3

1 Use the data of example 1 to regress the mass of a snail (x g) on its foot area (y mm^2).

Mass (g), X	0.64	0.21	0.85	0.53	0.18	0.06	0.20	0.07	0.01	0.05
Foot area (mm^2), Y	29	16	35	25	20	7	13	7	3	10

Mass (g), X	0.02	0.01	0.21	0.81	0.53	0.18	0.06	0.20	0.07	0.01
Foot area (mm^2), Y	4	1	16	35	25	20	7	13	7	1

Draw a scatter plot of the data and show this regression line and also the line $y = \hat{a} + \hat{b}x$ found in the solution to example 4. Write down the gradients of the two lines.

4.5.5 Spearman's rank correlation coefficient

In certain investigations a rank is more appropriate than a measure. For example, if you were testing brands of cola you might feel that you could put them in order of taste preference but would not care to allocate marks. This kind of investigation is common in psychology and it was a psychologist, Charles Spearman (1863–1945), who first developed a coefficient of correlation between rankings. The derivation of this coefficient is covered on the next tasksheet.

▶ 4.5 **Tasksheet E1 – Derivation of Spearman's rank correlation coefficient (page 316)**

Suppose that n candidates are ranked in two different ways. If d_i is the difference in the rankings for the ith candidate, then **Spearman's rank correlation coefficient** is

$$r_s = 1 - \frac{6 \sum d_i^2}{n(n^2 - 1)}$$

As with the product moment coefficient, $-1 \le r_s \le 1$.
$r_s \approx 1$ when the rankings are in close agreement.
$r_s \approx -1$ when one ranking is (roughly) the reverse of the other.

Example 5

In a competition, two judges ranked ten pianists as follows.

Competitor	1	2	3	4	5	6	7	8	9	10
Ranks { judge A	10	4	5	2	1	8	9	6	7	3
judge B	9	1	5	3	2	7	10	4	8	6
Difference in ranks	1	3	0	−1	−1	1	−1	2	−1	−3

How well do the two judges agree?

Solution

$$r_s = 1 - \frac{6 \times 28}{10 \times 99} = 0.83$$

The high positive value of r_s implies close agreement between the judges.

Tests do exist to assess the *significance* of correlation coefficients, although they are beyond the scope of this book. However, you should be able to appreciate that the interpretation of a coefficient depends on the number of data points.

4.5 Exercise 4

1 At a flower show, nine roses are ranked for quality and size of bloom, as follows.

Rose	1	2	3	4	5	6	7	8	9
Rank { quality	8	3	1	9	4	2	7	5	6
size	3	5	6	7	8	4	9	1	2

Calculate the value of r_s. Are the rankings in general agreement?

2 In example 5, take the rankings of judges A and B as being marks x and y, respectively. Calculate the product moment coefficient r for the two sets of marks and compare it with the rank coefficient r_s.

3 Twelve students took a test. After a refresher course they took a further test. The results were as follows.

Student	1	2	3	4	5	6	7	8	9	10	11	12
First mark, x	30	75	58	34	52	70	50	81	62	35	57	60
Second mark, y	22	59	78	50	41	71	32	60	49	40	55	61

(a) Calculate the product moment correlation coefficient r.

(b) Rank the marks x and the marks y.

(c) Calculate the rank correlation coefficient r_s.

(d) Comment on your answers to (a) and (c).

After working through section 4.5 you should be able to

1 explain the term **bivariate distribution**;

2 calculate **Pearson's product moment correlation coefficient** r and interpret its value;

3 understand the difference between correlation and causation;

4 fit **least squares regression lines** and use them for prediction;

5 calculate **Spearman's rank correlation coefficient** r_s and interpret its value.

Statistics in action

Miscellaneous exercise 4

1 A drug manufacturer claims that only 5% of patients experience any side-effects when given a new drug. In clinical trials, 250 patients were given the drug and 21 of them reported side-effects. Would you describe these results as significant at the 1% level?

2 In a manufacturing process, a machine produces rods which must have a diameter, x, between 7.9 mm and 8.1 mm.

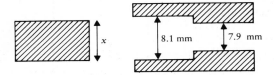

The rods are tested using the gauge shown in the diagram. Rods outside the required limits are rejected. At the end of a day's production the manufacturer finds that 7% of the rods are rejected, 6.6% being too large and 0.4% being too small.

(a) If you can assume $X \sim N(\mu, \sigma^2)$, estimate μ and σ from the information given.

(b) If the machine is adjusted so that the mean is 8.0 mm, calculate the proportion of rejected rods. (Assume the variance is unchanged.)

(c) A random sample of 10 rods is taken after the machine has been adjusted. The sample mean is 8.02 mm. Does the machine need readjusting?

3 On the hypothesis that 70% of people over the age of 21 drive a car, what is the probability that if you approach 100 such people, chosen at random, you will find that 65 or fewer of them can actually do so? Does this sample result cast doubt on the hypothesis?

4 A geographer is investigating the theory that, in the UK, at least 25% of people over the age of 40 have their home in the town in which they were born. What conclusion do you draw if only 40 out of a sample of 200 do so?

5 In a population of about 8000, you expect about 75% to be non-smokers. You want to be able to rule out the hypothesis 'one third or more smoke' at the 1% significance level. What size of sample should you take?

6 A particular mental ability test is constructed to have a mean of 100 and a standard deviation of 15. A medical student wishes to test whether sufferers from a disease he is investigating differ from the general public on their performance on this test. He chooses a random sample of 10 patients and their scores are

   120, 130, 98, 105, 124, 90, 120, 90, 103, 105

   Is the sample mean significantly different from the population mean?

7 A machine is producing components to a nominal dimension of 1.500 cm. The dimensions of components in a random sample of eight are found to be 1.502, 1.501, 1.504, 1.498, 1.503, 1.499, 1.505, 1.504. Give 95% confidence limits for the mean component dimension. Is the result consistent with the nominal dimension?

8 Past experience has shown that a certain machine, which can cut hacksaw blades to any required length, produces blades whose lengths are Normally distributed with variance 0.003 cm^2. An order for hacksaw blades of length 18 cm is received, and the first four blades produced when the machine is set to 18 cm have lengths 17.98, 17.82, 17.91 and 18.09 cm. Test whether the machine setting is giving significantly low values.

9 The annual rainfall in a town over the five-year period 1991–5, measured in millimetres, was

Year	1991	1992	1993	1994	1995
Rainfall	736	752	793	555	746

Use these data to give a 95% confidence interval for the mean annual rainfall. It is known that, in fact, the mean annual rainfall over the 100-year period 1895–1994 was 832 mm. Do the figures suggest that 1991–5 was a particularly dry period?

10 An experiment was performed to compare two methods of analysing the percentage impurity in a chemical. Tests were made on twelve different samples of the chemical, each sample being analysed by both methods. The results of the experiment were

Sample number	1	2	3	4	5	6	7	8	9	10	11	12
% impurity { method A	2.12	2.56	2.43	2.51	2.42	2.44	2.45	2.41	2.41	2.46	2.43	2.38
method B	2.26	2.65	2.46	2.44	2.55	2.56	2.45	2.36	2.50	2.52	2.48	2.42

Test the hypothesis that on average the two methods of analysis are equivalent.

11 Ten equal strips of metal were each divided into two, and one member of each pair was coated with a special lacquer intended to prevent corrosion. The specimens were left exposed to urban air for two years, and then the percentage change in weight was noted for each of the twenty pieces. Analyse the data.

Strip number	1	2	3	4	5	6	7	8	9	10
Treated	5.0	3.9	3.4	4.8	6.3	6.1	5.2	4.3	5.0	4.2
Untreated	4.6	4.6	4.7	5.1	7.5	5.0	6.4	5.7	5.9	3.1

12 In 1959, Dowdeswell published the results of an earthworm count. He measured the number of worms per unit area in samples from two plots, one well manured and the other not. Is there evidence that earthworms prefer manured ground?

Manured plot	5	9	12	9	10	7	5	8	4
Non-manured plot	4	3	6	8	5	3	4	5	

13 The breaking strengths in tension of five steel specimens taken from each of two consignments A and B are given in $N\,m^{-2} \times 10^{12}$. Use the t-test to compare the mean breaking strengths of the two consignments.

A	0.4751	0.4828	0.4951	0.4720	0.4735
B	0.4936	0.5029	0.4982	0.4951	0.4789

14 One group of mice was fed a normal diet and another group was fed a test diet. Examine the following data on body weight in grams for differences in the average weight in the two groups.

Normal diet	40	30	41	41	41	42	31
Test diet	34	28	41	38	34	41	35

15 In a test to determine the relative effectiveness of two diet plans, eight people were given diet plan A and nine were given diet plan B. The weight losses achieved (in kilograms) were as shown.

$$\text{Plan A:} \quad \bar{x}_A = 2.8; \quad s_A^2 = 1.2; \quad n_A = 8$$
$$\text{Plan B:} \quad \bar{x}_B = 3.8; \quad s_B^2 = 1.5; \quad n_B = 9$$

(a) Assuming that the population variances are equal, find the pooled estimate of the common variance.

(b) Conduct a two-tail t-test to see if there is any difference in the mean weight losses for the two diets.

16 The scores for two groups of students on a cognitive ability test are provided in the table below.

Group A	54	58	62	64		
Group B	48	50	50	58	60	65

Is there a significant difference in the performance of the two groups?

17 In a competition, there were ten candidates and the marks awarded by two judges, A and B, are shown in the table. Draw a scatter diagram of the data. Calculate also Spearman's rank correlation coefficient.

Competitor	1	2	3	4	5	6	7	8	9	10
Judge A	36	34	24	38	20	37	22	28	30	32
Judge B	20	26	8	30	13	19	17	11	15	25

[London]

18 Ten varieties of tea, labelled A, B, C, ..., J, were tasted by two groups of people, and were ranked from best to worst as in the table.

Group 1	G	H	C	D	A	E	B	J	I	F
Group 2	C	B	H	G	J	D	I	E	F	A

Calculate a coefficient of rank correlation for the data.

[Cambridge]

19 The table gives the altitude x (in metres) above sea level, and mean air temperature y (in °C), for weather stations.

x	2	7	12	40	76	99	135	163	235	307
y	9.7	10.7	9.9	10.4	9.5	9.2	9.2	9.4	8.7	7.5

Calculate the equation of the regression line of y on x.

Estimate the mean air temperature at a place 200 m above sea level.

[Cambridge]

20 The ages, x years, and heights, y cm, of 10 boys were as follows.

x	6.6	6.8	6.9	7.5	7.8	8.2	10.1	11.4	12.8	13.5
y	119	112	116	123	122	123	135	151	141	141

Calculate the equation of the regression line of y on x, and use it to estimate the height of a boy who is 9.0 years old.

Find the value of y given by the regression line when $x = 30$ and comment upon your answer.

[Cambridge]

Cumulative frequency diagrams

The **cumulative frequency** is the total frequency up to a particular value, or class boundary.

The heights of 340 sunflower plants were measured six weeks after planting. From the frequency table it is easy to draw up a cumulative frequency table.

Height (cm)	Frequency
3–6	10
7–10	21
11–14	114
15–18	105
19–22	54
23–26	36

Height (cm)	Cumulative frequency
up to 6.5	10
up to 10.5	$10 + 21 = 31$
up to 14.5	$31 + 114 = 145$
up to 18.5	$145 + 105 = 250$
up to 22.5	$250 + 54 = 304$
up to 26.5	$304 + 36 = 340$

It can be helpful to plot cumulative frequencies on a cumulative frequency diagram or **ogive**.

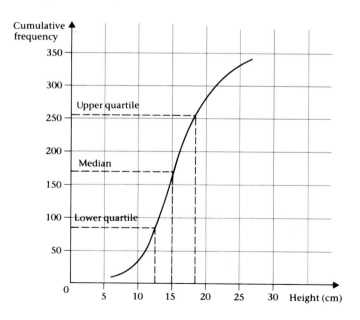

Using the cumulative frequency diagram, the median can be estimated quite easily. For 340 plants, the median (or middle plant) will be approximately the 170th plant. By finding 170 on the cumulative frequency axis you can read off the corresponding height on the horizontal axis. The median height is 15 cm.

The lower quartile can be found by reading off the height for the 85th plant. The upper quartile can be found by reading off the height of the 255th plant.

1 Find the values of the lower and upper quartiles.

2 A gardener collected 150 worms from her garden and recorded their lengths to the nearest millimetre. The results are given below.

Length (mm)	95–109	110–124	125–139	140–154	155–169	170–184	185–199	200–214
No. of worms	4	10	19	36	43	26	9	3

(a) Write down the cumulative frequency table and draw a cumulative frequency curve to illustrate this information.

(b) Use the curve to estimate the median and interquartile range.

(c) What percentage of worms are less than 150 mm in length?

The Hardy–Weinberg law

Children take after their parents. Such passing on of characteristics, determined by genes, is called genetic inheritance. The characteristics of the parents may be opposite in kind, for example, having six toes (*S*) and having the normal number of toes (*N*).

Offspring inherit an allele (gene-type) from each parent. The various possibilities for number of toes are shown in the table.

		Mother	
		S	*N*
Father	*S*	*SS*	*SN*
	N	*NS*	*NN*

The pairs *SN* and *NS* are indistinguishable. Which parent contributes which allele is usually immaterial.

Suppose that at a particular time for a particular population the probability of inheriting *S* from either parent is p. Then the probabilities of the various allele pairs in offspring are shown in the tree diagram.

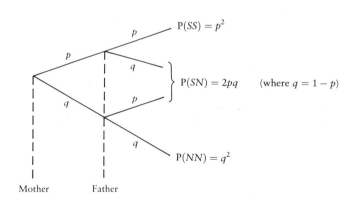

You will see that the second generation has a population in which:

- the event *SS* occurs with probability p^2
- the event *NN* occurs with probability q^2
- the event *SN* occurs with probability $2pq$

Individuals with allele-pair (or **genotype**) *SS* or *NN* are called **homozygotes** (*homo* means the same) and those with allele-pair *SN* are called **heterozygotes** (*hetero* means different).

1 Show that the probabilities given in the tree diagram for the offspring total 1.

2 Suppose that the distribution of the genotypes in the population is given by

$$P(SS) = p^2, \qquad P(SN) = 2pq, \qquad P(NN) = q^2$$

Assume also that a heterozygote (SN) has an equal chance of passing either characteristic (S or N) forward to the next generation.

Consider the probabilities of the various allele-pairs in the following generation.

(a) Explain the entries in this table.

Event	P(Event)	Assuming the event		
		P(SS)	P(SN)	P(NN)
Both parents SS	p^4	1	0	0
One SS, the other SN	$4p^3q$	$\frac{1}{2}$	$\frac{1}{2}$	0
One SS, the other NN				
Both SN	$4p^2q^2$	$\frac{1}{4}$	$\frac{1}{2}$	$\frac{1}{4}$
One SN, the other NN				
Both NN				

(b) Complete the table.

(c) Find the probabilities of the various allele-pairs.

3 Explain why the model results in a stable distribution of genotypes in the population. [This is the **Hardy–Weinberg law**.]

4 Suppose that six-toedness is a dominant characteristic; that is, that any individual with either one or two S alleles will have six toes. If at any time in a stable population 20% have six toes, what percentage would be SS genotypes?

You may be interested to discover how the incidence of other characteristics change from one generation to another. Haemophilia and sickle-cell anaemia would be worth investigating.

Sampling without replacement

1   Ten marbles are placed in a bag. Four are red and the rest are blue. Three
    marbles are removed and the number of reds is recorded. These are replaced
    in the bag which is then shaken and the procedure is repeated 50 times. The
    results are as follows.

Number of reds	Number of samples
0	7
1	22
2	17
3	4
Total	50

(a) Using these sample data, calculate the mean and standard deviation of the
     number of reds.

     Complete the tree diagram below and hence find the predicted frequencies
     from 50 trials based on the probability model.

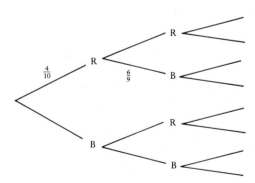

(b) Find the mean and variance from the probability model.

2   Repeat question 1 starting with three red and seven blue marbles (or
    equivalent equipment).

3   Start with 2 red and 8 blue marbles. Select one marble at a time without replacement until a red marble is chosen. Record the number of marbles required to obtain a red (e.g. for the sequence BBBR record the number 4; for BR record 2). What is the smallest number you might record? What is the largest? What do you anticipate will be the mean score?

From a tree diagram, or otherwise, find the probabilities of each score, the predicted frequencies from a total of 90 trials and the predicted mean.

4   Repeat question 3, but this time replacing each marble in the bag after noting its colour.

5   Suggest what results you would expect if question 3 is repeated starting with:

(a) 4 red and 16 blue marbles,

(b) 20 red and 80 blue marbles.

6   Repeat question 1 'with replacement', i.e. for each trial take one marble, note its colour, return it to the bag, shake the bag and repeat three times.

7   Are political opinion poll samples chosen with or without replacement? Does it matter?

8   A die is thrown repeatedly until an even number is obtained. What is the probability that this takes four throws? How many throws will be needed on average?

Answer the same questions if the die is thrown until a six appears.

9   Find out about the St Petersburg paradox.

Boxes of matches

Boxes of matches often have on the side a statement such as:

Suppose you want to check whether this is true and find out more information about the distribution of the number of matches in a box. The obvious thing to do is to take a random sample of perhaps 1000 matchboxes and count the matches in each. You could then work out the average number of matches in a box and the standard deviation of the number of matches. You could get some idea of the shape of the population distribution by drawing a frequency diagram for your sample of 1000 boxes. This would take a good deal of time and you might find you could only deal practically with a very much smaller number of matchboxes; so it would be useful to see what information can be obtained from much smaller samples.

Taking the problem to its opposite extreme, consider what information could be obtained from a sample of size 2, just two matchboxes, whose contents are counted. Suppose that one box contained 47 matches and other contained 48 matches. The sample of two boxes has a mean of 47.5 and you can work out the variance as 0.25. To see what can be inferred from this sample you can look at the problem the other way around and assume that you know what the population looks like (its distribution, mean and variance). You can then investigate possible samples of size 2.

Use a simple model for the population: assume that 20% of boxes contain 47 matches, 60% contain 48 matches and 20% contain 49 matches.

x	47	48	49
$P(X = x)$	0.2	0.6	0.2

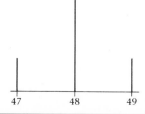

1 Show that the population mean is 48, and find the population variance.

If a random sample of two boxes is chosen from the population, then there are just 9 possibilities.

> A sample of (48, 49) has probability 0.12

Probabilities	47	48	49
47	0.04	0.12	0.04
48	0.12	0.36	0.12
49	0.04	0.12	0.04

Values of $\bar{x}$	47	48	49
47	47.0	47.5	48.0
48	47.5	48.0	48.5
49	48.0	48.5	49.0

Values of s^2	47	48	49
47	0.00	0.25	1.00
48	0.25	0.00	0.25
49	1.00	0.25	0.00

2 Show that the probability of obtaining a sample having $\bar{x} = 48.5$ is 0.24.

Both $\bar{x}$ and s^2 have distributions:

Sample mean $\bar{x}$					
x	47.0	47.5	48.0	48.5	49.0
$P(\bar{x} = x)$	0.04	0.24	0.44	0.24	0.04

Sample variance s^2

y	0	0.25	1
$P(s^2 = y)$	0.44	0.48	0.08

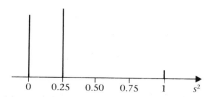

The original distribution was symmetrical. Note that $\bar{x}$ has a symmetrical distribution, but that s^2 does not.

3 (a) Show that the mean value of the distribution of $\bar{x}$ is 48.

(b) Show that the mean value of the distribution of s^2 is 0.2.

Comparing these values with $\mu = 48$ and $\sigma^2 = 0.4$, you can see that if you took a large number of samples of size 2, the distribution of their means ($\bar{x}$) would be symmetrical and have mean value μ; but the distribution of their variance (s^2) would have a mean value of only $\frac{1}{2}\sigma^2$.

4 Investigate, taking samples of size 2 from the other populations of matches (below).

Rectangular

x	47	48	49
$P(X = x)$	$\frac{1}{3}$	$\frac{1}{3}$	$\frac{1}{3}$

Asymmetrical

x	47	48	49
$P(X = x)$	0.6	0.3	0.1

U-shaped

x	47	48	49
$P(X = x)$	0.5	0	0.5

Comment on your findings and produce unbiased estimates for the mean and variance of the population from which the original sample of two boxes was drawn.

You could use a computer simulation to investigate samples of size other than 2.

Programming the binomial

It can be convenient to calculate binomial probabilities by developing a step-by-step or iterative method.

You know that

$$P(X = r) = \binom{n}{r} p^r q^{n-r}$$

and

$$\binom{n}{r} = \frac{n!}{r!\,(n-r)!}$$

You need to find a relationship between $P(r+1)$ and $P(r)$.

1 Show that

$$\frac{r!}{(r-1)!} = r$$

2 Find, in terms of r, expressions for:

(a) $\dfrac{(r+1)!}{r!}$

(b) $\dfrac{(r+1)!}{(r-1)!}$

(c) $\dfrac{(r+2)!}{r!}$

(d) $\dfrac{(r+n)!}{r!}$

3 Show that

$$\frac{\binom{n}{r+1}}{\binom{n}{r}} = \frac{n-r}{r+1}$$

Hence show that

$$P(r+1) = \left(\frac{n-r}{r+1}\right) \frac{p}{q} P(r)$$

The following expression is ideal for programming a computer or calculator.

$$P(r + 1) = \frac{(n - r)}{(r + 1)} \frac{p}{q} P(r)$$

An outline of an algorithm for doing this is as shown.

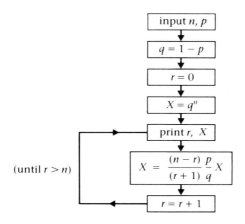

Use this to program your computer or calculator. Check your program by calculating B(10, 0.25), the distribution of which is given in the table.

X	P(X = r)
0	0.0563
1	0.1877
2	0.2816
3	0.2503
4	0.1460
5	0.0584
6	0.0162
7	0.0031
8	0.0003
9	0.0000
10	0.0000

You might like to retain this program for future use.

4 Use the program to calculate the following probability distributions:

(a) B$(3, \frac{1}{4})$ (b) B$(4, \frac{1}{3})$

From binomial to Poisson

You have seen that the binomial distribution $N(n, p)$ appears to 'tend to' the Poisson distribution $P(\lambda)$, when

$$\lambda = np \quad \text{and} \quad n \to \infty$$

As a mathematician you will want to know why!

You showed (on 3.2 tasksheet E1) that, for a binomial random variable,

$$P(X = r + 1) = \left(\frac{n - r}{r + 1}\right)\frac{p}{q}P(X = r) \quad \text{and} \quad P(X = 0) = q^n$$

1 For a Poisson random variable, show that

$$P(X = r + 1) = \frac{\lambda}{r + 1}P(X = r) \quad \text{and} \quad P(X = 0) = e^{-\lambda}$$

You need to show that as $n \to \infty$ and $p \to 0$, with $np = \lambda$,

$$q^n \to e^{-\lambda} \qquad \qquad ①$$

$$\frac{n - r}{r + 1}\frac{p}{q} \to \frac{\lambda}{r + 1} \qquad ②$$

The Maclaurin series for e^x is

$$e^x = 1 + \frac{x}{1!} + \frac{x^2}{2!} + \frac{x^3}{3!} + \dots$$

2 Write down the Maclaurin series for $e^{-\lambda}$.

3 Show that

$$q^n = \left(1 - \frac{\lambda}{n}\right)^n$$

Find the first four terms of the binomial expansion.

4 Deduce that as $n \to \infty$, $q^n \to e^{-\lambda}$. This demonstrates ①.

5 To demonstrate ②, show that

$$\frac{(n - r)p}{q} = \frac{\left(1 - \dfrac{r}{n}\right)}{\left(1 - \dfrac{\lambda}{n}\right)}\lambda$$

Deduce that as $n \to \infty$, $\dfrac{(n - r)p}{q} \to \lambda$ and hence

$$\frac{(n - r)}{(r + 1)}\frac{p}{q} \to \frac{\lambda}{r + 1}$$

Combining random variables

General proofs for the results

$$E[X + Y] = E[X] + E[Y]$$

and

$$V[X + Y] = V[X] + V[Y]$$

are difficult because of the complexity of the notation. However, the working below illustrates how the proof would proceed.

Consider two discrete random variables X and Y. Suppose X can take only the values x_1, x_2 and x_3 and Y only y_1 and y_2. The probability distributions of X and Y are

x	x_1	x_2	x_3
$P(X = x)$	a	b	c

y	y_1	y_2
$P(Y = y)$	d	e

There are only six possible values of the variable $X + Y$, having probabilities r, s, t, u, v, w, for example.

1 List the six possible values of $X + Y$.

The probabilities associated with each of the possible values are shown in the table below.

	X values				
	x_1	x_2	x_3		
Y values $\quad y_1$	r	s	t	d	$P(x_3 + y_2) = w$
y_2	u	v	w	e	$u + v + w = e$
	a	b	c	1	

$s + v = b$

2 Explain why:

   (a) $r + u = a$ (b) $r + s + t = d$ (c) $d + e = 1$

Using the probabilities defined in the table,

$$E[X + Y] = (x_1 + y_1)r + (x_2 + y_1)s + (x_3 + y_1)t$$
$$+ (x_1 + y_2)u + (x_2 + y_2)v + (x_3 + y_2)w$$
$$= x_1(r + u) + x_2(s + v) + x_3(t + w)$$
$$+ y_1(r + s + t) + y_2(u + v + w)$$
$$= x_1 a + x_2 b + x_3 c + y_1 d + y_2 e$$
$$= E[X] + E[Y]$$

Notice that you do *not* need to assume independence here.

To obtain the variance relationship, use the result

$$V[X] = E[X^2] - (E[X])^2$$

So,

$$V[X + Y] = E[(X + Y)^2] - (E[X + Y])^2$$
$$= E[X^2] + E[Y^2] + 2E[XY] - (E[X] + E[Y])^2$$
$$= E[X^2] - (E[X])^2 + E[Y^2] - (E[Y])^2$$
$$+ 2E[XY] - 2E[X]E[Y] \qquad ①$$

3 If X and Y are *independent* random variables, $P(xy) = P(x)P(y)$. Using this result, and the relationships between the various probabilities shown in the table, prove that $E[XY] = E[X]E[Y]$.

For *independent* random variables X and Y, $E[XY] = E[X]E[Y]$ and so the expression ① simplifies to

$$V[X + Y] = E[X^2] - (E[X])^2 + E[Y^2] - (E[Y])^2$$
$$= V[X] + V[Y]$$

(X and Y *must* be independent variables).

A more general proof extends to n values for X $(x_1, x_2, \ldots, x_i, \ldots, x_n)$ and m values for Y $(y_1, y_2, \ldots, y_j, \ldots, y_m)$.

4 If X takes the values $x_1, x_2, \ldots, x_n$, prove that:

(a) $E[aX] = aE[X]$

(b) $E[X + b] = E[X] + b$

Some proofs

Of the three discrete distributions considered in section 3.4 – geometric, binomial and Poisson – a proof of the results for the mean and variance has, so far, only been given for the binomial. On this tasksheet, you will consider the other two distributions.

The geometric distribution
If $X \sim G(p)$, then $E[X]$ is the number of trials needed until the required event occurs.

1 How long do you think you would wait, on average, until you score a six when you throw a die?

If $X \sim G(p)$, then $E[X] = \sum_i x_i P(x_i)$

Writing this out in full gives

$$E[X] = 1p + 2pq + 3pq^2 + \ldots$$
$$= p(1 + 2q + 3q^2 + \ldots)$$

2 Confirm that the expression in brackets is the binomial expansion of $(1 - q)^{-2}$.

$$E[X] = \frac{p}{(1 - q)^2} = \frac{1}{p}$$

For throwing a six with a die, $X \sim G(\frac{1}{6})$. You would expect to wait six throws on average because $E[X] = 6$.

The Poisson distribution
Suppose X is a Poisson variable, $X \sim P(\lambda)$.

$$E[X] = \sum_i x_i P(x_i) \qquad \text{where } P(X = r) = \frac{e^{-\lambda} \lambda^r}{r!}$$

In the proofs which follow you will need the series expansion for e^x:

$$e^x = 1 + x + \frac{x^2}{2!} + \frac{x^3}{3!} + \ldots + \frac{x^n}{n!} + \ldots$$

3 Complete the following proof.

$$E[X] = \frac{0 \times e^{-\lambda}\lambda^0}{0!} + \frac{1 \times e^{-\lambda}\lambda}{1!} + \ldots$$

$$= e^{-\lambda}\{(\ldots) + (\ldots) + (\ldots) + \ldots\}$$

$$= \lambda e^{-\lambda}\{\ldots + \ldots + \ldots + \ldots\}$$

$$= \lambda e^{-\lambda}e^{\lambda} \qquad \text{using the expansion of } e^x$$

$$= \lambda$$

To obtain the variance, you will need to use

$$V[X] = E[X^2] - (E[X])^2 \qquad \text{where } E[X] = \lambda$$

Finding $E[X^2]$ is awkward here. It is best to use an algebraic 'trick' and to work with $E[X(X-1)]$.

4 Show that

$$E[X^2] = E[X(X-1)] + E[X]$$

To use this result, you need to find an expression for $E[X(X-1)]$.

$$E[X(X-1)] = \sum_i x_i(x_i - 1)P(x_i)$$

$$= \frac{2 \times 1 \times e^{-\lambda}\lambda^2}{2!} + \frac{3 \times 2 \times e^{-\lambda}\lambda^3}{3!} + \ldots$$

5 Complete the proof, showing that

(a) $E[X(X-1)] = \lambda^2$

and hence

(b) $V[X] = \lambda$

This confirms the result stated for Poisson variables, i.e. that the mean and the variance are equal.

Plotting t-distributions

The equation of a t-distribution is

$$f(t) = c_\nu \left(1 + \frac{t^2}{\nu}\right)^{-\frac{(\nu+1)}{2}}$$

where c_ν is a constant such that

$$\int_{-\infty}^{\infty} f(t)\,dt = 1$$

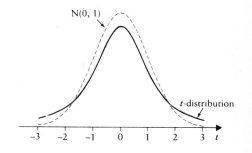

1 (a) Use a numerical method or the substitution $t = \sqrt{5}\tan x$ to show that

$$\int_{-\infty}^{\infty} (1 + \tfrac{1}{5}t^2)^{-3}\,dt \approx 2.63$$

  (b) Explain why this shows that $c_5 = 0.380$ (to 3 s.f.)

  (c) Use a similar method to evaluate c_ν when $\nu = 10$, 20 and 50.

2 (a) Write down the equation of the t-distribution when the degrees of freedom are:

  (i) $\nu = 3$ (ii) $\nu = 5$ (iii) $\nu = 10$
  (iv) $\nu = 20$ (v) $\nu = 50$

  (b) Use a graph plotter to plot the graph of the Standard Normal variable,

$$f(z) = \frac{1}{\sqrt{(2\pi)}}e^{-\frac{1}{2}z^2}$$

  (c) Superimpose the graphs of the t-distributions obtained in (a).

  (d) Describe and discuss the significance of what you find.

As a point of mathematical interest, it can be shown that the t-distribution with $\nu = 1$ has equation

$$f(t) = \frac{1}{\pi(1 + t^2)}$$

This distribution is known as the **Cauchy distribution** and is of particular interest because it can further be shown that while its mean is zero (by symmetry) its variance is infinitely large.

Derivation of Spearman's rank correlation coefficient

In a 'beautiful poodle' competition there are eight competitors and two judges, A and B. Each judge assigns a ranking to the competitors as follows.

Poodle		1	2	3	4	5	6	7	8
Rank	Judge A (x)	4	7	1	5	2	3	8	6
	Judge B (y)	8	4	3	7	5	1	6	2
Difference in ranks		-4	3	-2	-2	-3	2	2	4

1 Explain why the sum of the differences is zero.

2 For each judge in turn find the mean and variance of the rank numbers.

3 (a) Now generalise: if there were n dogs instead of 8, what would be the mean and variance? You will need the result that

$$\sum_{i=1}^{n} i^2 = \tfrac{1}{6}n(n+1)(2n+1).$$

(b) Use the result for $\sum i^2$ to show that

$$\sum_{i=1}^{n} d_i^2 = \tfrac{1}{3}n(n+1)(2n+1) - 2\sum_{i=1}^{n} x_i y_i$$

4 In the particular case quoted with 8 dogs, find the covariance of the rankings and the product moment coefficient r.

5 Show that in the general case, with n dogs, $r = 1 - \dfrac{6\sum d_i^2}{n(n^2 - 1)}$.

6 What value does r take when the judges:

(a) agree exactly in their rankings;   (b) disagree totally?

[The last answer is not unexpected but not easy to prove.]

SOLUTIONS
1 LIVING WITH UNCERTAINTY

1.1 Statistics and data analysis
1.1.1 Introduction

1.1 Exercise 1

1 1986, about 22%
1993, about 33%

The figure is highest in the North and the North West. It is lowest in East Anglia.

2 (a) (i) 116.5

(ii) 88.1

(b) There are clear regional differences in GDP. The highest figures are found in London and the surrounding areas with a fall-off as you move north. Wales and Northern Ireland each have a low GDP in relation to the English regions and to Scotland.

3 (a) (i) About 25% (ii) about 36%

(iii) about 25%

(b) No. Note also that the figures are for the clear up of *reported* crime. Much crime is unreported and so cannot be 'cleared up'.

(c) (i) It takes time for a crime to be solved. You could find the percentage clear-up rate by considering at some time the number of crimes reported – say, in a given month – and the number of these crimes solved after, say, six months. Once a suitable method is defined, each region must follow it carefully.

(ii) Data on *reported* crime could be collected easily from each region and suitably classified. It would be more difficult to obtain information on the hidden pool of unreported crime.

4 (a) Smoking in all regions shown has declined since 1980. There seems to be no obvious regional distinction.

(b) Directing advertising at suitable age groups might be sensible. You would need information on smoking habits, related to age groups and perhaps gender.

1.1.2 Exploratory data analysis

1.1 A

Intervals of 10 °C

```
3 |
2 | 0000111122222 3335667
1 | 678889
0 |
```
2 | 1 means 21 °C

Intervals of 1 °C   Intervals of 2 °C

```
      ↑ etc.              2 | 667
2 | 0000               2 | 5
1 | 9                  2 | 22222333
1 | 888                2 | 00001111
1 | 7                  1 | 8889
1 | 6                  1 | 67
1 |
```

1 | 7 means 17 °C   2 | 5 means 25 °C

The interval of 2 °C is probably the best. In the first plot, it is not possible to see any pattern – the grouping is too coarse. The plot using intervals of 1 °C also shows little pattern because it is very broken up.

1.1 Exercise 2

1 (a) By considering the data values alone it is difficult to say which of the two sets of heights is more variable. Certainly the male heights seem to be generally greater, but picking out which is the more variable is much harder.

(b) (i) Husbands

```
18 | 0 2 4
17 | 1 1 3 3 3 3 4 4 5 5 7 8 9
16 | 1 4 5 8
15 |
14 |
13 |
```
17 | 3 means 173 cm

Wives

```
18 |
17 | 0 1
16 | 1 2 3 4
15 | 2 4 5 6 6 8 8 8 9 9 9
14 | 2 3
13 | 9
```
14 | 2 means 142 cm

(ii) There is an impression, from the diagrams, that the heights of the wives are more variable.

(iii) The husbands have the higher middle value.

(iv) Husbands: median = 173.5 cm
Wives: median = 158 cm

(c) Heights of 40 adults

```
18 | 0 2 4
17 | 0 1 1 1 3 3 3 3 4 4 5 5 7 8 9
16 | 1 1 2 3 4 4 5 8
15 | 2 4 5 6 6 8 8 8 9 9 9
14 | 2 3
13 | 9
```
16 | 5 means 165 cm

The stem and leaf diagram has two peaks. The distribution is said to be bimodal, as opposed to the unimodal distributions of part (b)(i).

(d) (iv), as this reflects the indication of the stem and leaf plot. Such a distribution often occurs when two distinct populations are mixed.

2   Examination marks

Class 1		Class 2
	9	1
7 4 0	8	0 1 3
9 8 8 6 6 5 1	7	1 3 3 5 9
9 6 5 4 2 0	6	2 4 4 8 9
9 8 6 3 1 0	5	1 5 6 8 9
	4	5 8
1	3	4

```
       6 | 4 means 64 marks
     3 | 5      means 53 marks
```

(a) Disregarding the 91 mark in class 2, class 1 seem to have done marginally better, with more marks in the upper 70s and 80s.

(b) Both have approximately symmetrical distributions. The marks for class 1 are slightly more closely bunched than those for class 2.

3   Graduate starting salaries

```
16 | 0
15 | 0
14 | 0
13 | 0 0
12 | 0 0 0
11 | 0 0 0 0
10 | 0 0 0 0
 9 | 0 0 0 5
 8 | 0 0 5 5
 7 | 0 5
```
10 | 0 means £10 000

The distribution is skewed towards the lower end. The bulk of salaries are in the range £7000–£13 000, but there are a few very highly paid jobs. The median is £10 000.

1.1.3 Numerical representation of data

1.1 B

1 $y = |x - 2| + |x - 4| + |x - 5| + |x - 5| + |x - 6|$

Minimum at $x = 5$

Median $= 5$

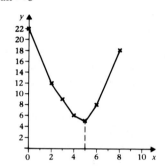

2 (a) (i) Median $= 3$

(ii)

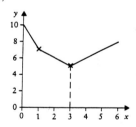

$y = |x - 1| + |x - 3| + |x - 6|$
Minimum $x = 3$

(b) In all cases, the total of the distances from x is least when x is equal to the median.

3 (a) (i)

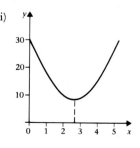

$y = (x - 1)^2 + (x - 2)^2 + (x - 5)^2$
$\quad = 3x^2 - 16x + 30$
Minimum at $x = 2\frac{2}{3}$

(ii) This is the mean value of the data set 1, 2, 5.

(b) The sum of the squared distances from x is least when x is the mean value of the data set.

1.1 Exercise 3

1 Mean $= \frac{1}{50}(41 \times 0 + 6 \times 1 + 3 \times 2) = \frac{12}{50}$

Mode $= 0$ \qquad Median $= 0$

The mode is most sensible measure of the average in this case.

2 (a) Mean $= \frac{1052}{19} = 55.4$ seconds \quad (to 3 s.f.)

Median $= 52$ seconds

It would probably be better to quote the mean as this better reflects the individual values, some of which are very low and some high.

(b) Although the person did not complete the jigsaw, the data should be included. It will significantly affect the mean; if you credit this person with a time of 148 seconds the mean is 60 seconds. The median is much less affected by an extreme value such as this. (Here, in fact, it is still 52 seconds.)

3 The distribution has two peaks – it is bimodal. Any of the measures of average might be used, but data such as these emphasise that you need to know more about a population than simply a measure of its average value, which can disguise a great deal of hidden detail. There is no particular merit in any of the measures here.

1.1.4 Box and whisker diagrams

1.1 Exercise 4

1 The range of A is greater overall although it has a smaller interquartile range. The average speed of B is greater than that of A. B has a relatively symmetric distribution whereas A's is skewed.

2 (a) The highest recorded temperature was 83 °F, in Copenhagen. London was generally hotter, with a median temperature of 66 °F against Copenhagen's 63 °F. London's lower quartile is only 1 °F less than Copenhagen's upper quartile.

(b) Copenhagen had the greater range of temperatures overall even though the interquartile range for London is much greater than that for Copenhagen. The interquartile range is not particularly useful when planning a trip – you need the full range when deciding what to pack. From that point of view, Copenhagen is the more variable.

London has a more symmetric distribution than Copenhagen.

3 (a) There was very little sunshine in January. There was a much more varied amount in July.

(b)

	January	July
(i) Median	0.4	5.7
(ii) Lower quartile	0	2.6
(iii) Upper quartile	2.1	7.7

(c)

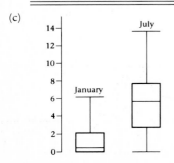

(d) There was a much greater range of sunshine hours in July and the average sunshine was much higher. In January there was no recorded sunshine on at least a quarter of the days.

4

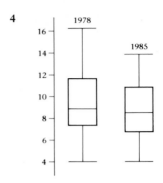

Although following a similar pattern, total alcohol consumption has dropped slightly. There has been a more pronounced drop in heavy drinking.

1.2 Data analysis revisited
1.2.1 Grouping data

1.2 **A**

Number of households lacking at least one basic amenity (per 1000 households) for metropolitan districts

29	3
28	9
27	0
26	
25	
24	7 8
23	8
22	3
21	0
20	0 0 1 1 6 6
19	1 5
18	2 3 3 6 8
17	5
16	4
15	4 6 8 8
14	6
13	4 8
12	3
11	3 6 8
10	
9	
8	
7	
6	
5	
4	4
3	
2	5

19 | 1 means 191 substandard households (per 1000 households)

The stem and leaf diagram still gives a useful pictorial representation. It is, however, tedious to construct, even with the relatively small data set here.

1.2 **B**

1 If the intervals are too narrow, then it can be difficult to notice any features of the data. The extreme case of an interval of width 1 should illustrate this point! Conversely, if the intervals are too wide then much of the information contained in the data will be lost.

2 There is no one 'correct' grouping of the data on the non-metropolitan counties. You should apply the principles above when choosing your grouping.

1.2.2 Representing grouped data – histograms

1.2 **Exercise 1**

1 (a) (i) $10 \times 1 = 10$ (ii) $10 \times 2 = 20$
   (iii) $20 \times 1 = 20$

   (b) Total frequency $= 50$

2 Total frequency $= (25 \times 0.2) + (50 \times 0.4)$
   $+(50 \times 0.2) = 35$

3 (a)

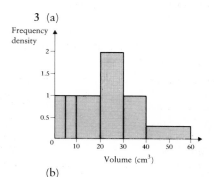

4 (b)

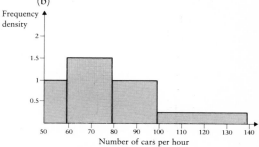

4 (a) See the table in (b). The choice of grouping should reflect the principles established in the previous discussion.

(b)

| | | North | |
Rainfall (mm)	Width	Frequency	Frequency density
40–69	30	1	$\frac{1}{30} = 0.033$
70–79	10	4	$\frac{4}{10} = 0.4$
80–89	10	9	$\frac{9}{10} = 0.9$
90–99	10	4	$\frac{4}{10} = 0.4$
100–109	10	11	$\frac{11}{10} = 1.1$
110–119	10	6	$\frac{6}{10} = 0.6$
120–129	10	5	$\frac{5}{10} = 0.5$
130–139	10	1	$\frac{1}{10} = 0.1$
140–149	10	5	$\frac{5}{10} = 0.5$
150–229	80	4	$\frac{4}{80} = 0.05$

| | | South | |
Rainfall (mm)	Width	Frequency	Frequency density
40–69	30	10	$\frac{10}{30} = 0.33$
70–79	10	9	$\frac{9}{10} = 0.9$
80–89	10	11	$\frac{11}{10} = 1.1$
90–99	10	8	$\frac{8}{10} = 0.8$
100–109	10	6	$\frac{6}{10} = 0.6$
110–119	10	4	$\frac{4}{10} = 0.4$
120–129	10	1	$\frac{1}{10} = 0.1$
130–139	10	0	0
140–149	10	0	0
150–229	80	1	$\frac{1}{80} = 0.012$

As the readings are to the nearest mm, the true intervals are 39.5–69.5, 69.5–79.5, and so on. The positioning of the bars on the histogram should reflect this.

(c)

Rainfall in the north of England

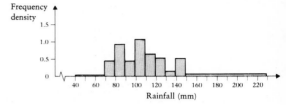

Rainfall in the south of England

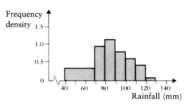

(d) The south of England has more readings in the 40–69 mm range and in general appears to have had a drier month than the north of England. This result needs to be interpreted cautiously as it does not mean that the south has a drier climate than the north. It only indicates what happened in one particular month.

The 100 weather stations chosen were fairly equally divided between the east and the west of England to avoid any east–west differences affecting the result. The line from the Wash to the Bristol Channel was chosen as the north–south boundary for the purposes of this study.

5

Non-metropolitan counties

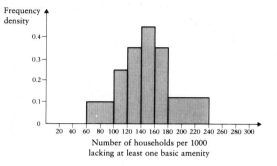

It is clear from the histograms that there is a much higher proportion of substandard housing in the metropolitan districts than in the non-metropolitan counties.

1.2.3 Averages and spread

1.2 **C**

1 9.7, 0.13 and 9.3, 0.41

2 (a) 0. The points are all the same and have no spread. This is shown by a standard deviation of zero.

(b) 1.4 (to 2 s.f.)

(c) 1.7 (to 2 s.f.). Set (c) is slightly more spread out than (b) and has a correspondingly higher standard deviation.

(d) 2.8 (to 2 s.f.). Set (d) is twice as spread out as set (b) and has twice the standard deviation.

3 (a) If all the values are increased by the same number, then the mean is also increased by this number but the standard deviation is unchanged.

(b) If all the values are multiplied by the same number, then the mean and the standard deviation are also multiplied by that number.

1.2 **Exercise 2**

1 (a) Mean = 54.2, standard deviation = 0.473 (both results to 3 s.f.)

(b) New mean = $54.2 \div 1.10 = 49.3$ (to 3 s.f.)
New standard deviation = $0.473 \div 1.10$
$= 0.430$ (to 3 s.f.)

2 0.25 years
The standard deviation is unchanged.

3 Fahrenheit mean: $\frac{9}{5} \times 12 + 32 = 53.6$ °F
Fahrenheit standard deviation:
$\frac{9}{5} \times 0.5 = 0.9$ °F

1.2.4 Formulas for variance and standard deviation

1.2 **D**

1 (a) 2.125

(b) 68.$\dot{2}$

2 The calculation of $(x - \bar{x})^2$ for all values of x would prove to be cumbersome for large collections of data, making the algorithm very labour-intensive! Also, it requires two 'runs' through the data.

1.2 Exercise 3

1 Mean = 6.0 years; s.d. = 2.45 years

2 (a) Mean = 51.0 kg; s.d. = 2.2 kg

(b) 96 or 97 (to allow for variability)

3 (a) $\sum w = 350$ kg; $\sum w^2 = 25\,000$ kg^2

(b) Mean = 67.5 kg;

$$\text{s.d.} = \sqrt{\left(\frac{25\,000 - 80^2}{4} - 67.5^2\right)}$$

$$= 9.68\,\text{kg}$$

4 1116.3 g^2; 2527.5 g^2; 7.1 g

5E (a) Hint: $\bar{y} = \frac{1}{n}\sum(x + k)$;

$\text{Var}(y) = \frac{1}{n}\sum(x + k - \bar{y})^2$

(b) Hint: $\bar{z} = \frac{1}{n}\sum kx$;

$\text{Var}(z) = \frac{1}{n}\sum(kx)^2 - (\bar{z})^2$

1.2.5 The mean and variance for grouped data

1.2 E

You will need to refer to your calculator manual to obtain information about how to use the statistical functions on your calculator. It is important that you can use these functions confidently.

1.2 Exercise 4

1 (a) The mean is approximately 23.3 and the standard deviation is approximately 12.5.

(b) The average length of rally has increased; coaching has been of some benefit!

2 (a) The total population is 53 511 000.

(b) The population mean is approximately 41 years.

(c) The population variance is approximately 580. Therefore, the standard deviation is approximately 24 years.

3 (a) The upper boundary must be taken somewhere! There are so few people aged over 100 that this seems a reasonable upper value.

(b) The mean is 38.1 years, standard deviation 22.9 years.

(c) The total population (50 063 000 in 1986) is expected to increase by about $3\frac{1}{2}$ million and the average age is expected to rise from 38 years to 41 years. There is little change in the spread of ages.

4 Taking the upper value as 70 words gives a mean sentence length of 23.4 words and a standard deviation of 11.5 (to 3 s.f.).

The grouping into intervals mostly of width 10 involves a loss of accuracy. Also, the sample might not be representative.

1.3 Probability models
1.3.1 Order from chaos

1.3 A

1

2 There are 6 cases.

3 There are 16 cases.

4 (a) $\frac{4}{16}$ (b) $\frac{2}{16}$ (c) $\frac{6}{16}$

1.3 B

1, 2 Statistical data can never prove a theory; they can only indicate its likelihood or otherwise. If you tossed a coin ten times and obtained seven heads, then this would not be 'out of the ordinary' and would certainly not imply that the coin was biased. Even ten heads from ten throws occurs occasionally with a fair coin. However, large amounts of data can make certain conclusions more likely than others. For instance, obtaining over 70 heads out of 100 with an unbiased coin is very unlikely, and so would provide strong evidence of bias; over 700 out of 1000 would provide even stronger evidence.

It is the accumulation of statistical evidence which supports belief in certain theories. For example, there were initially no scientific reasons to suggest that smoking caused lung cancer. It was only when large amounts of statistical evidence were collected which compared the incidence of cancer in smokers and non-smokers that the connection was made. This in itself does not prove a causal connection; it simply makes the lack of such a connection extremely unlikely.

In the cartoon, *neither* statement is correct. You can never 'prove' how lucky or unlucky you are, but you can investigate the chances of certain things happening. In games such as poker, the concept of 'luck' is less important than the ability to weigh up the chances of certain events occurring. For this reason, gambling played an important role in motivating the initial development of probability theory.

1.3.2 Making probability models

1.3 Exercise 1

1

s	1	2	3	4	5	6
$P(s)$	$\frac{1}{6}$	$\frac{1}{6}$	$\frac{1}{6}$	$\frac{1}{6}$	$\frac{1}{6}$	$\frac{1}{6}$

2

x	0	1	2	3	4 or over
$P(x)$	0.14	0.20	0.51	0.10	0.05

3

s	0	1
$P(s)$	$\frac{1}{2}$	$\frac{1}{2}$

4

y	1	2	3	4	5	6	7	8	9	10
$P(y)$	$\frac{1}{13}$	$\frac{1}{13}$	$\frac{1}{13}$	$\frac{1}{13}$	$\frac{1}{13}$	$\frac{1}{13}$	$\frac{1}{13}$	$\frac{1}{13}$	$\frac{1}{13}$	$\frac{4}{13}$

5

t	0–1	1–2	2–3	3 or over
$P(t)$	0.155	0.282	0.323	0.241

6

x	0	1	2	3	4	5
$P(x)$	$\frac{6}{36}$	$\frac{10}{36}$	$\frac{8}{36}$	$\frac{6}{36}$	$\frac{4}{36}$	$\frac{2}{36}$

7

h	0	1	2	3
$P(h)$	$\frac{1}{8}$	$\frac{3}{8}$	$\frac{3}{8}$	$\frac{1}{8}$

1.3.3 The mean and variance of a random variable

1.3 C

1 £800. You should charge at least £2 for each go!

2 Total winnings
$= £(1 \times 400 + 2 \times 300 + 3 \times 200 + 4 \times 100)$
$= £2000$

So mean winnings $= £\frac{2000}{1000}$
$= £2$ per game

3 (a)

b	1	2	3	4
$P(b)$	$\frac{1}{4}$	$\frac{1}{2}$	$\frac{1}{4}$	0

(b) Mean $(\mu) = 2$

1.3 Exercise 2

1

d	1	2	3	4	5	6
$P(d)$	$\frac{1}{6}$	$\frac{1}{6}$	$\frac{1}{6}$	$\frac{1}{6}$	$\frac{1}{6}$	$\frac{1}{6}$

Mean $(\mu) = 3.5$
Variance $(\sigma^2) = 2.917$

2

x	10	20	50
$P(x)$	0.4	0.4	0.2

Mean $(\mu) = 22$ pence
Variance $(\sigma^2) = 216$

3 (a) $\mu = 2$ (b) $\mu = 1.4$ (c) $\mu = 2$
    $\sigma^2 = \frac{2}{3}$ $\sigma^2 = 0.64$ $\sigma^2 = 2\frac{1}{3}$

4

Score x	1	2	3	4	5	6	7	8	9	10
$P(x)$	$\frac{4}{52}$	$\frac{4}{52}$	$\frac{4}{52}$	$\frac{4}{52}$	$\frac{4}{52}$	$\frac{4}{52}$	$\frac{4}{52}$	$\frac{4}{52}$	$\frac{4}{52}$	$\frac{16}{52}$

Mean $= 6.538$,   variance $= 9.94$

5 The random variable is the journey time in minutes. My mean journey time is 29 minutes.

6 (a) Let $X =$ expected gain.

x	0	10	50
$P(x)$	0.5	0.25	0.25

$\mu = 0 \times 0.5 + 10 \times 0.25 + 50 \times 0.25$
$\quad = 15p$

(b) The centre of the coin must land inside the square shown. As the target square is a quarter of the area of the square in total, the probability of this happening is 0.25. This divides the probability of winning 10p or 50p by four, so the expected gain is reduced to 3.75p.

1.4 More probability models
1.4.1 Compound events

1.4 A

1 $40 \times 40 = 1600$ possible pairs

2 (a) $16 \times 10 = 160$ possible double ones

(b) (i) $12 \times 10 = 120$ double twos
    (ii) $8 \times 10 = 80$ double threes
    (iii) $4 \times 10 = 40$ double fours

(c) $160 + 120 + 80 + 40 = 400$

3 (a) P(double one) $= \frac{160}{1600} = \frac{1}{10} = 0.1$

(b) $\frac{120}{1600} = \frac{3}{40} = 0.075$

(c) $\frac{400}{1600} = \frac{1}{4} = 0.25$

4 The probability of, say, double two is:
P(Yellow 2 *and* Red 2)
$\quad = $ P(Y2) $\times$ P(R2)
$\quad = 0.3 \times 0.25$
$\quad = 0.075$

The probability of a double is as follows:
P(double one *or* double two *or* ...)
$\quad = $ P(double one) $+$ P(double two) $+ \dots$
$\quad = $ P(Y1 and R1) $+$ P(Y2 and R2) $+ \dots$
$\quad = 0.4 \times 0.25 + 0.3 \times 0.25 + 0.2 \times 0.25$
$\quad\quad + 0.1 \times 0.25$
P(double one *or* double two *or* ...) $= 0.25$

5 Snap occurs when you obtain:
(B1 *and* Y1) or (B2 *and* Y2) or (B3 *and* Y3)
So P(Snap)$= \left(\frac{1}{4} \times \frac{4}{10}\right) + \left(\frac{1}{2} \times \frac{3}{10}\right) + \left(\frac{1}{4} \times \frac{2}{10}\right)$

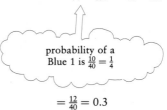

probability of a Blue 1 is $\frac{10}{40} = \frac{1}{4}$

$= \frac{12}{40} = 0.3$

1.4 B

(a) The two events are probably dependent, i.e. I am more likely to walk to work if the weather is fine. They are very unlikely to be mutually exclusive!

(b) My cutting an ace and your cutting a king are independent events if the ace is replaced in the pack before you cut. They are *not* mutually exclusive.

(c) If Dan's Delight wins, Andy's Nag cannot – the events are mutually exclusive. They must therefore be dependent as the occurrence of one obviously affects the other.

(d) There is no relationship. The events are independent. They are *not* mutually exclusive.

(e) Since Mrs Smith having toothache is not likely to influence whether Mr Smith has one also, the events are likely to be independent. They are not mutually exclusive.

(f) There is likely to be some connection here and the events are probably not independent, nor are they mutually exclusive.

1.4 Exercise 1

1 (a) $\frac{1}{36}$ (b) $\frac{11}{36}$ (c) $\frac{5}{18}$

2 (a) $\frac{1}{26}$ (b) $\frac{2}{13}$ (c) $\frac{2}{13}$

3 (a) $\frac{4}{13}$ (b) $\frac{1}{2}$

4 0.005

5 $0.12^2 = 0.0144$

6 $\frac{1}{144}$

7 (a) 0.8464   (b) 0.0064

1.4.2 Tree diagrams

1.4 Exercise 2

1

f	0	1	2	3
P($F = f$)	0.504	0.398	0.092	0.006

2 (a) (i) $\frac{1}{64}$ (ii) $\frac{1}{16}$

  (b) (i) $\frac{13}{52} \times \frac{12}{51} \times \frac{11}{50} = 0.0129$ (ii) 0.0518

3 (a) 0.382   (b) 0.867   (c) 0.750

4 (a) $\frac{65}{81}$ (b) $\frac{11}{27}$

Yes. The assumption of independence is probably not justified: if one line is busy, calls may be transferred to a free line.

5 $\frac{90}{156} = \frac{15}{26}$

1.4.3 The binostat

1.4 C

1 There are three routes; each one is equally likely and each has probability $\frac{1}{8}$. Therefore P(slot 2) $= \frac{3}{8}$.

2

x	0	1	2	3
P($X = x$)	$\frac{1}{8}$	$\frac{3}{8}$	$\frac{3}{8}$	$\frac{1}{8}$

3 For 400 balls you would expect $400 \times \frac{1}{8} = 50$ in slot 0, and so on:

Slot x	0	1	2	3
Expected number	50	150	150	50

4

x	0	1	2
P($X = x$)	$\frac{1}{4}$	$\frac{1}{2}$	$\frac{1}{4}$

Expected frequencies are 100, 200, 100.

5 The ball will hit 4 pins. The probability of a particular route is $\left(\frac{1}{2}\right)^4 = \frac{1}{16}$.

6 Routes to P = 1. Routes to Q = 3.

There are therefore $1 + 3 = 4$ routes to slot 1. $P(\text{slot } 1) = \frac{4}{16} = \frac{1}{4}$.

7

Slot x	0	1	2	3	4
Routes	1	4	6	4	1

x	0	1	2	3	4
$P(x)$	$\frac{1}{16}$	$\frac{4}{16}$	$\frac{6}{16}$	$\frac{4}{16}$	$\frac{1}{16}$

1.4 Exercise 3

1 (a) 35 (b) 21 (c) 15 (d) 10

(e) 2 (f) 35 (g) 5 (h) 1

2 (a) 21 (b) 21

If exactly 2 heads are obtained in 7 throws then exactly 5 tails must also occur. This tells you that $\binom{7}{2}$ and $\binom{7}{5}$ must be equal.

3 $\frac{28}{256}$

4 $\frac{5}{16}$

5 (a) $\frac{1}{32}$ (b) $\frac{5}{16}$

6 $\frac{252}{1024} = 0.246$ (to 3 s.f.)

1.4.4 The binomial probability model

1.4 D

1 The ball is deflected R L R. The probability that the ball will take the route shown is $0.4 \times 0.6 \times 0.4 = 0.096$.

Assume that each deflection (L or R) is independent of previous ones.

2 Other routes are R R L and L R R. The probabilities are both $0.4^2 \times 0.6 = 0.096$.

3 $P(\text{slot } 2) = 3 \times 0.096 = 0.288$

There are 3 equally likely ways to arrive in slot 2.

4 $P(\text{slot } 0) = 1 \times (0.6)^3 = 0.216$
  Route: L L L
$P(\text{slot } 1) = 3 \times (0.6)^2(0.4) = 0.432$
  Routes: L L R, L R L, R L L
$P(\text{slot } 3) = 1 \times (0.4)^3 = 0.064$
  Route: R R R

5 The expected frequencies are

Slot	0	1	2	3
Number of balls	108	216	144	32

6

x	$P(x)$	
0	$1 \times (0.6)^5$	$= 0.07776$
1	$5 \times (0.4) \times (0.6)^4$	$= 0.2592$
2	$10 \times (0.4)^2 \times (0.6)^3$	$= 0.3456$
3	$10 \times (0.4)^3 \times (0.6)^2$	$= 0.2304$
4	$5 \times (0.4)^4 \times (0.6)$	$= 0.0768$
5	$1 \times (0.4)^5$	$= 0.01024$

7

x	$P(x)$	
0	$1 \times (0.2)^3$	$= 0.008$
1	$3 \times (0.8) \times (0.2)^2$	$= 0.096$
2	$3 \times (0.8)^2 \times (0.2)$	$= 0.384$
3	$1 \times (0.8)^3$	$= 0.512$

1.4 Exercise 4

1 S = the number of sixes when 4 dice are thrown

The probability of no sixes

$$= \frac{5}{6} \times \frac{5}{6} \times \frac{5}{6} \times \frac{5}{6}$$

The probability of 1 six

$$= \binom{4}{1} \times \frac{1}{6} \times \left(\frac{5}{6}\right)^3$$

The probability of 2 sixes

$$= \binom{4}{2} \times \left(\frac{1}{6}\right)^2 \times \left(\frac{5}{6}\right)^2$$

The probability of 3 sixes

$$= \binom{4}{3} \times \left(\frac{1}{6}\right)^3 \times \frac{5}{6}$$

The probability of 4 sixes

$$= \binom{4}{4} \times \left(\frac{1}{6}\right)^4$$

s	0	1	2	3	4
$P(S = s)$	0.482	0.386	0.116	0.015	0.001

2 (a) If Wizzo is no better or worse than Wow then the probability that 1 person prefers Wizzo is $\frac{1}{2}$.

The probability that exactly 8 prefer

Wizzo is $\binom{10}{8} \times \left(\frac{1}{2}\right)^{10} = 0.044$

The probability that 9 prefer Wizzo

is $\binom{10}{9} \times \left(\frac{1}{2}\right)^{10} = 0.010$

The probability that all 10 prefer Wizzo

is $1 \times \left(\frac{1}{2}\right)^{10} = 0.001$

So the probability of 8 or more is
$0.044 + 0.010 + 0.001 = 0.055$

(b) P(8 or more prefer Wizzo) = 0.678
(to 3 s.f.)

3 0.298

4 0.284 (to 3 s.f.)

Since what happens in one year could influence the next (there may be the same crews for example) the assumption of independence is very weak. It is likely that the probability of Cambridge's success is *not* the same each year.

5 (a) 0.0355 (to 3 s.f.)

(b) 0.000 17 (to 2 s.f.)

This is a very unlikely event, so you should doubt the player's honesty!

6 P(9 *or more* wins) = 0.0107 (to 3 s.f.)

The captain is therefore extremely lucky.

7 The probability of rain on 6 or more days out of 7 is

$$\binom{7}{6} \times \left(\frac{1}{3}\right)^6 \times \left(\frac{2}{3}\right) + \left(\frac{1}{3}\right)^7$$
$$= 0.0069 \quad \text{(to 2 s.f.)}$$

The Wilsons were very unlucky with the weather. The model is almost certainly not appropriate – the assumption of independence is weak.

8 If both drinks were the same you would expect the probability that 7 or more out of 8 would prefer the new flavour to be

$$\binom{8}{7} \times \left(\frac{1}{2}\right)^8 + \left(\frac{1}{2}\right)^8 = 0.0352 \quad \text{(to 3 s.f.)}$$

This result is clearly unlikely and suggests that the new flavour is preferred.

9 (a) The probability that at least one seed will germinate out of the five planted is the same as

1 − probability that *no* seeds germinate
$$= 1 - (0.8)^5$$
$$= 0.672\,32$$

(b) $1 - (0.8)^n = 0.9$
$$0.1 = (0.8)^n$$

This can be solved by 'trial and improvement' on a calculator, or you can take natural logarithms of both sides.

$$\ln(0.1) = n \ln(0.8)$$

$$n = \frac{\ln(0.1)}{\ln(0.8)}$$

$$n = 10.3$$

Thus 11 or more seeds must be planted to ensure a 90% chance of at least one germination.

1.5 An introduction to sampling
1.5.1 Random samples

1.5 A

1 As the same number of trains run east as west the answer must have something to do with the time the trains arrive at the station.

Suppose the westbound train arrives 10 minutes after the eastbound train. The following diagram should help to explain the paradox in the case when eastbound trains arrive on the hour, every hour.

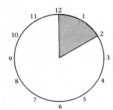

There are ten minutes when the next train will be westbound (shaded) and fifty minutes when the next train will be eastbound (unshaded).

2 The princess ensures that her favourite suitor's coin is in one of the urns on its own. All the other suitors' coins are in the second urn. The king has a 50:50 chance of choosing the urn with the princess' favourite suitor's coin.

1.5 B

2 It is quite likely that neither sampling procedure gives particularly close estimates to the true mean (μ). Neither sampling method is likely to give a representative sample, due in part to the way in which the data are listed on the sheet. Method A will always give a sample of five students of the same sex, while method B will sometimes give a mixed group. Neither will give a sample of five independently selected individuals. If a particular sixth-former is selected, then the other members of the sample are adjacent or close by on the list.

3 To obtain a more representative sample, you must ensure that each member of the population has an equal and independent chance of being included. This type of sample is called a **random sample**. An elementary but time-consuming way of obtaining such a sample would be to number the sixth-formers from 1 to 300 and then to draw five numbers from 300 well-mixed raffle tickets.

A computer or calculator can be used to rapidly generate random numbers in the range 1 to 300. Some calculators generate random integers in the range 0 to 9, so three such numbers taken together give a number in the range 000 to 999, each with an equal probability of occurring. If each sixth-former is allocated one number you would not be able to make a selection if any of random numbers 301–999 appeared. To avoid this wastage you can allocate three numbers to each person.

	Numbers allocated		
Student 1	001	301	601
Student 2	002	302	602
....	...	...	...
....	...	...	...
Student 300	300	600	900

In this scheme only the numbers 000 and 901–999 remain unused. However, it is not possible to allocate these numbers, as each sixth former must have an equal number of 'chances' so that each has an equal probability of $\frac{1}{300}$ of being included in the sample.

1.5 Exercise 1

1 The sample is biased.

If you assume that each floor is equally populated, then the lift is more likely to be above floor 3 than below floor 3. Similarly, the lift is more likely to be below the 10th floor than above it.

2 The sample is biased.

Possible reasons are:

(a) One elderly person with a contagious disease is more likely to pass it on to another elderly person in the residential home than if he or she were living alone.

(b) People in a residential home are more likely to be in need of medical attention.

(c) Elderly people living in a residential home are likely to have better living conditions (food, heating etc.) than those not living in a residential home.

(d) If the home is fee-paying then residents are unlikely to be representative of the general population.

3 The sample was biased.

In fact Truman won the 1948 US Presidential Election. The incorrect forecast of the opinion poll was attributed to the fact that the majority of telephone owners in the US in 1948 were Republican voters. Those who owned telephones did not form a representative sample of the voting population.

4 The sample is biased.

In November the main reason for absences is likely to be illness. Truancy and interviews are more likely to be reasons in the spring and summer terms.

1.5.2 Sample size

1.5 C

1, 2 You should find that the distribution of $\bar{x}$ for random samples of size 10 is a more compact and symmetrical distribution than that for $\bar{x}$ from random samples of 5. Your results should be close to these.

Size of random sample	Mean of $\bar{x}$	Variance of $\bar{x}$
5	167.4	8.63
10	167.4	4.31

3 Your distribution of sample means will have a mean close to the population mean. The sample means for the samples of $n = 10$ will have a smaller variance than those for $n = 5$.

4 (a) Results for both samples of size 5 and size 10 are likely to be close to the true mean.

(b) A crucial part of the theory underpinning the use of samples is that as the sample size increases, the distribution of the sample mean becomes increasingly clustered around the true value of the population mean. This is reflected in the smaller variance of the distribution of $\bar{x}$ for samples of size 10 as compared to samples of size 5. The estimates generated by larger random samples are less variable than those generated by smaller random samples so, as you might expect, unusual results from large samples tend to be more **significant** than those from small samples.

1.5.3 Testing claims based on sample evidence

1.5 D

1 (a) You would expect those who regularly commute to the centre to be in favour – also perhaps shop owners.

(b) A total of 48 replied.

(i) 5   (ii) 23   (iii) 20

2 A sampling procedure ideally should be just as likely to choose one particular member of the population as it is any other, but often this is impracticable.

The sample of 48 were, in fact, the people who filled in a coupon accompanying a previous article on the monorail proposal. Such a sampling procedure is almost bound to introduce bias. In this case, it could be argued that people opposed to new proposals are much more likely to take the trouble to write in than people who feel favourably about them. A better method would be to conduct a random sample of the population of the city and its surrounding districts.

A dictionary might define a bias as a predisposition or prejudice. Thus a die is biased if it is predisposed to show a particular face more than any other. A telephone poll could be predisposed to selecting relatively prosperous members of society.

1.5 E

1 Since no samples in the simulation produced a result as low as five supporting the scheme, it seems highly likely that the actual percentage in support is less than 50%.

2 This shows that in a poll of 48 people, obtaining 5 or fewer in support of the project is very unlikely. The poll would therefore provide strong evidence that the majority of the population are against the monorail *if* you could be confident that the method of conducting the poll has not introduced bias.

3 A result of 22 is in or near the middle of the distribution – it is the sort of result you would expect if the initial assumption was valid. It would then be quite likely that around 50% of the population were in favour of the monorail.

1.5 Exercise 2

1 (a) $P(6 \text{ correct}) = \binom{8}{6}\left(\frac{1}{2}\right)^6\left(\frac{1}{2}\right)^2$

$$= 28\left(\frac{1}{2}\right)^8$$

$$= \frac{28}{256} (\approx 11\%)$$

(b) $P(6 \text{ or more}) = \binom{8}{6}\left(\frac{1}{2}\right)^8 + \binom{8}{7}\left(\frac{1}{2}\right)^8$

$$+ \binom{8}{8}\left(\frac{1}{2}\right)^8$$

$$= \frac{28}{256} + \frac{8}{256} + \frac{1}{256}$$

$$= \frac{37}{256} (\approx 14\%)$$

Random guessing would produce a result of 6 or more correct 'predictions' in about 14% of cases. 7 or 8 correct results would have been more convincing.

2 Assuming that the taster cannot tell the difference, and is 50% likely to be correct each time,

$P(7 \text{ or more correct})$
$$= \frac{120 + 45 + 10 + 1}{1024} = \frac{176}{1024} (\approx 17\%)$$
$P(8 \text{ or more correct})$
$$= \frac{45 + 10 + 1}{1024} = \frac{56}{1024} (\approx 5\%)$$
$P(9 \text{ or more correct})$
$$= \frac{10 + 1}{1024} = \frac{11}{1024} (\approx 1\%)$$
8 or more correct is quite convincing. 9 or 10 correct would make you more certain that they are not guessing.

1.6E Further probability
1.6.1 Conditional probability

1.6 **A**

1 Of the 1000 adults you should expect 1000×0.03 to be colour blind, i.e. 30 individuals.

(a) $500 \times 0.05 = 25$ (b) $500 - 25 = 475$

(c) $30 - 25 = 5$ (d) $500 - 5 = 495$

2 $P(C|M) = 0.05$

3 $P(C'|F)$ is the probability of not being colour blind given that the subject is female.
It is $\frac{495}{500} = 0.99$.

4

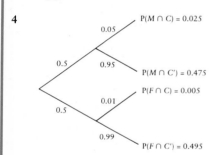

$P(M \cap C) = 0.025$

0.05

0.5

0.95

$P(M \cap C') = 0.475$

$P(F \cap C) = 0.005$

0.01

0.5

0.99

$P(F \cap C') = 0.495$

5 $\dfrac{P(M \cap C)}{P(M)} = \dfrac{0.025}{0.5} = 0.05 = P(C|M)$

6 (a) $P(C'|M) = \dfrac{P(M \cap C')}{P(M)}$

(b) $P(C|F) = \dfrac{P(F \cap C)}{P(F)}$

(c) $P(C'|F) = \dfrac{P(F \cap C')}{P(F)}$

7 $P(C) = P(M \cap C) + P(F \cap C)$
$\qquad = P(M)P(C|M) + P(F)P(C|F)$

1.6 **Exercise 1**

1 (a) $P(A \cap B) = P(A)P(B)$ or $P(B|A) = P(B)$
or $P(A|B) = P(A)$

(b) $P(A \cup B) = P(A) + P(B)$

2 (a) $P(A) + P(A') = 1$

(b) $P(A|B) + P(A'|B) = 1$

(c) $P(A'|B)P(B) = P(A' \cap B)$

(d) $P(A \cup B) + P(B')P(A'|B')$
$= P(A \cup B) + P(A' \cap B')$
$= P(A \cup B) + P[(A \cup B)']$
$= 1$

3 Let B stand for blue-eyed and L for left-handed.

$P(L|B) = \frac{1}{7}$ $P(B|L) = \frac{1}{3}$ $P(L' \cap B') = \frac{4}{5}$

You have to find $P(L \cap B)$.

$$P(L|B) = \frac{P(L \cap B)}{P(B)} \text{ and } P(B|L) = \frac{P(L \cap B)}{P(L)}$$

So, putting $P(L \cap B) = x$, $P(B) = 7x$
and $P(L) = 3x$

Now, $P(L' \cap B') = P[(L \cup B)'] = \frac{4}{5}$,
so $P(L \cup B) = \frac{1}{5}$

But $P(L \cup B) = P(L) + P(B) - P(L \cap B)$
i.e. $\frac{1}{5} = 3x + 7x - x = 9x$

Hence $P(L \cap B) = x = \frac{1}{45}$

4 (a)   (i) $P(A \cap B) = P(B)P(A|B) = \frac{1}{3} \times \frac{1}{4} = \frac{1}{12}$

(ii) $P(A \cup B) = P(A) + P(B) - P(A \cap B)$
$= \frac{1}{2} + \frac{1}{3} - \frac{1}{12} = \frac{3}{4}$

(iii) $P(A' \cap B') = P[(A \cup B)']$
$= 1 - P(A \cup B) = \frac{1}{4}$

(b) Since A and C are independent,
$P(A \cap C) = P(A)P(C)$, hence

$$P(C) = \tfrac{1}{12} \div \tfrac{1}{2} = \tfrac{1}{6}$$

Then to show that B and C are mutually exclusive you can now verify that

$$P(B \cup C) = P(B) + P(C)$$

1.6.2 Bayes' theorem

1.6 B

1 If A is to be executed, then the other is equally likely to be B or C. If A is not to be executed, then B and C are to be executed and the jailer is equally likely to name either. In both possible cases the probability of the jailer choosing to name B is $\frac{1}{2}$.

2 The formula is a symbolic form of the explanation just given. The value of the expression is

$$\tfrac{2}{3} \times \tfrac{1}{2} + \tfrac{1}{3} \times \tfrac{1}{2} = \tfrac{1}{2}$$

1.6 Exercise 2

1 Let F stand for fiction and H for hardback.

$$P(F) = 0.4 \qquad P(F') = 0.6 \qquad P(F \cap H) = 0.1$$

$$P(H) = 0.5$$

$$P(F|H) = \frac{P(F \cap H)}{P(H)} = 0.2$$

2 Abbreviations used (for night drivers) are D for drinking and A for accident.

$$P(D) = \tfrac{1}{4} \qquad P(A|D') = 4 \times 10^{-5}$$

$$P(A|D) = 2 \times 10^{-3}$$

First you have to find $P(A)$.

$$P(A) = P(D)P(A|D) + P(D')P(A|D')$$

$$= \tfrac{1}{4} \times 2 \times 10^{-3} + \tfrac{3}{4} \times 4 \times 10^{-5}$$

$$= 5.3 \times 10^{-4}$$

The probability that the policeman's guess is correct is $P(D|A)$.

By Bayes' theorem,

$$P(D|A) = \frac{P(D)P(A|D)}{P(A)}$$

$$= \frac{\tfrac{1}{4} \times 2 \times 10^{-3}}{5.3 \times 10^{-4}} \approx 0.94$$

1.6.3 Further applications of Bayes' theorem

1.6 Exercise 3

1 $P(D|F) = \dfrac{P(D)P(F|D)}{P(F)} = \dfrac{0.3 \times 0.2}{0.56} = \dfrac{3}{28}$

$P(R|F) = \dfrac{P(R)P(F|R)}{P(F)} = \dfrac{0.1 \times 0.2}{0.56} = \dfrac{1}{28}$

$\dfrac{6}{7} + \dfrac{3}{28} + \dfrac{1}{28} = 1$

2 Abbreviations used are B for 'New Sudso is better than Kleenrite' and F for a favourable report.

Prior probability $P(B)$ is 0.9 and conditional probabilities $P(F|B)$ and $P(F|B')$ are 0.8 and 0.2 respectively.

You have to find $P(B|F)$. From Bayes' theorem,

$$P(B|F) = \frac{P(B)P(F|B)}{P(B)P(F|B) + P(B')P(F|B')}$$

$$= \frac{0.9 \times 0.8}{(0.9 \times 0.8) + (0.1 \times 0.2)} \approx 0.97$$

The example shows how a not very reliable survey can be a powerful reinforcement of a hunch.

3 Abbreviations used are A and B for 'resistors come from machines A and B', and E for 'sample of three are all good'.

(a) $P(E|A) = (0.9)^3 = 0.729$

Similarly, $P(E|B) = (0.8)^3 = 0.512$

(b) $P(A|E) \approx 0.77$

4 $P(L|G)$

$$= \frac{P(L)P(G|L)}{P(L)P(G|L) + P(H)P(G|H) + P(M)P(G|M)}$$

$$= \frac{0.5 \times 0.2}{(0.5 \times 0.2) + (0.25 \times 0.5) + (0.25 \times 0.9)}$$

$$\approx 0.222$$

Similarly, $P(L|G') = 0.727$, $P(H|G) = 0.278$, $P(H|G') = 0.227$, $P(M|G) = 0.500$, $P(M|G') = 0.045$ (all to 3 d.p.)

5 Taking $P(E) = 0.5$

$\quad P(E|F) \approx 0.82$

Taking $P(E) = 0.7$

$\quad P(E|F) \approx 0.91$

(a) In both cases a conjecture is strongly supported by a contingent event. As the prior probability increases by 0.2, the posterior probability increases by rather less than 0.1; the weaker the conjecture, the greater is the strengthening effect.

(b) Much scientific progress is based on this idea. Theories are tested by experiment and reinforced, weakened or rejected as a result.

Medical diagnosis proceeds according to the same model. Jaundice may make a doctor suspect gallstones. Using knowledge of other symptoms of this complaint the doctor asks questions and performs tests which may lead to reinforcement of the original suspicion. If necessary an X-ray examination will virtually settle the matter.

Miscellaneous exercise 1

1 With: Lower quartile = 18, median = 20.5, upper quartile = 22
Without: 11, 15, 17

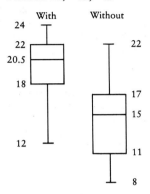

2 (a) $m = 33.4$, $s = 7.35$ (b) 0.12

(c) about 32 minutes

3 Mean = 81.375 kg, s.d. = 4.21 kg

4 (b) Mean = 194 g, s.d. = 25.8 g

5 Mean = 1.95 kg, s.d. = 0.05 kg

6 (a) Mean = 60, s.d. = 12

(b) Mean = 99, s.d. = 21.6

(c) Mean = 115, s.d. = 24

7 (a) (i) $0.8^3 \times 0.2^2 = 0.0205$ (ii) 0.205

(b)

N	0	1	2	3	4	5
$P(N = n)$	0.000 32	0.0064	0.0512	0.2048	0.4096	0.327 68

Mean = 4, s.d. = 0.894 (to 3 s.f.)

8 (a) 68% (b) 17.6% (c) 43.8%

9 (b) Mean = 1.37 days, s.d. = 0.87 days

10 P(at least 1 double six) $= 1 - \left(\frac{35}{36}\right)^{24} = 0.49$

It would not be a particularly good bet.

11 0.75

12 (b) $\frac{31}{63}$

13 $\frac{4}{35}$

14 £180

15 (a) Expected winnings per month $= 0.45$ jiks.

Rick would expect to lose 0.55 jiks per month, or 6.60 jiks per year.

(b) (i) 0.280 (to 3 s.f.)

(ii) Possibilities are 0 and (25 or 100)

or (25 or 100) and (any)

or (10) and (10)

Thus P(at least 10) $= 0.0144$ (to 3 s.f.)

16 (a) $\left(\dfrac{a}{N}\right)^3$ (b) $\dfrac{a(a-1)(a-2)}{N(N-1)(N-2)}$

17 (a) $\dfrac{2a(N-a)}{N^2}$ (b) $\dfrac{2a(N-a)}{N(N-1)}$

18 (a) $\frac{98}{125}$ (b) $\frac{36}{125}$

19 (a) (i) 0.078 (ii) $0.88^4 = 0.60$

(b) $0.98^4 + (4 \times (0.98)^3) \times 0.98^4 = 0.99$ (to 2 s.f.)

20 0.0156 (to 3 s.f.)

2 THE NORMAL DISTRIBUTION

2.1 An important distribution

2.1.1 Introduction

2.1 A

1 From a sample of adult males you would expect a distribution similar to the one below.

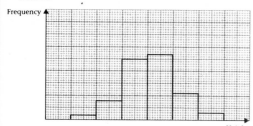

There are few men who are *very* tall or *very* short. Most men are somewhere in the middle.

2 (b) ±1 s.d. covers approximately the range of values 7.04 to 7.24. There are about 72 observations (or about 70% of the observations) within ±1 s.d. of the mean.

You are looking for weights between 6.94 and 7.34. There are about 96 observations in this range.

2.1.2 Standardising data

2.1 B

1 $\bar{x} = \dfrac{9 + 9 + 10 + 12 + 14 + 16 + 16 + 18}{8} = 13$

Variance $= \frac{1}{8}\{(9 - 13)^2 + (9 - 13)^2 + \ldots\}$

s.d. $= \sqrt{10.75} = 3.28$ (to 3 s.f.)

2

Original score	9	9	10	12	14	16	16	18
Standardised score	−1.22	−1.22	−0.915	−0.305	0.305	0.915	0.915	1.52

4 Other data sets will produce the same results for the mean and the standard deviation. In each case the mean of standardised data is 0 and the standard deviation is 1, although rounding errors in the calculations will lead only approximately to these values.

2.1 Exercise 1

1 (a) −1   (b) −2.833   (c) 1   (d) $\dfrac{x - m}{d}$

2 (a)

	Standardised scores	
	Mathematics	Economics
Karen	0.833	0.375
Alex	−2.708	−3.375
Melanie	0	0
Chris	−7.083	−5.375

(b) Mathematics 64 (2.08 standardised);

Economics $\dfrac{x - 68}{8} = 2.08 \Rightarrow x \approx 85$

(c) $\dfrac{x - 54}{4.8} = \dfrac{x - 68}{6} \Rightarrow x = 33$

3 (a) The man is relatively taller.

Male: $\dfrac{-1}{2.8} = -0.36$; Female: $\dfrac{-1}{2.4} = -0.42$

(b) 5 ft 9 in

4 Let the original observations be $x_1, x_2, \ldots, x_n$ (mean $= \bar{x}$, s.d. $= s$).

$z_1 = \dfrac{x_1 - \bar{x}}{s}, \quad z_2 = \dfrac{x_2 - \bar{x}}{s}, \quad \ldots$

$\bar{z} = \displaystyle\sum_{i=1}^{n} \left(\dfrac{x_i - \bar{x}}{s} \right) = \dfrac{1}{s} \sum (x_i - \bar{x})$

$= \dfrac{1}{s} \left(\sum x_i - n\bar{x} \right)$

But $\sum x_i = n\bar{x}$

So $\bar{z} = 0$

$$V(z) = \frac{1}{n} \sum z_i^2 - (\bar{z})^2$$

$$= \frac{1}{n} \sum z_i^2$$

$$= \frac{1}{n} \sum \left(\frac{x_i - \bar{x}}{s}\right)^2$$

$$= \frac{1}{ns^2} \sum (x_i^2 - 2x_i\bar{x} + (\bar{x})^2)$$

$$= \frac{1}{ns^2} \left(\sum x_i^2 - 2\bar{x} \sum x_i + n(\bar{x})^2\right)$$

$$= \frac{1}{ns^2} \left(\sum x_i^2 - n(\bar{x})^2\right)$$

$$= \frac{1}{ns^2} (ns^2) = 1$$

2.1.3 Considering the area

2.1 C

1 (a) The total relative frequency is 1 and will always be so for any data set.

(b) The area of each block is

height of block × width

= relative frequency for the block

The total area of the histogram is the sum of the areas of the separate blocks, which is the same as the sum of the relative frequencies. The area of a relative frequency density histogram is therefore 1.

2 The relative frequency density histogram is illustrated.

2.1.4 The 'Normal' curve

2.1 D

1 $f(x) = k\,e^{-ax^2}$

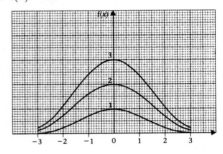

Graphs of the functions e^{-x^2}, $2e^{-\frac{1}{2}x^2}$ and $3e^{-\frac{1}{4}x^2}$ are shown and clearly display the basic shape that is required.

If k is negative, then the graphs obtained are mirror images of those shown with a positive value for k. Therefore k must be positive.

2 The area under the curve should be 1. This idea can be used to find k by plotting $f(x)$ for different values of k and obtaining the total area under each curve using, say, the trapezium rule. You can keep adjusting k until the area is (approximately) 1.

2.2 Applying the Normal distribution
2.2.1 Area and probability

2.2 A

1 Your values should be approximately

a	b	Area
0	1	0.341
1	2	0.136
2	3	0.0215

2 The area between ±1 s.d. is 0.682.

The area between ±2 s.d. is 0.954.

The area between ±3 s.d. is 0.997.

3 (a) 0.68   (b) 0.023   (c) 0.001

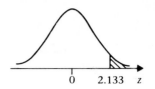

The percentage with an IQ of 132 or more is 1.7%.

2.2.2 Tables for the Standard Normal function

2.2 Exercise 1

1 (a) 0.092

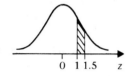

(b) (i) 0.067   (ii) 0.977

(c) (i) 0.947   (ii) 0.929   (iii) 0.055

(d) (i) 0.045   (ii) 0.775   (iii) 0.242

2 (a) 0.683   (b) 0.954   (c) 0.997

3 (a) $z = 1.22$ (b) $z = 0.44$ (c) $z = 1.50$

(d) $z = -0.04$ (e) $z = -1.15$

4 (a) $z = -1.52$ (b) $z = -1.18$

(c) $z = 0.77$ (d) $z = 0.35$ (e) $z = -0.07$

2.2.3 Other Normal distributions

2.2 Exercise 2

1 $z = \dfrac{132 - 100}{15} = 2.133$;

$\Phi(2.133) = 0.983$ (to 3 s.f.)

2 $z = \dfrac{1.52 - 1.5}{0.01} = 2$;

$\Phi(2) = 0.9772$

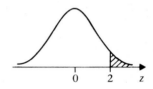

The proportion rejected as being over 1.52 cm is 2.3%.

3 $\Phi(z) = 0.03$; $z = -1.88$

$-1.88 = \dfrac{1 - m}{0.0025}$

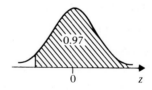

The mean must be 1.005 kg.

4 $\Phi(z) = 0.005$; $z = -2.575$

$\dfrac{1.5 - 1.53}{\sigma} = -2.575$

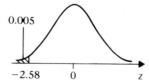

The standard deviation must be less than 0.0117.

5 19.1

6 The standard deviation must be 4.44.

7 $\dfrac{498.5 - 500}{4} < z < \dfrac{500.5 - 500}{4}$

$-0.375 < z < 0.125$

19.6% of tubs will weigh between 498.5 g and 500.5 g.

8 35.7% of the girls are between 150 cm and 155 cm tall.

9 Mean = 48.9, standard deviation = 16.5.

2.3 From binomial to Normal
2.3.2 More detailed considerations

2.3 Exercise 1

1 (a) $B(100, \frac{1}{2})$ is approximated by $N(50, 25)$.
$P(X \geq 52)$ is the area to the right of 51.5.

$z = \dfrac{51.5 - 50}{5} = 0.3$

$P(Z > 0.3) = 0.382$

(b) 0.109   (c) 0.00

2 $B(200, 0.7)$ is approximated by $N(140, 42)$.

$z = \dfrac{149.5 - 140}{\sqrt{42}} = 1.466$

$P(Z > 1.466) = 0.071$

3 (a) $\dbinom{30}{5}\left(\dfrac{1}{6}\right)^5\left(\dfrac{5}{6}\right)^{25} = 0.192$

(b) $B(30, \frac{1}{6})$ is approximated by $N(5, 4.167)$.
$P(X = 5)$ is the area between 4.5 and 5.5.

$\dfrac{4.5 - 5}{\sqrt{4.167}} < z < \dfrac{5.5 - 5}{\sqrt{4.167}}$

$P(-0.245 < Z < 0.245) = 0.194$

4 0.455

5 (a) 0.035   (b) 0.455

6 0.0561

7 0.208

8 0.527

9 (a) 0.286   (b) 0.588

10 (a) 0.650   (b) 0.480

2.4 Sampling distribution of the mean
2.4.1 Sample and population

2.4 A

1 Your own solution will differ from this example, which is provided as an illustration.

Sample mean weight (g)	Tally	Frequency
6.80 –		0
6.85 –		0
6.90 –	||	2
6.95 –		0
7.00 –	|||	3
7.05 –	ⱶⱶ ⱶⱶ ||	12
7.10 –	ⱶⱶ ⱶⱶ |||	13
7.15 –	ⱶⱶ ⱶⱶ ⱶⱶ		16
7.20 –	||	2
7.25 –	||	2
7.30 –		0
7.35 –		0
7.40 –		0

3 The mean of the distribution of sample means is 7.12. The variance of the distribution is 0.0049.

4 The mean of the distribution of the sample means is very close to the population mean, but the variance of the sample means is smaller than the population variance.

2.4.2 The Central Limit Theorem

2.4 Exercise 1

1 $X \sim N(166, 6^2)$

Sample size 5, $\quad \bar{X} \sim N\left(166, \dfrac{6^2}{5}\right)$

$z = 1.49$

$P(-1.49 < Z < 1.49) = 0.864$

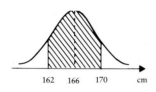

Sample size 8, $\quad \bar{X} \sim N\left(166, \dfrac{6^2}{8}\right)$

$z = 1.886$

$P(-1.886 < Z < 1.886) = 0.941$

2 $X \sim N(980, 120^2)$

Sample size 10, $\quad \bar{X} \sim N\left(980, \dfrac{120^2}{10}\right)$

(a) $P(970 < \bar{X} < 1010)$
$= P(-0.264 < Z < 0.791) = 0.39$

(b) $P(950 < \bar{X} < 1030)$
$= P(-0.791 < Z < 1.318) = 0.69$

(c) $P(940 < \bar{X} < 1040)$
$= P(-1.054 < Z < 1.581) = 0.80$

3 $X \sim N(162, 3.5^2)$

Sample size n, $\quad \bar{X} \sim N\left(162, \dfrac{3.5^2}{n}\right)$

(a) $\dfrac{163.5 - 162}{3.5/\sqrt{n}} = 1.96$

$n = 20.9$

A sample of size 21 must be taken.

(b) A sample of 48 must be taken.

4 (a) 26   (b) 234

5 0.030

6 (a) 0.401   (b) 0.193

2.5 Estimating with confidence
2.5.1 The standard error

2.5 Exercise 1

1 (a) 0.4   (b) 0.095

2 (a) $\bar{x} = 5.57 \quad n = 6 \quad$ s.e. $= 0.816$

(b) $\bar{x} = 6.75 \quad n = 20 \quad$ s.e. $= 0.447$

3 $\bar{x} = 3.7 \quad n = 40 \quad$ s.e. $= 0.079$

3 s.e. above the mean would give a value of 3.94.

This is still well below the normal pH of 5.7, which suggests that there is excess acid in the rain.

2.5.2 Confidence intervals

2.5 Exercise 2

1 (a) Clean Valley Primary School:

$\bar{x} = 8.15 \quad n = 25 \quad \sigma^2 = 0.5$

s.e. $= \dfrac{\sigma}{\sqrt{n}} = 0.141$

68% confidence interval (8.01, 8.29)
95% confidence interval (7.87, 8.43)

(b) Clean Valley Water Authority:

$\bar{x} = 7.8 \quad n = 100 \quad \sigma^2 = 0.5$

s.e. $= \dfrac{\sigma}{\sqrt{n}} = 0.071$

68% confidence interval (7.73, 7.87)
95% confidence interval (7.66, 7.94)

2 $n = 9$ $\sigma = 10$ $\bar{x} = 20$ s.e. $= 3.33$

90% confidence interval (14.52, 25.48)
95% confidence interval (13.47, 26.53)
99% confidence interval (11.41, 28.59)

3 The confidence intervals would be smaller.

$n = 25$ $\sigma = 10$ $\bar{x} = 20$ s.e. $= 2$

90% confidence interval (16.71, 23.29)
95% confidence interval (16.08, 23.92)
99% confidence interval (14.84, 25.16)

4 (a) (12.59, 13.61)   (b) (2.53, 2.77)

 (c) (201.62, 208.38)

5 (a) (0.0999, 0.160)   (b) (20.51, 21.29)

 (c) (842.3, 847.7)

6 Sample: $n = 50$ $\bar{x} = 26$ $\sigma^2 = 6$

$$\text{s.e.} = \frac{\sqrt{6}}{\sqrt{50}} = 0.346$$

The 95% confidence interval is 26 ± 1.96 s.e.
i.e. (25.3, 26.7)

7 $\sigma = 9.5$ $n = 10$ s.e. $= 3.004$ $\bar{x} = 117.1$

90% confidence interval (112.16, 122.04)

8 (a) Width of 95% confidence interval is 3.92;

 (b) width of 95% confidence interval is 2.77;

 (c) width of 95% confidence interval is 1.96.

For a width of 1, a sample of 1537 would
have to be taken.

2.5.3 Estimating a population variance

2.5 A

1 This can be checked simply by using the statistics functions on your calculator. Alternatively,

x	-1	1
$x - \mu$	-1	1
$(x - \mu)^2$	1	1
$P(X = x)$	$\frac{1}{2}$	$\frac{1}{2}$

$$\sigma^2 = 1 \times \tfrac{1}{2} + 1 \times \tfrac{1}{2} = 1$$

2 $s^2 = \tfrac{1}{2} \sum_1^2 x_i^2 - (\bar{x})^2$

$$= \tfrac{1}{2}(1^2 + (-1)^2) - 0^2 = 1$$

3 The sample $(-1, -1)$ consists of 2 males.

$$P(\text{male and male}) = \left(\tfrac{1}{2}\right)^2 = \tfrac{1}{4}$$

The mean of the sample is -1. Its variance is zero; similarly for other values in the table.

4

Sample	$(-1, -1, -1)$	$(-1, -1, 1)$	$(-1, 1, 1)$	$(1, 1, 1)$
Probability	$\frac{1}{8}$	$\frac{3}{8}$	$\frac{3}{8}$	$\frac{1}{8}$
Sample mean, $\bar{x}$	-1	$-\frac{1}{3}$	$\frac{1}{3}$	1
Sample variance	0	$\frac{8}{9}$	$\frac{8}{9}$	0

5 For both $n = 2$ and $n = 3$, the distributions of sample means have mean 0, illustrating the fact that $\bar{x}$ is an unbiased estimator of μ.

2.5 Exercise 3

1 (a) $s^2 = 0.0017$, $\left(\dfrac{n}{n-1}\right)s^2 = 0.0019$

 (b) $s^2 = 33.05$, $\left(\dfrac{n}{n-1}\right)s^2 = 36.72$

2 (a) $s^2 = 2.038$, $\left(\dfrac{n}{n-1}\right)s^2 = 2.061$

(b) $s^2 = 1829$, $\left(\dfrac{n}{n-1}\right)s^2 = 1925$

3 Estimate of mean is 1.501
Sample variance $\approx 8.2 \times 10^{-6}$
Estimate of σ^2 is 9.9×10^{-6}

2.5.4 Populations with unknown variance

2.5 B

1 To find the standard error you must know the population standard deviation.

2 You do not know the value of the population standard deviation.

You have seen that $\dfrac{ns^2}{n-1}$ is an unbiased

estimator of the population variance and this could be used instead of the unknown value.

3 If the sample size is large enough then the distribution of mean remission times will be Normal, whatever the distribution of the parent population.

2.5 Exercise 4

1 (a) Population variance (estimated)

$$= \dfrac{n}{n-1}s_n^{\,2} = \dfrac{36}{35} \times 4 = 4.11$$

A 95% interval is 10 ± 1.96 s.e.

$$= 10 \pm 1.96 \dfrac{\sigma}{\sqrt{n}}$$

$$= 10 \pm 1.96 \times 0.338$$

$$= (9.34, 10.7) \text{ to 3 s.f.}$$

(b) $(19.4, 20.6)$ to 3 s.f.

(c) $(19.9, 20.1)$ to 3 s.f.

The answer is likely to be inaccurate because the sample size is small.

2 $n = 59$ $\bar{x} = 114$ $s_{n-1} = 4.14$ s.e. $= 0.538$
A 90% confidence interval is $(113, 115)$ to 3 s.f.

3 $n = 891$ $\bar{x} = 3.856$ $s_{n-1} = 1.286$

s.e. $= 0.043$

A 95% confidence interval is $(3.77, 3.94)$

The actual mean age of the fish is unknown. However, this single sample provides an interval which you can be confident contains the mean: if you took a large number of samples of this size, even though *each* would generate *its own* confidence interval for the mean, in 95% of cases you could expect that confidence interval to contain the true mean.

4 (a) $n = 10$ $\bar{x} = 10$ $s_{n-1} = 4.22$ s.e. $= 1.33$

A 90% confidence interval is $(7.8, 12.2)$

(b) The sample is small, so you can only say that the distribution of sample means is approximately Normal.

2.5.5 Estimating a population proportion

2.5 C

Part of inequality ① is

$$400p - 1.96\sqrt{(400p(1-p))} < X$$

$$\Rightarrow 400p < X + 1.96\sqrt{(400p(1-p))}$$

$$\Rightarrow p < \dfrac{X}{400} + 1.96\sqrt{\left(\dfrac{p(1-p)}{400}\right)}$$

The other half of inequality ① is

$$X < 400p + 1.96\sqrt{(400p(1-p))}$$

$$\Rightarrow X - 1.96\sqrt{(400p(1-p))} < 400p$$

$$\Rightarrow \dfrac{X}{400} - 1.96\sqrt{\left(\dfrac{p(1-p)}{400}\right)} < p$$

Combining the two inequalities for p gives inequality ②.

2.5 Exercise 5

1 (a) (i) $p = 0.178 \qquad q = 0.822 \qquad n = 10\ 284$

$$0.178 - 1.96\sqrt{\left(\frac{(0.178)(0.822)}{10\ 284}\right)}$$

$$< p <$$

$$0.178 + 1.96\sqrt{\left(\frac{(0.178)(0.822)}{10\ 284}\right)}$$

$$\Rightarrow 0.171 < p < 0.185$$

i.e. between 17.1% and 18.5%

(ii) $p = 0.418 \qquad q = 0.582 \qquad n = 10\ 284$
The 95% confidence interval is
$(40.8\%, 42.8\%)$

(b) $p = 0.573 \qquad q = 0.427 \qquad n = 10\ 284$
The 90% confidence interval is
$(56.8\%, 57.8\%)$

(c) $p = 0.555 \qquad q = 0.445 \qquad n = 1119$
The 99% confidence interval is
$(51.7\%, 59.3\%)$

(d) From (a), it can be seen that a 95% confidence interval is approximately of the form $p \pm 1\%$.

If p were rounded to the nearest 1%, this would increase the possible error to $\pm 1.5\%$, which would not be sensible. Conversely, it would be unreasonable to give p to $\pm 0.01\%$, given a band as wide as $\pm 1\%$. To 1 d.p. therefore seems the most appropriate precision.

2 (a) (i) For males, the 95% confidence interval is

$$0.67 \pm 1.96\sqrt{\left(\frac{0.67 \times 0.33}{444}\right)}$$

i.e. 0.63 to 0.71

(ii) For females, the interval is

$$0.72 \pm 1.96\sqrt{\left(\frac{0.72 \times 0.28}{306}\right)}$$

i.e. 0.67 to 0.77

(b) $0.19 \pm 1.645\sqrt{\left(\frac{0.19 \times 0.81}{313}\right)}$

i.e. 0.15 to 0.23

3 (a) Point estimate $p = 0.5$
The council requires $p \pm 0.02$
The 90% interval for p is $p \pm 1.645$ s.e.

$$1.645\sqrt{\left(\frac{0.5 \times 0.5}{n}\right)} \leq 0.02 \Rightarrow n \geq 1692$$

The council should select a sample of at least 1692 people.

(b) $0.02 \geq 1.96\sqrt{\left(\frac{0.5 \times 0.5}{n}\right)} \Rightarrow n \geq 2401$

Miscellaneous exercise 2

1 0.933

2 0.03

3 4.5 days

4 0.78 months,   99

5 (a) 49   (b) 52   (c) 9

6 0.184
  (a) 0.005   (b) about 0

7 0.097

8 0.081;   8 flights a year

9 0.059

10 0.053

11 (a) 0.006   (b) 0.013

12 (a) 0.06   (b) 0.096

13 (a) 0.23   (b) 0.013

14 0.24 to 0.37

15 (a) 0.24 to 0.36
   (b) Increase by a factor of 4.

16 0.56 to 0.74

17 39.9 to 40.1

18 9.74 m s^{-2} to 9.86 m s^{-2}

19 57 kg to 79 kg

20 $x = 23.6$, $s_n = 1.8$,   22.6 ohms to 24.6 ohms

3 PROBABILITY MODELS FOR DATA

3.1 Goodness of fit: the chi-squared test
3.1.1 Deterministic and probabilistic models

3.1 A

(a) Probabilistic model.

(b) There is a great deal of uncertainty concerning the value of the pound and models to predict its value in the future need to assign probabilities to various possible outcomes. Models are therefore likely to be probabilistic, but once certain assumptions have been made, deterministic models may be used.

(c) Deterministic model.

(d) Probabilistic model.

(e) The rate of a nuclear reaction can be modelled with a deterministic mathematical model as it involves huge numbers of molecules and statistical fluctuations would 'even out'. The underlying process is again probabilistic.

(f) Probabilistic model.

3.1 B

1 The likelihood of a baby being a boy is almost the same as its being a girl. If you consider the sex of a child as being independent of the sex of other children in a family, then the sex of the first child would not affect that of subsequent children. You could investigate this assumption by looking at a large number of families and counting the number of male and female children in each family.

2 These data would seem to suggest that if the first child is a boy then the second child is more likely to be a boy also. It will also seem that the second child is more likely to be a girl if the first child is a girl. In a sample of 100 families, you would expect about 25 in each of the cells. You should consider whether the variation from 25 is sufficient for you to reconsider your ideas in question 1. Are you just seeing *random* fluctuations, or do the data indicate something significant?

3 If you assume that a baby is equally likely to be a boy or girl and that the sex of the second child is independent of the first, then the probability of

$$\text{boy, boy} = \tfrac{1}{2} \times \tfrac{1}{2} = 0.25$$
$$\text{boy, girl} = \tfrac{1}{2} \times \tfrac{1}{2} = 0.25$$
$$\text{girl, boy} = \tfrac{1}{2} \times \tfrac{1}{2} = 0.25$$
$$\text{girl, girl} = \tfrac{1}{2} \times \tfrac{1}{2} = 0.25$$

3.1 C

1 (a) and (b) You may find that your sequence contains more $(0, 1)$ and $(1, 0)$ pairings than $(0, 0)$ and $(1, 1)$.

(c) If the sequence were random, the probability of obtaining each of the number pairs $(0, 0)$, $(0, 1)$, $(1, 0)$ and $(1, 1)$ would be 0.25. The expected frequencies would be 25 for each pair.

(d) A possible result might be

	Expected frequencies	Observed frequencies
$(0, 0)$	25	16
$(0, 1)$	25	30
$(1, 0)$	25	30
$(1, 1)$	25	24

The sequence obtained naturally produces different results from the expected frequencies. Here, there are fewer $(0, 0)$ pairs than you might expect. Again, this may be acceptable random variation or a conscious effort on your part to avoid following a zero with a zero. It is difficult to decide without some objective measure.

2 (a) Some pairs obtained from a typical calculator-generated random sequence are

Number pair	Frequency
$(0, 0)$	29
$(0, 1)$	24
$(1, 0)$	25
$(1, 1)$	22

Obviously, your results will be different.

(b) (i) and (ii)
In order to decide whether the calculator was producing truly random sequences, you would need to consider some *measure* of the difference between the values you would *expect* if it were fair and those you actually achieve in practice. You will further investigate this **difference measure** in the rest of this section.

3.1.2 How good is the model?

3.1 D

1 The probability of throwing a one is $\frac{1}{6}$, so the expected number of ones is $\frac{1}{6} \times 1200 = 200$. Similarly, the expected number of sixes is also 200.

2 Dice A and C are possibly biased, but you cannot be sure. The results for die B seem too good to be true! Die D appears biased because the 'other' scores appear too low.

3 (a)

	1	6	Other
Observed	182	238	780
Expected	200	200	800
Deviation between O and E	-18	38	-20

Sum of deviations $= 0$

(b) This is not satisfactory as the positive and negative values cancel one another out.

4 (a) Die A: $\sum (O - E)^2$
$$= 18^2 + 38^2 + 20^2 = 2168$$

Die B: $\sum (O - E)^2 = 1^2 + 1^2 + 0^2 = 2$

Die C: $\sum (O - E)^2$
$$= 20^2 + 18^2 + 38^2 = 2168$$

Die D: $\sum (O - E)^2$
$$= 20^2 + 18^2 + 38^2 = 2168$$

(b) Comparing results for die C and die D gives the same value, but this calculation does not take into account the fact that die D was only thrown 600 times, whereas die C was thrown 1200 times.

(c) Comparing results for dice A and C also gives the same value, whereas, intuitively, you would expect different results.

5 (a) Die B:
$$X^2 = \frac{(201 - 200)^2}{200} + \frac{(199 - 200)^2}{200}$$
$$+ \frac{(800 - 800)^2}{800} = 0.01$$

Die C:
$$X^2 = \frac{(220 - 200)^2}{200} + \frac{(218 - 200)^2}{200}$$
$$+ \frac{(762 - 800)^2}{800} = 5.425$$

Die D:
$$X^2 = \frac{(120 - 100)^2}{100} + \frac{(118 - 100)^2}{100}$$
$$+ \frac{(362 - 400)^2}{400} = 10.85$$

(b) In order of increasing value of X^2, the dice are B, C, A and D.

3.1 Exercise 1

1 (a) (i) With $P(\text{boy}) = \frac{1}{2}$ the expected frequencies would be

	Boy first	Girl first
Boy second	25	25
Girl second	25	25

So $X^2 = \dfrac{(31-25)^2}{25} + \dfrac{(21-25)^2}{25}$
$+ \dfrac{(22-25)^2}{25} + \dfrac{(26-25)^2}{25}$
$= 2.48$

(ii) With P(boy) = 0.513 the expected frequencies would be

	Boy first	Girl first
Boy second	26.3	25.0
Girl second	25.0	23.7

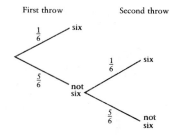

$100 \times P(GB) = 100 \times 0.487 \times 0.513 = 25.0$

$X^2 = \dfrac{(31-26.3)^2}{26.3} + \dfrac{(21-25)^2}{25}$
$+ \dfrac{(22-25)^2}{25} + \dfrac{(26-23.7)^2}{23.7}$
$= 2.06$

(b) Model (ii) fits these data better.

2 (a)

First throw   Second throw

$\tfrac{1}{6}$ six
$\tfrac{1}{6}$ six
$\tfrac{5}{6}$ not six
$\tfrac{5}{6}$ not six

(i) $P(N = 1) = \tfrac{1}{6}$

(ii) $P(N = 2) = \tfrac{5}{6} \times \tfrac{1}{6}$

(iii) $P(N = 3) = \tfrac{5}{6} \times \tfrac{5}{6} \times \tfrac{1}{6}$

(b)

N	1	2	3	4	5	6+
$P(N = n)$	0.167	0.139	0.116	0.096	0.08	0.402
Expected frequencies	33.4	27.8	23.2	19.2	16	80.4

(c) $X^2 = 4.5$

3 1560 books were loaned.

Expected number loaned per day $= \dfrac{1560}{6} = 260$

$X^2 = \dfrac{(200-260)^2}{260} + \dfrac{(290-260)^2}{260} + \dots$
$= 20.6$

4 (a) A probability model for this situation would assume that:

- each coin was equally likely to come down head or tail;
- each trial is independent.

On this basis, P(no heads in three cases)
$= \left(\tfrac{1}{2}\right)^3 = \tfrac{1}{8}$

In 800 such throws, the expected frequency is $800 \times \tfrac{1}{8} = 100$.

Similarly,

$P(\text{1 head}) = \begin{pmatrix} 3 \\ 1 \end{pmatrix} \left(\tfrac{1}{2}\right) \left(\tfrac{1}{2}\right)^2 = \tfrac{3}{8}$;

expected frequency $= 300$

$P(\text{2 heads}) = \begin{pmatrix} 3 \\ 2 \end{pmatrix} \left(\tfrac{1}{2}\right)^2 \left(\tfrac{1}{2}\right) = \tfrac{3}{8}$;

expected frequency $= 300$

$P(\text{3 heads}) = \left(\tfrac{1}{2}\right)^3 = \tfrac{1}{8}$;

expected frequency $= 100$

(b) $X^2 = 24.0$ (to 3 s.f.)

3.1.3 The chi-squared distribution

3.1 E

1 (a) 26.22   (b) 11.07

2 (a) 0.025   (b) 5%

3 (a) $a = 18.31$ (b) $b = 20.48$

3.1.4 Testing a model: the chi-squared test

3.1 F

1 (a) Total number of girls
$$= (1 \times 17) + (2 \times 21) + (3 \times 4) = 71$$

(b) In 51 families which contain 3 children there will be a total of 153 children. The proportion of girls is therefore $\frac{71}{153} = 0.464$ (to 3 s.f.).

(c)

Number of girls per family	0	1	2	3
Probability	0.154	0.400	0.346	0.100
Expected frequency	7.85	20.4	17.65	5.1

2 (a) $X^2 = \dfrac{(9 - 7.85)^2}{7.85} + \dfrac{(17 - 20.4)^2}{20.4}$

$$+ \dfrac{(21 - 17.65)^2}{17.65} + \dfrac{(4 - 5.1)^2}{5.1}$$

$$= 1.61$$

(b) The lower value of X^2 suggests that this second model is a better fit than the binomial model with $p = 0.5$.

3

Number of girls	0	1	2	3
Observed	9	17	x	y

$$9 + 17 + x + y = 51$$
$$x + y = 25$$
$$(0 \times 9) + (1 \times 17) + (2 \times x) + (3 \times y) = 71$$
$$2x + 3y = 54$$

Solving for x and y gives $x = 21$ and $y = 4$.

3.1 Exercise 2

1

Sample	1	2	3	4	5	6
O	40	35	30	28	25	20
E	30	30	30	30	30	30

$X^2 = 8.47$

There are six cells, giving five degrees of freedom. $\chi^2 < 9.24$ in 90% of samples, so there is insufficient evidence to disprove the hypothesis. The difference is not significant.

2

Pea classification	RY	WY	RG	WG
O	55	20	16	9
E	56.25	18.75	18.75	6.25

W = wrinkled, R = round, Y = yellow, G = green

$X^2 = 1.72$

There are four cells, giving three degrees of freedom. $\chi^2 < 6.25$ in 90% of samples, so you can conclude that these results agree with Mendelian theory.

3 The proportion of imperfect peaches is 15%.

No. of imperfect peaches in box	0	1	2	3	4	5	6
Expected frequency	35.13	40.15	19.12	4.86	0.69	0.05	0

No. of imperfect peaches in box	0	1	2	3 or more
O	49	24	14	13
E	35.13	40.15	19.12	5.60

$X^2 = 23.12$ The number of degrees of freedom is two (p is calculated from the data, and the total number of peaches is also fixed).

$\chi^2(2) > 13.81$ in fewer than 0.1% of samples. The difference is highly significant (at the 0.1% level). The model used does not give a good fit with the data collected.

4 (a) $X^2 = 5.43$ with four degrees of freedom. The critical $\chi^2(4)$ value is 9.49 (at the 5% significance level). The differences are not significant and the $B(4, \frac{1}{2})$ model is appropriate for the data.

(b) $p = \frac{219}{400} = 0.5475$

You need to combine the 0 and 1 groups so that the expected frequency is greater than 5 for the cell. This gives $X^2 = 1.45$ with two degrees of freedom (4 cells − 2 constraints). The model fits the data.

Both distributions are acceptable models for the data.

3.1.5 Contingency tables

3.1 G

1

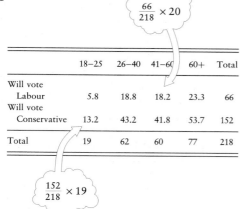

	18–25	26–40	41–60	60+	Total
Will vote Labour	5.8	18.8	18.2	23.3	66
Will vote Conservative	13.2	43.2	41.8	53.7	152
Total	19	62	60	77	218

2 $X^2 = 7.75$

3 There are 3 degrees of freedom.

From $\chi^2(3)$ tables, $\chi^2(3)$ exceeds 6.25 for 10% of samples and it exceeds 7.81 for 5% of samples.

A value of 7.75 is therefore not significant at the 5% level.

There is no clear evidence in this sample to suggest that voting intention is related to age.

3.1 Exercise 3

1 The model used assumes that there is no difference in grades awarded and gives the following table of expected grades.

	Grade				
	1	2	3	4	Total
College A	6.31	60.79	114.69	60.21	242
College B	4.69	45.21	85.31	44.79	180
Total	11	106	200	105	422

$$X^2 = 1.78 \qquad \nu = 3$$

$\chi^2(3) < 6.25$ in 90% of samples.

There is no evidence that there is any significant difference in grades awarded by the two colleges.

2 The proportion of staff who are satisfied overall is $\frac{92}{190}$.

From this, the expected frequencies of all types of staff can be calculated.

	Satisfied	Not satisfied	Total
Doctors	34	36	70
Nurses	29	31	60
Ancillary staff	29	31	60
Total	92	98	190

The initial assumption is that job satisfaction is not related to the job done.

$$X^2 = 34 \qquad \text{number of degrees of freedom} = (3-1)(2-1) = 2$$

$\chi^2(2) > 13.82$ in less than 0.1% of samples. The evidence against the initial assumption is highly significant, suggesting that job satisfaction is related to job done.

3 An initial assumption that the drug is not effective would give the following expected frequency table.

	Drug	Placebo	Total
Improved	95.5	95.5	191
Not improved	104.5	104.5	209
Total	200	200	400

$$X^2 = 22.13 \qquad \text{degrees of freedom} = 1$$

At the 1% level, $\chi^2 = 6.64$. Thus there is significant evidence to disprove the initial assumption and you can conclude that the drug is effective in improving the condition.

4 $X^2 = 7.15$ degrees of freedom $= 1$

The difference in behaviour is significant at the 1% significance level.

3.2 Probability distributions for counting cases
3.2.1 The geometric distribution

3.2 A

1

0.487 G

0.487 G

0.513 B

0.487 G

0.513 B

0.487 G

0.513 B and so on

You must assume that the probabilities remain constant throughout – that each birth is independent of all other births.

2 (a) 0.487

(b) $(0.513)(0.487) = 0.250$

(c) $(0.513)^4(0.487) = 0.0337$

(d) $(0.513)^{n-1}(0.487)$

3

x	1	2	3	4	5	6	7	8	...
P(x)	0.487	0.250	0.128	0.0657	0.0337	0.0173	0.008 88		...

4 $P(X \geq 8) = 1 - P(x < 8)$

$$= 1 - [P(X = 1) + P(X = 2)$$
$$+ \ldots + P(X = 7)]$$
$$= 0.009\,35$$

Alternatively, if eight or more children are needed for the first girl, then the first seven must have been boys.

$$P(7 \text{ boys}) = (0.513)^7 = 0.009\,35$$

5 (a) If $X = 1$ then the event occurs at the first trial. So $P(X = 1) = p$

(b) The event of interest occurs on the third trial. $P(X = 3) = q \times q \times p = q^2 p$

(c) $P(X = n) = \boxed{q \times q \times q \times \ldots} \times p$

$(n - 1$ non-occurrences)
$$= q^{n-1}p$$

3.2 Exercise 1

1 (a) $P(X = 3) = (0.8)^2(0.2) = 0.128$

(b) $P(X < 3) = P(X = 1) + P(X = 2)$
$$= 0.2 + (0.8)(0.2) = 0.36$$

(c) $P(X \geq 3) = 1 - P(X < 3) = 0.64$

2 Let X denote the number of trials until the right key is selected.

(a) (i) $P(X = 2) = \frac{3}{4} \times \frac{1}{3} = \frac{1}{4}$
   (ii) $P(X = 4) = \frac{3}{4} \times \frac{2}{3} \times \frac{1}{2} = \frac{1}{4}$

(b) $X \sim G(\frac{1}{4})$
   (i) $P(X = 2) = \frac{3}{4} \times \frac{1}{4} = \frac{3}{16}$
   (ii) $P(X > 2)$
   $$= 1 - (P(X = 1) + P(X = 2))$$
   $$= 1 - (\frac{1}{4} + \frac{3}{16}) = \frac{9}{16}$$

(c) The first strategy is better as it guarantees finding the correct key within 4 trials. Also, the first strategy has a higher probability for 2, 3 and 4 trials than the second strategy.

3 (a) Let X denote the number of attempts required to pass. Then $X \sim G(0.4)$.
   $$P(X = 3) = (0.6)^2(0.4) = 0.144$$

(b) $P(X > 5) = 1 - P(X \leq 5)$

$$= 1 - [P(X = 1) + P(X = 2)$$
$$+ P(X = 3) + P(X = 4)$$
$$+ P(X = 5)]$$
$$= 1 - [0.4 + (0.4)(0.6)$$
$$+ (0.4)(0.6)^2 + (0.4)(0.6)^3$$
$$+ (0.4)(0.6)^4]$$
$$= 1 - 0.922\,24 = 0.077\,76$$

4 (a) $\left(\frac{9}{10}\right)^5 = 0.590\,49$

$$= 0.59 \qquad \text{(to 2 s.f.)}$$

(b) Having to select more than 20 digits to obtain the first zero means that all of the first 20 digits are non-zero.

$$P(20 \text{ non-zero digits}) = \left(\frac{9}{10}\right)^{20}$$
$$= 0.122$$

3.2.2 The binomial distribution revisited

3.2 B

1 The random variable (X) is the number of boys in the ten cots. X is a discrete variable which may take any of the values $0, 1, 2, \ldots, 10$. On the assumption that babies are equally likely to be male or female, the appropriate binomial model for X is $X \sim B\left(10, \frac{1}{2}\right)$.

2 As discussed in section 3.2.1 the binomial and geometric variables have a number of factors in common. However, the geometric has an infinite number of possible outcomes, while for a binomial variable, the number of outcomes is finite. The geometric distribution counts the number of cases until an event occurs (including the occurrence of the event itself).

3.2 Exercise 2

1 X denotes the number of times the team won the toss.

$$X \sim B(5, 0.5)$$

(a) $P(X = 3) = \binom{5}{3}(0.5)^2(0.5)^3$

$$= \frac{5!}{3!\,2!}(0.5)^5 = 0.3125$$

(b) $\quad P(X \geq 3) = P(X = 3) + P(X = 4)$
$$+ P(X = 5)$$

$$P(X = 4) = \binom{5}{4}(0.5)^5 = 5(0.5)^5$$
$$= 0.156\,25$$

$$P(X = 5) = \binom{5}{5}(0.5)^5 = 0.031\,25$$

$$\Rightarrow P(X \geq 3) = 0.3125 + 0.156\,25$$
$$+ 0.031\,25 = 0.5$$

[This result could have been obtained by symmetry.]

2 $X \sim B\left(8, \frac{2}{3}\right)$

$$P(X = 0) = \left(\frac{1}{3}\right)^8 = 0.000\,15$$

$$P(X = 1) = \binom{8}{1}\left(\frac{2}{3}\right)\left(\frac{1}{3}\right)^7 = 0.002\,44$$

Similarly,

$P(X = 2) = 0.017\,07$	$P(X = 3) = 0.068\,28$
$P(X = 4) = 0.170\,71$	$P(X = 5) = 0.273\,13$
$P(X = 6) = 0.273\,13$	$P(X = 7) = 0.156\,07$

$$P(X = 8) = 0.039\,02$$

So 5 and 6 are the values which are most likely to occur.

3 You can approach this question by seeing how likely the outcome is if there is no preference for A or B.

Let X denote the number of people who prefer brand B. Then $X \sim B(6, 0.5)$.

$$P(X \geq 5) = \binom{6}{5}(0.5)(0.5)^5 + (0.5)^6$$

$$= 7(0.5)^6 = 0.1094$$

i.e. just over 1 in 10.

In practice this would not be considered to be sufficiently small to discard the assumption that A and B are equally well-liked.

4 Let X denote the number of correct questions. Then $X \sim B(20, \frac{1}{3})$.

$$P(X \geq 15) = 0.000\ 167 \qquad \text{(to 3 s.f.)}$$

5 P(same number of heads on first 4 throws as last 4)

$$= P(X = 0, Y = 0) + P(X = 1, Y = 1)$$

$$+ P(X = 2, Y = 2) + P(X = 3, Y = 3)$$

$$+ P(X = 4, Y = 4)$$

(where X and Y denote the number of heads on the first and last four throws respectively)

$$= \left[(0.5)^4\right]^2 + \left[4(0.5)^4\right]^2 + \left[\binom{4}{2}(0.5)^4\right]^2$$

$$+ \left[\binom{4}{3}(0.5)^4\right]^2 + \left[(0.5)^4\right]^2$$

$$= 0.273$$

By symmetry, the probability that there are more tails on the first four throws than the last four $= \dfrac{1 - 0.273}{2} = 0.36$ (to 2 s.f.).

3.2.3 The Poisson distribution

3.2 C

1 (a) The mean of $B(n, p)$ is np.
$$np = 12 \times \tfrac{1}{3} = 4$$

(b)

x	0	1	2	3	4	5	6
$P(X = x)$	0.008	0.046	0.127	0.212	0.238	0.191	0.111

x	7	8	9	10	11	12
$P(X = x)$	0.048	0.015	0.003	0.000	0.000	0.000

2 (a) There are 48 intervals of 15 minutes. On average, there are four requests in 12 hours.

P(request in a 15-minute interval) $= \frac{4}{48} = \frac{1}{12}$

(b) $X \sim B(48, \frac{1}{12})$

The distribution of X is as shown. Compare these values with those for $B(12, \frac{1}{3})$.

x	0	1	2	3	4	5	6
$P(X = x)$	0.015	0.067	0.143	0.199	0.204	0.163	0.106

x	7	8	9	10	11	12
$P(X = x)$	0.058	0.027	0.011	0.004	0.001	0.000

3 $X \sim B(720, \frac{1}{180})$

x	0	1	2	3	4	5	6
$P(X = x)$	0.018	0.073	0.146	0.196	0.196	0.157	0.104

x	7	8	9	10	11	12
$P(X = x)$	0.060	0.030	0.013	0.005	0.002	0.001

4 $X \sim B(7200, \frac{1}{1800})$

x	0	1	2	3	4	5	6
$P(X = x)$	0.018	0.073	0.147	0.195	0.195	0.156	0.104

x	7	8	9	10	11	12
$P(X = x)$	0.060	0.030	0.013	0.005	0.002	0.001

5 np is the mean value.
For $X \sim B(48, \frac{1}{12})$ the mean is $48 \times \frac{1}{12} = 4$.
Similarly, $np = 4$ for the other distributions.

6 The 4 represents the mean number of requests. In the general expression for $P(X = r)$,

$$P(X = r) = \frac{e^{-\lambda}\lambda^r}{r!} \quad \text{where } \lambda \text{ is the mean value}$$

7 $P(X = 0) = \dfrac{e^{-4}4^0}{0!} = e^{-4} = 0.0183$

$$P(X = 1) = \frac{e^{-4}4^1}{1} = 4e^{-4} = 0.073$$

$$P(X = 2) = \frac{e^{-4}4^2}{2!} = 0.147$$

and so on.

Your results should confirm that the distributions are identical and that the given distribution provides a very good approximation to the binomial under the conditions indicated.

8 $P(X \geq 4) = 1 - P(X < 4)$

$$= 1 - P(X = 0, 1, 2, 3)$$

$P(X = 0) = e^{-4} = 0.0183$

$P(X = 1) = 4e^{-4} = 0.073$

$P(X = 2) = \dfrac{4^2 e^{-4}}{2!} = 0.147$

$P(X = 3) = \dfrac{4^3 e^{-4}}{3!} = 0.195$

$P(X \geq 4) = 0.567$

3.2 Exercise 3

1 (a) $P(0) = e^{-1.4} = 0.247$ (to 3 s.f.)

   (b) $P(2 \text{ or more}) = 1 - P(0) - P(1)$

           $P(1) = 1.4e^{-1.4}$

    $\Rightarrow P(2 \text{ or more}) = 0.408$ (to 3 s.f.)

2 (a) 2

   (b) (i) $P(0) = \dbinom{100}{0}(0.02)^0(0.98)^{100}$

            $= (0.98)^{100} = 0.133$ (to 3 s.f.)

      (ii) $P(\text{at least one}) = 1 - P(0)$

              $= 0.867$ (to 3 s.f.)

   (c) Mean $= np = 2$

     $P(0) = e^{-2} = 0.135$ (to 3 s.f.)

     $P(\text{at least one}) = 1 - 0.135$

             $= 0.865$ (to 3 s.f.)

3 (a) 0.006 74   (b) 0.0842

   (c) 0.960   (to 3 s.f.)

4 Let X be the number of customers arriving at the check-out in one minute.

   $X \sim P(2.4)$

   $P(X > 3) = 0.221$ (to 3 s.f.)

5 0.549, 0.329, 0.099, 0.023

6 0.323

7 0.125

8 0.185

3.3 Selecting and testing the models
3.3.1 Choosing a suitable model

3.3 A

1 (a) It is not binomial as there is no fixed value for n, the number of trials. It is not Poisson as $X \neq 0$ and the events do not occur over a continuous interval of time. The geometric distribution is the most suitable as it is measuring the number of trials before an event occurs.

   (b) To use the geometric distribution, you must assume that successive attempts are independent.

2 (a) Binomial. Assume each die is independent.

     $X \sim B\left(5, \frac{1}{6}\right)$

   (b) Geometric. Assume independence.

     $X \sim G\left(\frac{1}{6}\right)$

   (c) Binomial. Assume births are independent.

     $X \sim B(4, 0.5)$ or $X \sim B(4, 0.513)$

     assuming that $P(\text{boy}) = 0.513$ as stated in 3.2A on page 186.

   (d) Poisson. Assume radioactive emissions occur randomly, singly and independently. λ would be defined as the average number of emissions in a five-second interval.

(e) Geometric. To specify the model in further detail you need to know the probability of a goal being scored in a home match.

3.3 Exercise 1

1 (a) The binomial distribution is a possible model as each event has two possible outcomes (boy or girl) and births can be regarded as being independent. If it is assumed that boys and girls are equally likely outcomes, then $p = \frac{1}{2}$. As there are five children in each family, $n = 5$.

(b)

		Expected values
$P(X = 0) =$ $\left(\frac{1}{2}\right)^5 = 0.03125$	$300 \times P(X = 0) =$	9.375
$P(X = 1) =$ $5\left(\frac{1}{2}\right)^5 = 0.15625$	$300 \times P(X = 1) =$	46.875
$P(X = 2) = 10\left(\frac{1}{2}\right)^5 = 0.3125$	$300 \times P(X = 2) =$	93.75
$P(X = 3) = 10\left(\frac{1}{2}\right)^5 = 0.3125$	$300 \times P(X = 3) =$	93.75
$P(X = 4) =$ $5\left(\frac{1}{2}\right)^5 = 0.15625$	$300 \times P(X = 4) =$	46.875
$P(X = 5) =$ $\left(\frac{1}{2}\right)^5 = 0.03125$	$300 \times P(X = 5) =$	9.375

$$X^2 = \sum \frac{(O - E)^2}{E} = 11.04$$

There are six cells and therefore five degrees of freedom.

$\chi^2(5) = 11.07$ at the 5% level

So there is insufficient evidence to reject the model.

(c) Number of boys $= 809$
Number of children $= 1500$

So $p = \dfrac{809}{1500}$. Put $q = -p$.

		Expected values
$P(X = 0) = q^5$	$= 0.021$	6.22
$P(X = 1) = 5pq^4$	$= 0.121$	36.43
$P(X = 2) = 10p^2q^3$	$= 0.284$	85.31
$P(X = 3) = 10p^3q^2$	$= 0.333$	99.88
$P(X = 4) = 5p^4q$	$= 0.195$	58.47
$P(X = 5) = p^5$	$= 0.046$	13.69

$$X^2 = \sum \frac{(O - E)^2}{E} = 1.135$$

$\chi^2(4) = 9.49$ at the 5% level

The fit appears to be much better. Note that there are only four degrees of freedom as there are two constraints. p is estimated from the data and the total is the same for both expected and observed frequencies.

(d) The second model gives the best fit. You would expect this as p is estimated from the data.

2 (a) N has a binomial distribution as it has only two possible outcomes (point up or down) and you can assume that each drawing pin lands independently of the others.

(b) (i) Number of pins
landing point up $= 690$
Number of trials $= 1200$
So an estimate of p is $\frac{690}{1200} = 0.575$

(ii) Assume $N \sim B(4, p)$.

		Expected values
$P(N = 0) = q^4$	$= 0.032$	9.79
$P(N = 1) = 4pq^3$	$= 0.177$	52.97
$P(N = 2) = 6p^2q^2$	$= 0.358$	107.49
$P(N = 3) = 4p^3q$	$= 0.323$	96.96
$P(N = 4) = p^4$	$= 0.109$	32.79

$$\chi^2 = \sum \frac{(O - E)^2}{E} = 3.5$$

There are three degrees of freedom (5 cells − 2 constraints).

$\chi^2(3) = 7.81$ at the 5% level

So the model is suitable.

3.3.2 The geometric distribution as a model

3.3 B

1 For 200 trials, you would expect results similar to

1	2	3	4	...
20	18	16	15	...

2 You must assume that successive numbers are independent. There are 10 possible outcomes. If the numbers are chosen at random then each is equally likely and so

P(zero is chosen) $= \frac{1}{10}$.

3 You will find it necessary to group a number of cells. The more data you collect, the better.

4 For your data you should calculate

$$\frac{\text{total number of runs of length one}}{\text{total number of trials}}$$

5 The second model should be a better fit as p is generated using *all* the data.

6 The mean run length of your data should be approximately 10.

3.3.3 Fitting a Poisson distribution to data

3.3 Exercise 2

1 (a) $\bar{x} = \text{mean} = \dfrac{81}{60} = 1.35$

Variance $= \dfrac{1}{n}\left(\sum x^2\right) - \bar{x}^2 = 1.19$
(to 3 s.f.)

(b) You can consider the arrival of customers as random and independent and the variance as close to the mean.

2 (a) As the disease is not known to be infectious, you can assume that its outbreak is random and independent. Since the values of the mean, 1.26, and variance, 1.57, are reasonably close, a Poisson model is reasonable.

(b)

X	0	1	2	3	4	5	6	7
P(X)	0.28	0.36	0.23	0.09	0.03	0.008	0.002	0.0003
E	28.4	35.7	22.5	9.46	2.98	0.75	0.16	0.028

13.4

Group these cells together to make the expected frequency greater than 5.

(c) $\sum \dfrac{(O - E)^2}{E} = 0.341$

There are 4 cells and 2 constraints, giving 2 degrees of freedom.

$\chi^2(2) = 5.99$ at the 5% level

The model is a good fit.

3 (a) $\lambda = \text{mean} = 9.4$ Variance $= 10.2$

(b) Regroup the data to avoid having expected numbers smaller than 5.

Number of water fleas	0 to 6	7	8	9	10	11	12 or more
Probability	0.173	0.106	0.125	0.131	0.123	0.105	0.237
Expected	8.64	5.32	6.25	6.53	6.14	5.25	11.87
Observed	8	6	7	4	5	7	13

$$\sum \frac{(O - E)^2}{E} = 2.11$$

There are 7 cells and 2 constraints, so there are 5 degrees of freedom.

$\chi^2(5) = 11.07$ (at the 5% level)

The model appears to be a good fit.

4 228, 211, 98, 30, 7, 2 (for 5 or more).

$X^2 = 1.2$

d.f. $= 3$ (you need to combine 2 groups)
The differences are not significant.

5 (a) $\lambda = \dfrac{196}{280} = 0.7$

(b)

	E
P(X = 0) = 0.497	139.0
P(X = 1) = 0.348	97.3
P(X = 2) = 0.122	34.1
P(X = 3) = 0.028	7.95 ⎫
P(X = 4) = 0.005	1.39 ⎬ 9.60
P(X ≥ 5) = 0.0007	0.26 ⎭

The fit appears to be reasonable.

(c) $\sum \dfrac{(O - E)^2}{E} = 1.92$

There are 4 cells with 2 constraints, so there are 2 degrees of freedom.

$\chi^2(2) = 5.99$ at the 5% level, suggesting that the model is satisfactory.

3.4 Forming new variables
3.4.1 Combining random variables

3.4 A

1 (a) $P(Y + B = 5) = P(Y_4, B_1) + P(Y_3, B_2)$
$$+ P(Y_2, B_3)$$
$$= 0.1 \times 0.25 + 0.2 \times 0.5$$
$$+ 0.3 \times 0.25 = 0.20$$
$$P(2) = P(Y_1, B_1) = 0.10$$
$$P(4) = P(Y_2, B_2) + P(Y_3, B_1)$$
$$+ P(Y_1, B_3) = 0.30$$
$$P(7) = P(Y_4, B_3) = 0.025$$

Score $Y + B$	Probability
2	0.1
3	0.275
4	0.3
5	0.2
6	0.1
7	0.025

(b) $\text{Mean}(Y + B) = 4.0$
$\text{Variance}(Y + B) = 1.5$
Note that
$\text{mean}(Y + B) = \text{mean}(Y) + \text{mean}(B)$
and $\text{variance}(Y + B)$
$\quad = \text{variance}(Y) + \text{variance}(B)$

2

$2b$	2	4	6
$P(2b)$	0.25	0.5	0.25

$\text{Mean}(2B) = 2 \times 0.25 + 4 \times 0.5 + 6 \times 0.25$
$$= 4 = 2 \,\text{mean}(B)$$
$\text{Variance}(2B) = 2 = 2^2 \,\text{variance}(B)$

$3y$	3	6	9	12
$P(3y)$	0.4	0.3	0.2	0.1

$\text{Mean}(3Y) = 6 = 3 \,\text{mean}(Y)$
$\text{Variance}(3Y) = 9 = 3^2 \,\text{variance}(Y)$

3.4 B

1

Score on die (D)	1	2	3	4	5	6
Probability	$\frac{1}{6}$	$\frac{1}{6}$	$\frac{1}{6}$	$\frac{1}{6}$	$\frac{1}{6}$	$\frac{1}{6}$

$\text{Mean}(D) = \frac{1}{6}(1 + 2 + 3 + 4 + 5 + 6)$
$$= 3.5$$
$\text{Variance}(D)$
$$= \frac{1}{6}(1^2 + 2^2 + 3^2 + 4^2 + 5^2 + 6^2) - (3.5)^2$$
$$\approx 2.9$$

Option 1
$\text{Mean}(D_1 + D_2) = 2 \,\text{mean}(D) = 7$
$\text{Variance}(D_1 + D_2)$
$$= \text{variance}(D) + \text{variance}(D)$$
$$= 2 \,\text{variance}(D) \approx 5.8$$

Option 2
$\text{Mean}(2D) = 2 \,\text{mean}(D) = 7$
$\text{Variance}(2D) = 2^2 \,\text{variance}(D)$
$$= 4 \,\text{variance}(D) \approx 11.7$$

The expected winnings are the same for each option. Your prize money would be 7p minus the cost to play. If it cost less than 7p per go, then you would expect (in the long term) to win on both options.

The variance (variability) is much greater with option 2. You have a chance of winning (or losing) more per go.

More cautious players might prefer option 1!

2 (a) $\text{Mean}(A) = 1 \qquad \text{Mean}(B) = 1.5$
$\quad \text{Variance}(A) = 0.4 \quad \text{Variance}(B) = 0.25$

$A - B$	-2	-1	0	1
$P(A - B)$	0.1	0.4	0.4	0.1

$\text{Mean}(A - B) = -0.5$
$\text{Variance}(A - B) = 0.65$

(b) (i) Mean(A) − mean$(B) = 1 - 1.5$

$$= -0.5$$

$$= \text{mean}(A - B)$$

(ii) Variance(A) + variance(B)

$$= 0.4 + 0.25$$

$$= 0.65$$

$$= \text{variance}(A - B)$$

3.4 Exercise 1

1

x	1	2	5	8
$P(X = x)$	$\frac{1}{4}$	$\frac{1}{4}$	$\frac{1}{4}$	$\frac{1}{4}$

(a) (i) Mean(X)

$$= (1 \times \tfrac{1}{4}) + (2 \times \tfrac{1}{4}) + (5 \times \tfrac{1}{4}) + (8 \times \tfrac{1}{4})$$

$$= \tfrac{1}{4} \times 16 = 4$$

(ii) Variance(X)

$$= (1^2 \times \tfrac{1}{4}) + (2^2 \times \tfrac{1}{4}) + (5^2 \times \tfrac{1}{4})$$

$$+ (8^2 \times \tfrac{1}{4}) - 4^2$$

$$= \tfrac{1}{4}(1 + 4 + 25 + 64) - 16$$

$$= \tfrac{94}{4} - 16 = 7.5$$

(b) Mean$(2X) = 2\,\text{mean}(X) = 2 \times 4 = 8$

Variance$(2X) = 4V(X)$

$$= 4 \times 7.5 = 30$$

(c) Mean$(3X) = 3\,\text{mean}(X) = 3 \times 4 = 12$

$V(3X) = 9V(X)$

$$= 9 \times 7.5 = 67.5$$

(d) Mean$(X_1 + X_2) = \text{mean}(X_1) + \text{mean}(X_2)$

$$= 2\,\text{mean}(X) = 8$$

Variance$(X_1 + X_2) = V(X_1) + V(X_2)$

$$= 2V(X) = 15$$

2

x	1	2	3	4
$P(X = x)$	$\frac{1}{6}$	$\frac{2}{6}$	$\frac{2}{6}$	$\frac{1}{6}$

(a) Mean $= 2.5$ Variance $= 0.917$

(b) Mean$(2X) = 2\,\text{mean}(X) = 5$

Variance$(2X) = 4V(X) \approx 3.7$

(c) Mean$(X_1 + 2X_2) = 7.5$

Variance$(X_1 + 2X_2) \approx 4.6$

3 (a) $\frac{20}{3}$ (b) $\frac{80}{3}$ (c) $\frac{40}{3}$ (d) $\frac{100}{3}$

4 Mean $= \frac{21}{6}$

5 (a) $Y = -1 \Rightarrow (X_1, X_2, X_3) = (-1, -1, -1)$

or $(-1, -1, 0)$ (in any order)

or $(-1, -1, 1)$ (in any order)

Adding probabilities

$$\Rightarrow \quad P(Y = -1) = 0.104$$

$P(Y = 1) = 0.104 \qquad P(Y = 0) = 0.792$

(b) Mean$(Y) = 0$ Variance$(Y) = 0.208$

3.4.2 Combining Poisson variables

3.4 Exercise 2

1 (a) Mean$(A + B)$ $= \mu_A + \mu_B$

Variance$(A + B) = \sigma_A{}^2 + \sigma_B{}^2$

(b) Mean$(2A)$ $= 2\mu_A$

Variance$(2A) = 4\sigma_A{}^2$

(c) Mean$(3A - B)$ $= 3\mu_A - \mu_B$

Variance$(3A - B) = 9\sigma_A{}^2 + \sigma_B{}^2$

2 (a) Mean$(X + Y) = \text{mean}(X) + \text{mean}(Y) = 7$

(b) $X + Y \sim P(\lambda)$ where $\lambda = 7$

$P(X + Y < 4) = 0.0818$

3 (a) $X \sim P(3)$ Mean$(X) = 3$ Variance$(X) = 3$
$Y \sim P(2)$ Mean$(Y) = 2$ Variance$(Y) = 2$
Mean$(X + Y) = 3 + 2 = 5$
Variance$(X + Y) = 3 + 2 = 5$

(b) $X + Y \sim P(5)$

(i) 0.006 74   (ii) 0.875

4 (a) (i) 0.008   (ii) 0.857

(b) 0.046

3.4.3 Expectation

3.4 C

(a) $E[aX] = \sum ax_i P(x_i) = a \sum x_i P(x_i)$

$= aE[X]$

(b) $V[aX] = E[a^2 X^2] - (F[aX])^2$

$= a^2 E[X^2] - a^2 (E[X])^2$

$= a^2 \{E[X^2] - (E[x])^2\}$

$= a^2 V[X]$

3.5 Continuous random variables
3.5.1 The Normal probability density function

3.5 A

It is useful to be able to make approximate calculations with the Normal distribution based on the knowledge that 68% of the values should be within one standard deviation of the mean and 98% within two standard deviations. Recall also that a sketch always helps in solving problems on the Normal distribution.

1 Underweight bags are at least one standard deviation below the mean.

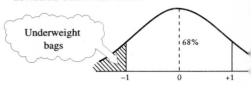

So 32% (approximately) are more than one standard deviation, with 16% beyond +1 and 16% below −1 standard deviation.

About 16% of bags are underweight.

2

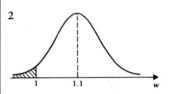

Let W = weight of sugar

$z = \dfrac{1 - 1.1}{0.1} = -1$

$P(W < 1.0 \, \text{kg}) = \Phi(-1)$

$= 1 - \Phi(1)$

$= 1 - 0.8413$

$= 15.9\%$ (to 3 s.f.)

3.5 Exercise 1

1 Let the total journey time be T minutes.

$T \sim N(20, 5^2)$

$P(T > 26)$ is required.

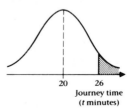

Standardising, $z = \dfrac{26 - 20}{5} = 1.2$

$P(T > 26) = 1 - \Phi(1.2)$

$\qquad = 1 - 0.885 \quad \text{(from tables)}$

$\qquad = 0.115$

I will be late on about 12% of journeys.

2 (a) 0.726 (b) 0.104

3 The standard deviation is about 4.4 days.

4 0.22

3.5.2 General probability density functions

3.5 Exercise 2

1 (a) $0 \leq X \leq 3$

(b)
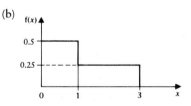

$\text{Area under } f(x) = 1 \times \frac{1}{2} + 2 \times \frac{1}{4} = 1$

(c) (i) $P(X \geq 1) \qquad = \frac{1}{2}$

(ii) $P(X \geq \frac{1}{2}) \qquad = \frac{3}{4}$

(iii) $P(\frac{1}{2} \leq X \leq 2) = \frac{1}{2}$

(iv) $P(X \leq 3) \qquad = 1$

2 (a) The area under the curve must equal 1.

$\text{Area of triangle} = \frac{1}{2} \text{ base} \times \text{height}$

$\qquad\qquad\qquad = \frac{1}{2} \times 2 \times k = k$

$\qquad\qquad \Rightarrow \; k = 1$

(b) (i) $P(X \geq 1.5) = 0.125$

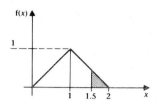

(ii) $P(X \leq 0.5) = 0.125$

(iii) $P(0.5 \leq X \leq 1.5) = 0.75$

3 $0 \leq X \leq 10 \quad \text{and} \quad f(x) = 0.0012x^2(10 - x)$

(a) $P(X > 5) = \displaystyle\int_5^{10} f(x)\,dx$

$\qquad = 0.0012 \displaystyle\int_5^{10} x^2(10 - x)\,dx$

$\qquad = 0.0012 \left[\frac{10}{3}x^3 - \frac{1}{4}x^4\right]_5^{10}$

$\qquad = 0.0012[(833.3) - (260.4)]$

$\qquad = 0.687 \quad \text{(to 3 s.f.)}$

(b) $P(1 < X < 2) = \displaystyle\int_1^2 f(x)\,dx$

$\qquad = 0.0012 \left[\frac{10}{3}x^3 - \frac{1}{4}x^4\right]_1^2$

$\qquad = 0.0235$

3.5.3 The mean and variance

3.5 Exercise 3

1 (a) $\qquad 1 = \displaystyle\int_0^1 kx^2\,dx$

$\qquad\qquad = k\left[\frac{1}{3}x^3\right]_0^1 = k(\frac{1}{3} - 0)$

$\qquad\qquad \Rightarrow \; k = 3$

(b) $\mu = \int_0^1 x f(x) \, dx$

$= 3 \int_0^1 x^3 \, dx$

$= 3 \left[\tfrac{1}{4} x^4 \right]_0^1$

$= 3 \left[\left(\tfrac{1}{4} \right) - (0) \right] = \tfrac{3}{4}$

$\sigma^2 = E(X^2) - \mu^2$

$E(X^2) = 3 \int_0^1 x^2 f(x) \, dx$

$= 3 \int_0^1 x^2 x^2 \, dx$

$= 3 \left[\tfrac{1}{5} x^5 \right]_0^1 = \tfrac{3}{5}$

$\Rightarrow \sigma^2 = \tfrac{3}{5} - \left(\tfrac{3}{4} \right)^2 = 0.0375$

(c) $P(X \geq 0.5) = 3 \int_{0.5}^1 x^2 \, dx$

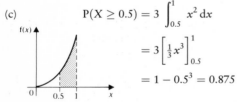

$= 3 \left[\tfrac{1}{3} x^3 \right]_{0.5}^1$

$= 1 - 0.5^3 = 0.875$

2 (a) $\int_5^{15} \dfrac{k}{x^3} \, dx = 1$

$\Rightarrow k = 56.25$

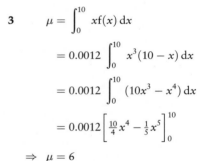

(b) $\mu = 7.5$

(c)

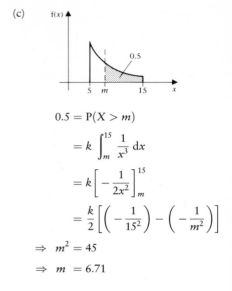

$0.5 = P(X > m)$

$= k \int_m^{15} \dfrac{1}{x^3} \, dx$

$= k \left[-\dfrac{1}{2x^2} \right]_m^{15}$

$= \dfrac{k}{2} \left[\left(-\dfrac{1}{15^2} \right) - \left(-\dfrac{1}{m^2} \right) \right]$

$\Rightarrow m^2 = 45$

$\Rightarrow m = 6.71$

3 $\mu = \int_0^{10} x f(x) \, dx$

$= 0.0012 \int_0^{10} x^3 (10 - x) \, dx$

$= 0.0012 \int_0^{10} (10 x^3 - x^4) \, dx$

$= 0.0012 \left[\tfrac{10}{4} x^4 - \tfrac{1}{5} x^5 \right]_0^{10}$

$\Rightarrow \mu = 6$

The mean distance travelled is 6 metres.

4 (b) $m = 1.45$

(c) 0.450

5 (a) $k = -6$

(b) The graph of f(x) is symmetric; the median divides the area under f(x) into two equal portions.

(c) 0.156

3.5.4 The exponential distribution

3.5 Exercise 4

1 (a)

(b) (i)

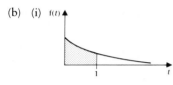

(ii)

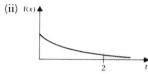

(c) (i) $P(T < 1) = \int_0^1 f(t)\, dt$

$$= \int_0^1 e^{-t}\, dt$$

$$= \left[-1\, e^{-t} \right]_0^1$$

$$= 0.632$$

(ii) $P(T > 2) = \int_2^\infty e^{-t}\, dt$

$$= \left[-e^{-t} \right]_2^\infty$$

$$P(T > 2) = e^{-2}$$

$$= 0.135$$

2 (a) P(arrival in 1st minute) $= 2 \int_0^1 e^{-2t}\, dt$

$$= 2 \left[\frac{e^{-2t}}{-2} \right]_0^1$$

$$= 0.865$$

(b) $2 \int_1^2 e^{-2t}\, dt = 2 \left[\frac{e^{-2t}}{-2} \right]_1^2 = 0.117$

3E (a) $E[X] = \int_0^\infty x f(x)\, dx$

$$= \lambda \int_0^\infty x\, e^{-\lambda x}\, dx$$

Integration by parts leads to $E[X] = \dfrac{1}{\lambda}$

(b) $V[X] = \int_0^\infty x^2 f(x)\, dx - (\text{mean})^2$

$$= \lambda \int_0^\infty x^2\, e^{-\lambda x}\, dx - \left(\frac{1}{\lambda} \right)^2$$

Again, integration by parts (where you can use your results from (a)) leads to

$$V[X] = \frac{1}{\lambda^2}$$

3.5.5 Combining Normal random variables

3.5 Exercise 5

1 $X \sim N(14, 0.02)$ $Y \sim N(9, 0.01)$
Let the total length be L.
$L = X + Y \sim N(23, 0.03)$

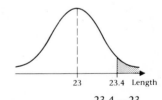

Standardising, $z = \dfrac{23.4 - 23}{\sqrt{(0.03)}}$

$$= 2.31$$

$$P(L > 23.4) = 1 - \Phi(2.31)$$

$$= 0.0104$$

2 $X \sim N(3, 0.003)$ $Y \sim N(20, 0.06)$
Let the total length of the cap plus bottle be L.
$L = X + Y \sim N(23, 0.063)$

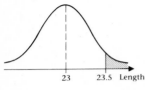

Standardising, $z = \dfrac{23.5 - 23}{\sqrt{(0.063)}}$

$= 1.99$

$P(L > 23.5) = 1 - \Phi(1.99)$

$= 0.0233$

2.33% will not fit on the shelf.

3 $X \sim N(1.9, 0.01)$
$X + X + \ldots \sim N(12 \times 1.9, 12 \times 0.01)$
$\sim N(22.8, 0.12)$

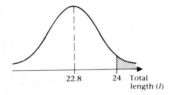

Standardising, $z = \dfrac{24 - 22.8}{\sqrt{(0.12)}}$

$= 3.46$

$P(L > 24) = 1 - \Phi(3.46)$

$= 0.0003$

0.03% of boxes are too small.

4 $X \sim N(79, 1.25)$
$X + X + \ldots \sim N(5 \times 79, 5 \times 1.25)$
$\sim N(395, 6.25)$

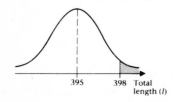

$z = \dfrac{398 - 395}{\sqrt{(6.25)}}$

$= 1.20$

$P(L \leq 398) = \Phi(1.20)$

$= 0.885$

5 $X \sim N(10, 0.013)$ $Y \sim N(9.5, 0.013)$
$X - Y \sim N(0.5, 0.026)$

(a)

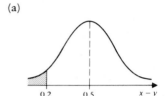

Standardising, $z = \dfrac{0.2 - 0.5}{\sqrt{(0.026)}}$

$= -1.86$

$P(X - Y < 0.2) = \Phi(-1.86)$

$= 1 - \Phi(1.86)$

$= 0.0314$

3.14% of bolts jam.

(b)

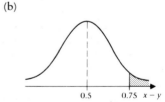

Standardising, $z = \dfrac{0.75 - 0.5}{\sqrt{(0.026)}}$

$= 1.55$

$P(X - Y > 0.75) = 1 - \Phi(1.55)$

$= 0.0606$

6.06% of bolts are too loose.

6 $X \sim N(18, 0.005)$ $Y \sim N(18.2, 0.005)$
$Y - X \sim N(0.2, 0.01)$

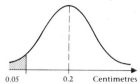

0.05   0.2   Centimetres

Standardising, $z = \dfrac{0.05 - 0.2}{\sqrt{(0.01)}}$

$$= -1.5$$

$P(\text{gap} < 0.05) = \Phi(-1.5)$

$$= 1 - \Phi(1.5)$$

$$= 0.0668$$

6.68% of lids do not fit.

Miscellaneous exercise 3

1 (a) 40 on each day

(b) $X^2 = 8.6$;   d.f. = 4

This is not significant at the 5% level; there is no evidence to contradict the model.

2 This is *not* a contingency table problem (although it looks like one) – the 1937–46 data are taken as the underlying model, against which the 1947 data are to be compared.

Of the 598 people infected before 1947, 78.1% were between 0 and 14 years old and 21.9% were over 15 years old. Of the 702 cases in 1947, you would therefore expect 548 aged 0–14 years and 154 aged 15 and over.

$$X^2 = \frac{(453 - 548)^2}{548} + \frac{(249 - 154)^2}{154} = 75$$

There is one degree of freedom.

This result is significant at the 99% level and suggests that the age distribution was significantly different in the epidemic year.

3 $X^2 = 1.77$;   d.f. = 3

There is no significant difference in results between the colleges.

4 $X^2 = 9.28$;   d.f. = 6

There is no significant difference between the results in various divisions.

5 (a) 1   (b) $\dfrac{1}{k}$ (c) $\frac{1}{4}$ (d) $(1 - k)^n$

6 (a) Mean = 2.5;   s.d. = 1.48

(b) 8.21, 20.52, 25.65, 21.38, 13.36, 6.68, 4.20 (for 6 or more)
$X^2 = 2.89$ with 5 degrees of freedom. A Poisson model is acceptable.

(c) The variance is low. For a Poisson model, mean and variance are equal, but the data have mean 2.5 and variance 2.19.

7 Fitting a Poisson with mean 2 gives $X^2 = 9.24$ with 4 degrees of freedom (combining '5 or more' into a single group), which is just below the critical value at the 5% significance level. There are insufficient grounds to reject the model.

8 Mean = 3.023
2.14, 6.47, 9.78, 9.86, 7.45, 4.50, 3.84
$X^2 = 1.13$;   d.f. = 5

The results are not significant; a Poisson model is acceptable.

9 750 g;   625 g^2

10 (a) 0.323   (b) 0.130   (c) 0.934

11E Mean = b;   standard deviation = $\dfrac{b}{\sqrt{6}}$

12 (a) $k = 2$

(b) Mean = $2 \ln 2 \approx 1.39$; Variance = 0.0782

13 $k = (295\,245\,000)^{-1}$;   0.098

14 (a) $k = \frac{1}{1200}$ (b) 0.189   (c) 2763 hours

15 (a) $A = 0.05$

(b) 0.223

About 22% of gamma rays will pass through the shield.

16 $k = 20$;   mean $= \frac{2}{3}$;   variance $= \frac{2}{63}$

    $P(\mu - \sigma < X < \mu + \sigma) = 0.652$

17 (a) 12   (b) 0.6, 0.04   (c) 0.4752

18 (a) Mean $= 20\,$s. (This is based on the assumption that the times are evenly spread over each interval, so that they can be supposed for the purposes of calculation to be located at the centre of the interval. In this example it is likely that they will be concentrated more densely towards the left of each interval, so that this value for the mean is probably an over-estimate.)

   (b) $A = \lambda$

   (c) Choose $\lambda = 0.05$. The probability of a time interval between a seconds and b seconds is, on this model, $e^{-\lambda a} - e^{-\lambda b}$, giving expected frequencies 63.3, 29.9, 14.1, 6.7, 6.0 (grouping the last two frequencies).

      $X^2 = 1.81$;   d.f. $= 3$

      There is satisfactory agreement between the experimental data and the model.

19 (a) 0.648   (b) 0.544

20 $S - A \sim N(5, 4^2)$
    P(less than 1 cm difference) $= 0.159$,
    P(more than 7 cm) $= 0.309$; so required probability is $0.159 + 0.309 = 0.468$.

21 0.04   (i.e. 4% of poles will be more than 2 cm too short.)

22 Total weight of box of sweets $\sim N(870, 160)$

   (a) 0.943   (b) approximately 0

4 STATISTICS IN ACTION

4.1 Hypothesis testing

4.1.1 Making a decision: the null hypothesis

4.1 **A**

1 If the die is 'fair', the number of sixes out of 60 is $R \sim B\left(60, \frac{1}{6}\right)$.

The Normal approximation is $X \sim N(10, 8\frac{1}{3})$.

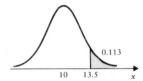

    $P(R \geq 14) \approx P(X > 13.5)$

$$\approx P\left(Z > \frac{13.5 - 10}{\sqrt{\left(8\frac{1}{3}\right)}}\right)$$

$$\approx P(Z > 1.212) \approx 0.113$$

There is a probability of 0.113 that a fair die will be wrongly classified as 'loaded'.

2 If the die is 'loaded', the number of sixes out of 60 is $R \sim B\left(60, \frac{1}{4}\right)$.

The Normal approximation is $X \sim N(15, 11\frac{1}{4})$.

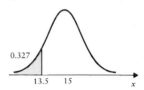

    $P(R < 14) \approx P(X < 13.5)$

$$\approx P\left(Z < \frac{13.5 - 15}{\sqrt{\left(11\frac{1}{4}\right)}}\right)$$

$$\approx P(Z < -0.447) \approx 0.327$$

There is a probability of 0.327 that a biased die will be wrongly accepted as 'fair'.

3 (a) For a fair die, $X \sim N(10, 8\frac{1}{3})$.

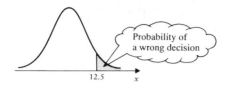

Probability of a wrong decision

$$z = \frac{12.5 - 10}{\sqrt{(8\frac{1}{3})}} = 0.866$$

$P(Z > 0.866) = 0.193$

The probability of wrongly classifying a fair die as 'loaded' is

$P(Z > 0.866) \approx 0.193$

The probability of wrongly classifying a loaded die as 'fair' is

$P(Z < -0.745) \approx 0.229$

(b) The probability of wrongly classifying the die 'loaded' $\approx P(Z > 1.559) \approx 0.059$

The probability of wrongly classifying the die 'fair' $\approx P(Z < -0.149) \approx 0.440$

(c) The 'best' threshold value is open to discussion.

4 Although it would be very unlikely that a number as low as (or lower than) this might occur, it is possible. It is unlikely to happen if the die is 'fair', but it is even more unlikely to happen with a 'loaded' die, so you should conclude that the die is 'fair'.

4.1 B

The student's friend only claims to be able to 'taste the difference'. If she had none correct, she would have identified every one incorrectly. She could still claim to be able to 'taste the difference'; she simply did not know which was which. The correct alternative hypothesis in this case is $H_1 : p \neq \frac{1}{2}$.

4.1.2 Making the wrong decision

4.1 C

1 $P(X > 10) = P\left(Z > \dfrac{10 - 6.2}{1.8}\right)$

$\qquad\qquad\quad = P(Z > 2.111)$

$\qquad\qquad\quad \approx 0.0174$

2 The probability of a type II error is

$P\left(Z < \dfrac{10 - \mu}{1.8}\right).$

You cannot evaluate this unless you know μ.

3 $P(X > 9) \approx P(Z > 1.556) \approx 0.060$

4 The probability of a type II error will decrease.

5 $P(Z > 1.645) = 0.05$ so

$\dfrac{x - 6.2}{1.8} = 1.645 \Rightarrow x = 9.161$

4.1.3 Level of significance

4.1 Exercise 1

1 $H_0 : p = \frac{1}{5}$

$H_1 : p > \frac{1}{5}$

Level of significance: 5%

If $R \sim B(120, \frac{1}{5})$ then the Normal approximation is $X \sim N(24, 19.2)$. The critical region is $X > 24 + 1.645\sqrt{19.2}$ or $X > 31.2$.

H_0 is rejected for $R \geq 32$. A candidate is unlikely to be answering purely by guesswork if he or she obtains 32 or more correct answers.

2 The null hypothesis is that the probability that a digit is even is $\frac{1}{2}$.

$H_0 : p = \frac{1}{2}$

$H_1 : p \neq \frac{1}{2}$

Level of significance: 5%

If R is the number of even digits out of fourteen, then $R \sim B\left(14, \frac{1}{2}\right)$.

The data give $R = 4$. This is obviously not in the upper critical region but could be in the lower critical region.

$P(R \leq 4) \approx 0.09$. This is greater than $2\frac{1}{2}\%$ and so H_0 is *not* rejected.

3 $H_0 : \mu = 1300$

$\quad H_1 : \mu < 1300$

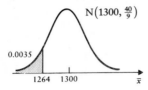

The data give $\bar{x} = 1264$

$P(\bar{X} < 1264) = P(Z < -2.7)$

$\qquad\qquad \approx 0.0035$

This is significant at the 1% level but not the 0.1% level. There is very significant evidence that the breaking strain is lower than expected.

4 If the machine is out of adjustment then the mean can be either too large or too small, so a two-tail test is appropriate.

$H_0 : \mu = 3.00$

$H_1 : \mu \neq 3.00$

Level of significance: 5%

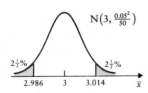

As $3.01 < 3.014$, $\bar{x} = 3.01$ is *not* in the critical region; therefore H_0 is not rejected at the 5% level of significance. The machine does not need adjusting. However, the results are so marginal that perhaps the machine should be checked anyway.

5 $H_0 : \mu = 0.85$

$\quad H_1 : \mu > 0.85$

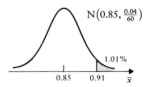

$$P(\bar{X} > 0.91) = P\left(Z > \frac{0.91 - 0.85}{\sqrt{\left(\frac{0.04}{60}\right)}}\right)$$

$$= P(Z > 2.324)$$

$$\approx 0.0101$$

The result is in the 'significant' 5% critical region but not quite in the 'very significant' 1% critical region. The evidence would therefore be described as 'significant'. (You should note that the sample mean, $\bar{x} = 0.91$, has probably been rounded. A more accurate value could be used and the evidence might then become 'very significant'.)

4.1.4 Population proportions

4.1 D

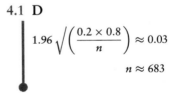

$$1.96 \sqrt{\left(\frac{0.2 \times 0.8}{n}\right)} \approx 0.03$$

$$n \approx 683$$

4.1 Exercise 2

1 $H_0 : p = 0.46$

$H_1 : p > 0.46$

Level of significance: 5%

$$z = \frac{p_s - p}{\sqrt{\left(\dfrac{p(1-p)}{n}\right)}} \approx \frac{0.06}{\sqrt{\left(\dfrac{0.46 \times 0.54}{400}\right)}}$$

$$\approx 2.41$$

$2.41 > 1.645$ and so H_0 is rejected. There is significant evidence that there has been an increase in the Labour vote.

2 $H_0 : p = 0.338$

$H_1 : p \neq 0.338$

Level of significance: 5%

$$z = \frac{0.36 - 0.338}{\sqrt{\left(\dfrac{0.338 \times 0.662}{400}\right)}}$$

$$\approx 0.93$$

$0.93 < 1.96$ and so H_0 is not rejected. The discrepancy is not significant.

3 $H_0 : p = 0.5$

$H_1 : p < 0.5$

Level of significance: 5%

$$z = \frac{0.43 - 0.5}{\sqrt{\left(\dfrac{0.5 \times 0.5}{200}\right)}}$$

$$\approx -1.98$$

$-1.98 < -1.645$ and so H_0 is rejected. There is significant evidence that the manufacturers are overstating the proportion of people who prefer their product.

4.2 The Student t-distribution
4.2.2 Small samples

4.2 A

1 x: 62, 63.5, 65, 62.5

$\bar{x} = 63.25$, $\quad s_{n-1}^{2} = 1.75$, $\quad \mu = 65.535$

$$t = \frac{63.25 - 65.535}{\sqrt{(1.75/4)}} = -3.455$$

2 (a) $z = \dfrac{63.25 - 65.535}{\sqrt{(6.540/4)}} = -1.787$

(b) $\bar{X} \sim N\left(\mu, \dfrac{\sigma^2}{n}\right) \Rightarrow \bar{X} - \mu \sim N\left(0, \dfrac{\sigma^2}{n}\right)$

$$\Rightarrow Z \sim N(0, 1)$$

3 Replacing the constant, σ^2, by a random variable S_{n-1}^{2} adds 'uncertainty' to the distribution, so you might expect the distribution of T to be more 'spread out' (i.e. have a greater variance) than a Standard Normal distribution.

4 You would not expect so many values with magnitude greater than 2 in a Standard Normal distribution. The general shape, although still 'bell-shaped', is narrower around the peak and more spread out in the tails.

5 (a) Substituting $\nu = 3$, you obtain

$$c_3 \left(1 + \frac{t^2}{3}\right)^{-\frac{(3+1)}{2}} = c_3 \left(1 + \frac{t^2}{3}\right)^{-2}$$

(b) A sketch of the function shows that the area under the graph for $|t| > 10$ is negligible. A numerical method such as the mid-ordinate rule shows that

$$\int_{-10}^{10} \left(1 + \frac{t^2}{3}\right)^{-2} dt \approx 2.715 \quad \text{(to 4 s.f.)}$$

The substitution gives $\frac{1}{2}\pi\sqrt{3} \approx 2.72$

(c) $\displaystyle\int_{-\infty}^{\infty} f(t)\, dt = 1$

$$\Rightarrow \int_{-\infty}^{\infty} c_3 \left(1 + \frac{t^2}{3}\right)^{-2} dt = 1$$

$$\Rightarrow c_3 = 1 \div \int_{-\infty}^{\infty} \left(1 + \frac{t^2}{3}\right)^{-2} dt$$

$$\approx 1 \div 2.715$$

$$\approx 0.368 \quad \text{(to 3 s.f.)}$$

4.2 B

1

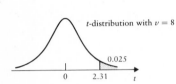

t-distribution with $\nu = 8$

0.025

0   2.31 t

2 If $X \sim N(\mu, \sigma^2)$ and $T = \dfrac{\bar{x} - \mu}{s_{n-1}/\sqrt{9}}$ where $\bar{x}$ and s_{n-1} are calculated from a random sample of 9 x-values, then $P(T > 2.31) = 0.025$.

3 These values are precisely the same as the values of z where $Z \sim N(0, 1)$. This suggests that a t-distribution with $\nu \to \infty$ is a Standard Normal distribution.

4.2 Exercise 1

1 (a) If $n = 6$ then $\nu = 5$. From the table, $t = 3.36$ for $p = 0.01$.

(b) If $n = 15$ then $\nu = 14$. From the table, $t = 2.14$ for $p = 0.025$.

2 $H_0 : \mu = 0$

$H_1 : \mu \neq 0$

Level of significance: 10%

For the sample, $\bar{x} = 21.5$, $s_{n-1} = 51.32$ and $n = 10$

$$t = \frac{21.5 - 0}{(51.32/\sqrt{10})} = 1.32$$

Accept H_0 as $1.32 < 1.83$. The evidence for a difference in times is not significant at the 10% level.

3 $H_0 : \mu = 1000$

$H_1 : \mu < 1000$

Level of significance: 5%

As the sample size is large, assume that $T \sim N(0, 1)$.

$$t = \frac{997 - 1000}{(13/\sqrt{200})} = -3.26$$

As $-3.26 < -1.645$, you should reject H_0 in favour of H_1. (As the sample size is *very* large, the test is very sensitive and although the result is undoubtedly significant, an average shortfall of three hours in the life of a battery is unlikely to produce a storm of protest!)

4.2.3 Confidence intervals

4.2 C

1 Looking at each part of the inequality separately gives

$$-2.2 < \frac{\bar{x} - \mu}{(s_{n-1}/\sqrt{12})}$$

and $\dfrac{\bar{x} - \mu}{(s_{n-1}/\sqrt{12})} < 2.2$

$$\Rightarrow -2.2 \left(\frac{s_{n-1}}{\sqrt{12}}\right) < \bar{x} - \mu$$

and $\bar{x} - \mu < 2.2 \left(\dfrac{s_{n-1}}{\sqrt{12}}\right)$

$$\Rightarrow \mu < \bar{x} + 2.2 \left(\frac{s_{n-1}}{\sqrt{12}}\right)$$

and $\bar{x} - 2.2 \left(\dfrac{s_{n-1}}{\sqrt{12}}\right) < \mu$

$$\Rightarrow \bar{x} - 2.2 \left(\frac{s_{n-1}}{\sqrt{12}}\right) < \mu < \bar{x} + 2.2 \left(\frac{s_{n-1}}{\sqrt{12}}\right)$$

2 $s_{n-1} = 31.80$

3 $107.9 - 2.2 \times \dfrac{31.8}{\sqrt{12}} < \mu < 107.9 + 2.2 \times \dfrac{31.8}{\sqrt{12}}$

$\Rightarrow 87.7 < \mu < 128.1$

The 95% confidence interval is (87.7, 128.1).

4 The 90% confidence interval is (91.4, 124.4).

Note that the table does not show critical t-values for $\nu = 11$ and so you have to estimate the value by interpolation, knowing that the critical value is 1.81 for $\nu = 10$ and 1.78 for $\nu = 12$. A good estimate for $\nu = 11$ is therefore $(1.81 + 1.78) \div 2 = 1.795$.

4.2 Exercise 2

1 If X is the weight of a peach, assume that $X \sim N(\mu, \sigma^2)$.

(a) For the sample, $\bar{x} = 132$ and $s_{n-1} = 18.6$. As the sample size is $n = 10$, the number of degrees of freedom is $\nu = 9$.

The 90% confidence interval for μ is

$$\left(132 - 1.83 \times \frac{18.6}{\sqrt{10}}, \quad 132 + 1.83 \times \frac{18.6}{\sqrt{10}}\right)$$

$$= (121.2, 142.8)$$

(b) The 95% confidence interval for μ is (118.7, 145.3).

The 99% confidence interval for μ is (112.9, 151.1).

2 Assume that $X \sim N(\mu_x, \sigma_x^2)$ and that $Y \sim N(\mu_y, \sigma_y^2)$.

For each sample, $n = 15$ and so the resulting t-distribution will have $\nu = 14$ degrees of freedom.

For the sample without alcohol: $\bar{x} = 11.7$ and $s_{n-1} = 2.05$

The 95% confidence interval for μ_x is

$$\left(11.7 - 2.14 \times \frac{2.05}{\sqrt{15}}, \quad 11.7 + 2.14 \times \frac{2.05}{\sqrt{15}}\right)$$

$$= (10.6, 12.8)$$

For the sample with alcohol: $\bar{y} = 17.1$ and $s_{n-1} = 4.97$

The 95% confidence interval for μ_y is (14.4, 19.8).

As the confidence intervals do not overlap it is very unlikely that $\mu_x = \mu_y$. The alcohol does appear to have slowed down the second group.

4.2.4 Matched pairs t-test

4.2 D

1 $\bar{x} = -0.5; \quad s_{n-1} = 0.852$

$$T = \frac{\bar{X} - \mu}{S_{n-1}/\sqrt{8}} \text{ has a } t\text{-distribution with } \nu = 7.$$

$$t = \frac{-0.5 - 0}{0.852/\sqrt{8}} = -1.66$$

As $-1.66 > -1.89$, you should *not* reject H_0.

2 No. The probability of accepting H_0 when H_1 is in fact true (a type II error) can be quite large, especially if the mean decrease in weight, μ, is small.

4.2 Exercise 3

1 If X is the difference in corrosion ('uncoated' − 'coated'), then assume that $X \sim N(\mu, \sigma^2)$.

$H_0 : \mu = 0 \qquad H_1 : \mu > 0$

Level of significance: 1%

$$T = \frac{\bar{X} - \mu}{S_{n-1}/\sqrt{9}} \text{ has a } t\text{-distribution with } \nu = 8.$$

The sample gives x:

16, 12, −4, −1, −2, 6, 20, 3, 12

Then $\bar{x} = 6.89, \quad s_{n-1} = 8.54$ and

$$t = \frac{6.89 - 0}{8.54/3} = 2.42$$

As $2.42 < 2.90$, you should not reject H_0. The sample does not provide very significant evidence in support of the claim.

2 If X is the improvement in score, then assume that $X \sim N(\mu, \sigma^2)$. (Note that this is a simplification since X is actually discrete and takes relatively small values.)

$H_0 : \mu = 0 \qquad H_1 : \mu > 0$

Level of significance: 5%

$T = \dfrac{\bar{X} - \mu}{S_{n-1}/\sqrt{15}}$ will have a t-distribution with $\nu = 14$.

The sample gives x:

  1, −1, 1, 3, −1, 2, 3, 4, 1, −1, 4,
  3, 1, 0, 3

Then $\bar{x} = 1.53$, $s_{n-1} = 1.77$ and

$$t = \dfrac{1.53 - 0}{1.77/\sqrt{15}} = 3.35$$

As $3.35 > 1.76$, H_0 is rejected in favour of H_1. The sample provides significant evidence to support the claim that the course of instruction improves recall.

3 If D kg is the difference in weight loss, then assume that $D \sim N(\mu, \sigma^2)$.

$H_0 : \mu = 0$

$H_1 : \mu \neq 0$

Level of significance: 5%

d: 3.2, 1.3, −0.6, 3, 1.2,
  −2.4, 3.8, −1, 1.1, −3.6

Then $\bar{d} = 0.6$, $s_{n-1} \approx 2.46$ and

$$t = \dfrac{0.6}{2.46/\sqrt{10}} \approx 0.77 \text{ with } \nu = 9$$

As $0.77 < 2.26$, you should not reject H_0. The evidence of a difference in weight loss is not significant at the 5% level.

4.3 Two-sample tests
4.3.1 Testing the equality of two means

4.3 Exercise 1

1 H_0 : The average age at which men in countries A and B first marry is the same; $\mu_A = \mu_B$

H_1 : On average, men marry later in life in country B than in country A; $\mu_A < \mu_B$

A 1% one-tail test is to be applied. H_0 is to be rejected if $z < -2.33$.

$$\bar{A} - \bar{B} \sim N\left(\mu_A - \mu_B, \dfrac{\sigma_A{}^2}{80} + \dfrac{\sigma_B{}^2}{100}\right)$$

The test statistic is $z = \dfrac{\bar{a} - \bar{b}}{\sqrt{\left(\dfrac{\sigma_A{}^2}{80} + \dfrac{\sigma_B{}^2}{100}\right)}}$

Substituting $\bar{a} = 24.5$, $\bar{b} = 26.1$, $\sigma_A{}^2 = 3.2^2$, $\sigma_B{}^2 = 2.8^2$

$$z = \dfrac{-1.6}{0.45} = -3.5$$

H_0 is rejected in favour of H_1; there is strong evidence that men marry later in life in country B than in country A.

2 Let the population of annual costs be £X for the first model and £Y for the second.

H_0 : Cars of both models have the same average maintenance costs; $\mu_X = \mu_Y$

H_1 : The second model is more expensive to maintain than the first; $\mu_X < \mu_Y$

A 5% one-tail test is to be applied. H_0 is to be rejected if $z < -1.645$.

$$\bar{X} - \bar{Y} \sim N\left(\mu_X - \mu_Y, \dfrac{\sigma_X{}^2}{20} + \dfrac{\sigma_Y{}^2}{11}\right)$$

The test statistic is $z = \dfrac{\bar{x} - \bar{y}}{\sqrt{\left(\dfrac{\sigma_X{}^2}{20} + \dfrac{\sigma_Y{}^2}{11}\right)}}$

Substituting $\bar{x} = 540$, $\bar{y} = 710$, $\sigma_X{}^2 = 90^2$, $\sigma_Y{}^2 = 110^2$

$$z = \dfrac{-170}{38.8} = -4.38$$

Since $-4.38 < -1.645$, H_0 is rejected in favour of H_1. The company should be advised to use only the first model.

There is no evidence that the parent populations are Normally distributed and, for such small samples, the assumption that the sample means are Normally distributed is not justified. Nevertheless, as a result of the test the company would probably phase out the use of the second model (assuming there were no other factors affecting the decision).

3 $H_0 : \mu_B = \mu_G$

$H_1 : \mu_B > \mu_G$

The test is 1% one-tail. H_0 is to be rejected if $z > 2.33$.

$z = 2.72$

Therefore H_0 is rejected. Assuming that the mean levels of ability in logical thinking of boys and girls are equal, there is strong evidence that the test is biased in favour of boys.

4 $H_0 : \mu_X = \mu_Y$

$H_1 : \mu_X \neq \mu_Y$

The test is 5% two-tail. H_0 is to be rejected if $z < -1.96$ or $z > 1.96$.

$z = 1.875$

Therefore H_0 is accepted. There is no significant change in mean length.

5 $H_0 : \mu_U = \mu_O$

$H_1 : \mu_U < \mu_O$

The test is 5% one-tail. H_0 is to be rejected if $z < -1.645$.

$\bar{u} = 7.96, \quad \bar{o} = 10.66$

$z = -4.78$

Therefore H_0 is rejected.

4.3.2 Confidence intervals

4.3 **Exercise 2**

1 Let the distributions be $X \sim N(10.3, 25)$ and $Y \sim N(8.2, 36)$.

$$(10.3 - 8.2) \pm 1.96 \sqrt{\left(\frac{25}{50} + \frac{36}{72} \right)} = 2.10 \pm 1.96$$

The 95% confidence interval is (0.14, 4.06).

2 The required interval is $(-3.81, -1.59)$.

3 The required interval is (0.06, 2.70).

4 Assume that the tar content in milligrams of brand A is $X \sim N(9.9, 1.6^2)$ and that the tar content in milligrams of brand B is $Y \sim N(8.9, 1.6^2)$. Then,

$$1 \pm 2.575 \sqrt{\left(\frac{1.6^2}{100} + \frac{1.6^2}{100} \right)} = 1 \pm 0.58$$

The required interval is (0.42, 1.58).

4.3.3 The pooled variance estimator

4.3 **A**

1 (a) $\frac{15}{14} s_A{}^2 \approx 271.4$

(b) $\frac{12}{11} s_B{}^2 \approx 311.0$

(c) $\dfrac{15 s_A{}^2 + 12 s_B{}^2}{25} \approx 288.8$

2 Each estimator has its own distribution. All three estimates are unbiased and so the three distributions all have mean σ^2.

The values given above simply represent individual points in each distribution and cannot therefore be expected to be the same. Because the pooled estimate uses more data, its distribution can be expected to be more closely grouped around σ^2 and therefore any particular pooled estimate is likely to be close to σ^2.

4.3.4 Two-sample t-tests

4.3 **B**

The pooled variance estimator is 288.82.

$$t = \frac{68.40 - 83.42}{\sqrt{288.82} \sqrt{\left(\frac{1}{15} + \frac{1}{12} \right)}} \approx -2.28; \quad \nu = 25$$

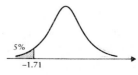

5%

−1.71

H_0 is rejected in favour of H_1. There is significant evidence that drug A is more effective.

4.3 Exercise 3

1 (a) $\dfrac{6 \times 1.2 + 8 \times 1.7}{6 + 8 - 2} \approx 1.73\,\text{kg}^2$

(b) $H_0 : \mu_A = \mu_B$
$H_1 : \mu_A \neq \mu_B$

Level of significance: 5%

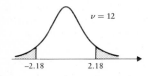
$\nu = 12$
$-2.18 \qquad 2.18$

$$t = \frac{3.3 - 4.1}{\sqrt{1.73}\sqrt{\left(\frac{1}{6} + \frac{1}{8}\right)}} \approx -1.13$$

There is no significant difference between the mean weight losses.

2 (a) $\bar{a} = 26.775; \quad s_A{}^2 \approx 0.307; \quad n_A = 4$
$\bar{b} = 25.55; \quad s_B{}^2 \approx 0.629; \quad n_B = 6$

A pooled estimate of variance is $s^2 \approx 0.625$.

(b) $H_0 : \mu_A = \mu_B$
$H_1 : \mu_A > \mu_B$

Level of significance: 5%

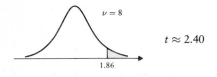
$\nu = 8$
$t \approx 2.40$
1.86

At the 5% level, H_0 should be rejected in favour of H_1. There is significant evidence that trout from the Arn have a greater average length than those from the Bate.

3 $H_0 : \mu_1 = \mu_2$
$H_1 : \mu_1 \neq \mu_2$

Level of significance: 5%

$\bar{x}_1 = 3.1; \quad s_1{}^2 = 0.275; \quad n_1 = 4$
$\bar{x}_2 = 3.5; \quad s_2{}^2 = 0.093; \quad n_2 = 6$

A pooled estimate of variance is $s^2 \approx 0.2075$.

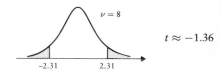
$\nu = 8$
$t \approx -1.36$
$-2.31 \qquad 2.31$

The difference between the means of the two samples is not significant.

4 $H_0 : \mu_A = \mu_J$
$H_1 : \mu_A \neq \mu_J$

$\bar{a} = 2.148; \quad s_A{}^2 \approx 0.002\,06; \quad n_A = 5$
$\bar{j} = 2.084; \quad s_J{}^2 \approx 0.001\,34; \quad n_J = 7$
$s^2 \approx 0.001\,97; \quad t \approx 2.5$

The evidence for a difference in playing ability is significant at 5% but not at 1%.

4.4 Non-parametric tests
4.4.1 The sign test

4.4 A

1 The median divides a probability distribution into two equal areas, each equal to a half.

$$P(T > 4.8) = P(T < 4.8) = \tfrac{1}{2}$$

Therefore, under H_0, the plus signs occur with probability $\frac{1}{2}$. As there are 36 'trials' when a plus sign can occur, $R \sim B\left(36, \frac{1}{2}\right)$.

2 The data give $r = 22$.

For $R \sim B\left(36, \frac{1}{2}\right)$, you must calculate $P(R \geq 22)$. Using a Normal approximation, you should find that $P(R \geq 22) \approx 0.12$. As $P(R \geq 22)$ is greater than $2\frac{1}{2}\%$, the result is not significant and H_0 is not rejected.

3 If the probability density function of T is $f(t)$, then $P(T = 4.8) = \int_{4.8}^{4.8} f(t)\, dt = 0$.

4 In practice, data items are measured to a specified degree of accuracy. If data items are measured to one decimal place accuracy, then the data item $T = 4.8$ would have an actual value $4.75 \leq T < 4.85$, and

$$P(4.75 \leq T < 4.85) = \int_{4.75}^{4.85} f(t)\, dt \neq 0$$

4.4 Exercise 1

1 H_0 : median $= 1.82$

H_1 : median $\neq 1.82$

Level of significance: 5%

The data give $r = 12$.

If $R \sim B(20, \frac{1}{2})$, then, using a Normal approximation, $P(R \geq 12) \approx 0.25$ (25%)

As $25\% > 2.5\%$, $r = 12$ is not in the critical region and H_0 is not rejected in favour of H_1. There is no significant difference from the findings of the Gallup poll.

2 H_0 : median $= 28$

H_1 : median $\neq 28$

Level of significance: 5%

For the data given, $r = 3$.

If $R \sim B(13, \frac{1}{2})$ then $P(R \leq 3) = 0.046$ (4.6%)

As $4.6\% > 2.5\%$, $r = 3$ is not in the critical region and H_0 is not rejected. (Had this been a one-tail test, then H_0 would have been rejected.) The locusts bred in captivity can be assumed to have a median lifetime of 28 days.

3 H_0 : median improvement $= 0$

H_1 : median improvement > 0

Level of significance: 5%

The data give $r = 8$.

If $R \sim B(9, \frac{1}{2})$ then $P(R \geq 8) = 0.020$ (2%)

As $2\% < 5\%$, $R = 8$ is in the critical region and so H_0 is rejected in favour of H_1. There is significant evidence to support the maker's claim.

4.4.2 The Wilcoxon signed-rank test

4.4 B

1 If the null hypothesis is true you would expect the sum of ranks corresponding to positive differences to be roughly equal to the sum corresponding to negative differences. If the null hypothesis is false you would expect the sums to differ substantially. Therefore, the smaller the value of T, the stronger will be the evidence for rejecting the null hypothesis.

2 From the table of critical values for the Wilcoxon signed-rank test, the critical value is 17.

$T > 17$ and so H_0 is accepted. The locusts bred in captivity can be assumed to have a median lifetime of 28 days.

4.4 Exercise 2

1 H_0 : median $= 24$

H_1 : median > 24

Level of significance: 5%

Difference	-1	3	4	-4	2	2	0	-7	14	0	9	15
Rank	1	4	5.5	5.5	2.5	2.5	–	7	9	–	8	10

$T = 1 + 5.5 + 7 = 13.5; \quad n = 10$

The critical value is 10 and so H_0 is accepted. The data do not provide significant evidence that the median is greater than 24.

2 H_0 : median $= 60$

H_1 : median < 60

Level of significance: 5%

$T = 7$
For $n = 7$, the critical value at the 5% level is
3 and so the evidence for a lower median
score is not significant.

3 H_0 : median $= 0$

H_1 : median $\neq 0$

Level of significance: 5%

Differences	8	3	2	4	6	5	6	7	−1	−4
Rank	10	3	2	4.5	7.5	6	7.5	9	1	4.5

$T = 1 + 4.5 = 5.5$

For $n = 10$, the critical value at the 5% level
for a two-tail test is 8 and so there is
significant evidence for a difference in time.

4.5 Correlation and regression
4.5.1 Bivariate distributions

4.5 A

In the case illustrated by (1) there is a strong
negative correlation between X and Y. A good
model for the correlation would be a linear one
such as $y + x = c$.

(2) illustrates a case where there would again be
a strong negative correlation. However, the best
model would not be linear; possibly the
relationship between X and Y is one of inverse
proportionality, $X \propto \dfrac{1}{Y}$

In the case illustrated by (3) there is neither
positive nor negative correlation; X and Y are
unrelated.

4.5 B

1 From the scatter plots it should appear that for:

- sample P   there is a strong negative
correlation between X and Y;
- sample Q   there is a strong positive
correlation;
- sample R   there is little or no correlation.

2 (a) In quadrants A and C

(b) (i) $x - \bar{x} > 0$ (ii) $y - \bar{y} > 0$
(iii) $(x - \bar{x})(y - \bar{y}) > 0$

For (x, y) in quadrant B the answers are:

(i) $x - \bar{x} < 0$ (ii) $y - \bar{y} > 0$
(iii) $(x - \bar{x})(y - \bar{y}) < 0$

If (x, y) is in quadrant C,
$(x - \bar{x})(y - \bar{y}) > 0$

If (x, y) is in quadrant D,
$(x - \bar{x})(y - \bar{y}) < 0$

(c) If X, Y are positively correlated, most
points will be in quadrants A and C and
$\sum (x_i - \bar{x})(y_i - \bar{y})$ will be positive.

If X, Y are negatively correlated, most
points will be in quadrants B and D and
$\sum (x_i - \bar{x})(y_i - \bar{y})$ will be negative.

If X, Y are unrelated, then points should
be equally distributed in the four quadrants
and $\sum (x_i - \bar{x})(y_i - \bar{y})$ will be small.

3 Values of $\bar{x}$, $\bar{y}$ are:

for P: 26.5, 6.39
for Q: 19.8, 11.4
for R: 36.6, 3.58

4 Values of $\sum (x_i - \bar{x})(y_i - \bar{y})$ are:

for P: −93
for Q: 138
for R: 7.4

These figures support the conclusion from the
scatter plots in question 1.

5 The scaling factor $\dfrac{1}{n}$ ensures that covariance is
not affected simply by the *size* of the sample
being considered.

4.5.2 The product moment correlation coefficient

4.5 C

1 The sample covariance will be multiplied by a scale factor of $5 \times 4 = 20$.

2 r is unchanged, since $s_X s_Y$ is increased by the same scale factor as $\text{Cov}(X, Y)$. Note also that r is a pure number; the dimensions in which X and Y are measured cancel out in the expression for r.

4.5 D

1 In general, you would expect tall people to have a relatively heavy bone structure and to weigh more than short people. You would therefore expect a positive correlation between height and weight.

Height and weight both depend upon the genetic make-up and early nutrition of the individual. However, weight can be independently changed by diet and lifestyle. The relationship is therefore described by a combination of the second and third categories.

2 Without further evidence, the example would be placed in the third category; the increases appear causally unrelated. It is possible that the same changes in society have caused both increases and then the example would fall into the second category.

4.5 Exercise 1

1 (b) $r = 0.989$

The temperatures are strongly correlated.

2 For both sets, $r = -1$

Both sets of points lie exactly on straight lines having gradient -2 and -4 respectively.

3 (a) $r = 0.646$

(b) $r > 0$ but is not very close to 1. The correlation is not strong.

4 (a) $r = 0.991$

(c) Despite the high value of r, as you can check, the relationship between l and T is not linear. You should find that the relationship between l and T^2 is almost linear.

5

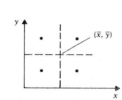

$r = 0$
The points are at the four corners of a square.
The diagram shows why the covariance is zero.

6E (a) $a^2 + b^2 - 2ab = (a - b)^2 \geq 0$
$$\Rightarrow a^2 + b^2 \geq 2ab$$

(b) (i) $(x_1{}^2 + x_2{}^2)(y_1{}^2 + y_2{}^2) - (x_1 y_1 + x_2 y_2)^2$
$$= x_1{}^2 y_2{}^2 + x_2{}^2 y_1{}^2 - 2x_1 x_2 y_1 y_2$$
$$= (x_1 y_2 - x_2 y_1)^2 \geq 0$$

Hence the required result.

(ii) $(x_1{}^2 + x_2{}^2 + x_3{}^2)(y_1{}^2 + y_2{}^2 + y_3{}^2)$
$$- (x_1 y_1 + x_2 y_2 + x_3 y_3)^2$$
$$= x_1{}^2 y_2{}^2 + x_2{}^2 y_1{}^2 - 2x_1 x_2 y_1 y_2$$
$$+ x_1{}^2 y_3{}^2 + x_3{}^2 y_1{}^2 - 2x_1 x_3 y_1 y_3$$
$$+ x_2{}^2 y_3{}^2 + x_3{}^2 y_2{}^2 - 2x_2 x_3 y_2 y_3$$
$$= (x_1 y_2 - x_2 y_1)^2 + (x_1 y_3 - x_3 y_1)^2$$
$$+ (x_2 y_3 - x_3 y_2)^2 \geq 0$$

(c) In general, $\sum x_i{}^2 \sum y_i{}^2 \geq \left(\sum x_i y_i \right)^2$

[This is known as the Cauchy–Schwarz inequality.]

Similarly,
$$\sum (x_i - \bar{x})^2 \sum (y_i - \bar{y})^2$$
$$\geq \left[\sum (x_i - \bar{x})(y_i - \bar{y}) \right]^2$$

which establishes the result that

$$[\text{Cov}\,(X, Y)]^2 \leq s_X{}^2 s_Y{}^2$$

Then

$$r^2 = \frac{[\text{Cov}\,(X, Y)]^2}{s_X{}^2 s_Y{}^2} \leq 1$$

$$\Rightarrow -1 \leq r \leq 1$$

4.5.3 A line of best fit

4.5 Exercise 2

1 (a) $r = -0.955$ so there is a strong negative correlation between Y and X.

(c) $y = 819.4 - 2.66x$

(e) When $x = 95$,
$y = 819.4 - (2.66 \times 95) = 567$

(f) $x = 60$ is outside the range of validity of the trial. It is possible that the reaction time is not being governed by the heart rate but by some other effect of the drug. Other ways of affecting the heart rate, such as exercise, might be tried instead of the drug.

2 (a) $r = 0.902$

(b) $y = -1.634 + 0.276x$

(c) The yield increases slowly until about 25 g of fertiliser is used, then more rapidly. Two different lines for the ranges $10 \leq x \leq 25$ and $25 < x \leq 32$ would provide a better model.

4.5.4 Regressing X on Y

4.5 Exercise 3

1 The equation of the regression line of X on Y is

$$x = 0.024y - 0.108$$

The gradients are respectively $\hat{b} = 37.6$ and $\dfrac{1}{\hat{d}} = 41.7$. Both lines pass through $(\bar{x}, \bar{y})$ and therefore the two lines are in close agreement for values of x near to $\bar{x}$.

4.5.5 Spearman's rank correlation coefficient

4.5 Exercise 4

1

Quality	8	3	1	9	4	2	7	5	6
Size	3	5	6	7	8	4	9	1	2
Difference	5	−2	−5	2	−4	−2	−2	4	4

$$r_s = 1 - \frac{6 \times 114}{9 \times 80} = 0.05$$

The rankings do not show general agreement.

2 $r = r_s = 0.83$

Spearman's rank correlation coefficient is simply the product moment correlation coefficient applied to rankings.

3 (a) $r = 0.669$

(b)

x rank	12	2	6	11	8	3	9	1	4	10	7	5
y rank	12	5	1	7	9	2	11	4	8	10	6	3
Difference	0	−3	5	4	−1	1	−2	−3	−4	0	1	2

(c) $r_s = 1 - \dfrac{6 \times 86}{12 \times 143} = 0.699$

(d) Although very similar, the coefficients are not the same. As seen in question 2, if rankings are taken as scores then $r = r_s$. If rankings are found from given scores, then generally $r \neq r_s$.

Miscellaneous exercise 4

1 $H_0 : p = 0.05$
$H_1 : p > 0.05$

$X \sim N(12.5, 11.875)$ is the Normal approximation to $R \sim B(250, 0.05)$.

$P(R \geq 21) \approx 0.0102$

As $P(R \geq 21)$ is greater than 1% the result is *not* significant so H_0 is not rejected. (The result is significant at the 5% level.)

2 (a) Using Normal tables,
$\mu + 1.506\sigma = 8.1$, $\mu - 2.65\sigma = 7.9$
Hence $\mu = 8.027$, $\sigma = 0.0481$

(b) Approximately 3.8% of rods will be rejected.

(c) $H_0 : \mu = 8.0$
$H_1 : \mu \neq 8.0$

The evidence does not suggest that the machine needs adjusting.

3 0.164;   no

4 The hypothesis is just acceptable at the 5% level.

5 150 at the 1% significance level

6 $z = 1.79$;   the difference is not significant at the 5% level since this is a two-tail test.

7 $1.502 \pm 2.36 \left(\dfrac{0.002\,345}{\sqrt{7}} \right)$ i.e. (1.4999, 1.5041)
It is consistent.

8 Probability is 0.034, significant at the 5% level. But a larger sample would give more reliable information and would not be too expensive.

9 Between 601 mm and 832 mm; it might seem that the mean rainfall of 832 mm is just consistent with the interval estimate obtained from the sample. However, the confidence interval is based on a two-tail test. But to test the hypothesis '1991–5 was a typical period' against '1991–5 was drier than a typical period', a one-tail test would be used. On this basis, the null hypothesis would be rejected if the mean rainfall is below 744 mm for the five-year period. The actual mean was 716.4 mm, so the conclusion is that 1991–5 was an unusually dry period.

10 For the differences (method B – method A), $m = 0.0525$ and $t = 0.70$. At the 5% significance level, $t = 2.20$ so the hypothesis is acceptable.

11 $t = 1.54$; the effectiveness of the lacquer is not proven.

12 $t = 2.68$; $\nu = 15$;
significant at the 5% level

13 $t = 2.39$; $\nu = 8$

The consignments have significantly different mean breaking strengths, at the 5% level.

14 $t = 0.82$; $\nu = 12$

The difference in weight is not significant.

15 (a) 1.54

(b) $t = -1.66$; the critical value for $t = 2.13$ (15 d.f., two-tail test). The differences are not significant.

16 $\bar{x}_A = 59.5$; $s_A{}^2 = 14.75$
$\bar{x}_B = 55.17$; $s_B{}^2 = 38.81$

Pooled variance estimate ≈ 36.5; $t \approx 1.11$; not significant at the 5% level

17 0.76

18 0.48

19 $y = 10.26 - 0.007\,85x$;
when $x = 200, y = 8.69$

20 $y = 87.4 + 4.46x$

For a boy aged 9 years the formula gives a height of 127.6 cm.

Substituting $x = 30$ gives $y = 221$ cm – not a sensible estimate of height. Clearly the formula does not extend to age 30; you would not expect it to apply beyond the late teens in any case.

Cumulative frequency diagrams

1 The lower quartile is approximately 12.5 cm.
   The upper quartile is approximately 18.5 cm.

2 (a)

Length (mm)	Cumulative frequency
Up to 109.5	4
Up to 124.5	14
Up to 139.5	33
Up to 154.5	69
Up to 169.5	112
Up to 184.5	138
Up to 199.5	147
Up to 214.5	150

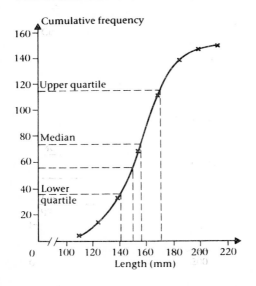

(b) The median is 156 mm.
     The interquartile range is 30 mm.

(c) 56 worms are less than 150 mm in length; that is 37%.

The Hardy–Weinberg law

1 $p^2 + 2pq + q^2 = (p+q)^2 = 1$, since $p + q = 1$.

2 (a) Second line:

$$P(\text{father } SS, \text{mother } SN) = p^2 \times 2pq = 2p^3q$$

$$P(\text{mother } SS, \text{father } SN) = p^2 \times 2pq = 2p^3q$$

$$\Rightarrow P(\text{one } SS, \text{other } SN) = 4p^3q$$

One parent always provides an S allele. The other has equal chances of providing an S or an N allele.

Similar explanations can be given for the other lines.

(b)

Event	P(Event)	Assuming the event		
		P(SS)	P(SN)	P(NN)
SS, SS	p^4	1	0	0
SS, SN	$4p^3q$	$\frac{1}{2}$	$\frac{1}{2}$	0
SS, NN	$2p^2q^2$	0	1	0
SN, SN	$4p^2q^2$	$\frac{1}{4}$	$\frac{1}{2}$	$\frac{1}{4}$
SN, NN	$4pq^3$	0	$\frac{1}{2}$	$\frac{1}{2}$
NN, NN	q^4	0	0	1

(c) From the table, for the following generation,

$$P(SS) = p^4 + \tfrac{1}{2}(4p^3q) + \tfrac{1}{4}(4p^2q^2)$$

$$= p^4 + 2p^3q + p^2q^2$$

$$= p^2(p^2 + 2pq + q^2) = p^2(p+q)^2 = p^2$$

Similarly, $P(SN) = 2pq$ and $P(NN) = q^2$

3 From question 2 it may be concluded that in the case when the probability distribution is p^2, $2pq$, q^2, with random pairing the distribution remains stable. To show that the distribution always tends to the stable form might be a suitable topic for a project.

4 The SS and NS alleles together have probability $p^2 + 2pq$. Hence
$p^2 + 2pq = 0.2$

Then $p^2 + 2p(1 - p) = 0.2$

So $p^2 - 2p + 0.2 = 0$

$$p = 1 - \sqrt{0.8}$$

$$\approx 0.011 \quad \text{(ignoring the root } p > 1)$$

The percentage of SS genotypes would be 1.1%.

Sampling without replacement

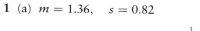
Commentary

1 (a) $m = 1.36$, $s = 0.82$

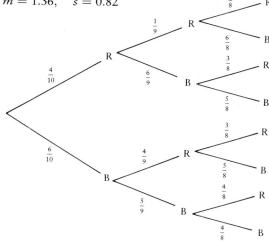

Number of reds	Probability	Predicted frequency
0	$\frac{120}{720} = \frac{5}{30}$	$\frac{5}{30} \times 50 \approx 8$
1	$\frac{360}{720} = \frac{15}{30}$	25
2	$\frac{216}{720} = \frac{9}{30}$	15
3	$\frac{24}{720} = \frac{1}{30}$	$\frac{1}{30} \times 50 \approx 2$
Totals	1	50

(b) $\mu = 1.2$ $\sigma^2 = 0.56$

2 (a)

Number of reds	Probability	Predicted frequency
0	$\frac{210}{720}$	15
1	$\frac{378}{720}$	26
2	$\frac{126}{720}$	9
3	$\frac{6}{720}$	0
Totals	1	50

(b) $\mu = 0.9$ $\sigma^2 = 0.49$

3 The smallest possible score is 1 and the largest is 9. Since small numbers are more likely than large ones (as will become clear), the mean will be nearer 1, between 3 and 4. For example,

$$P(4) = \frac{8}{10} \times \frac{7}{9} \times \frac{6}{8} \times \frac{2}{7} = \frac{6}{45}$$

Score	1	2	3	4	5	6	7	8	9
Probability	$\frac{9}{45}$	$\frac{8}{45}$	$\frac{7}{45}$	$\frac{6}{45}$	$\frac{5}{45}$	$\frac{4}{45}$	$\frac{3}{45}$	$\frac{2}{45}$	$\frac{1}{45}$
Predicted frequency	18	16	14	12	10	8	6	4	2

Predicted mean $= \mu = 3\frac{2}{3}$

4 This time there is no theoretical maximum score.

Score	1	2	3	4	5	6	...
Probability	$\frac{1}{5}$	$\left(\frac{4}{5}\right)\left(\frac{1}{5}\right)$	$\left(\frac{4}{5}\right)^2\left(\frac{1}{5}\right)$	$\left(\frac{4}{5}\right)^3\left(\frac{1}{5}\right)$	$\left(\frac{4}{5}\right)^4\left(\frac{1}{5}\right)$	$\left(\frac{4}{5}\right)^5\left(\frac{1}{5}\right)$	...
Predicted frequency	18	14.4	11.5	9.2	7.4	5.9	...

The theoretical mean (the calculation of which involves a simple program or summing an infinite series) is now 5.

5 For each score, the predicted frequency will lie between the corresponding ones for questions 3 and 4, depending on how significant the replacement effect is. In (a), they will be closer to those of question 3, while in (b), the results will be similar to those of question 4.

For example, in (b),

$$P(4) = \frac{80}{100} \times \frac{79}{99} \times \frac{78}{98} \times \frac{20}{97} \approx \frac{4}{5} \times \frac{4}{5} \times \frac{4}{5} \times \frac{1}{5}$$

6

Number of reds	Probability	Predicted frequency
0	$\left(\frac{6}{10}\right)^3$	10.8
1	$3\left(\frac{6}{10}\right)^2\left(\frac{4}{10}\right)$	21.6
2	$3\left(\frac{6}{10}\right)\left(\frac{4}{10}\right)^2$	14.4
3	$\left(\frac{4}{10}\right)^3$	3.2
Totals	1	50

$\mu = 1.2, \quad \sigma^2 = 0.72$

7 Sampling with replacement means that a name may be picked for a sample more than once and the opinion expressed should then be counted accordingly. As in question 5(b), when the 'parent population' is large enough, it does not matter in practice whether samples are taken with or without replacement.

8 The probability that four throws are needed to obtain an even number is $\frac{1}{16}$.

On average, $\sum x \, P(x) = 1 \times \frac{1}{2} + 2 \times \frac{1}{4} + 3 \times \frac{1}{8} + \ldots = 2$

(A calculator can easily be programmed to add, for example, 20 terms of this series.)

Throwing until a six appears, $P(4) = \left(\frac{5}{6}\right)^3 \left(\frac{1}{6}\right)$

Now, $\mu = \sum x \, P(x) = 6$

The series for μ converges less rapidly now, and more terms must be taken to obtain a convincing answer.

9 The St Petersburg paradox is based upon a gambling game reputed to have been played by the aristocrats of St Petersburg. The game can be played as follows.

For the payment of an initial stake, a player has the right to toss a coin repeatedly until a head appears. If it comes down head first time, the player wins 1p; the sequence T H gains 2p, T T H is worth 4p, T T T H 8p and so on. If the first head occurs after n tails, the player wins 2^np.

The surprising result which intrigued the gamblers of St Petersburg was that no original stake could be large enough to make the game fair, assuming unlimited resources of time and money. You might like to check this result by simulating the game on a computer or programmable calculator.

On average, a player wins

$$\sum x \, P(x) = 1 \times \frac{1}{2} + 2 \times \frac{1}{4} + 4 \times \frac{1}{8} + \ldots$$
$$= \frac{1}{2} + \frac{1}{2} + \frac{1}{2} + \ldots$$

The player can therefore expect to win, on average, an infinite amount.

Boxes of matches

Commentary

1 $\sigma^2 = 0.4$

2 $\bar{x} = 48.5$ when one box contains 48 matches and the other box contains 49 matches. The probability of box 1 having 48 and box 2 having 49 is 0.12, as is the probability of box 1 having 49 and box 2 having 48.
Thus the probability that $\bar{x}$ is $48.5 = 2 \times 0.12 = 0.24$.

3 (a) The mean value of the distribution of $\bar{x}$ is

$$47 \times 0.04 + 47.5 \times 0.24 + 48 \times 0.44 + 48.5 \times 0.24 + 49 \times 0.04 = 48$$

(b) The mean value of the distribution of s^2 is

$$0 \times 0.44 + 0.25 \times 0.48 + 1 \times 0.08 = 0.2$$

4 For the **rectangular** population, $\mu = 48$, $\sigma^2 = \frac{2}{3}$.

	Probabilities		
	47	48	49
47	$\frac{1}{9}$	$\frac{1}{9}$	$\frac{1}{9}$
48	$\frac{1}{9}$	$\frac{1}{9}$	$\frac{1}{9}$
49	$\frac{1}{9}$	$\frac{1}{9}$	$\frac{1}{9}$

Sample mean, $\bar{x}$:

x	47	47.5	48	48.5	49
$P(\bar{X} = x)$	$\frac{1}{9}$	$\frac{2}{9}$	$\frac{3}{9}$	$\frac{2}{9}$	$\frac{1}{9}$

The mean value of the distribution of $\bar{x}$ is 48.

Sample variance, s^2:

y	0	0.25	1
$P(s^2 = y)$	$\frac{3}{9}$	$\frac{4}{9}$	$\frac{2}{9}$

The mean value of the distribution of s^2 is $\frac{1}{3}$.

For the **asymmetrical** population, $\mu = 47.5$, $\sigma^2 = 0.45$

	Probabilities		
	47	48	49
47	0.36	0.18	0.06
48	0.18	0.09	0.03
49	0.06	0.03	0.01

Sample mean, $\bar{x}$:

x	47	47.5	48	48.5	49
$P(\bar{X} = x)$	0.36	0.36	0.21	0.06	0.01

The mean value of the distribution of $\bar{x}$ is 47.5.

Sample variance, s^2:

y	0	0.25	1
$P(s^2 = y)$	0.46	0.42	0.12

The mean value of the distribution of s^2 is 0.225.

For the **u-shaped** population, $\mu = 48$, $\sigma^2 = 1$.

	Probabilities		
	47	48	49
47	0.25	0	0.25
48	0	0	0
49	0.25	0	0.25

Sample mean, $\bar{x}$:

x	47	47.5	48	48.5	49
$P(\bar{X} = x)$	0.25	0	0.5	0	0.25

The mean value of the distribution of $\bar{x}$ is 48.

Sample variance, s^2:

y	0	0.25	1
$P(s^2 = y)$	0.5	0	0.5

The mean value of the distribution of s^2 is 0.5.

In all of these populations you will have found that:

- the mean value of the distribution of $\bar{x}$ is μ;
- the mean value of the distribution of s^2 is $\frac{1}{2}\sigma^2$.

Programming the binomial

Commentary

1 $\dfrac{r!}{(r-1)!} = \dfrac{r(r-1)(r-2)\ldots3 \times 2 \times 1}{(r-1)(r-2)\ldots3 \times 2 \times 1} = r$

2 (a) $\dfrac{(r+1)!}{r!} = r+1$ **(b)** $\dfrac{(r+1)!}{(r-1)!} = (r+1)r$

(c) $\dfrac{(r+2)!}{r!} = (r+2)(r+1)$ **(d)** $\dfrac{(r+n)!}{r!} = (r+n)(r+n-1)\ldots(r+1)$

3 $\dbinom{n}{r+1} \Big/ \dbinom{n}{r} = \dfrac{n!}{(n-r-1)!(r+1)!} \Big/ \dfrac{n!}{(n-r)!r!}$

$= \dfrac{n!}{(n-r-1)!(r+1)!} \cdot \dfrac{(n-r)!r!}{n!}$

$= \dfrac{(n-r)!}{(n-r-1)!} \cdot \dfrac{r!}{(r+1)!} = \dfrac{n-r}{r+1}$

$\dfrac{P(r+1)}{P(r)} = \dfrac{\dbinom{n}{r+1}p^{r+1}q^{n-r-1}}{\dbinom{n}{r}p^r q^{n-r}} = \dfrac{\dbinom{n}{r+1}}{\dbinom{n}{r}} \dfrac{p}{q}$

$= \left(\dfrac{n-r}{r+1}\right)\dfrac{p}{q}$, hence the result.

Your program should be similar to the one given here.

```
"N"? → N: "P"? → P
1-P → Q:0 → R
Q  x^y  N → X
Lbl 1:R◢
X◢
(N-R) × P × X ÷ ((R+1) × Q) → X
R+1 → R
R≤N ⇒ GOTO 1
```

4 (a)

x	0	1	2	3
$P(X=x)$	0.42	0.42	0.14	0.02

(b)

x	0	1	2	3	4
$P(X=x)$	0.20	0.40	0.30	0.10	0.01

From binomial to Poisson   Commentary

1 $P(X = r + 1) = \dfrac{e^{-\lambda}\lambda^{r+1}}{(r+1)!}$

$$= \dfrac{\lambda}{(r+1)} \dfrac{e^{-\lambda}\lambda^r}{r!} = \dfrac{\lambda}{r+1} P(X = r)$$

$$P(X = 0) = \dfrac{e^{-\lambda}\lambda^0}{0!} = e^{-\lambda}$$

2 $e^{-\lambda} = 1 - \dfrac{\lambda}{1!} + \dfrac{\lambda^2}{2!} - \dfrac{\lambda^3}{3!} + \ldots$

3 Define $\lambda = np$,   so $p = \dfrac{\lambda}{n}$.

Now $q = 1 - p$,   so $q^n = \left(1 - \dfrac{\lambda}{n}\right)^n$

$$\Rightarrow q^n = 1 - \dfrac{n\lambda}{n} + \binom{n}{2}\dfrac{\lambda^2}{n^2} - \binom{n}{3}\dfrac{\lambda^3}{n^3} + \ldots$$

$$= 1 - \lambda + \dfrac{n(n-1)}{2!}\dfrac{\lambda^2}{n^2} - \dfrac{n(n-1)(n-2)}{3!}\dfrac{\lambda^3}{n^3} + \ldots$$

$$= 1 - \lambda + \dfrac{\lambda^2}{2!}\left(1 - \dfrac{1}{n}\right) - \dfrac{\lambda^3}{3!}\left(1 - \dfrac{1}{n}\right)\left(1 - \dfrac{2}{n}\right) + \ldots$$

4 As $n \to \infty$, $\left(1 - \dfrac{1}{n}\right) \to 1$, $\left(1 - \dfrac{2}{n}\right) \to 1$ and so on.

Then $q^n \to 1 - \lambda + \dfrac{\lambda^2}{2!} - \dfrac{\lambda^3}{3!} + \ldots$ i.e. $q^n \to e^{-\lambda}$

5 $\dfrac{(n-r)p}{q} = \dfrac{\left(1 - \dfrac{r}{n}\right)np}{q} = \dfrac{\left(1 - \dfrac{r}{n}\right)\lambda}{q} = \dfrac{\left(1 - \dfrac{r}{n}\right)\lambda}{1 - p} = \dfrac{\left(1 - \dfrac{r}{n}\right)\lambda}{1 - \dfrac{\lambda}{n}}$

$\Rightarrow$ as $n \to \infty$, $\dfrac{(n-r)p}{q} \to \lambda$

so $\dfrac{(n-r)p}{(r+1)q} \to \dfrac{\lambda}{r+1}$

Combining random variables   Commentary

1 $(x_1 + y_1), (x_1 + y_2), (x_2 + y_1), (x_2 + y_2), (x_3 + y_1), (x_3 + y_2)$

2 (a) $P(x_1) = P(x_1y_1 \text{ or } x_1y_2)$

$\qquad\qquad = P(x_1y_1) + P(x_1y_2)$

$\qquad a = r + u$

(b) $P(y_1) = P(y_1x_1 \text{ or } y_1x_2 \text{ or } y_1x_3)$

$\qquad\qquad = P(y_1x_1) + P(y_1x_2) + P(y_1x_3)$

$\qquad d = r + s + t$

(c) y_1 or y_2 must occur in the sum $X + Y$, hence $P(y_1 \text{ or } y_2) = 1$.

3 $E[XY] = (x_1y_1)r + (x_1y_2)u + (x_2y_1)s + (x_2y_2)v + (x_3y_1)t + (x_3y_2)w$ ②

But $\quad r = P(x_1y_1) = P(x_1)P(y_1)$ as X and Y are independent

$\qquad\qquad = ad$

Similarly for the other probabilities, i.e. $s = bd$, $t = cd$ etc.
So ② becomes

$E[XY] = (x_1y_1)ad + (x_1y_1)ae + \ldots$

$\qquad = (x_1a)(y_1d) + (x_1a)(y_1e) + \ldots$

$\qquad = (x_1a)(y_1d + y_1e) + (x_2b)(y_1d + y_1e) + \ldots$

$\qquad = (x_1a)(E[Y]) + (x_2b)(E[Y]) + (x_3c)(E[Y])$

$\qquad = E[X]E[Y]$

4 (a) $X = x_1, x_2, \ldots, x_i, \ldots x_n$

$\qquad aX = ax_1, ax_2, \ldots$

$\qquad E[aX] = \sum_{i=1}^{n} ax_iP(x_i) = a\sum_{1}^{n} x_iP(x_i) = aE[X]$

(b) $E[X + b] = \sum_{1}^{n} (x_i + b)P(x_i) = \sum_{1}^{n} x_iP(x_i) + b\sum_{1}^{n} P(x_i) = E[X] + b$

Some proofs

Commentary

The geometric distribution

1 6 throws

2 $(1-q)^{-2} = 1 + (-2)(-q) + \dfrac{(-2)(-3)}{2!}(-q)^2 + \dots$

$\qquad = 1 + 2q + 3q^2 + \dots$

The Poisson distribution

3 $\text{E}[X] = \dfrac{0\,\text{e}^{-\lambda}\lambda^0}{0!} + \dfrac{1\,\text{e}^{-\lambda}\lambda}{1!} + \dfrac{2\,\text{e}^{-\lambda}\lambda^2}{2!} + \dfrac{3\,\text{e}^{-\lambda}\lambda^3}{3!} + \dots$

$\qquad = \text{e}^{-\lambda}\left(\lambda + \dfrac{2\lambda^2}{2!} + \dfrac{3\lambda^3}{3!} + \dots\right)$

$\qquad = \lambda\,\text{e}^{-\lambda}\left(1 + \dfrac{\lambda}{1!} + \dfrac{\lambda^2}{2!} + \dots\right)$

$\qquad = \lambda\,\text{e}^{-\lambda}\,\text{e}^{\lambda} = \lambda$

4 Taking the right-hand side of this equation,

$\text{E}[X(X-1)] + \text{E}[X] = \text{E}[X^2 - X] + \text{E}[X]$

$\qquad\qquad = \text{E}[X^2] - \text{E}[X] + \text{E}[X] = \text{E}[X^2]$

5 (a) $\text{E}[X(X-1)] = \displaystyle\sum_i [x_i(x_i - 1)]\text{P}(x_i)$

$\qquad = 2 \times 1\,\text{e}^{-\lambda}\dfrac{\lambda^2}{2!} + 3 \times 2\,\text{e}^{-\lambda}\dfrac{\lambda^3}{3!} + 4 \times 3\,\text{e}^{-\lambda}\dfrac{\lambda^4}{4!} + \dots$

$\qquad = \lambda^2\,\text{e}^{-\lambda}\left(1 + \dfrac{\lambda}{1!} + \dfrac{\lambda^2}{2!} + \dots\right)$

$\qquad = \lambda^2\,\text{e}^{-\lambda}\,\text{e}^{\lambda} = \lambda^2$

(b) $V[X] = \text{E}[X(X-1)] + \text{E}[X] - (\text{E}[X])^2$

$\qquad = \lambda^2 + \lambda - \lambda^2 = \lambda$

Plotting t-distributions

Commentary

1 (a) A sketch of the function on a graph plotter suggests that the area under the graph for $|t| > 10$ is negligible. A numerical method for integration such as the mid-ordinate rule shows that

$$\int_{-10}^{10} \left(1 + \frac{t^2}{5}\right)^{-3} dt \approx 2.634 \quad \text{(to 4 s.f.)}$$

(b) When $\nu = 5$, $\quad f(t) = c_5 \left(1 + \frac{t^2}{5}\right)^{-3}$

So $\displaystyle\int_{-\infty}^{\infty} f(t)\, dt = 1 \Rightarrow c_5 \int_{-\infty}^{\infty} \left(1 + \frac{t^2}{5}\right)^{-3} dt = 1$

$$\Rightarrow c_5 \approx \frac{1}{2.634} \approx 0.380$$

(c) $c_{10} \approx 0.390; \quad c_{20} \approx 0.394; \quad c_{50} \approx 0.397$

2 (a) (i) $\nu = 3; \quad f(t) = 0.368\left(1 + \frac{t^2}{3}\right)^{-2}$ (see question 5, page 251)

   (ii) $\nu = 5; \quad f(t) = 0.380\left(1 + \frac{t^2}{5}\right)^{-3}$

   (iii) $\nu = 10; \quad f(t) = 0.389\left(1 + \frac{t^2}{10}\right)^{-5.5}$

   (iv) $\nu = 20; \quad f(t) = 0.394\left(1 + \frac{t^2}{20}\right)^{-10.5}$

   (v) $\nu = 50; \quad f(t) = 0.397\left(1 + \frac{t^2}{50}\right)^{-25.5}$

(d) You should find that the graph of the t-distribution approaches that of a Standard Normal distribution as the value of ν (the degrees of freedom) increases. The graphs are virtually indistinguishable when $\nu = 50$. This implies that the random variable

$$T = \frac{\bar{X} - \mu}{\left(\dfrac{S_{n-1}}{\sqrt{n}}\right)}$$

can be assumed to have $N(0, 1)$ distribution for $n > 50$. In practice, the Normal approximation to the t-distribution is often used for a sample size $n \geq 30$.

Derivation of Spearman's rank correlation coefficient

Commentary

1 $\sum d = \sum (x - y)$

$\qquad = \sum x - \sum y$

$\qquad = 36 - 36$

2 The mean is $\frac{9}{2}$ and the variance is $\frac{21}{4}$ in both cases.

3 (a) The mean would be $\frac{1}{2}(n + 1)$.

The variance would be

$$\frac{1}{n} \sum_{i=1}^{n} i^2 - \left[\frac{1}{2}(n + 1)\right]^2 = \frac{1}{n} \times \frac{1}{6} n(n + 1)(2n + 1) - \frac{1}{4}(n + 1)^2$$

$$= \frac{1}{12}(n^2 - 1)$$

(b) $\sum d^2 = \sum (x - y)^2 = \sum x^2 + \sum y^2 - 2 \sum xy$, where

$$\sum x^2 = \sum y^2 = \sum_{i=1}^{n} i^2 = \frac{1}{6} n(n + 1)(2n + 1)$$

So $\sum d^2 = 2 \times \frac{1}{6} n(n + 1)(2n + 1) - 2 \sum xy$

$$= \frac{1}{3} n(n + 1)(2n + 1) - 2 \sum xy$$

4 Cov $(x, y) = \frac{9}{8}$; $r = 0.214$

5 $r = \dfrac{\sum xy - n\bar{x}\bar{y}}{\sqrt{[(\sum x^2 - n\bar{x}^2)(\sum y^2 - n\bar{y}^2)]}}$

Since $\sum x^2 = \sum y^2 = \frac{1}{6} n(n + 1)(2n + 1)$ and $\bar{x} = \bar{y} = \frac{1}{2}(n + 1)$, the denominator becomes $\frac{1}{6} n(n + 1)(2n + 1) - \frac{1}{4} n(n + 1)^2 = \frac{1}{12} n(n^2 - 1)$. Substituting from the result of question 3(b), the numerator is

$$\frac{1}{6} n(n + 1)(2n + 1) - \frac{1}{2} \sum d^2 - \frac{1}{4} n(n + 1)^2$$

$$= \frac{1}{12} n(n^2 - 1) - \frac{1}{2} \sum d^2$$

Hence $r = 1 - \dfrac{6 \sum d^2}{n(n^2 - 1)}$

6 (a) If the judges agree totally then $d_i = 0$ for all i, so $r = 1$.

(b) If they disagree totally, then the rankings are as follows.

X	n	$(n-1)$	$(n-2)$	...	2	1
Y	1	2	3	...	$(n-1)$	n
d	$(n-1)$	$(n-3)$	$(n-5)$	...	$(3-n)$	$(1-n)$

Note that for *total* disagreement n must be even. This affords an excuse to show the calculation only in the even case! Then

$$\sum d^2 = (n-1)^2 + (n-3)^2 + \ldots + (3-n)^2 + (1-n)^2$$

$$= 2[1^2 + 3^2 + \ldots + (n-1)^2]$$

$$= 2\left[\sum_{i=1}^{n} i^2 - (2^2 + 4^2 + \ldots + n^2)\right]$$

$$= 2\left[\sum_{i=1}^{n} i^2 - 4\sum_{i=1}^{\frac{1}{2}n} i^2\right]$$

$$= \tfrac{1}{3}n(n+1)(2n+1) - \tfrac{1}{3}n(n+1)(n+2)$$

$$= \tfrac{1}{3}n(n^2 - 1)$$

and $r = 1 - \dfrac{6\sum d^2}{n(n^2-1)} = -1$

[In fact, the odd case is fairly similar to this calculation.]

Appendix

Deriving the equation for the line of best fit

See section 4.5.3, page 287.

To find the values of a and b which minimise $\sum_{1}^{n}(y_i - (a + bx_i))^2$ it is convenient to work relative to the mean values $\bar{x}$ and $\bar{y}$. It is also convenient to consider the mean of the squared deviations.

$$\frac{1}{n}\sum_{1}^{n}(y_i - (a + bx_i))^2 = \frac{1}{n}\sum_{1}^{n}((y_i - \bar{y}) - b(x_i - \bar{x}) + (\bar{y} - a - b\bar{x}))^2$$

Expanding the right-hand side gives six terms:

$$\frac{1}{n}\sum_{1}^{n}(y_i - \bar{y})^2 = \text{Var}(Y)$$

$$\frac{1}{n}\sum_{1}^{n}b^2(x_i - \bar{x})^2 = b^2\,\text{Var}(X)$$

$$\frac{1}{n}\sum_{1}^{n}(\bar{y} - a - b\bar{x})^2 = (\bar{y} - a - b\bar{x})^2$$

$$-\frac{2b}{n}\sum_{1}^{n}(y_i - \bar{y})(x_i - \bar{x}) = -2b\,\text{Cov}(X, Y)$$

$$\frac{2}{n}\sum_{1}^{n}(y_i - \bar{y})(\bar{y} - a - b\bar{x}) = \frac{2}{n}(\bar{y} - a - b\bar{x})\sum_{i}(y_i - \bar{y}) = 0$$

$$-\frac{2b}{n}\sum_{1}^{n}(x_i - \bar{x})(\bar{y} - a - b\bar{x}) = 0$$

It is therefore required to minimise

$$\text{Var}(Y) - 2b\,\text{Cov}(X, Y) + b^2\,\text{Var}(X) + (\bar{y} - a - b\bar{x})^2$$

The parameter a appears only in the squared term and so must be chosen to make

$$\bar{y} - a - b\bar{x} = 0$$

The regression line therefore passes through the point $(\bar{x}, \bar{y})$ as might have been expected.

The expression to be minimised is then a quadratic in b,

$$\text{Var}\,(Y) - 2b\,\text{Cov}\,(X, Y) + b^2\,\text{Var}\,(X)$$

The quadratic is minimised when

$$b = \frac{\text{Cov}\,(X, Y)}{\text{Var}\,(X)}$$

Substituting this value for b, the mean of the squared deviations is then equal to

$$\text{Var}\,(Y) - \frac{\text{Cov}^2\,(X, Y)}{\text{Var}\,(X)} = \text{Var}\,(Y)(1 - r^2)$$

where r is the product moment correlation coefficient. From this expression, it can be seen that the line of best fit is good (i.e. the sum of squared deviations is small) when $r^2 \approx 1$, i.e. when $r \approx +1$ or $r \approx -1$.

Tables

Table 1   The Standard Normal distribution

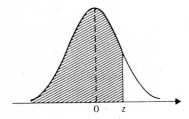

The table opposite gives the area to the left of (or below) any given z-value. z is the number of standard deviations from the mean value.

z	.00	.01	.02	.03	.04	.05	.06	.07	.08	.09
.0	.5000	.5040	.5080	.5120	.5160	.5199	.5239	.5279	.5319	.5359
.1	.5398	.5438	.5478	.5517	.5557	.5596	.5636	.5675	.5714	.5753
.2	.5793	.5832	.5871	.5910	.5948	.5987	.6026	.6064	.6103	.6141
.3	.6179	.6217	.6255	.6293	.6331	.6368	.6406	.6443	.6480	.6517
.4	.6554	.6591	.6628	.6664	.6700	.6736	.6772	.6808	.6844	.6879
.5	.6915	.6950	.6985	.7019	.7054	.7088	.7123	.7157	.7190	.7224
.6	.7257	.7291	.7324	.7357	.7389	.7422	.7454	.7486	.7517	.7549
.7	.7580	.7611	.7642	.7673	.7704	.7734	.7764	.7794	.7823	.7852
.8	.7881	.7910	.7939	.7967	.7995	.8023	.8051	.8078	.8106	.8133
.9	.8159	.8186	.8212	.8238	.8264	.8289	.8315	.8340	.8365	.8389
1.0	.8413	.8438	.8461	.8485	.8508	.8531	.8554	.8577	.8599	.8621
1.1	.8643	.8665	.8686	.8708	.8729	.8749	.8770	.8790	.8810	.8830
1.2	.8849	.8869	.8888	.8907	.8925	.8944	.8962	.8980	.8997	.9015
1.3	.9032	.9049	.9066	.9082	.9099	.9115	.9131	.9147	.9162	.9177
1.4	.9192	.9207	.9222	.9236	.9251	.9265	.9279	.9292	.9306	.9319
1.5	.9332	.9345	.9357	.9370	.9382	.9394	.9406	.9418	.9429	.9441
1.6	.9452	.9463	.9474	.9484	.9495	.9505	.9515	.9525	.9535	.9545
1.7	.9554	.9564	.9573	.9582	.9591	.9599	.9608	.9616	.9625	.9633
1.8	.9641	.9649	.9656	.9664	.9671	.9678	.9686	.9693	.9699	.9706
1.9	.9713	.9719	.9726	.9732	.9738	.9744	.9750	.9756	.9761	.9767
2.0	.9772	.9778	.9783	.9788	.9793	.9798	.9803	.9808	.9812	.9817
2.1	.9821	.9826	.9830	.9834	.9838	.9842	.9846	.9850	.9854	.9857
2.2	.9861	.9864	.9868	.9871	.9875	.9878	.9881	.9884	.9887	.9890
2.3	.9893	.9896	.9898	.9901	.9904	.9906	.9909	.9911	.9913	.9916
2.4	.9918	.9920	.9922	.9925	.9927	.9929	.9931	.9932	.9934	.9936
2.5	.9938	.9940	.9941	.9943	.9945	.9946	.9948	.9949	.9951	.9952
2.6	.9953	.9955	.9956	.9957	.9959	.9960	.9961	.9962	.9963	.9964
2.7	.9965	.9966	.9967	.9968	.9969	.9970	.9971	.9972	.9973	.9974
2.8	.9974	.9975	.9976	.9977	.9977	.9978	.9979	.9979	.9980	.9981
2.9	.9981	.9982	.9982	.9983	.9984	.9984	.9985	.9985	.9986	.9986
3.0	.9987	.9987	.9987	.9988	.9988	.9989	.9989	.9989	.9990	.9990
3.1	.9990	.9991	.9991	.9991	.9992	.9992	.9992	.9992	.9993	.9993
3.2	.9993	.9993	.9994	.9994	.9994	.9994	.9994	.9995	.9995	.9995
3.3	.9995	.9995	.9995	.9996	.9996	.9996	.9996	.9996	.9996	.9997
3.4	.9997	.9997	.9997	.9997	.9997	.9997	.9997	.9997	.9997	.9998

Joint Matriculation Board

Tables

Table 2   Upper percentage points for χ^2 distributions

The tabulated value is $\chi^2{}_p$, where
$P(X^2 > \chi^2{}_p) = p$, when X^2 has a
χ^2 distribution with ν degrees of freedom.

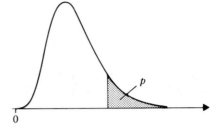

p	.1	.05	.025	.01	.005	.001
$\nu = $ 1	2.71	3.84	5.02	6.63	7.88	10.83
2	4.61	5.99	7.38	9.21	10.60	13.81
3	6.25	7.81	9.35	11.34	12.84	16.27
4	7.78	9.49	11.14	13.28	14.86	18.47
5	9.24	11.07	12.83	15.09	16.75	20.52
6	10.64	12.59	14.45	16.81	18.55	22.46
7	12.02	14.07	16.01	18.48	20.28	24.32
8	13.36	15.51	17.53	20.09	21.95	26.12
9	14.68	16.92	19.02	21.67	23.59	27.88
10	15.99	18.31	20.48	23.21	25.19	29.59
12	18.55	21.03	23.34	26.22	28.30	32.91
14	21.06	23.68	26.12	29.14	31.32	36.12
16	23.54	26.30	28.85	32.00	34.27	39.25
18	25.99	28.87	31.53	34.81	37.16	42.31
20	28.41	31.41	34.17	37.57	40.00	45.31
25	34.38	37.65	40.65	44.31	46.93	52.62
30	40.26	43.77	46.98	50.89	53.67	59.70
40	51.81	55.76	59.34	63.69	66.77	73.40
50	63.17	67.50	71.42	76.15	79.49	86.66
60	74.40	79.08	83.30	88.38	91.95	99.61
100	118.5	124.3	129.6	135.8	140.2	149.4

Joint Matriculation Board

Tables

Table 3   Upper percentage points for the *t*-distribution

The tabulated value is t_p, where $P(X > t_p) = p$, when X has a t-distribution with ν degrees of freedom.

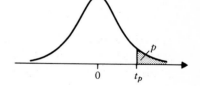

p	.05	.025	.01	.005	.001	.0005
$\nu = 1$	6.31	12.71	31.82	63.66	318.3	636.6
2	2.92	4.30	6.96	9.92	22.33	31.60
3	2.35	3.18	4.54	5.84	10.21	12.92
4	2.13	2.78	3.75	4.60	7.17	8.61
5	2.02	2.57	3.36	4.03	5.89	6.87
6	1.94	2.45	3.14	3.71	5.21	5.96
7	1.89	2.36	3.00	3.50	4.79	5.41
8	1.86	2.31	2.90	3.36	4.50	5.04
9	1.83	2.26	2.82	3.25	4.30	4.78
10	1.81	2.23	2.76	3.17	4.14	4.59
12	1.78	2.18	2.68	3.05	3.93	4.32
14	1.76	2.14	2.62	2.98	3.79	4.14
16	1.75	2.12	2.58	2.92	3.69	4.01
18	1.73	2.10	2.55	2.88	3.61	3.92
20	1.72	2.09	2.53	2.85	3.55	3.85
25	1.71	2.06	2.48	2.79	3.45	3.72
30	1.70	2.04	2.46	2.75	3.39	3.65
40	1.68	2.02	2.42	2.70	3.31	3.55
60	1.67	2.00	2.39	2.66	3.23	3.46
120	1.66	1.98	2.36	2.62	3.16	3.37
∞	1.64	1.96	2.33	2.58	3.09	3.29

Joint Matriculation Board

Tables

Table 4 Critical values for the Wilcoxon signed-rank test

The table shows the critical values of T for a significance level of 5%.

n	Two-tail test	One-tail test
5		0
6	0	2
7	2	3
8	3	5
9	5	8
10	8	10
11	10	13
12	13	17
13	17	21
14	21	25
15	25	30
16	29	35
17	34	41
18	40	47
19	46	53
20	52	60
21	58	67
22	65	75
23	73	83
24	81	91
25	89	100
26	98	110
27	107	119
28	116	130
29	126	140
30	137	151

Index